Developments in French Politics 5

Developments titles available from Palgrave Macmillan

Alistair Cole, Sophie Meunier and Vincent Tiberj (eds)
DEVELOPMENTS IN FRENCH POLITICS 5

Maria Green Cowles and Desmond Dinan (eds)
DEVELOPMENTS IN THE EUROPEAN UNION 2

Richard Heffernan, Philip Cowley and Colin Hay (eds)
DEVELOPMENTS IN BRITISH POLITICS 9

Erik Jones, Paul M. Heywood, Martin Rhodes and Ulrich Sedelmeier (eds)
DEVELOPMENTS IN EUROPEAN POLITICS 2

Stephen Padgett, William E. Paterson and Gordon Smith (eds)
DEVELOPMENTS IN GERMAN POLITICS 5*

Gillian Peele, Christopher J. Bailey, Bruce Cain and B. Guy Peters (eds)
DEVELOPMENTS IN AMERICAN POLITICS 6

Stephen White, Judy Batt and Paul Lewis (eds)
DEVELOPMENTS IN CENTRAL AND EAST EUROPEAN POLITICS 5*

Stephen White, Richard Sakwa and Henry E. Hale (eds)
DEVELOPMENTS IN RUSSIAN POLITICS 7*

If you have any comments or suggestions regarding the
above or other possible *Developments* titles, please write to
Steven Kennedy, Palgrave Macmillan, Houndmills,
Basingstoke, RG21 6XS, UK or e-mail s.kennedy@palgrave.com

---

* Rights world excluding North America

Developments in French Politics 5

Edited by
Alistair Cole
Sophie Meunier
and
Vincent Tiberj

palgrave
macmillan

This edition first published 2013 by
PALGRAVE MACMILLAN

Palgrave Macmillan in the UK is an imprint of Macmillan Publishers Limited,
registered in England, company number 785998, of Houndmills, Basingstoke,
Hampshire RG21 6XS.

Palgrave Macmillan in the US is a division of St Martin's Press LLC,
175 Fifth Avenue, New York, NY 10010.

Palgrave Macmillan is the global academic imprint of the above companies
and has companies and representatives throughout the world.

Palgrave® and Macmillan® are registered trademarks in the United States,
the United Kingdom, Europe and other countries

ISBN 978-0-230-34962-9   paperback

This book is printed on paper suitable for recycling and made from fully
managed and sustained forest sources. Logging, pulping and manufacturing
processes are expected to conform to the environmental regulations of the
country of origin.

A catalogue record for this book is available from the British Library.

A catalog record for this book is available from the Library of Congress.

Contents

List of Tables and Figures

Tables

Figures

List of Abbreviations

ANA	Afghan National Army
ATR	Administration Térritoriale de la République (Territorial Administration of the Republic)
ATTAC	Association pour la Taxation des Transactions pour l'Aide aux Citoyens (Association for Taxing Transactions for the Benefit of Citizens).
CAP	Common Agricultural Policy
CNRS	Centre National de Recherche Scientifique (National Scientific Research Centre)
CERES	Centre d'Études, de Recherches et d'Éducation Socialiste (Socialist Study, Research and Education Centre)
CESEDA	Code d'Entrée et de Séjour des Étrangers et des Demandeurs d'Asile (Asylum and Foreign Residency Code)
CEVIPOF	Centre d'Études sur la Vie Politique Française (Centre for the Study of French Politics).
CFDT	Confédération Française Démocratique du Travail (French Democratic Labour Confederation).
CGT	Confédération Générale du Travail (General Labour Confederation).
CNCDH	Commission Nationale Consultative des Droits de l'Homme (Consultative National Commission on Human Rights)
CPNT	Chasse, Peche, Nature et Tradition (Hunting, Fishing, Nature and Tradition)
CSA	Conseil Supérieur de l'Audiovisuel (The High Council for the Audiovisual Media)
CSM	Conseil Supérieur de la Magistrature (Higher Council of the Magistrature)
CT	Constitutional Treaty
DATAR	Délégation Interministérielle à l'Aménagement du Territoire et à l'Attractivité Régionale (Delegation for Territorial and Regional Planning).
DGCL	Direction Générale des Collectivités Locales (Directorate-General for Local Government)
DGD	Dotation Générale de la Décentralization (grant to local and regional authorities for undertaking decentralised competencies)
DGF	Dotation Globale de Fonctionnement (general block grant to local and regional authorities)

ECHR	European Court of Human Rights
ECOWAS	Economic Community of West African States
EDA	European Defence Agency
EDF–GDF	Electricité de France – Gaz de France (French Electricity – French Gas)
EELV	Europe Écologie les Verts (Europe Ecology – the Greens)
EPCI	Établissement Public de Coopération Intercommunale (Public Body for Intercommunal Cooperation)
EPR	European Pressurized Reactor
ESDP	European Security and Defence Policy
EU	European Union
FG	Front de Gauche (Left Front)
FN	Front National (National Front)
FNSEA	Fédération Nationale des Syndicats d'Exploitants Agricoles (National Federation of Farming Unions)
FPEU08	French Presidency of the European Union 2008
GDP	Gross Domestic Product
GMO	Genetically Modified Organisms
HADOPI	Haute Autorité pour la Protection des Œuvres et la Protection des Droits sur l'Internet
IMF	International Monetary Fund
INSEE	Institut National des Statistiques et des Études Économiques (National Institute for Statistics and Economic Research)
ISAF	International Stabilization and Assistance Force
LCR	Ligue Communiste Révolutionnaire (Revolutionary Communist League)
LGV	Ligne à Grandes Vitesse (high-speed train)
LO	Lutte Ouvrière (Workers' Struggle)
LRU	Loi Relative aux Libertés et Responsabilités des Universités
LT	Lisbon Treaty
MoDem	Mouvement Démocrate (Democratic Movement)
MRP	Mouvement Républicain Populaire (Popular Republican Movement)
NATO	North Atlantic Treaty Organization
NC	Nouveau Centre (New Centre)
NPA	Nouveau Parti Anticapitaliste (New Anti-Capitalist Party)
OECD	Organisation for Economic Co-operation and Development
OIF	Organisation Internationale de la Francophonie (International Organisation for Francophonie)
PCF	Parti Communiste Français (French Communist Party)
PG	Parti de Gauche (Left Party)
PS	Parti Socialiste (Socialist Party)
QPC	Question Prioritaire de Constitutionnalité (Prior Constitutional Question)

RATP	Régie Autonome des Transports Parisiens (Paris Public Transportation Office)
RéATE	Réforme de l'Administration Territoriale de l'État (Reform of the Territorial State)
RGPP	Révision Générale des Politiques Publiques (Comprehensive Policy Review)
RMC	Radio Monte Carlo
RMI	Revenu Minimum d'Insertion (Minimal Income)
RPR	Rassemblement pour la République (Rally for the Republic)
RSA	Revenu de Solidarité Active (Active Solidarity Income)
RTL	Radios et Télévisions de Luxembourg (Luxembourg Radio and Television Group)
RTT	Réduction du Temps de Travail (Reduction in the Working Week)
SGAE	Secrétariat Général aux Affaires Européennes (General Secretariat for European Affairs)
SGAR	Secrétariat Général aux Affaires Régionales (General Secretariat for Regional Affairs)
SNCF	Société Nationale des Chemins de fer Français (National Company of French Railways)
SNESup	Syndicat National de l'Enseignement Supérieur (National Trade Union for Higher Education)
SUD–Rail	Solidaire, Unitaires et Démocratiques, Rail (Solidarity, Unity, Democracy – railway workers' branch)
TSCG	Treaty on Stability, Growth and Governance
UDF	Union pour la Démocratie Française (Union for French Democracy)
UDR	Union des Démocrates pour la République (Union of Democrats for the Republic)
UK	United Kingdom
UMP	Union pour un Mouvement Populaire (Union for a Popular Mouvement)
UN	United Nations
UNEF	Union Nationale des Étudiants de France (National Union of Students in France)
UNR	Union pour la Nouvelle République (Union for the New Republic)
USM	Union Syndicale des Magistrats (Trade Union of Magistrates)
UNSC	United Nations Security Council
UPM	Union pour la Méditerranée (Union for the Mediterranean)
US	United States
VAT	Value Added Tax

Notes on the Contributors

Sylvain Brouard is Senior Research Fellow at Centre Émile Durkheim, Sciences Po Bordeaux, France, having worked previously at the Center of Political Research of Sciences Po, Paris. His research focuses on law-making in Western democracies and on minority politics. He is currently co-director of the French Agendas Project.

Alistair Cole is Professor of Politics at Cardiff University, Wales, UK. He has published widely on French and European politics. He is the author of *Governing and Governance in France* (Cambridge University Press, 2008) and co-editor (with Romain Pasquier and Sebastien Guigner) of the *Dictionnaire des politiques territoriales* (Presses de Sciences Po, 2011). He is a fellow of the Academy of Social Sciences.

Olivier Costa is a Centre National de la Recherche Scientifique (CNRS) senior research fellow at Sciences Po, Bordeaux, France. He is the author of many books, articles and editorial contributions dealing with European institutions, policies and parliaments. He runs the European studies section of the French Political Science Association. He is a member of the editorial board of the *Journal of European Integration*.

Helen Drake is Professor of French and European Studies at Loughborough University, UK. Her research interests cover contemporary French politics, culture and society, and European integration. She is the author of *Contemporary France* (Palgrave Macmillan, 2011).

Robert Elgie is the Paddy Moriarty Professor of Government and International Studies at Dublin City University, Ireland. He is the co-editor of the journal *French Politics* (published by Palgrave Macmillan). He is the author of *Political Institutions in Contemporary France* (Oxford University Press, 2003), and the lead co-editor of the forthcoming *Oxford Handbook of French Politics* (Oxford University Press).

Arthur Goldhammer is a scholar, writer and translator, and a senior affiliate of the Center for European Studies at Harvard University, USA. He has translated more than 120 books from French and has received numerous awards for his translations, including Tocqueville's *Democracy in America* and Pierre Rosanvallon's *Democratic*

Legitimacy. Together with George Ross, he contributed the chapter on France to a volume entitled *What's Left of the Left?* (Duke University Press, 2012). He is also the author of the widely read blog 'French Politics'.

Florent Gougou has just finished his doctoral thesis ('Comprendre les mutations du vote des ouvriers. Vote de classe, transformation des clivages et changement électoral en France et en Allemagne depuis 1945' [Understanding the changing voting behaviour of workers. Class voting, the transformation of cleavages and electoral change in France and Germany since 1945]) at Sciences Po, Paris, France. He is the author of numerous articles in the journal *French Politics* and has published chapters in several books on electoral behaviour.

Florence Haegel is CNRS Director of Research at the Centre for European Studies (Centre d'Études Européennes) at Sciences Po, Paris, France. She is the author of numerous publications on French parties, including her recent monograph *Les droites en fusion* (Presses de Sciences Po, 2012).

Jolyon Howorth has been Visiting Professor of Political Science at Yale University, USA, since 2002. He is also Jean Monnet Professor *ad personam* of European Politics and Emeritus Professor of European Studies at the University of Bath. His books include *Security and Defence Policy in the European Union* (Palgrave Macmillan, 2007; 2nd edition 2013) and *Defending Europe: The EU, NATO and the Quest for European Autonomy* (Palgrave Macmillan, 2003, co-editor).

Eric Kerrouche is a Professor and Researcher at Sciences Po, Bordeaux, France. He is part of the LEA-CODE, a cooperative project between the University of Stuttgart and Sciences Po to analyse European democratic systems in the context of the enhancement of the European Union. His research interests range from local politics, elected officials and territorial reforms to methods in social science.

Raymond Kuhn is Professor of Politics in the School of Politics and International Relations at Queen Mary University, London, UK. He has published widely on French media policy and political communication. He is the author of *The Media in Contemporary France* (Open University Press, 2011).

Simon Labouret is a specialist in the field of elections and teaches at Sciences Po, Grenoble, France. He is the author of numerous articles in the journal *French Politics*, 2012.

Sophie Meunier is Research Scholar in the Woodrow Wilson School of Public and International Affairs at Princeton University and Co-Director of the EU Program at Princeton. She is the author of *Trading Voices: The European Union in International Commercial Negotiations* (Princeton University Press, 2005) and co-author with Philip Gordon of *The French Challenge: Adapting to Globalization* (Brookings Institution Press, 2001), winner of the 2002 France-Ameriques book award. She is also the editor of several books on Europe and globalization. Her current work deals with the politics of hosting Chinese investment in Europe.

Romain Pasquier is CNRS Director of Research at Sciences Po, Rennes, France. His numerous publications on territorial politics include *Le Pouvoir régional* (Presses de Sciences Po, 2012).

Frédéric Sawicki is Professor of Politics at the University of Paris 1 – Sorbonne-Pantheon, France. He is the co-author, with Remy Lefebvre, of *La Société des socialistes. Le PS aujourd'hui* (Editions du croquant, 2006).

Patrick Simon is Director of Research at the National Institute for the Study of Demography (Institut National d'Études Demographiques) and is a research fellow at the Centre for European Studies (CEE) at Sciences Po, Paris, France. He studies integration and discrimination against immigrants in France and in international comparisons. His publications include 'Collecting Ethnic Statistics in Europe: A Review' (*Ethnic and Racial Studies*, 2012).

Timothy B. Smith is Professor of History at Queen's University, Kingston, Ontario, Canada, where he teaches modern European history and the history of public policy. He is the author of *France in Crisis* (Cambridge University Press, 2004) and *Creating the Welfare State in France, 1880–1940* (McGill/Queen's University Press, 2003). He is working on a general history of the welfare state in rich nations since 1945.

James Stimson is Raymond Dawson Professor of Political Science at the University of North Carolina, Chapel Hill, USA. He is the author of numerous books and articles on American politics and, more specifically, on public opinion and the concept of the policy mood. He is a fellow of the American Academy of Arts and Sciences.

Yves Surel is Professor of Political Science at the University Panthéon-Assas (Paris II), France. He is also Associate Researcher and Co-director of the Centre for the Study of Political and Administrative

Science (Centre d'Études et de Recherches de Sciences Administratives et Politiques, CERSA, Paris, France). He has co-edited, with Jacques de Maillard, *Les politiques publiques sous Sarkozy* (Presses de Sciences Po, 2012).

Cyrille Thiébaut is working towards his doctorate in political science at the University of Paris 1 (Panthéon-Sorbonne), France. He is a member of the Sorbonne Centre for Political Research (Centre de la Recherche Politique de la Sorbonne).

Vincent Tiberj has been Associate Research Professor at Sciences Po, Paris, France, since 2002, where he specializes in comparative electoral behaviour (in France, the USA and Europe), the political psychology of ordinary citizens, the sociology of inequalities, the politics of immigration and integration, and survey research and methodology. He has been a visiting scholar at Stanford University and Oxford University. He also co-ordinates the methodological curricula in the PhD programme of Sciences Po.

Chapter 1

From Sarkozy to Hollande: The New Normal?

ALISTAIR COLE, SOPHIE MEUNIER AND
VINCENT TIBERJ

This is the fifth volume of *Developments in French Politics*. While every chapter is new, the overall aim remains the same as that of its predecessors: to provide an integrated and systematic assessment of current trends in French politics, drawing on the latest research but giving sufficient background to make the book accessible to those without a detailed knowledge of French politics. Two central questions guide this present volume.

First, is there still a 'French exception', a uniquely French path to identity and globalization – if there ever was one? Second, do the presidencies of Nicolas Sarkozy and François Hollande represent mostly rupture or continuity with French political and cultural traditions? To answer these questions, rather than identifying a single encompassing theme, the book sets out to capture the past decade or so of French politics across five main dimensions: the core political and institutional evolutions; processes of partisanship, citizenship, communication and mediation; political attitudes and elections; domestic policy reforms; and the multi-level, regional and international contexts. Though there is no overarching conclusion, the key approach underpinning most chapters is one of France's contingent governance – the country caught between converging economic, European and international pressures and the robust defence of a particular model of republican integration.

The main purpose of this introductory chapter is to provide a temporally specific overview that integrates the five dimensions mentioned above and contributes to our understanding of the evolution of the French polity. This holistic overview will be engaged primarily via a narrative of the presidency of Conservative Nicolas Sarkozy (2007–12) and, where applicable, updated and contrasted with that of the presidency of Socialist François Hollande, who was elected in May 2012. This introductory chapter thereby contains a full analysis

1

of the leadership context of the Sarkozy presidency (upon which very little has been written in English since 2007) and provides insights into the early period of the Hollande presidency. References and comparisons are made to other times and places where appropriate. In this chapter we examine claims that Sarkozy was an inappropriate president, a paradoxical president and a crisis president. By contrast, Hollande based his 2012 campaign on being a 'normal' president. However, early observation of his presidency suggests that normality was a clever political construction, designed to rally anti-Sarkozy feeling, and which was based on the sharp contrast between the two personalities. The image of the 'normal' president did not long resist the exercise of power, which required sustained presidential intervention.

President Sarkozy, 2007–12: an inappropriate president

Sarkozy was elected on the premise that fresh style and fresh policies were connected: because he was bringing a different style to the Elysée palace, he would also bring about policy reforms. His hyperactive personality (especially compared to his predecessor the Conservative Jacques Chirac), his unconventional pedigree as the son of a Hungarian émigré (though he was as bourgeois as Chirac or the Socialist François Mitterrand) and his exposed private life were part of the package that he offered to French voters in 2007. Yet he was barely elected before accusations of inappropriateness surfaced with a vengeance. By the end of his five-year term, during which he had to face a succession of personal and international crises, the prevailing interpretation was that he had been, above all, an 'inappropriate president'.

Nicolas Sarkozy acted in a way, especially during his first 18 months, which was deemed 'unsuitable' for the presidential office, as tailor-made by the iconic General de Gaulle and only slightly modified by his successors. In the first few months of his presidency, the 'bling-bling' president engaged in personal excesses that provoked widespread disapproval, from the post-election celebration at Fouquet's to the luxury holidays offered by close business allies. Sarkozy's personal, especially romantic, life was propelled to the heart of his governing style; in an intensely mediatized age, French electors were invited to share his personal misfortunes and joys (his divorce from Cecilia, his quick courtship and marriage to Carla, the birth of their daughter Giulia). More than the temporary extolling of the virtues of enrichment, Sarkozy was brought low by suspicions of nepotism, most obviously in relation to his own son, Jean Sarkozy, who was being groomed to head the body governing the Défense business district in Paris before public uproar forced the president to abandon his plan. This explicit importing of family life into the operation of the Elysée and the public representation of the Elysée office was novel. There was much less respect than under previous presidents for the traditional boundary between public and private.

While in part a comment on Sarkozy's style, this blurring of public and private can also be read as a sign of the times, when a stolen image on a mobile phone can instantaneously reach a worldwide audience. Herein lay one of the principal paradoxes of the Sarkozy period, as Raymond Kuhn shows in Chapter 8. On the one hand, there was a tightly planned strategy of media control, evidenced by a far closer involvement with the media than at any period since the 1960s (Padis, 2007; Kuhn, 2011). On the other hand, even the most tightly planned media strategy could not cope with the spontaneity of presidential interventions, such as Sarkozy's infamous *casse-toi pauv' con* ('get lost loser') outburst at the Paris Agricultural Salon in 2008, which challenged the sense of appropriate behaviour and decorum commonly associated with the presidency.

In more subtle ways, also, the Sarkozy style broke with established presidential practices. His use of the triangulation strategy (adopting and adapting policies put on the agenda by political opponents, such as the Tobin Tax on financial transactions) was unusual for a French president, as it implied a detailed involvement in day-to-day politics. Moreover, this strategy was not typically French but had been inspired by the US Democrats and by Britain's New Labour Prime Minister Tony Blair. Blurring the boundaries between left and right (by triangulation and even more by opening up the first government of UMP Prime Minister François Fillon to socialists and representatives of civil society) was successful in the short term, but ultimately produced confusion and dissension within Sarkozy's own camp.

Aware of the bad reputation acquired by his initial handling of the presidency, Sarkozy tried to correct and transform his presidential image to shore up his sagging popularity from 2009 onwards. After each mistake a new Sarkozy was spun in the media. He worked hard to learn from his errors and adapt his behaviour in a way broadly deemed appropriate for the office, especially after the fateful first 18 months. The new behaviour was manifest in a conscious and rather successful retrenchment of his personal life from the public sphere. It also took the form of a series of successive, often failed, efforts by Sarkozy to detach himself from the day-to-day management of domestic policies.

The 2007–12 period witnessed an evolution from the early highly interventionist president to the consciously more focused figure seeking to symbolize national unity and crisis management. Initially ambivalent about Gaullist symbols, Sarkozy had embraced the Gaullist model by the end of his term as a means of restoring the authority of the office itself (Landrin, 2009). Like many political leaders before him, Sarkozy looked to salvation in the European Union (EU), in the international political economy or in foreign policy interventions (such as that in Libya) to make a difference, through adopting the regalien posture that only the Head of State can assume. If reshaping the presidency was central to his 2007 campaign message, by late 2011 the office had almost tamed Sarkozy.

Yet most French voters could not forget the early years of the presidency, and the 2012 presidential election was in many ways an anti-Sarkozy referendum and a repudiation as much of the man as of his policies. What was the meaning of this personal unpopularity? Did it signify the rejection of an individual deemed inappropriate to exercise the highest office? Or was it a consequence of the new rules of presidential leadership introduced by the *quinquennat* (five-year term)? Or did it reflect a demand for different policies? Answers to these questions are provided in the chapters by Stimson, Tiberj and Thiébault (Chapter 11) and Gougou and Labouret (Chapter 10). Whichever interpretation is preferred, the low poll ratings were a harsh verdict on the president's style of governing, especially as premier Fillon remained more popular than Sarkozy for most of the five-year period – a highly unusual feat for a French prime minister. In the perception of most French voters, Sarkozy had been the one actually governing for five years and was therefore the one held accountable for the policy outcomes.

In some accounts, the Sarkozy presidency was reduced to being an inappropriate transgression of the key personal and institutional codes, most notably via a deeply political reading of the office, whereby the political leader dispensed with the discourse of national unity, slated opponents and invited unpopularity in response to detailed interventionism in politics and policy-making (Giesbert, 2011; Nay, 2012). But it makes more sense to reason in terms of a paradoxical president. The Sarkozy period was replete with the paradoxes of the 'hyperpresident' who undertook a thoroughgoing reform of the institutions and the neo-liberal who gave a new lease of life to *dirigiste* practices. Sarkozy's downfall might ultimately have been due more to the lack of a consistent legitimizing discourse for a substantial reform programme than to any lingering doubts about his personal fitness for office.

President Sarkozy, 2007–12: a paradoxical president

The election of Nicolas Sarkozy as President of the French Republic on 6 May 2007 was clear and unambiguous. He fought the campaign on a platform of decline and revival (beside his particular focus on immigration and the restoration of national identity). Decline, he argued, was the consequence of an overprotected and under-productive public sector, a level of personal and business taxation that was too high, a social model that discouraged employment, and a centralized and inefficient education system. The prognosis was barely less straightforward. To restore its economic position and political influence, France had to reform its social model, control public expenditure, reduce the number of civil servants and challenge the conservatism and corporatism of French society. In this narrative, the core concerns were economic, but the remedies were those of political leadership. The Sarkozy presidency was inaugurated in 2007 with a discourse of reform, indeed of *rupture*, with existing political practices, established interests and the general feeling that the state can do everything – this was an ironic turn of events since Sarkozy was proposing a break with the government that preceded him, yet was dominated by his own party.

Sarkozy started with a reform of the presidency itself. As soon as he was elected, he set up a commission, chaired by former Prime Minister Edouard Balladur, tasked with the mission of exploring the prospects for institutional reform, notably a stronger presidential form of government. The constitutional reform package, narrowly agreed by a Congress of the two Chambers in July 2008, is discussed in its various dimensions by Elgie (Chapter 2), Brouard, Costa and Kerrouche (Chapter 3) and Surel (Chapter 4). The landmark set of reforms enhanced parliamentary and judicial checks and balances as the counterpart to the strengthening of the executive and, specifically, presidential power.

Paradoxically, Sarkozy's practice of the presidency seemed at odds with the spirit of the reform he had launched and strongly defended (Knapp, 2013). Once elected, he pushed furthest the break with the inherited roles of the presidential office, dispensing almost entirely with the fiction of a supra-partisan, non-interventionist president that was the principal legacy of de Gaulle. The instruments of Sarkozy's presidential 'power' (and their limitations) are analysed by Elgie (Chapter 2).

Did Sarkozy succeed in bringing about a reform of public policy as well? A clearer presidential mandate gave rise to a more explicitly assumed policy leadership. Most of the key reforms of the 2007–12 period were directly associated with Sarkozy; from the reforms to the 35-hour week and flexible working time (2007) and the tax shield (2007), through the detailed interventions in the fields of state reform (Révision Générale des Politiques Publiques (RGPP), 2007–12), universities (2007), the environment (2008), local government (2009–10) and pensions reform (2010) (de Maillard and Surel, 2012). These reforms are considered in more detail in this volume, especially in the chapters by Goldhammer (Chapter 9) and Smith (Chapter 12). But there was no consistent specific policy style associated with Sarkozy. If the RGPP was implemented in a top-down manner, the ambitious programme of environmental reforms (the 'Grenelle') was conceived as part of a protracted process of negotiation with key economic and environmental interests, as illustrated by Goldhammer (Chapter 9). And if the key 2010 reform to pensions was implemented against the bitter opposition of the trade unions, the latter were regular visitors to the Elysée and associated with other important changes (for example, the rules for determining which union lists are representative in professional elections). The overall evaluation of Sarkozy's reformist record, tempered by the impact of economic crisis, is rather paradoxical. If his presidency was a reformist one, almost all of the key reforms introduced in 2007–08 had been modified or abandoned by 2012.

The 'hyper-presidentialist thesis' also accounts with difficulty for the revival of dissidence within the governing presidential party, the UMP. Traditionally, the linkage between presidential power and the party system took the form of the emergence of the presidential party – successively the Union des démocrats pour la République (UDR), the Union pour la démocratie française (UDF), the Parti socialiste (PS) and the UMP – the heart of the presidential *majorité* to support the governments named by the president. The presidentialization of the French party system, though never complete, was encouraged by the strengthening of the presidency as the key institution after the 1962 referendum, as well as by the use of the majoritarian-based second-ballot electoral system in presidential and parliamentary elections and by the prestige of the presidential contest as the 'decisive' election that oriented the results of parliamentary elections that followed immediately after the presidential contest.

Sarkozy's election as president in 2007 represented a new phase in the history of the French presidency. In the June 2007 parliamentary elections, following the presidential contest, the UMP by itself had an absolute majority, with 313 deputies out of 577. This powerful result demonstrated the political ascendancy of the decisive presidential election over the parliamentary one. Bringing into line the presidential and parliamentary elections from 2002 has strengthened presidential control over elections (whereas all previous presidents had had to face mid-term elections) but also made the president into a far more hands-on, contestable figure. The president used to stay outside of the realm of day-to-day politics, but now he is at the heart of media and opposition attention; if he fails, he takes his party and its elected officials down with him (even at the local level).

As Haegel demonstrates in Chapter 6, one of the core paradoxes of the 2007–12 period lay in the distancing of powerful forces within the UMP from Sarkozy, though he had rescued and renovated the party from 2004 onwards. Rather like the Rassemblement pour la République (RPR) for former president, Jacques Chirac, in 1976, the

UMP became a powerful electoral machine for Sarkozy and proved its mobilizing capacity in the 2007 presidential election. The role of the presidential party has evolved in the post-2007 environment. Far from the older style *parti de godillots* ('party of yes-men'), representatives of the UMP, anxious to secure re-election, saw themselves as scrutineers of effective presidential performance. Generational ambition, and the new timescale of the *quinquennat*, produced a far more instrumental relationship with the incumbent president. There emerged a clear sense of positioning on behalf of a younger generation of ambitious UMP politicians (Jean-François Copé, François Baroin, Nathalie Kosciusko-Morizet, Valérie Pécresse, Laurent Wauquiez), with their eyes on the 2017 presidential election contest and with no particular affective link to Sarkozy. The 2012 presidential campaign, driven almost entirely from the Elysée, proved highly divisive. It was criticized by leading figures within the UMP: implicitly by Prime Minister Fillon, and more openly by former Prime Minister Raffarin, or by other figures closely associated with the Sarkozy years such as former Justice Minister Rachida Dati. The speed with which hostilities broke out in the UMP even before the results of the June 2012 parliamentary elections were known, and the lingering divisions, leading to the hotly contested election for the leadership of the UMP in November 2012, suggested the Sarkozy era had definitively passed.

President Sarkozy, 2007–12: a crisis president

One of the core distinctions in the literature on political leadership is that between transactional versus transformational leadership styles (Burns, 1978). The transactional leader drives bargains and fosters compromises, while the transformational style is one based on clear goals and vision. Which type of leader was Sarkozy?

In domestic politics, the new interventionism of Sarkozy, who was elected on a platform of rupture and had vowed to enact quickly a series of major policy reforms breaking with the past, paradoxically produced in practice a transactional style of leadership, one where the president was forced to bargain with interests, compromise with parliament and party and make bargains on the details of domestic policy (as illustrated in Chapter 5 by Cole and Pasquier in the field of local government reform). Arguably, the supra-partisan presidential aura was diminished by the attempt to intervene in matters of day-to-day politics. The effects of the economic crisis after 2008 strengthened the impression of the perceived unfairness of some of the early measures, such as the tax shield (*bouclier fiscal*), which forced the French Treasury to reimburse very wealthy people who had paid too much tax. More generally, there was a gradual calling into question of the symbolic measures of the first year under the weight of a major economic crisis.

At the same time, Sarkozy's presidency was gradually transformed by having to respond to a series of international crises, from the 2008 Georgia crisis through to the seemingly interminable sovereign debt and euro crises from 2010. This provided opportunities for reverting to a more transformational conception of the presidency – or at least offered a transformational moment in 2008 and 2009. Sarkozy's direct leadership style was successful, or at least significant, in some key respects, as shown by Drake (Chapter 14), Meunier (Chapter 15) and Howorth (Chapter 16). The French leader demonstrated considerable political skill in mobilizing the opportunities provided by these crises.

France's presidency of the European Council from July to December 2008, analysed by Drake, represented a major opportunity for this ambitious president (Chapter 14). It provided Sarkozy with the opportunity to act decisively and rapidly to respond to international diplomatic and economic crises. Speed, for once, was of the essence. He reacted very rapidly to the outbreak of the war in Georgia in August 2008, travelling to Moscow to meet with Dmitry Medvedev and Vladimir Putin, and agreeing a deal that recognized Russia's 'right' to defend its borders, in return for forestalling a full-scale occupation of Georgia. The French president had no mandate from the Council, or the Commission, but acted immediately and presented a fait accompli.

In terms of the financial crisis, Sarkozy also acted fast, as analysed by Meunier (Chapter 15). Using the crisis as a personal resource, he distanced himself from US and international capitalism, called for new economic regulations (notably against tax havens), fiscal coordination and a more protective role for the state. At the UN on 23 September 2008, thanks to the ongoing US elections, Sarkozy took the initiative to call for a G20 Summit, comprising leaders from 20 major economies across the planet, a meeting that eventually took place in November 2008. He cooperated closely with UK Prime Minister Gordon Brown; by mid-October, the key EU countries had agreed a plan to save the banks. The international turn allowed Sarkozy to reposition himself in domestic politics and to move on from the early portrayals of him as a Gallic version of the neo-liberal Margaret Thatcher. By attempting to place the French presidency at the centre of crisis operations, within and beyond Europe, Sarkozy renewed explicitly traditional French perspectives whereby French presidents should be intimately involved in shaping key history-making decisions.

Sarkozy's belief that only governments could act in a crisis revived Franco-German leadership claims. By November 2008, Sarkozy and German Chancellor Angela Merkel were jointly calling for a relaxation of the EU's Stability and Growth Pact rules. Three years later, Sarkozy and Merkel were admonishing Greece for proving itself incapable of respecting the terms of the euro bailout fund. While these positions were diametrically opposed, in practice public opinion was invited to draw the lesson that the Franco-German 'couple' were once again in charge of the European ship. Between 2008 and 2011, however, there was an important shift in the balance of the Franco-German relationship. The banking crisis of 2008 called forth Keynesian economic instincts from British Prime Minister Gordon Brown that were supported by Sarkozy (and, later, by US President Barack Obama) and produced a massive state-led public investment programme (mainly to rescue the banks and the car industry). The rapid deterioration in public finances in countries such as Spain, the UK and Greece also played out in France and Germany. As the credit crunch became a debt and (euro) currency crisis, Merkel, Chancellor of the key creditor nation in the eurozone, exercised an increasingly iron grip. The euro crisis ultimately produced the 2011 Fiscal Compact that represented an almost complete victory for German positions over French ones. By 2012, the ongoing and highly unpredictable economic crisis had sapped the popularity of most incumbent governments, including that of the French.

The above analysis reveals another paradox of the Sarkozy period. Never before had European and foreign policy been so concentrated amongst the Elysée staff, or supervised more closely by the president. By the end of the Sarkozy period, however, there was a widespread belief that power within Europe had shifted eastwards and that the cherished Franco-German relationship was above all valued for the image it gave of France as a great power, sharing a seat at the table, rather than as an equal partner driving the substance of European governance. Sarkozy attempted to play the role of the transformational leader until the end. But not even a successful and highly personal war in Libya in 2011, as analysed by Howorth in Chapter 16, could provide relief for the embattled Sarkozy, ultimately demonstrating the limits of foreign policy prestige in domestic politics.

Reverting to type? Sarkozy's 2012 presidential campaign

Running on a platform of rupture in 2012, as he had done in 2007, was no longer possible for Sarkozy as the incumbent president. But he had more campaign choices available than his rivals. One potential strategy was to focus on his record as 'captain of the ship' sailing through turbulent waters, the image of *La France forte* ('a strong France') on his campaign posters. He could have argued that he preserved, and even amplified, France's voice in the world, from the handling of the financial crisis to the Libya intervention. He could legitimately boast that France alone, of all the major EU nations, had not undergone a recession since 2008. He could point to his record as co-steerer of EU destiny, via the close relationship formed with Germany's Chancellor Angela Merkel. The temptation was strong; the early campaign was framed in terms of the necessary alignment with and convergence to the German model. But, in the process of the transition from president to candidate in February 2012, all sense of balance, achievement and caution were thrown to the wind in a manner characteristic of Sarkozy's personal style.

A clear divorce was assumed between the President of all the French and the activist candidate who presented himself as a challenger. As in 2007, Sarkozy was convinced that France had moved to the right, that only domestic politics really mattered and that Marine Le Pen, leader of the resurgent far-right National Front (FN), represented a danger to his chances of re-election. A strategic choice was made to focus primarily on the large proportion of the French electorate worried about globalization, European integration, immigration and national identity, as noted by Meunier (Chapter 15). There were two versions of this orientation of a protective France, represented by two rival teams of Elysée advisers around Henri Guaino and Patrick Buisson respectively. The former orientation focused on social and economic issues, identifying internal and external threats to the well-being of French people and proposing clear remedies to assuage these fears. This national and social strand underpinned the Villepinte speech in mid-March 2012. It involved an affirmation of European and national preference, going so far as to call into question existing EU treaties and going beyond Hollande's promise to renegotiate the Fiscal Compact. The second variant of Sarkozy's protective France campaign focused on the core 'values' of France, namely work, family, national identity and security. These values were identified as representing the preoccupations of popular voters, tempted by the FN, whose support would be needed to ensure Sarkozy's presence in the second round and eventual victory. This strategy arguably backfired. Centring the campaign on issues such as halal meat (initially raised by Le Pen), proposing two referenda targeting the rights of the unemployed, and limiting welfare rights for immigrants appeared withdrawn from the preoccupations of the popular electorate, which had been destabilized by the crisis. The national populist tone of the campaign was heightened after the first round, when Le Pen came in a strong third.

Sarkozy was the first incumbent President of the Fifth Republic seeking re-election who did not lead in the first ballot round, and this created a psychologically very damaging effect. Though he gained ground between the two ballots and benefited from a differential mobilization of first round abstentions, these gains were not enough to overturn the logic of the first round vote, as reported by Gougou and Labouret (Chapter 10) and by Stimson, Tiberj and Thiébault (Chapter 11).

The 2012 campaign was quite consistent, in short, with Sarkozy's instrumental use of electoral programmes and ideology. Built on limitless personal energy and activism, based on one announcement a day and negative campaigning, the 2012 campaign was the embodiment of Sarkozy's fast governing style. His campaign relied on the electorate's short attention span, though most French voters had not forgotten the previous five years. In this way, the 2012 presidential election had features of an anti-Sarkozy referendum.

François Hollande: the accidental president?

In some ways François Hollande might be considered as an accidental president. When he finally ceded his place as First Secretary of the French Socialist Party in 2008, after 11 years at the helm, virtually no-one would have accredited the idea that he would ever be elected president. His reputation thus far had been of a fairly consensual party leader lacking authority and personality. Closely allied with First Secretary Lionel Jospin during the decade of socialist government (1981–86, 1988–93), Hollande became party First Secretary in 1997, when Lionel Jospin became Prime Minister in the plural left government. An important behind-the-scenes player, Hollande did not form part of the Jospin government – and never had any ministerial experience for that matter. Was he, at least, a successful party leader? The verdict is mixed. Perhaps his main achievement was to have held the party together throughout a turbulent decade which included the highs of electoral victory in 1997 and the lows of the Socialists failing to reach the second round of the presidential election in 2002. His stewardship of the PS had a curate's egg quality. He obtained a substantial victory in the 2004 regional and European elections, for instance, but was disavowed by a large proportion of the party's electorate in the 2005 referendum on the draft EU Constitutional Treaty. And in spite of winning a mandate in favour of the 'Yes' vote from party members, he was unable to ensure the acquiescence of party heavyweights such as former Prime Minister Laurent Fabius, the socialist leader of the 'No' campaign. From his time as First Secretary, however, Hollande developed a deeper knowledge than anybody else of the internal workings of the Socialist Party, a network he used effectively to win the PS primary in 2011 and then to rally the party to his presidential candidacy (see Sawicki, Chapter 7).

Hollande's emergence as a serious political player was linked to an underlying self-confidence and three fortuitous events. Paradoxically, his failure to unite the party in 2005 meant that he was excluded as a serious player in the PS internal primaries in 2006, eventually won by his former partner and mother of their four children, Ségolène Royal. With the benefit of hindsight, this appeared as a blessing in disguise. Following Royal's failure against Sarkozy in 2007, Hollande was defeated at the Reims congress in 2008, when the PS leadership was captured by the mayor of Lille, Martine Aubry, in a tough battle against Royal. Breaking the umbilical cord with the Socialist Party organization provided Hollande with a window of opportunity. He displayed a constant self-belief in his prospects of winning the presidential election in 2012. He declared his intentions early on in 2009 and linked his re-election as President of the Corrèze departmental council in the 2010 cantonal elections to the pursuit of his candidacy. Surpassing this initial obstacle, he then benefited from two key accidental events: first, the disgrace of the socialist front-runner, Dominique Strauss-Kahn, after the 'events' in a Sofitel hotel room in New York on 14 May 2011; second, the decision to push ahead with primary elections in October 2011 to select the Socialist Party's candidate. The Strauss-Kahn affair not only disqualified the former head of the International Monetary Fund from seeking the PS nomination, but it also challenged First Secretary Aubry, who had previously agreed to a pact with Strauss-Kahn. Second, the Socialist primaries were an unexpected success, mobilizing almost three million voters and designating a clear victor – Hollande. The internal primary also laid to rest the claims of Royal as another potential rival.

If Sarkozy made the strategic gamble that he could win the election by focussing on boundaries and identity, Hollande made a very different calculation: that, for once, the public would favour an economically realistic social-democratic campaign message (particularly the Bayrou supporters). Though the campaign was consistent with the verbal radicalism of the French left's discursive tradition (hence the attacks on 'faceless finance' in the Le Bourget speech in January 2012 and the proposed 75 per cent marginal tax on very high incomes), Hollande deliberately avoided making too many promises. The campaign was based as much on process (the call to renegotiate the Fiscal Compact treaty, repeal the RGPP, restore social dialogue or undertake a new decentralization reform) as on the substantive promises in the '60 engagements' which, once presented in February 2012, provided a roadmap from which the candidate rarely deviated (except for the taxation of the wealthy, which was a response to the growing weight of the Left Front candidate Jean-Luc Mélenchon during the campaign). Hollande was nonetheless accused of storing up problems for later – by Brussels, as well as by domestic rivals such as Bayrou and Sarkozy. The growth assumptions underpinning the 60 engagements certainly appeared highly optimistic; and how the public debt would be eliminated by 2017 was not elucidated.

If Hollande's campaign drew lessons from the past, these concerned mainly the need for a much closer link between candidate and party. His 60 engagements drew liberally on the Socialist Programme adopted in 2011, unlike Royal's earlier programme in the 2007 election which was her own. Hollande displayed strategic skill in healing the wounds that might have festered after the primary campaign by reaching out to Pierre Moscovici (a Strauss-Kahn supporter), Aubry (the First Secretary of the party) and Fabius (former First Secretary), all of whom had harshly criticized him in the past. Hollande fought the campaign as a compromise candidate between the various families of the French left; personally he was strongly pro-European and social democratic (which is seen as a handicap for the French left) and he was deeply conscious of the need to reach out to the France du Non that had captured a majority of PS voters in the 2005 EU referendum. Finally, the success of his campaign might be explained by his anticipating the equilibria of multiparty bipolar competition. The Socialist candidate made few explicit promises that might endanger his courtship of the centre and centre-right electorate in the second round. For all the hue and cry, the Left Front candidate Jean-Luc Mélenchon's voters were unlikely to back any candidate other than Hollande in the second round.

François Hollande: a normal president?

The choice to focus the campaign on the record of the Sarkozy years was defensive, designed to preserve an opinion poll lead that was mainly built upon a popular rejection of Sarkozy. If the 2012 election was considered by many to be an anti-Sarkozy referendum, the Socialist candidate did little to challenge this reading. Hollande's candidacy was based on his strategic political positioning as being a 'normal' candidate and president, a style deliberately adopted to be the counterpart of the flamboyant Sarkozy. Such a construction served an obvious short-term purpose. The analysis undertaken by Jaffré (2012) suggests that this was by far the best electoral strategy for Hollande in 2012, even though Jospin had lost on a similar premise of switching to a more normal (i.e. less vertical) presidential style in 2002.

With Hollande (narrowly) elected on an anti-Sarkozy platform, the first 100 days of the new presidency were defined symbolically as the counterpart of the preceding five years, in terms of substance and, above all, in terms of style. Normality signified a return to a more traditional reading of the dual executive in the Fifth Republic. Presidential–prime ministerial relations would revert to 'type', whereby the president would concentrate upon the sphere of foreign and European policy and the prime minister would lead and coordinate governmental policy. Superficially, at least, such a classic division of labour was respected in the early months of the Hollande presidency. The new president, with no experience of ministerial office, was forced to concentrate his presidential activity during the first three months on the 'reserved' presidential sphere of foreign policy and European Union affairs, themes developed by Elgie (Chapter 2), Drake (Chapter 14), Meunier (Chapter 15) and Howorth (Chapter 16). Such international activism bore testament as much to the pressing weight of the EU and foreign policy cycle as to any conscious choice by the incoming president. Normality was also ostensibly assured by the return to a more balanced pattern of inner executive relations. Prime Minister Jean-Marc Ayrault initially gave the impression of steering and coordinating government policy, making a series of authoritative judgements, chairing the July 2012 meetings designed to indicate budgetary ceilings and defending the government's position in the July 2012 extraordinary session of parliament. The prime minister's leadership was seriously challenged over the next few months, however, as his authority was undermined by independent-minded and popular ministers such as Manuel Valls (Interior) and Arnaud Montebourg (Industrial Revival) and the negative public image portrayed of an uncoordinated executive branch.

The traditional mechanisms of prime ministerial subordination were also very much in evidence from the outset. By choosing Ayrault, a consensual political figure representative of Grand-Ouest politics, as his first prime minister, Hollande selected a close and loyal lieutenant, a good manager and former head of the Socialist deputies, who would implement the president's programme. In turn Ayrault called on electors to make a 'coherent' choice and return a pro-presidential majority in the June 2012 National Assembly election. The June 2012 parliamentary elections, which duly produced an overall majority of PS deputies to support the president, were another textbook example of presidential supremacy since 2002. The key portfolios in the first two Ayrault governments were decided by the new president and clearly followed campaign choices and declarations, such as a gender balanced 'parity' government (in the number of portfolios, if not their importance) and a Socialist-led government with Green and left radical allies but without the participation of the (much reduced) Communists or the Left Party led by Mélenchon. Moreover, there was evidence of pressure being placed on the Socialist Party leadership under Martine Aubry to demonstrate its support for the newly elected president; the announcement made in July 2012 that there would be a Aubry–Ayrault motion for the October 2012 PS conference created rumblings of discontent from the left of the party (see Chapter 7).

President Hollande, however, soon became trapped by his self-presentation as a normal president. The 'normal' facade crumbled quickly and unexpectedly on the personal front. As a candidate he had pledged not to allow his personal life to interfere with his presidential practice; unlike Sarkozy, close members of his family were given no special treatment at the inauguration ceremony. It did not take long, however, for Hollande's private life to spill over into the public domain. The provocative tweet sent by the president's current partner, *Paris Match* journalist Valérie Trierweiler, in support of a dissident Socialist candidate running against Ségolène Royal in the La Rochelle constituency in the 2012 National Assembly elections, challenged the notion of a president with a normal private life and opened up the floodgates to ridicule and comedy. It became a running joke, calling into question Hollande's ability to steer his own life, let alone the country. Rather like during the early days of the Sarkozy presidency (Nay, 2012), Hollande's partner was also suspected of getting involved with the selection of presidential advisors and vetoing a number of mooted appointments.

The second danger with the 'normal presidency' frame was the accusation that the new government was all style and no substance. The early focus of governmental activity was on enacting a few symbolic measures by governmental decree to enhance the prospects of victory in the June 2012 parliamentary election, such as raising the minimum wage, restoring the right for certain categories of employees to retire at age 60 and blocking rents for private rented property. However, the extraordinary parliamentary session of July 2012 was much calmer than the equivalent under Sarkozy five years earlier, the key measure being to reintroduce a law penalizing sexual harassment, a previous one having been declared as unconstitutional by the Constitutional Council. Against the social generosity of the early measures, a much harder edge was already making itself felt. In the emergency 'budgetary perspectives' of July 2012, €10 billion of tax rises were identified (via a raising of stamp duty, a strong increase in the wealth tax and the limitation of exoneration of gifts from taxation). These decisions were taken in part to compensate the decision not to implement the VAT increase planned by the previous government. These corrective measures presaged some tough political and economic choices ahead, which are discussed in Meunier's chapter. In November 2012, Hollande announced a further, more substantial cut in public expenditure and a rise in VAT.

A normal president, as Howorth demonstrates in Chapter 16, is not necessarily the best equipped to deal with extraordinary situations, such as the conflict in Syria. Back home, Hollande was relieved by the decision taken by the Constitutional Council, in August 2012, that a ratification of the Fiscal Compact Treaty would not require a constitutional revision. But the decision to ratify the treaty, much-derided during the election campaign, not only raised the ire of the Left Front around Mélenchon, but also created deep unease within the ruling

Socialist Party and provoked a decision by the Greens not to support this specific action. On the 100-day anniversary of his election, Hollande was faced with growing unpopularity as a result of the continuing economic crisis, a sharp rise in unemployment and the uncertainty produced by the ongoing euro crisis. One survey carried out to mark the 100 days since Hollande's election suggested that a majority of French electors (54 against 46 per cent) were dissatisfied with his actions as president (*Le Figaro*, 12 August 2012). Was this the new normality?

Conclusion

With the benefit of hindsight, two main lessons emerged from the 2012 presidential election campaign. First, the leading candidates converged in dissociating the main campaign themes from the key developments in European politics and the international political economy. Second, the Socialist François Hollande was elected on the basis of a strong rejection of the outgoing president, but with less powerful personal or policy endorsement than his predecessor five years earlier; the vote was more a verdict against Sarkozy than it was a mandate for Hollande.

The 2012 election took place in a difficult international economic context characterized by an ongoing economic slump in the United States, competition from emerging economies not always playing by the rules, major structural power shifts in the global economy, and of course the seemingly never-ending crisis of the euro. Yet the electoral campaign, but for the period between the two rounds, was like a moment suspended in time, largely disconnected from the reality that any new government would have to face.

This book asks whether there is still a 'French exception', a uniquely French path to identity and globalization. To varying degrees, the contributors to this volume concur that the Sarkozy presidency and the 2012 electoral campaign represented, to some extent, evidence that there is still a "French exception" when it comes to globalization –a collective demonization of the phenomenon and an ostrich-like quality of political rhetoric, pretending either that France is victimized by the globalized economy or that it can be ignored and that politicians can protect the French population so that everything can be like it used to be. Despite the salience and gravity of these international economic realities, the main candidates were trapped in a narrative that prevented them from tackling the most pressing issues of the day and precluded them from addressing fundamentally the underlying causes of the loss of French competitiveness – which resulted in the end in the sending of mixed and vacuous messages. Neither Sarkozy nor Hollande confronted head on the real problems. They did not discuss how to adjust the French economy so it could compete and thrive in the globalized world, nor did they address the real risks of the European sovereign debt crisis to French banks or any meaningful political reform of European governance. Instead, the campaign revolved around empty promises and scapegoat issues, such as immigration, halal meat and the cost of a driver's licence.

This book also asks whether the presidencies of Nicolas Sarkozy and François Hollande represented mostly rupture or continuity within the French political and cultural traditions. On the surface, Sarkozy projected himself initially, and was perceived subsequently, as a different breed of politician, one who could initiate a true break, both through his individual style and through his policies. But, as the contributors to this volume show, in hindsight his presidency exhibited more continuity than rupture. On the personal level, his style quickly rubbed up the French the wrong way and, deemed an inappropriate president, he had to revert back to more traditional ways of conducting himself. On the policy level, he came into office with a heavy agenda of reforms, but these quickly fizzled out, both for internal reasons and because of the financial crisis and the sovereign debt crisis in Europe. President Hollande demonstrated more continuity than change with his predecessor's European agenda. Within six months of his election, he had secured the passage through the French parliament of the EU Fiscal Compact Treaty, including the 'golden rule' of balanced budgets that he had criticized so vigorously during the campaign.

The second lesson of the 2012 election was that Hollande was elected with no particular mandate. Sarkozy did both too much and too little as president to be re-elected: too much, because his new personal style and policy hyperactivity were interpreted negatively; too little, because his interventions had not been enough to shield the French people from global economic forces. Though Hollande benefited in the short term from a strong anti-Sarkozy sentiment, and played his hand with great skill, the result was not an embrace of the left's policy proposals or values. The 2012 electoral series was fought in a crisis; voters were equally pessimistic about the ability of Hollande to 'improve the situation of the country' (26 per cent) as they were about Sarkozy (25 per cent) (Jaffré, 2012). Moreover, a majority of second-round voters (51 per cent, compared with 31 per cent in 2007) declared that they had voted negatively (for the candidate best placed to prevent the less preferred candidate from being elected) and only a minority declared they had voted positively for their candidate (49 per cent, compared with 69 per cent in 2007). The logic of institutional conformity ensured that President Hollande would have the means to govern after the victory in the June 2012 National Assembly elections. But he appeared to have been elected more on the basis of a strong rejection of the outgoing president than as a result of a powerful personal or policy endorsement. This made for a short honeymoon period. President Hollande soon, in turn, became subject to deep unpopularity. The ongoing economic crisis had already 'cost' outgoing executives in a number of European countries (including Sarkozy in France, Brown in the UK, Zapatero in Spain and Berlusconi in Italy). Within a few months, Hollande's popularity had plunged and public opinion surveys were equating his 'normality' and cautiousness with a lack of capacity for action.

Reality quickly caught up with Hollande, and within six months of gaining the presidency he could no longer wait and see when dealing with the ongoing ravages of the economic crisis. Almost simultaneously in November 2012, the following occurred. Louis Gallois, a respected French industrialist and bona fide socialist, released a much publicized report on French competitiveness (and lack thereof); Moody's downgraded France's AAA credit rating; and the British magazine *The Economist* called France 'the time-bomb at the heart of Europe', warning about the dire state of the French economy and asking whether Hollande's proposed reforms to tackle structural economic challenges were ambitious enough. Like previous instances in the Fifth Republic, it may be the case that only a government from the left can actually implement drastic structural reforms without incurring the wrath of the demonstration-prone French population. Whether these reforms will go far enough to reinvigorate the French economy and whether Hollande will be able to implement these reforms, using stealth and distraction or through open and direct negotiation, remains to be seen.

Chapter 2

The French Presidency

ROBERT ELGIE

This chapter places the Sarkozy presidency (2007–12) in the context of presidential leadership from 1958 and reflects on the early months of the Hollande presidency. The main argument is that Sarkozy was able to operate a form of personalized governance because the institutions of the Fifth Republic encourage presidential leadership (Gaffney, 2012). However, it is important not to caricature either Sarkozy himself or his governing style. Many of the criticisms of the president's ostentatious lifestyle date from the early period of his presidency. Thereafter, he was careful to tone down the public manifestations of personal excess. Moreover, when he came to power he practised a policy of political '*ouverture*' (opening up), whereby the presidential majority was extended to include both centrists and former socialists. In addition, in 2008 he was the driving force behind constitutional reforms that aimed to increase the powers of parliament and decrease the powers of the presidency. Thus, the images of him as some sort of republican Croesus in his personal life and as an inveterate aggrandizer of personalized power in his political life need to be tempered somewhat. Even so, there is usually some truth to all myths. The Fifth Republic places the president at the centre of the political process and the system was undoubtedly presidentialized under Sarkozy. For his part, President Hollande has adopted a very different, much more restrained governing style. To date, though, the message seems to be that even if the French rejected the bling-bling president, they have not taken the 'normal' president fully to their hearts either.

The presidency under the Fifth Republic

The Constitution of the Fifth Republic created a dual executive, one in which both the president and the prime minister are important political actors (Elgie, 2003). A literal reading of the text might suggest that there is a system of prime ministerial government. Article 20 states that the government decides and directs the policy of the nation and that it has the administration and the armed forces at its disposal. Moreover, Article 21 states that the prime minister is in general charge of the government's work and is responsible for national defence and for the implementation of laws. Thus, the prime minister is placed at the head of a government, which is charged with the day-to-day realization and implementation of public policy. That said, the 1958 constitution also provides a basis for presidential leadership. For example, Article 8 states that the president appoints the prime minister. If the political conditions are right, and they usually are, the president will appoint a loyal or at least subordinate prime minister, thus giving the president an indirect influence over the system as a whole by way of being the head of the government. In addition, the president has particular responsibilities in foreign and defence policy. Article 52 states that the president is responsible for negotiating and ratifying international treaties. Also, Article 15 states that the president is the head of the armed forces. Even though the prime minister is responsible for national defence, the president's finger is on the nuclear button. Overall, while the Constitution of the Fifth Republic created a system in which both the president and the prime minister are important political actors, in practice the president, through the prime minister, is usually in control.

The 1958 constitution ensured that the president would be a significant constitutional figure. However, the 1962 constitutional reform that introduced the direct election of the president ensured that thereafter he or she would be the dominant political actor within the executive. The introduction of direct election changed the dynamic of the system in two ways. Firstly, it provided the president with a direct link to the people. He or she is elected by a two-ballot majority system, which means that the successful candidate will, necessarily, have won more than 50 per cent of the votes cast. For this reason, the president can justifiably claim to be speaking on behalf of France. This gives him or her an authority that no other actor in the system can hope to equal. Secondly, to win the election candidates put forward policy programmes. Once elected, the new president expects to implement his or her programme. In this way, the presidential election sets the policy agenda for the country. The prime minister heads a government that decides and directs the policy of the nation, but the policies are those identified by the successful candidate at the presidential election.

That said, the direct election of the president is a necessary but not a sufficient political condition for presidential leadership. The prime minister is accountable to the National Assembly and most legislation must be passed through parliament. Thus, the parliamentary majority remains key to the functioning of the system. In December 2000 a constitutional reform reduced the president's term of office from seven to five years, the same as the term for the National Assembly. The electoral calendar was also adjusted such that the presidential election now takes place a few weeks prior to the legislative election. The de facto synchronization of the presidential and legislative terms means that there is a very strong likelihood that any new president will also enjoy majority support in the legislature for the full term of his or her office. In other words, even though the 2000 constitutional reform gave the presidency no new powers, it made the president a more powerful political actor by increasing the likelihood that the parliamentary majority would support him or her for the full presidential term. However, the introduction of the so-called *quinquennat* also increased the pace of political life. Presidents now have less time to implement their campaign promises.

In May 2007 Nicolas Sarkozy was elected as president. In June 2007 his UMP party won an overall majority in the legislature. Thus, the constitutional and political conditions were set for a period of presidential leadership. In this regard, President Sarkozy did not disappoint.

The presidency after the 2008 constitutional reform

The presidential election sets the policy agenda for the next five years. In 2007, Nicolas Sarkozy's programme was called '*Ensemble tout devient possible*' ('Together, anything is possible'). In this document, Sarkozy committed himself to a series of constitutional reforms. In relation to the presidency, he promised a two-term presidential limit. He also promised to increase the role of parliament in relation to the president. In particular, he promised to ensure that parliament would have the right to hold hearings for nominees to state-sector posts, including presidential nominees. The aim was to send out the message that he would not be an all-powerful president and that he would reinforce the system of checks and balances. True to his word, once elected the necessary constitutional amendments were prepared. The result was a wide-ranging set of proposals that affected more than 20 articles of the 1958 Constitution. The reforms were passed by just one vote in a special parliamentary congress in July 2008.

The reforms included the specific promises that Sarkozy had made at the presidential election the previous year. Like the US president, the French president can now serve only two consecutive terms. Similar to the US system, parliament now also has the right to veto presidential nominations. The president's right to exercise emergency powers under Article 16 was also limited somewhat. If he or she assumes emergency powers when there is a serious and immediate threat to the country, parliament now has the right after 30 days to ask the Constitutional Council to rule on whether the threat is still present. In addition, by convention, a member of the opposition now chairs the important Finance Committee in the National Assembly. In these respects, the president could claim to have kept his electoral promise, for the president's powers were reduced. However, the situation is not quite as neat as this story might seem to imply. For example, while parliament can veto presidential nominations, the constitutional reform states that there has to be a three-fifths majority in the parliamentary commission for the veto to be automatic. In effect, this means that the ruling party has to agree to the veto. However, since the ruling party is unlikely to vote against the president very frequently, the president's nominees are unlikely to be blocked. Moreover, while the use of Article 16 in 1961 was certainly controversial and candidates at successive presidential elections have campaigned to limit it, it is a very exceptional measure. Indeed, it has been invoked only once in the history of the Fifth Republic. Therefore, even though the president's potential abuse of emergency powers has been limited, this reform will not make a difference to day-to-day governance.

On the other hand, the reforms did introduce a new presidential power. Article 18 now allows the president to call a parliamentary congress and to deliver a declaration there. Previously, the president could only have a message read out in parliament. Now, though, he or she may convene parliament and make a personal declaration, setting the parliamentary agenda and lobbying in favour of particular reforms. In June 2009 President Sarkozy invoked this article for the first time. He made a wide-ranging declaration covering a series of highly contested political issues. There was only a brief debate afterwards, but the president had made his point. In summary, even though Sarkozy could justifiably claim that, as promised, he had passed constitutional reforms limiting the powers of the president, arguably he emerged from the changes no less powerful in practice. In fact, there is a case to be made that the president is actually more powerful now than previously.

The same story can be told about the way in which the reforms aimed to increase the powers of parliament. In total, no fewer than ten articles relating to the government's relationship with parliament were amended. For example, the role of parliamentary committees was increased. These committees debate legislation proposed by the government and they routinely amend the legislation they receive. Previously, though, the government could ignore a committee's amendments when the bill was debated in the chamber as a whole. Now, for most legislation, the chamber debates the bill as it was amended by the parliamentary committee. Therefore, the committees have more opportunity to shape the wording of legislation than before. In addition, each chamber of parliament now has more control over its own order of business. Previously, the government determined the order of business in each chamber, and so parliament had to debate what the government wanted. Now, each chamber has more opportunity to set its own priorities in this regard. Overall, President Sarkozy could reasonably claim that he had kept another of his election promises and that the system included more checks and balances than before.

Once again, though, the story is a little more complex than it first appears (François, 2009). In practice, the reforms have strengthened the position of the parliamentary majority rather than parliament as a whole. For instance, the parliamentary majority enjoys not merely, by definition, a majority in the chamber as a whole, but also in parliamentary committees. Therefore, even though the chamber now debates the bill as amended by the committee, in practice the chamber is debating the bill as amended by the representatives of the majority in the committee, who, typically though, look to the president for leadership. Indeed, in France it is common to talk of the 'presidential majority', rather than the parliamentary majority, as if it were separate from the president. If the constitutional reforms have the effect of increasing the role of the presidential majority, then the main loser from the reform process is not the president but the prime minister (Pierre-Caps, 2009).

Undoubtedly the government's powers in relation to parliament have decreased, but this is not necessarily the case for the president's powers. To the extent that the head of the parliamentary majority and the majority itself is loyal to the president, then the constitutional changes may even have strengthened the president's control over the parliamentary process. Overall, therefore, the extent to which the 2008 reforms have increased the role of parliament should not be overestimated (Benetti and Sutter, 2009, p. 377). Rather, they have emphasized the importance of the relationship between the president, the president's party and the majority in parliament generally.

The president, the party and the parliamentary majority

The 1958 Constitution provides the president with a basis for political leadership; the direct election of the president provides the incumbent with a personal legitimacy and the country with a policy agenda; and the legislative election provides a majority for the passage of the president's policy programme in parliament. In June 2007 the legislative election returned an overall majority for President Sarkozy's UMP party. In the National Assembly, the UMP parliamentary group comprised 320 deputies. There are 577 seats in the chamber as a whole. Therefore, the UMP could have governed alone. However, the president chose to implement the policy of *ouverture*. Most notably, the new government, which was headed by UMP Prime Minister François Fillon, included members of the New Centre (NC) party. The NC was separate from the UMP in parliament and had 23 deputies. Therefore, the government was technically an oversized coalition. In addition, it included individuals who were not associated with the UMP. For example, there were three left-wing figures, the most high profile of whom, Bernard Kouchner, a member of the Socialist Party (PS), was appointed as foreign minister. (The PS duly expelled him from the party.) The government also included Jean-Louis Borloo. He was the leader of the small Radical Party. The Radicals were then part of the UMP, but they maintained their own organization. They were a party within a party. Overall, the government was a good demonstration of the notion of a presidential majority. The president could have relied solely on the UMP for a majority in the National Assembly. However, having been elected by virtue of winning the support of people from beyond merely his own party, the new government reflected the diversity of the president's winning coalition.

The formation of a government of *ouverture* was a public sign that President Sarkozy was not simply a party president, but that he was president of France more broadly. Over time, though, this image of the president, if it was ever credible, began to fade. In November 2010, the policy of *ouverture* was seriously compromised. Notably, the representatives of NC left the government, leaving the UMP as the only party represented there. Jean-Louis Borloo also left the government. Both Borloo and Hervé Morin, the leader of NC, harboured presidential ambitions, though Borloo also sported prime ministerial ambitions and was disillusioned when Fillon was reappointed following a government reshuffle. In the run-up to the 2012 election, they wanted to give themselves the opportunity to be able to criticize the president. In the end, neither stood at the 2012 election, but their ambitions meant that they had to leave office. In addition, Bernard Kouchner stepped down as foreign minister. In return, Frédéric Mitterrand, nephew of the former president, joined the government. Unlike his uncle, he was not a socialist, though President Sarkozy could at least claim that he had appointed a figure from 'civil society'.

The president also tempted one of the senior figures from the MoDem party to join the government. This was a blow to the party's leader, François Bayrou, who made no attempt to hide his own presidential ambitions and who had stood at the 2012 election. Overall, though, in contrast to the government formed in 2007, this one, that was in place following the November 2010 reshuffle, was very much a partisan administration dominated by the UMP.

President Sarkozy's attempts to portray himself as someone who was above party politics, or at least as someone who represented a broad range of party political opinions, was also questioned right from the beginning of his administration by virtue of his very close relations with the UMP party. All presidents need the support of a well-organized party machine to be elected. True, they need to build a coalition beyond the confines of their own party, but it does provide the bedrock of their support. François Mitterrand was the leader of the PS. Jacques Chirac was the long-time leader of the Gaullist Party. Nicolas Sarkozy himself was the president of the UMP prior to the 2007 election.

When in office presidents cannot ignore the party, precisely because it is the transmission mechanism for the passage of their policy programme in the legislature. For example, President Mitterrand regularly held breakfast meetings with senior PS representatives. President Sarkozy was far more involved in party management than any other president of the Fifth Republic. He, too, had regular breakfast meetings with representatives of the parliamentary majority at the official presidential residence, the Elysée Palace. In contrast to his predecessors, though, President Sarkozy also chose to meet regularly with UMP deputies and senators at the Elysée. He would often give a speech at these meetings, praising party representatives for their decisions or cajoling them into action. That the official residency of the presidency was used so regularly for internal party meetings was a first under the Fifth Republic. Indeed, at the 2012 presidential election, François Hollande criticized Sarkozy during their second-round debate for holding such meetings and said that he would not operate in such a partisan way.

In fact, the president's involvement in party affairs went far beyond holding meetings at the Elysée. He was intimately involved in the minutiae of party business. He worked closely with Jean-François Copé, the leader of the UMP group in the National Assembly from 2007–10 and the party general secretary from 2010 onwards. One of the reasons why the president was so involved in party business was that there were tensions both within the UMP and between the UMP parliamentary group and the government. In particular, the relationship between Copé and Prime Minister Fillon was sometimes very difficult as the UMP group sought to wield its new-found parliamentary powers against the government. Indeed, there were occasions when Copé even appeared to want to distance himself publicly from the president. Given these tensions, the important role of the parliamentary group and the need for party support at the 2012 election, Sarkozy had a strong incentive to manage party business very closely. Overall, rather like the situation with regard to the 2008 constitutional amendments, he claimed to be above parties – yet he associated himself consistently and publicly with the UMP and its internal debates. Indeed, he did this more systematically than any previous president. At the 2012 election, this made it difficult for him to campaign as the president of a broad coalition. On the campaign trail, he was seen primarily as the representative of the UMP party.

Presidential–prime ministerial relations under Sarkozy and Fillon

The 1958 Constitution places the prime minister at the heart of the governmental process. The direct election of the president and the presence of a presidential majority in parliament combine to create the potential for presidential leadership, but such leadership cannot occur without the support of the prime minister. As head of the government, the prime minister is responsible for implementing the president's programme, for coordinating the government's policies and for managing the government's business in the legislature. In this role, the prime minister has to arbitrate between the conflicting demands of the various ministers. For example, when it comes to the budget, should priority be given to education or employment? Within education, what are the priorities to be? The budget minister and the minister of finance prepare the budget and hold meetings with the various spending ministers to work through these issues. However, ultimately, the prime minister has to arbitrate and reach a final decision. Thus, he or she is in a very privileged position. There is, though, a complication. The president is the arbiter of last resort. When the president and the prime minister work in tandem, the prime minister can be sure that the president will support his or her arbitration. However, if the president is unhappy with the prime minister's decision, then the president may overturn it. More insidiously, members of the president's staff may attend arbitration meetings and try to shape the decision in the way that the president wants, undermining the prime minister's authority (Foucaud, 2010). Thus, the president needs the prime minister, but the prime minister is dependent upon and, ultimately, subordinate to the president. Hence, the relationship between the president and prime minister is fundamental to the operation of the French dual executive.

In May 2007 President Sarkozy appointed François Fillon as prime minister. Fillon was a leading member of the UMP party. He was not a long-time Sarkozy loyalist, but he had supported him in his efforts to win the party's nomination for the 2007 presidential election and had helped him to draw up his campaign programme. As prime minister, Fillon served for the full five-year presidential term. This is almost unheard of under the Fifth Republic. By the time he resigned following Sarkozy's defeat at the 2012 election, Fillon had become the second longest-serving prime minister since 1958. He was extremely loyal to Sarkozy during this period. On a number of occasions he 'shielded' the president from potential political trouble. For example, in December 2009 he travelled to China to help repair Sino-French relations following President Sarkozy's comments about the situation in Tibet and his decision to meet the Dalai Lama in December 2008. Even though the prime minister's popularity ratings declined fairly steadily over his five-year term, he was consistently more popular than President Sarkozy himself. His reward was a seat in a Paris constituency at the 2012 legislative election. Having been a deputy in the Le Mans area for more than 30 years, his move to Paris was controversial and stepped on many toes within the UMP party. However, it was a sign that he had successfully used his time as prime minister to consolidate his position within the party.

As with so much of the Sarkozy presidency, though, this narrative tells only one side of the story. During Fillon's time as prime minister, relations with President Sarkozy were sometimes quite strained. On a number of occasions, the president publicly overruled the prime minister. For example, in September 2009 Fillon announced that the price of the new carbon tax would be €14 per ton of carbon dioxide. However, the presidency immediately denied that the price had been fixed and a few days later declared that it would be €17. At times, the president also seemed to be making decisions without even including the prime minister. In May 2008 and a number of times thereafter Sarkozy convened a meeting of a so-called 'septet' of ministers to discuss strategy. Officially, the prime minister said that he was unconcerned and that the meetings did not amount to a second Council of Ministers, but that they were ever held was a sign of the presidentialization of the political process. Most controversially of all, the president's advisers were perhaps more interventionist than any of those under the Fifth Republic previously. For instance, particularly in the early years of the Fillon premiership, the president's most senior advisers regularly appeared in the media to comment on government policy. When they did so they made it plain that they were speaking as the president's representatives. Given they were publicly stating the president's wishes, it then became very difficult for the prime minister to contradict their statements because if he did so, then it would appear as if he was challenging the president personally. The regular interventions of figures such as the president's most senior adviser, Claude Guéant, the General Secretary of the Presidency from 2007–11, were extremely difficult for the prime minister to accept.

At certain times in 2008–09 the relationship between the prime minister, on the one hand, and both the president and the president's advisers, on the other, became almost unbearable. Politically, Fillon did not want to resign because this would have hurt his position within the party. However, he must have come close and in 2010 he certainly expected to be replaced by someone else for the remainder of the Sarkozy presidency. In the end, he was indispensable enough to be reappointed as prime minister when the cabinet was reshuffled in November 2010. He was popular within the party and, notwithstanding the various slights he had experienced as prime minister, publicly he remained loyal to the president.

In one sense, the difficult coexistence between Fillon and Sarkozy was typical of prime ministerial–presidential relations in general under the Fifth Republic. The prime minister willingly acknowledged that his role was to implement the president's programme and he was happy to liken himself to the conductor of an orchestra in the way that his job was to coordinate the work of a potentially discordant set of political actors. At the same time, though, the presidency, through Sarkozy's personal interventions and through those of his advisers, was extremely interventionist during Fillon's five-year term. Fundamentally, while Fillon did say that he was a 'little bit annoyed' at Sarkozy's characterization of himself as the 'boss' and the prime minister as the president's 'collaborator', he was willing to accept that the president was in charge. Strategically, Fillon calculated that in the long term he had more to lose personally by challenging the president and being forced to resign than by accepting the constant slights to his own authority. This was probably a wise move, even if it meant a certain degree of humiliation at times.

Sarkozy on the European and world stage

As noted previously, the Constitution of the Fifth Republic gives the president particular responsibilities in foreign and defence policy. In particular, Articles 15 and 52 of the 1958 Constitution, combined with the precedent set by President Charles de Gaulle, helped to create a so-called 'reserved domain' for the presidency. More recently, European affairs have in effect been added to this domain. France remains a considerable power on the world stage with strategic interests in many parts of the globe. In Europe, the process of integration has been driven by the Franco-German alliance. Given the president's undisputed authority within the French decision-making system in relation to foreign and European affairs and defence policy, he or she inevitably becomes a prominent international figure and the success of the presidency is at least partly dependent upon how the incumbent president performs in this regard.

The substance of foreign policy and European affairs under President Sarkozy is analysed in detail in Chapters 15 and 16. Here, the focus is merely on the president's governing style. In this regard, there is no doubt that once again Sarkozy was a highly active president. For example, he was personally responsible for taking certain key decisions. He was the driving force behind the creation of the Union for the Mediterranean in July 2008, having proposed a similar organization in his 2007 election campaign, though in the end he was disappointed with the structure of the organization (Gillespie, 2011). There is also no doubt that he personally took the decision in March

2009 to reintegrate France into NATO's military command structure. He also became notorious for his 'solo runs', meaning that he was willing to commit France unilaterally to particular issues. For instance, in November 2007 he flew to Chad to broker an agreement for the release of seven people, including three French nationals, who had been detained in an alleged child kidnapping case there. In September 2008, when France held the presidency of the European Union, he intervened in the conflict between Russia and Georgia. He travelled to both Moscow and Tbilisi to try to broker a ceasefire. He was successful, though the terms and the implementation of the deal were subsequently criticized (Dehousse and Menon, 2009). In January 2009 he made a high-profile visit to Israel. In his meetings with Palestinian officials in Ramallah in the Gaza Strip, he is reported to have said that he would tell the Israeli prime minister that violence there must stop. In March 2009 he created an ongoing diplomatic row with Mexico when, on a visit there, he declared publicly that a French citizen, Florence Cassez, should be released from a Mexican jail, where she was serving a sentence for involvement in kidnappings, and be transferred to France. The Mexican government was annoyed at the external intervention in its internal affairs and at the implication that French justice was better than Mexican justice.

The style of the Sarkozy presidency manifested itself very clearly in France's response to the rebellion against the regime of Mu'ammer Gaddafi in Libya. In terms of decision-making, Sarkozy was instrumental in organizing international military support for the rebellion, and the decision to commit French air support was crucial to the eventual success of the operation. At the same time, it is perhaps no coincidence that in September 2011 he, with David Cameron, was the first foreign leader to visit Libya to support the new government there, thus personalizing the policy. Generally, like all of his presidential predecessors, Sarkozy was clearly in full charge of foreign and defence policy-making, but, perhaps more so than any previous president except Charles de Gaulle, he was willing to associate himself personally with high-profile but sometimes controversial foreign visits.

What was true of foreign and defence policy in general was even more true of European policy. France has often been at the forefront of European integration. For example, President Mitterrand was key to the negotiation and passage of the Maastricht Treaty in 1992. Even so, during the Sarkozy presidency France was more consistently at the centre of European affairs than perhaps ever before. There is a case to be made that his presidency reinforced the intergovernmental tendencies of the EU generally. Indeed, in a speech at Toulon in December 2011 he identified intergovernmentalism as the way forward for the EU. Therefore, his impact at this level may be very significant and long-standing.

Whatever the future developments, EU politics from 2008–12 will be forever remembered for the relationship between Sarkozy and Angela Merkel, the Chancellor of Germany. In one sense, the so-called 'Merkozy' partnership was forced upon both leaders. The eurozone problems were so deep and ongoing that each successive European Council meeting and Euro Summit was a crisis event. As the most important economic power and the most significant political player in Europe, Germany and France respectively had no option but to respond jointly to events in Greece, Spain, Portugal, Ireland and elsewhere. Thus, Sarkozy and Merkel were thrust into the European limelight. However, there was also a sense that President Sarkozy in particular relished the attention. A key element of his future re-election strategy could be that he had been able to save Europe from ruin and that the French economy was safe in his hands. Thus, he instrumentalized the eurozone crisis. The more he could associate himself with it, the more benefit he hoped to obtain from a successful resolution to it or at least the capable management of it. The problem for the president, though, was that the crisis refused to go away. As the EU lurched from one crisis meeting to another and the 2012 French presidential election came ever closer, his strategy began to unravel. Precisely because he had associated himself with events so closely, he had more difficulty communicating the message that the French and European economies were safe in his custody. Presidents rarely lose elections as a result of events in foreign and defence policy. However, European affairs are different. The fate of the French economy is now so intertwined with the state of the European economy and, in particular, the eurozone region that European events have a profound effect on domestic elections in France. This was a lesson that Sarkozy, the president-candidate, was soon to learn and to his cost.

Sarkozy, the president-candidate

As noted previously, the introduction in 2000 of the *quinquennat*, the five-year presidential term, made the president a more powerful political actor by increasing the likelihood that the parliamentary majority would support him or her for the full term. At the same time, the *quinquennat* also reduced the duration of the political cycle (Cole, 2012). In some senses, Nicolas Sarkozy was the first president to feel the full effects of the 2000 constitutional reform. His predecessor, Jacques Chirac, was re-elected in 2002 following the reform, but there was very little likelihood of him standing again in 2007. He was the French equivalent of a US lame-duck president. As a result, even though he governed with the support of a large presidential majority in the legislature, his second term in office was a quiet affair from the perspective of the presidency. Indeed, for much of the 2002–07 period media attention was focused on the hyperactive minister of the interior, Nicolas Sarkozy. As president, and, more specifically, as a president who had every intention of standing for re-election, Sarkozy had to work to the fast-paced rhythm of the *quinquennat*'s political time (ibid.). With the ever-present status of 'president-candidate', Sarkozy had a strong incentive to be consistently in the public's mind, to control the policy process, and to manage party affairs. Viewing the Sarkozy presidency in this way helps to explain some of the interventionist behaviour that has been outlined up to this point.

The *quinquennat* provides the president with only a very limited honeymoon period at the very start of the presidency. This was particularly noticeable during the Sarkozy presidency. For example, this was the period when his bling-bling aspect was most pronounced. More importantly, it was also the period when he introduced some of his most controversial reforms, notably the so-called '*bouclier fiscal*' ('taxation shield'), whereby a limit was placed on the total amount of taxes to which a person could be subject. This reform, which was originally passed in 2006 but which was extended in Sarkozy's first budget in 2007, was extremely controversial because it gave the impression of disproportionately benefitting the rich. Very quickly, though, the political timetable starts to concertina. The spectre of re-election soon comes into view. For the president-candidate, everything comes to be seen in terms of whether or not a particular policy reform, a certain foreign policy initiative or a stage-managed television intervention will be judged favourably by voters whose support will be needed to create a second-term presidential majority. Sarkozy's highly interventionist style was at least partly due to his position as a president-candidate. He needed to intervene across the range of political issues so that during this re-election campaign he could claim to have addressed the problems that the French were facing. He needed to keep a tight control over his party so that no challengers emerged. He needed to control the flow of government information so that it was focused on his own priorities. The management of the presidency from 2007–12 was part of a broader strategy for re-election in 2012.

In the end, the strategy failed. Governing is always difficult. In the context of a global and European financial crisis and major foreign policy upheavals, such as the Arab Spring, governing became more difficult still. Across Europe, incumbent leaders had been defeated. In 2012 Nicolas Sarkozy was added to this list. In some senses, he did well to come so close to being re-elected. However, in retrospect, there is a temptation to say that at least part of the blame for his defeat lies with Sarkozy himself and his governing style. In the most memorable moment of the second-round televised presidential debate, François Hollande was asked what type of president he would be if elected. For three minutes, Hollande took the opportunity to list the ways in which his presidency would be different. As President of the Republic, he said, he would not meet the members of the parliamentary majority at the Elysée; he would not classify his prime minister as a 'collaborator'; he would not try to take care of everything; he would make sure that his behaviour was exemplary at all times; and so on. Each phrase was designed to remind people of the type of president that Sarkozy had been. Remarkably, Sarkozy did not fight back. Hollande's intervention may not have won the election for him; the die had probably already been cast. However, the phrases did resonate.

The Hollande presidency

On 6 May 2012 François Hollande was elected President of the Republic, winning 51.6 per cent of the vote at the second round of the election and defeating Nicolas Sarkozy. On 15 May President Hollande appointed Jean-Marc Ayrault as prime minister. He had been the leader of the Socialist Party (PS) in the National Assembly from 1997 and was a close ally of the new president. Prime Minister Ayrault headed an imbalanced coalition that was dominated by the PS, but which also included representatives from the ecologists and the left-radicals. In June, elections to the National Assembly were held. The PS was confirmed as by far the largest party and the coalition emerged with a comfortable majority. The seemingly ineluctable logic of the Fifth Republic had once again been confirmed. The newly elected president had the support of a solid parliamentary majority and a loyal prime minister. The conditions for presidential pre-eminence were, it seemed, fully in place.

By October 2012, though, the Hollande presidency was already coming under criticism. If there had been a honeymoon period, then it had scarcely lasted beyond the legislative elections. The president's style of governing was being seriously questioned. As we have seen, during the election campaign Hollande benefited from being the antithesis of Sarkozy. The idea of a 'normal' presidency seemed seductive; and once elected, Hollande duly implemented his vision of the office. For example: in contrast to his predecessor, Prime Minister Ayrault was left to run the government; the president did not try to dominate the media; and there was no slew of policy announcements. To be sure, Hollande was still a major figure on the European stage. There was no talk of 'Merkollande', though at the first European summit of his presidency at the end of June the president was clearly able to bargain with the German Chancellor and a commitment to growth and employment was forthcoming. Even so, Hollande was deliberately crafting a different style of presidency to his predecessor.

The problem, though, was that while this was a winning campaign formula, in office the president was expected to govern. His hands-off strategy led to claims that he was too reactive. Gone was the hyper-president, but instead Hollande was giving the impression of being a mini-president: he was too hands-off. In all likelihood Hollande will have to amend his governing style and become more prominent if he wishes to stand a chance of re-election.

More profoundly, Hollande seemed out of step with the economic and political calendar. The economic crisis showed no sign of abating. To combat it, there was a real desire for change. However, his response was to adopt what seemed to be an 'it'll-be-alright-on-the-night' strategy. In a television interview at the beginning of September 2012, he reiterated his promise that unemployment would start to come down in a year's time and that the country would be on its feet in two years. This dampening of expectations was laudable, but it seemed out of tune with the economic and social situation that seemed to be worsening rapidly. Politically, too, the president seemed out of step. As noted previously, the introduction of the five-year presidential term has speeded up the electoral calendar. The president was only at the start of his term, but he already seemed to be operating at the wrong political pace. Indeed, he seemed to realize it himself. By the end of August, he was calling for the pace of reform to be accelerated. An extraordinary session of parliament that was planned for late September was brought forward. It would be a wild exaggeration to say that time was already running out, but, by his actions, or rather by his inaction, he was managing to give that impression.

It is far too early to reach a judgement on the Hollande presidency. There have been some early divisions within the government, notably between the socialists and the ecologists. However, this is little more than normal coalition politics. At present, there is nothing seriously to worry the president or the prime minister in this regard.

There have also been rumblings within the parliamentary majority. There is a certainly a fraction of the PS parliamentary group that does not support the European Fiscal Compact. The ecologists tend to be even more opposed to it. The fact that European issues are likely to remain at the top of the political agenda for some time means that such divisions may periodically re-emerge. However, the majority seems generally solid and Prime Minister Ayrault's experience as the leader of the PS group in the Assembly for so long is likely to serve him in good stead for the foreseeable future. In this context, it is all the more tempting to place the blame for the rather inauspicious start to the Hollande presidency at the feet of the head of state personally. He is, though, a canny political actor. He knows that in the end his presidency will be judged by tangible results. Whatever the criticisms of Sarkozy's lifestyle and his governing style, in the end he was overcome by the difficult economic conditions that he faced. Even if for very different reasons Hollande's own governing style has been questioned, his political fate will also be decided by the state of the economy. In this regard Hollande is playing a long game. The rhythm of the *quinquennat* may militate against such a strategy, but the president is not defeated just yet.

Conclusion

In France, the President of the Republic is the most important actor in the political process. His or her power comes from a mixture of constitutional, electoral and party political sources. In 2007 President Sarkozy took office on the basis of a decisive electoral victory and with the support of a large parliamentary majority. For the next five years, within the domestic political system, his authority was largely unchallenged. He dominated the decision-making process either directly or indirectly; he was in full charge of his party's affairs; and he was a high-profile actor on the European and world stage. And yet he was defeated in 2012. For the most part, this was the result of economic and social problems, the seeds of which were sown long before he came to power and which he was largely powerless to resolve during his time in office. Even so, arguably, Sarkozy was at least partly the architect of his own downfall. It is easy, too easy, to caricature Sarkozy in this regard. It should be remembered that President Giscard d'Estaing was also criticized for being too 'showy', that President de Gaulle created the template for foreign policy 'solo runs', and that President Mitterrand, in his first term at least, was keen to manage party affairs. In other words, President Sarkozy acted in ways that were very similar to his predecessors. All the same, there is little doubt that overall he pushed the boundaries of the presidency further than most. In part, this was a result of the five-year presidential term, which meant that he was a perpetual president-candidate (a lesson that President Hollande is learning very quickly); but it was mainly a result of his personal style of governing. France has a presidentialized system, but Sarkozy is likely to go down in history as the president who tried to push the system to its limits. For his part, President Hollande perhaps went too far in the other direction in the early months of his presidency. Soon, though, the rhythm of the *quinquennat* and the exigencies of being a candidate-president are likely to reassert themselves with full force.

Chapter 3

The 'New' French Parliament: Changes and Continuities

SYLVAIN BROUARD, OLIVIER COSTA AND
ERIC KERROUCHE

One of the main legacies of the French revolution of 1789 was to vest the undivided sovereignty of the people in an elected Assembly, though this foundational belief was observed more in theory than in reality, as the country veered between monarchy and republic for over one century from 1789 to 1875. The republican tradition that re-established itself from the late 1870s firmly embedded the belief in parliamentary sovereignty in the country's political culture. The Third (1875–1940) and Fourth (1946–58) Republics were known as *régimes d'Assemblée*, though they were subsequently lauded and denigrated in turn by the parliamentary and Gaullist traditions. The instability of the post-war Fourth Republic, which experienced 28 governments in its short 12-year existence, challenged the belief that Parliament had an absolute right to make and unmake governments. The constitution of the Fifth Republic, created under de Gaulle's leadership in 1958 (and some would say tailor-made for the General), set as one of its key objectives to limit drastically Parliament's influence and powers.

The Founding Fathers of the Fifth Republic gave a clear priority to the stability of the executive branch and its governing capacities over the traditional concern with parliamentary sovereignty. Worse, from a parliamentary perspective, the French Parliament suffered from de Gaulle's pretention to incarnate the will of the citizens regardless of the balance of parliamentary representation. This trend was confirmed in 1962 when the constitution was reformed in order to allow for the direct election of the president, which had not been envisaged in 1958. This 'presidentialization' of the regime soon became the most influential event of French political life and led to a clear bipolarization of the party system. Finally, the founders decided to increase the governing capacity of the executive branch (at least for the right-wing parties) by making the Senate, the second chamber, a structurally conservative assembly. Because of their mode of appointment, senators were expected to support any right-wing government or president and to temper the desire for reform or resistance by the National Assembly.

The conjunction of these factors has, for a long time, been described as a source of weakness for the French Parliament. However, its classification among the weakest parliaments needs to be seriously discussed again, for at least two reasons. First, most comments on the French regime suffer from a lack of empirical data: they are mainly based on analyses of constitutional arrangements, on experts' appreciations, and on actors' views – and not on a study of the chambers' concrete activities. Basically, little is known about the ability of the chambers to amend laws or to propose bills, nor about the efficiency of their control over the government and the administration.

Second, the French Parliament has undergone, at least from a formal point of view, many changes in recent years that have affected the chambers and their role in the regime. Parliament benefited from the constitutional reform of 2008, which modified more than half of the constitution's articles with the main objective of reinforcing Parliament. This reform in turn brought about modifications in the internal rules of both chambers. The changes have also been political: for the first time in the history of the Fifth Republic, the senatorial elections of 2011 led to a left-wing majority in the high chamber. The lower chamber also experienced a change in majority in June 2012, coming after a widespread redistricting. For the first time since 1958, there is today a unified left-wing government, including the two chambers, the Presidency of the Republic, and the cabinet. The left also control 21 of the 22 metropolitan regions and the vast majority of *départements* (provinces) and large towns.

The political and constitutional changes experienced by the Parliament in the recent period must incite political scientists to reconsider their appraisal of its role and to undertake more empirical research about the impact of the reforms. More concretely, can we still consider the French Parliament as weak?

Overview of the structural weakness of the French Parliament

The 1958 French constitutional inheritance

In Lijphart's terminology (1999), the French Fifth Republic has an incongruent and asymmetrical bicameral Parliament, composed of a lower chamber – the National Assembly – and a higher chamber – the Senate. French bicameralism is incongruent because MPs of both chambers are elected according to different systems. The French representatives or *députés* are elected by direct suffrage in a two-round majoritarian system: if no candidate gets an absolute majority of the valid votes (representing at least 25 per cent of the registered voters) in the first round, all the candidates with more than 12.5 per cent of the registered voters are then qualified for the second round. The candidate with the majority of votes in the second round is then elected. Senators are chosen by an electoral college made up of the various local elected representatives (and *députés*), according to two different rules, depending on the size of the constituency: the block vote system (the two-round majority system for each seat in plural member constituencies) for the constituencies with a limited number of seats allocated; and the proportional representation system for the remaining electoral districts.

French bicameralism is not only incongruent, but also asymmetrical: the two chambers do not have equal power. In the case of an enduring disagreement in the lawmaking process, the government may give the last word to the National Assembly (Article 45). Additionally, only the lower chamber may remove the government by denying confidence to it or by adopting a motion of censure by an absolute majority, as happened once in 1962.

As in many Parliaments in Europe, the French legislature has been challenged by the development of decentralization, the rise of judicial review, domestic devolution and EU integration. In the French case, the core constraint preceded the development of multilevel governance: Parliament was severely hampered by the 1958 Fifth Republic Constitution and its 1962 amendment (on the direct election of the presidency). It also suffered from the negative attitudes adopted by de Gaulle and his majority. A strong presidency and the 'rationalization' of parliamentarianism were the two main causes that weakened its role.

Several provisions in the Constitution and in the internal regulations of the chambers jointly acted to weaken the legislative role of Parliament. The most important ones were those defining the status of the law within the constitution, those organizing the rationalization of parliament, and those granting control of the parliamentary timetable to the government.

The first limitation of parliamentary power was as symbolic as it was concrete. The 1958 Constitution challenged the central character of law-making, which prevailed during the Third and Fourth Republics, by explicitly detailing the competences of Parliament. This meant that Parliament was not considered a sovereign institution anymore. Over and beyond this, the domain of the law was itself defined in a restrictive way by the Constitution (Article 34), which also provided an autonomous regulatory power that was conferred on the government (Article 37). Finally, the principle laid down at the beginning of Article 34 ('the Parliament votes the law') came up against the stumbling block not only of Article 38, authorizing the government to legislate using empowering statutes, but also of Articles 3 and 11, which stipulated that the law may also emanate from the people, via a referendum.

The 'rationalization' of Parliament found its full expression in two articles of the Constitution: Articles 49.3 and 44.3. The first one, relating to the question of confidence, allows the government to oblige the National Assembly to make a clear choice, by either accepting the law in discussion or censuring the government. Article 49.3 has been often used in combination with Article 45 to provide a way of going beyond Senate opposition to a bill by giving the last word to the lower chamber (Huber, 1996). Article 44.3 authorizes the government to impose a 'package vote' on the entirety of a bill, thus excluding any possibility of MPs amending the law. Four other measures have also limited the legislative power of MPs: Article 40 stipulates that all propositions and amendments from MPs which lead to a decrease in public resources, or to an increase in public payloads, are precluded ('financial irreceivability'); Article 41 allows the government to oppose a bill or an amendment which pertains to regulation and not to law; Article 44.2 allows the government to refuse to examine an amendment if it has not first been submitted to the competent parliamentary committee; Article 45.3 states that, when a text has been negotiated by a joint committee of the two chambers, the government must approve any amendment to it – though it can itself freely amend the text, even if the Constitutional Council has recently limited this ability.

Both chambers have also faced very strict organizational constraints. The number of parliamentary committees was initially limited to six by Article 43 (Duprat, 1996). There were provisions for the creation of committees of enquiry and control, but their powers were restricted. The vote of resolutions and petitions, which had formed one of the key features of the two preceding Republics, was also prohibited. Finally, the internal rules of the two chambers were subject to a strict control of conformity to the Constitution.

Even more fundamentally, before the 2008 constitutional revision, the subordination of the National Assembly resulted from the close control of the legislative agenda by the government, in accordance with Article 28. The Constitution stipulated that there were to be two parliamentary sessions (one lasting 80 days and the second less than 90 days) that limited drastically the working capacity of MPs. There were also internal time limits imposed on specific sectors of parliamentary activity; for instance, Article 47 of the constitution set a limit of 70 days for voting on the budget before the government was allowed to legislate by ordinance. So, not only was the Parliamentary agenda governed by strict time limits, but neither the National Assembly nor the Senate had control over its own agenda. Article 48.1 of the Constitution stipulated that government bills had priority over those of private members. Although the Conference of Presidents of the

National Assembly was charged with organizing the timetable for each new bill, the government maintained its control over the legislative calendar since it could delay this schedule by according MPs extra days for further debate. The Constitutional Council defended the prerogatives of the government in that respect by allowing it to make changes to the National Assembly's agenda and to introduce a new bill on the floor. Finally, according to Article 45.4, the government was, after only two readings by the National Assembly and the Senate (or even one in an emergency), to ask the National Assembly to reach a final decision. Conversely, the government was not subject to constraints as regards extending the legislative process, since Article 29 allowed members of the parliamentary majority and the prime minister to call for a special session. In other words, since the main characteristic of parliamentary time is scarcity, the government took control of this aspect of affairs (Couderc, 1981).

Beyond the content of the Constitution, it is the way it has been implemented, along with the structure of the party system and the rules of electoral competition, that have decisively shaped the semi-presidential political regime of the Fifth Republic. These combined factors have reinforced the influence of the government and the president, and undermined the status of Parliament. The President is de facto considered the most legitimate incumbent in France because of his national direct election. The strengthening of presidential leadership has had historical and political causes, directly linked to the personality of de Gaulle and to his conception of the function of the president. This trend was reinforced in 1962 when the Constitution was reformed, at de Gaulle's initiative, in order to provide a direct election for the president. This reform gave rise to the *fait majoritaire* (i.e. the emergence of a clear majority in the National Assembly, which strongly supports the government) and broke the monopoly of citizens' representation by the Parliament. The presidential election became the most influential event of French political life and led to a bipolarization of the party system behind the leadership of presidential contenders. Legislative elections soon appeared to be a confirmation of presidential ones, especially when they occurred immediately after. This tendency was strengthened by the constitutional reform of 2000 – which has reduced the presidential term to five years and, de facto, made it coincide with the term of the National Assembly – and by the decision to hold systematically the legislative elections after the presidential ones. Since 2000, electors have been deeply encouraged to confirm the choice they have made at presidential elections by giving the new president a clear majority in the National Assembly.

As a consequence of all these factors, the president, as the political leader of both the executive and the legislative majority (with the exception of periods of *cohabitation*, from 1986 to 1988, 1993 to

1995 and 1997 to 2002), has been the key decision-maker under the Fifth Republic, at the expense of Parliament.

The 2008 constitutional reform as a new step in improving Parliament's role

The Constitution of the Fifth Republic has been revised 24 times since 1958, nearly every two years on average. Several of those revisions were aimed at releasing the executive grip on Parliament. The 1995 reform had significantly improved Parliament's role: President Chirac, in a message to Parliament that year, considered that it would put Parliament 'at its right place, a central place, allowing restoration of the relationship between citizens and MPs'. The 2008 reform was designed as a new decisive step in that direction. It was inspired by the work of a 'committee of reflection and proposition on the modernization and rebalancing of the Fifth Republic's institutions' (*'comité de réflexion et de proposition sur la modernisation et le rééquilibrage des institutions de la Vème République'*). The Balladur committee, named after its chair, former Prime Minister Edouard Balladur, was created in June 2007 to bring forward constitutional reform. Its report was handed to the president on 29 October 2008. The project of 'constitutional law' that derived from it was discussed and voted on by the two chambers and then submitted to Congress, a meeting of all MPs and senators, on 21 July. This constitutional law is, with the modification of 47 articles, the most important revision ever of the 1958 Constitution, at least in quantitative terms. The modified articles concerned the role of the president, the government, Parliament and the relations between citizens and the administration. Here we deal only with the main modifications concerning Parliament.

In his presentation of the revision to Congress in 2008, Prime Minister François Fillon insisted on the need to reinforce Parliament through the adoption of this reform: 'is it normal, is it good, that the heart of our democracy does not beat more here [in Parliament]? I don't think so'.

The 2008 revision impacted upon the organization, activities and powers of the Parliament in many ways, especially regarding the chambers' agendas, legislative processes and control of the executive. First, the control of the timetable by the government was further relaxed. The 1995 constitutional revision had already established a unique annual session of a maximum of 120 days, as well as a parliamentary window reserved for private member's bills. Since 2008, one day of sitting per month is reserved for bills proposed by opposition and minority groups. The capacity of the government to control the legislative timetable has also been drastically decreased, given the fact that it now sets the agenda for only two weeks of sittings out of four. This proportion is rather misleading, however, as the constitution allows the government to request that either chamber consider finance bills, social security finance bills, bills concerning a state of emergency, requests for the authorization of military intervention and texts transmitted by the other House during their two week periods. Finally, the constitution stipulates that 'for one week of sittings out of four, priority shall be given to the monitoring of Government action and to the assessment of public policies'.

The government's control over the legislative process has also been substantially loosened. First, there is a radical limitation to the scope of Article 49.3 (the issue of confidence): its use is restricted to finance bills and social security finance bills, along with one other bill per session. Even more importantly, the discussion of both government and private members' bills in the plenary sitting is now based on the text adopted in committee, and no longer on the original proposal. Today, the discussion deals with the text presented by the government only for constitutional revision bills, finance bills and social security financing bills. A further improvement of the standing of parliamentary committees occurred with the increase of the maximum number of committees from six to eight.

Finally, the scrutinizing capacity of Parliament over the executive has been reinforced. The media and commentators have focused their attention on the right of the president to speak in front of Congress, which they have analysed as a new sign of Congress's domination over Parliament. But they have overlooked the new tools that have been given to Parliament in order to control the executive branch. For instance, to exert its appointment powers, the president must now consult the relevant standing committee of both chambers; he or she cannot make an appointment if the sum of the negative votes in each committee represents at least three-fifths of the votes cast by the two parliamentary committees. Today, the constitution also states that 'a declaration of war shall be authorized by Parliament'. The government should also inform Parliament of its decision to have the armed forces intervene abroad for more than a three-day period. If the intervention exceeds four months, the government must submit the extension to Parliament for authorization.

Is Parliament under the Fifth Republic a weak institution?

Since 1958, there has been a consensus, among academics, journalists and politicians, to underline the weakness of the French Parliament and to consider that its contribution to policy-making and governmental control is very limited. This goes with the idea that MPs of the opposition are powerless, and that those of the majority have no other choice than to approve governmental and presidential action –

according to the *fait majoritaire*. In fact, most of the analyses rely on an assumption of conflict between Parliament and the executive power, even if the government and the lower chamber cannot be held by diverging majorities. We need to call into question such a perspective to get a more balanced appraisal of the role of Parliament. To do so, we will scrutinize three key dimensions of parliamentary activities: the role of committees, amendments and private member' bills.

Considering the time which is usually needed for institutions and actors to adapt to institutional changes, it is too early to make a comprehensive assessment of the 2008 reform. However, we can mention straightaway at least one of its uncontested positive effects: majority and opposition MPs all acknowledge that the reform has improved the quality and importance of committee work, as well as the government's attention to that stage of the parliamentary process, since the discussions in plenary sessions are now based on the committee report. Even before the reform, parliamentary committees had continuously amended government bills on a large scale and with a high success rate (Kerrouche, 2006); this aspect of parliamentary work is largely overlooked, in part because scholars have not studied the role of parliamentary committees in France. For decades, only a minority of laws were not amended – these were mostly laws ratifying international agreements. Let us also recall that the success rate of governmental amendments between 1967 and 2010 (84 per cent) is not that much higher than the general rate for committee amendments (76.4 per cent). Moreover, from 1967 to 2010, the committees proposed 59,946 amendments, nearly three times more than the government (20,284): contrary to what is often said, the government does not have the initiative for the majority of adopted amendments, since 75.9 per cent of them come from the committees. Of course, the amendments are often the result of negotiations between the executive and Parliament, but such a bargaining process constitutes, per se, a recognition of the important role of the committees. In other words, at least through parliamentary committees, MPs have been able to influence lawmaking.

Beyond the role of committees and the number of adopted parliamentary amendments, the progressive easing of the government's control over the parliamentary agenda has had an observable impact on the proportion of private members' bills that have been adopted. Between 1978 and 1995, 7 per cent of the laws had, on average, originated from private members' bills; since 1995, this proportion has been much higher at 17 per cent. Even if the statutes originating from these bills are, on average, four times shorter than those issued in government bills, parliamentary legislative initiative has, without a doubt, been more lively than ever under the Fifth Republic. The recent worldwide attention to one of them, establishing penalties for contesting the Armenian genocide, is a striking example.

In 1967 André Chandernagor wrote a much-commented book entitled *A Parliament: What For?* (*Un parlement, pour quoi faire?*). The evidence presented above challenges the received view that the French parliament is endemically weak. The evidence in favour of a more affirmative parliament is even stronger if the growing forms of parliamentary activity, such as oversight, evaluation, control, opinion-building and agenda-setting (using, for example, parliamentary questions), are taken into account.

The political aspects of Parliament

For the first time under the Fifth Republic, France is experiencing a left-wing unified government. Compared to the 2002–11 period, the political context of 2012 appears to have been turned upside-down. After multiple cases of divided government in the 1980s and 1990s, and after nearly a decade of right-wing unified government, a left-wing majority emerged from the senatorial elections of September 2011, the presidential election of May 2012 and the legislative elections that followed in June 2012. The current situation is exceptional in France in terms of government control.

Patterns of government control in France

France has a semi-presidential regime with a bicameral legislature, a directly elected president and a prime minister leading the cabinet. As a consequence, the two chambers of the legislature and the executive branch may both be divided or unified; the pattern of government control in France is thus complex and may have different features. Unified government means that the majority party or coalition does not require the cooperation of any opposition party in order to legislate. Under divided government, the majority party or coalition does require such cooperation.

'Cohabitation' is a case of divided government that stems from a situation of a divided executive that occurs when the president and the prime minister are partisan rivals. The president is not devoid of all influence during these periods. According to the tradition of the 'reserved domain', an opposition president continues to play a pre-eminent role in the field of defence and foreign policy. He or she may also slow down the legislative process, using different institutional tools such as asking for a new reading of the law, refusing to sign ordinances or refusing the opening of a supplementary parliamentary session. But the core dynamic during cohabitation is parliamentary. Only the National Assembly and the prime minister are certain to belong to the same partisan camp, since the parliamentary character of the semi-presidential system implies that the prime minister (and the cabinet) and the lower chamber belong to the same coalition: in other words, the prime minister must have the confidence of the Assembly. The opposition can thus be defined as the parties or coalition of parties that are not part of the coalition supporting the cabinet.

As we have seen, France has also an incongruent bicameral Parliament (Lijphart, 1999). This institutional configuration favours the situation of divided government within the legislative branch. Even if the French bicameralism is also asymmetrical, an opposition controlled French Senate has some institutional powers that can put the government under pressure. Senators may use well-known instruments of parliamentary procedures (amendments, motions, quorum calls) to delay the usual lawmaking process and to influence the speed and outcomes of legislative proceedings. In addition, senators can de facto veto constitutional laws and organic laws (i.e. an intermediate form of statute between constitutional law and ordinary law dealing with the operation of public authorities) that relate to the Senate.

Situations of divided legislatures have existed several times in the history of the Fifth Republic, and not only during the cohabitation periods. For example, from 1958 to 1968, the Gaullists had a stable majority in the National Assembly but failed to do so in the Senate, where the moderate Christian right and moderate left held a large number of seats. Also, a right-wing majority controlled the Senate when the National Assembly was experiencing a leftwing majority (1981–86 and 1988–93). Finally, a new situation of divided legislature occurred between September 2011 and June 2012, with a conservative National Assembly and government, and a leftist Senate.

The unified or divided controls of the executive, on the one hand, and of the legislature, on the other, interact to shape the nature of government control in France. Table 3.1 summarizes the four possible situations that match real-world cases. The pinnacle of divided government was reached between 1997 and 2002, when both the legislature and the executive were divided. A divided executive and a unified legislature characterized the two periods of cohabitation under Mitterrand's presidency. Unified executive and divided legislature also happened during the Mitterrand era, when a left-wing coalition held a majority in the lower house (1981–86; 1988–93), though the Senate was dominated by the conservatives. At the end of the Sarkozy presidency, for the first time under the Fifth Republic, a left-wing coalition controlled the Senate and was in opposition at the National Assembly. This was the first step towards the new left-wing unified government that started in June 2012. So far, unified government has occurred only with right-wing majorities (1968–81; 1995–97; 2002–11). From this point of view, since 17 June 2012, France is experiencing a novel pattern of government. All national political institutions are today

Table 3.1 *Patterns of government control in France under the Fifth Republic*

	Divided legislature	Unified legislature
Divided executive	1997–2002	1986–1988
		1993–1995
Unified executive	1958–1968	1968–1981
	1981–1986	1995–1997
	1988–1993	2002–2011
	2011–2012	2012–

controlled by the left: the only national institution that is not majority controlled by the left is the Constitutional Council. The newness of the current political situation is also underscored by the original and large control of subnational governments by the left-wing coalition. This situation of domination is a final step regarding the possibilities allowed by the regime of the Fifth Republic. However founded the original criticisms were, the institutions of the 1958 Constitution have proved to be flexible enough to allow and cope with a variety of political situations, even the most unpredictable, such as a left-wing controlled Senate.

Alternating majorities in the Senate

Since 1968, at least, most scholars have agreed, at least implicitly, with a quotation attributed to Professor Guy Carcassone: 'when the left loses everything, they lose everything; when the right loses everything, they keep the Senate'. Politicians shared this point of view with scholars. Left-wing politicians were, of course, frustrated at this seemingly permanent bias in favour of the right (Boyer, 2007). In 1998, Prime Minister Lionel Jospin stated that 'the Senate is a democratic anomaly' (*Le Monde*, 21 April 1998). Another former socialist prime minister, Pierre Mauroy, agreed, arguing that the Senate is a 'chamber where a change of majority is impossible' (*Le Figaro*, 27 April 1998). But in September 2011, the alleged impossible happened: in the wake of the elections, the Senate finished up with a left majority. Out of 348 seats, 177 were held by the left-wing coalition, providing them with a majority of two seats and enabling the election of the socialist Jean-Pierre Bel as the president of the chamber. This event is a strong incentive to dedicate more attention to this traditionally neglected institution in France (one notable exception being that of Smith, 2009).

As shown in Figure 3.1, the left-wing majority in the Senate is the product of the progressive growth of the socialist group since the end of the 1980s. The left-wing representation in the Senate had declined between 1959 and the beginning of the 1970s, along with the transformation of the party system that had progressively decreased the electoral competitiveness of the left-wing centre 'radical' candidates, even in Senate elections. This trend was reversed in the 1970s, as the socialist group strengthened its position after a series of victories in local elections. The initial burst was short-lived; socialist influence drastically receded during the 1980s. Since then, however, the left-wing coalition has gained seats at each of the seven last Senate elections. Even if few thought that a change in the Senate majority was possible, the left-wing majority that came to prominence in 2011 was in part the incremental result of a long-run electoral trend. It was also facilitated by several changes that affected Senate elections over time.

As already mentioned, French senators are elected through indirect universal suffrage. Their electorate, approximately 150,000 officials ('great electors' – *grands électeurs*), is composed of city councillors, regional councillors, department councillors, mayors and deputies: 90 per cent of them are delegates appointed by municipal councils. This system is justified by Article 24 of the Constitution, which states that

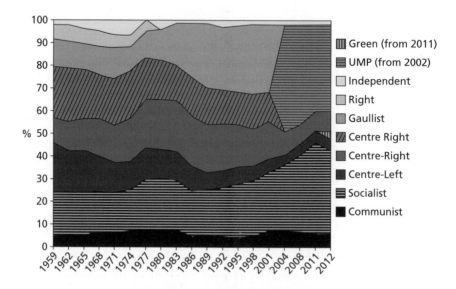

Figure 3.1   *Political composition of the Senate (1959–2012)*

the 'Senate shall ensure the representation of the territorial communities of the Republic', even if de facto it favours rural (traditionally more conservative) areas (Grangé, 1990).

In such a system all shifts in local majorities will affect the results of the senatorial elections. This is how the left got the Senate: since the setback of the 2001 municipal elections, it has won all the local elections, either at the municipal (2008), departmental (2004, 2008, 2011) or regional level (2004, 2010). In particular, the two landslides in 2004 and 2008 crucially affected the control of local governments and thus the political balance among the *grands électeurs*. They eventually led to a change of majority in the Senate.

The successive local victories of the left took time to be converted into Senate seats because of the over-representation of the (allegedly more conservative) delegates of small towns among the *grands électeurs* and of the partial renewal (every three years) of the chamber and the duration of the senatorial term. A bill introduced in the Senate and adopted by both chambers in 2003 reduced the duration of the Senate's term to six years – to be applied to all new senators from 2008 – and established a renewal of the Senate by half every three years. The implementation of the reform will, however, be complete only in 2014. Until 2011, only one-third of the Senate seats were up for election every three years. Moreover, for several Senate members elected in 2004 the length of the mandate is still officially nine years. These reasons combined to delay the victory of the left, but the unthinkable finally occurred in September 2011.

The electoral system has also been changed twice in the last decade. The constituencies are the *départements* and the number of senators elected in each constituency depends on the size of the population. In 2000, the block vote system (a two-round majority system for each seat in plural member constituencies) was limited to constituencies electing two senators or less, i.e. the least populated departments. Conversely, the use of proportional representation was extended from constituencies of five seats or more to constituencies of three seats or more. In a partial pull back, in 2003, constituencies with three senatorial seats were re-assigned to the block vote system. The effects of these changes in the electoral system have been important regarding the composition of the Senate (Kerrouche et al., 2001). In constituencies using the block vote system, there has been little diversity in terms of political affiliation of the incumbents: the extension of the proportional rule has thus enabled an increased diversity of representation that has benefitted the left-wing parties.

To what extent have these institutional and political changes affected the characteristics of Senate members? First, the turnover in the Senate has been rather high during the last three elections (44.5 per cent in 2004; 43.0 per cent in 2008; 46.5 per cent in 2011): only a minority of the newly elected senators were outgoing members. This means that the current Senate has been widely renewed in terms of membership since 2004: the turnover has even been higher than that of the lower chamber. This trend challenges the seniority feature that is commonly associated with Senate members. Furthermore, the turnover has also had an unexpected consequence in terms of political representation: despite its smaller size, in 2012 the Senate had a more diverse and balanced representation than the National Assembly. There are respectively 3.4 and 2.8 effective parliamentary parties (or groups) in the upper and lower chambers. This unexpected development calls into question the image of the Senate as a chamber well-known for its difficult access and its tendency to exclude small parties.

A honeymoon election (2012): a change of majority in the National Assembly

After the second round of the 2012 National Assembly elections, held on 10 and 17 June, 59 per cent of left-wing candidates belonging to the presidential coalition were elected to the National Assembly, in accordance with the honeymoon theory that stresses the link between presidential and legislative elections. The change of majority and its scope were indeed expected given the electoral cycle: Dupoirier and Sauger's (2010) observation that 'in the French case, the institutionalization of electoral cycles that begin with a presidential election and are immediately followed by a honeymoon legislative election shifts the balance in favor of the president' proved to be accurate once again.

French leaders have been discussing for years the possibility of introducing some element of proportional representation into legislative elections. In November 2012, once again, a committee chaired by former Prime Minister Lionel Jospin proposed that 10 per cent of MPs should be elected on a proportional basis, in order to increase the political representativity of the National Assembly. The 2012 elections were, however, still organized according to the majority two-round system that produces a huge disproportionality effect. As shown in Table 3.2, with 29.4 per cent of the valid votes in the first round, the Socialist Party obtained 280 seats, whereas UMP had only 194 with 27.1 per cent. Even more striking is that, despite polling 13.6 per cent of the votes, only two candidates from the National Front were elected. The socialist group obtained enough seats to have the majority by itself thanks to the numerous dissenting socialist candidates (who faced non-socialist candidates supported by the Socialist Party following national pre-electoral agreements) who joined the socialist group after the elections. The discrepancy between the number of effective electoral parties and the effective number of parliamentary parties (or groups) is still high at 5.3 and 2.8 respectively.

Table 3.2   *Results of the 2012 legislative elections*

Party	Number of seats	Valid votes at the first round (%)
Front de gauche	10	6.9
Parti socialiste	280	29.4
Parti radical de gauche	12	1.7
Europe-Ecologie-Les Verts	17	5.5
Le Centre pour la France	22	5.8
Union pour un Mouvement populaire	194	27.1
Front national	2	13.6

The left-wing shift in the control of the lower chamber paradoxically happened after a partial redistricting of the legislative constituencies that was criticized by the left-wing parties as heavily biased. This redistricting was substantial: only 238 constituencies out of 577 remained untouched. Figure 3.2 shows that most *départements* were affected by this process.

It is often considered that only a small pivotal number of MPs changes at each election. This is untrue. In 2012, around 40 per cent of

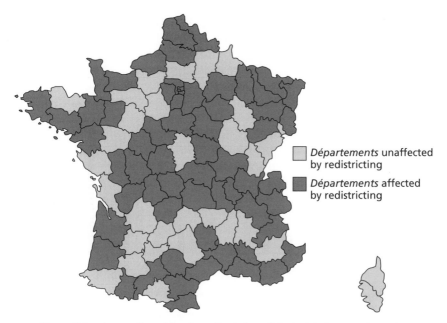

Figure 3.2   *Areas affected by the redistricting of the legislative constituencies*

Table 3.3   *Turnover in the National Assembly*

Legislature	Percentage of MPs elected at the parliamentary elections, who were MPs during the previous term	Percentage of outgoing MPs re-elected at the parliamentary elections
X (1993–1997)	52.5	47.1
XI (1997–2002)	53.4	49.6
XII (2002–2007)	61.0	54.9
XIII (2007–2012)	74.4	70.2
XIV (2012–)	60.0	56.2
1988–2012	60.2	55.6

seats changed their incumbent deputy (either because of the defeat of the sitting member or because of a change of candidate). By comparison with recent elections, the turnover in the 2012 election was certainly modest. As shown in Table 3.3, the level of turnover was weaker than during the changes of majority in the 1980s and 1990s, was similar to that of 2002 and was somewhat higher than that of 2007. Taken together, however, the figures presented in the table challenge the continuity belief.

Finally, it is worth emphasizing that the 2012 parliamentary election did introduce some noticeable changes, such as the increase in the proportion of women in both assemblies (Figure 3.3), following the imple-

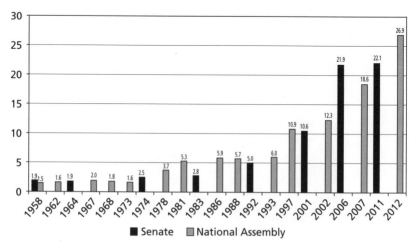

Figure 3.3   *Percentage of women among Senate and National Assembly members since 1958*

mentation of the law on gender parity. In June 2000, an Act was prom-
ulgated which, for the majority of elections, established that in certain
cases there must be an equal number of men and women candidates,
and in others that this male/female parity must apply to the outcome of
elections. With respect to the UMP, not respecting the parity principle in
legislative elections may lead to severe cuts on the funds given to political parties (which are based on the number of votes cast; see pp. 95–6).
If the situation is still far from parity, there has been a clear-cut progression since the second half of the 1990s.

Conclusion: a new wave of institutional change?

The French Parliament has experienced a number of fundamental
changes in recent years. These include: a new constitutional framework
for organizing parliamentary activity; a new majority in the lower
chamber, elected after an extensive redistricting; a novel left-wing
majority in a partially reformed Senate and, as a result, the first left-
wing unified government under the Fifth Republic. Notwithstanding
these changes, the French Parliament has also been characterized by
continuities. This is especially the case as far as the characteristics of
members of parliament are concerned. If we have witnessed some evolutions in terms of parity or the representation of visible minorities,
other features have remained more constant. In terms of age, despite the
change in majority, the Senate can still be characterized as an 'old
chamber'; even if the average age of senators has declined, it has been
stable since the 2008 election at around 62 years, almost five years
older than in the National Assembly. As expected, the two-step decrease
in the threshold age for being elected as a senator (from 35 to 30, and
finally to 24 years old) has not substantially affected this distribution.
As in the Senate, the age distribution in the National Assembly (Table
3.4) has been strongly biased against the young generation.

We could draw similar conclusions of stability regarding other
dimensions of the socio-biographic profiles of French members of
Parliament, be it education or occupation. The question of *cumul des
mandats* (holding several elected positions) also remains a stumbling

Table 3.4 *Percentage distribution of deputies in the National Assembly, 2002 and 2012 (by age)*

	Under 40	40–49	50–59	60 or over
2002	6.4	21.4	49.6	22.6
2012	9.5	21.1	33.2	36.3

block in French political life. Despite the attempts at regulation and the decision taken by the Socialist Party to limit it drastically, only 139 out of the 577 MPs elected in June 2012 exercised one elected mandate. Thus the *cumul* remains the rule for 76 per cent of French MPs, as is the case for 79 per cent of senators.

Such marks of conservatism may be challenged in the months and years to come because of the promises made by the new President Hollande during the campaign. Several campaign promises deal with institutional questions. For instance, Commitment 48 of Hollande's programme states that 'I shall increase the powers of initiative and control of the Parliament. I shall ensure that a law is voted on non-multiple office-holding. I shall strengthen parity between women and men by increasing the penalties against the political parties which do not respect it. I shall introduce an element of proportionality for the legislative elections'. Some of these topics are both highly controversial (including within the Socialist Party, especially as far as the question of *cumul* is concerned) and difficult to achieve without a majority in Congress (the combined meeting of the Senate and the National Assembly, where the left lacks 35 votes to achieve the required majority of three-fifths). They would however have an important impact on the French political system if they were implemented.

To achieve reform, President Hollande set up a committee headed by former Prime Minister Jospin, rather as Sarkozy had done after he was elected. This committee made several concrete proposals in November 2012 regarding, among other themes, the *cumul des mandats* and the introduction of a mixed electoral system for general elections. Some measures will be implemented; others will probably be forgotten, as was the case for most of the Balladur report. The president is not able to decide alone on institutional matters. He has to take into account many formal or informal veto players (political partners, advisors, high-ranking civil servants, members of the courts, agencies, lobbyists and MPs themselves) who are not all convinced that the situation of Parliament should be radically modified. As Henri Queuille, a former prime minister (President of the Council) during the Fourth Republic, once said: 'there is no urgent problem in politics which an absence of decision cannot solve'.

Chapter 4

Politics and Justice

YVES SUREL

The main aim of this chapter is to examine some recent trends in relations between politicians and judicial actors in the French political system. This relationship has sometimes appeared paradoxical over the past few years, especially under the Sarkozy presidency. On the one hand, several reforms have been decided and partially implemented, changing some important institutions or procedures within the judicial system. On the other hand, recurrent tensions and conflicts between political and judicial actors have resurfaced. The impression that the French political system is still unable to guarantee a real and lasting judicialization is a widely shared one. The relative importance of these contradictory trends will be assessed in this chapter, which starts with general observations about the place of judicial powers in France and provides some insights into the recent political context.

France is often depicted as an exception as regards its political–judicial relations, as it is more generally in other institutional respects. When they try to classify France in comparative studies, most political scientists encounter difficulties in making use of conventional typologies or categories. This is probably due to the fact that the common perception of the French political system is often still dominated by the idea that populism (majoritarian democracy), understood here as one of the two pillars of democratic regimes based on popular sovereignty (Leca, 1996), is in France more politically legitimate and more institutionally guaranteed than constitutionalism, a notion attached to the rule of law. In his classical analysis of democratic regimes, Lijphart stated that 'France was long considered the prime example of a country in which the principle of popular sovereignty was said to prevent any application of judicial review' (Lijphart, 1999, p. 225). As a (long) echo of the French Revolution, this asymmetry in its political institutions is often seen as one of the main characteristics of the country.

Nevertheless, as with many false ideas, this general characterization is rather paradoxical, not least since the Fifth Republic has also been described as the political regime in France which, institutionally, has done the most to ensure the respect of the rule of law. In fact, the Constitutional Council (Conseil Constitutionnel) remains an original creation of the Founding Fathers of the Fifth Republic in 1958 (Duhamel and Parodi, 1988). Since then, a number of major institutional initiatives have enlarged the scope of influence of the Constitutional Council. This was notably the case with the reform adopted in 1974, when a constitutional amendment provided 60 members of Parliament (deputies as well as senators) the power to appeal to the Constitutional Council. Moreover, with the effect of the European integration process, the French political system has been put under further pressure as it has Europeanized its domestic norms, laws and policies. Even if there is some controversy over the real impact of European law (Brouard et al., 2012), France has indeed to comply with this supranational legal lawmaking process (Surel, 2008).

This first set of general observations on the French political regime has to be complemented by several other common perceptions, this time related to the specific context of Nicolas Sarkozy's presidency. In fact, the period under examination in this book coincides for its most part with Sarkozy's term of office, which ended in May 2012 with François Hollande's victory in the presidential contest. Herein lies a paradox. This period has been described as one of 'hyper-presidentialization', and which logically favours the primacy of politics over the rule of law. But, at the same time, important institutional reforms were adopted under Sarkozy, some of them long awaited by promoters of constitutionalist principles and rules in the French political system. To take just one example, examined in more detail later, the adoption of the 2008 constitutional reform suppressed the rule which stated that the President of the Republic was also the President of the Council of the Magistrature (Conseil de la Magistrature), one of the main institutions of the judicial system in France. This disposition had long been seen as a symbol of the control that political actors have always exerted on judicial institutions; its suppression, long awaited, was well received. Those institutional adjustments might, then, legitimately be analysed as a reinforcement of traditional features of the rule of law in France, a country often depicted as a flawed democracy in this respect.

Taken as a whole, however, Sarkozy's presidency is often considered as comprising one long period of ever harsher conflicts between the chief of the executive and judicial actors. In fact, as in other domains of public policy surveyed in the introductory chapter, the Sarkozy period displayed a contradiction between, on the one hand, the promise of early institutional reforms and the belief that politics would refrain from detailed interference with the legal system and, on the other hand, a political practice that appeared to conflict with these early intentions. This period might be described as a new turn in the classical asymmetry between populism and constitutionalism in France.

In order to identify and analyse better these apparent contradictions and/or tensions, I will now refer to (and transform slightly) the notion of 'judicialization' as proposed variously by Alec Stone. In his extensive work on constitutional courts in Europe, as well as in his analyses of the European legal and judicial system, Stone elaborated the notion of judicialization as one of the main transformations of European political systems. More precisely, the dynamics of judicialization cover two different processes: '(a) the production, by constitutional judges, of a formal normative discourse that serves to clarify, on an ongoing basis, the constitutional rules governing the exercise of legislative power, and (b) the reception of these rules, and of the terms of this discourse, by legislators' (Stone, 2000, p. 195). On this basis, I will analyse the relations between politics and justice as a process of judicialization, which is determined both by the institutional evolution of norms and judicial organizations as well as by dominant perceptions of the rule of law in a given country. In the case of France, this means that we must look at the evolution of the legal norms which structure the judicial apparatus, but also take into account the political discourses, scandals or special events which also illustrate the quality of the rule of law over the past few years.

The domestic trends of justice in France

Most of the analysis of this section will be centred on the Sarkozy presidency, as it is too early to diagnose much of the activity that has occurred under President Hollande since May 2012. The Sarkozy period was especially rich in reforms of the justice system, as well as in terms of evolving political discourses and behaviours. In fact, under Sarkozy's presidency, some major shifts could be noticed in the way political actors organize, perceive and make use of the judicial institutions. Institutionally, Sarkozy himself was the initiator of important adjustments in the structuring and functioning of the judicial institutions, building to some extent on the reforms adopted at the end of Jacques Chirac's term. Somewhat paradoxically, the Sarkozy presidency also witnessed a serious deterioration in the quality of relations between judicial and political actors.

Some important institutional reforms

Even if Sarkozy often described his own presidency as characterized by a break with the past ('*la rupture*'), there was a real continuity with his predecessors on several institutional and policy issues. This was true in judicial matters. Following his election as president, Sarkozy announced several minor changes to a series of important reforms which had taken place in the 1990s and the 2000s. These reforms concerned the evolution of the penal responsibility of the president, further reforms to some of France's major judicial institutions, the creation of new norms and organizations and the transformation of several older ones.

The president's penal responsibility (accountability) has often been considered as one of the peculiarities and one of the weaknesses of the French political regime. For most of the Fifth Republic, the president was viewed as being non-accountable in judicial matters for the duration of his term of office, a special status that was sometimes depicted as an inheritance of the country's monarchical past (Mény, 2008). But, with the multiplication of political scandals and affairs in the 1980s and 1990s, this political custom was strongly criticized. There were also a number of constitutional and legal reforms in the 1990s and 2000s that sought to reform this anomaly. A constitutional revision adopted in 2007, just before the end of Jacques Chirac's presidential term of office, introduced some important modifications to the principle of the penal non-responsibility of the president. More precisely, Chirac and his prime minister, Dominique de Villepin, initiated a new constitutional law, enacted in February 2007, which stated that 'the President of the Republic can only be relieved of office in the case of failure of his duties which are obviously incompatible with the exercise of his mandate. The dismissal is pronounced by the Parliament made up in the High Court' (Article 68 of the Constitution). This reform, even if it did not establish explicitly any penal responsibility, was nevertheless considered as an important step in favour of a new equilibrium between institutional powers in the French political system. However, the effective implementation of this new disposition was constantly delayed during Sarkozy's presidency. Rather like his predecessor, Sarkozy waited until the end of his term to introduce a law with constitutional status ('*loi organique*'), adopted in January 2012, that gave substance to this partial step in the direction of penal responsibility. Why did this take so long? The answer probably lies in the repeated conflicts that characterized the relations between Sarkozy and the judges, as we will discuss later.

This continuous ambiguity on this specific institutional issue might be one of the reasons why François Hollande seems eager to take new initiatives. At the beginning of November 2012, the former prime minister, Lionel Jospin, who had been nominated in July 2012 as chair of a specially convened Committee for the Renovation of Institutions (Commission sur la Rénovation et la Déontologie de la Vie Publique), published a report containing new propositions for the penal status of the president and similar dispositions for the members of the government. Two proposals are specifically relevant to this chapter: the first evoked the need to institutionalize a 'normal' judicial status for the president in private affairs (Propositions 17 and 18); the second (Proposition 19) argued in favour of the suppression of specific judicial institutions – such as the High Court of Justice of the Republic – which had been established solely to judge ministers as well as heads of government. Members of the executive should be judged by the ordinary courts, as any other citizen. It is too early to say whether these propositions have a real chance of being implemented in the months to come. They demonstrate that each president has been sensitive to institutional demands for reform, and Hollande is no exception in this regard.

Going back to the Sarkozy presidency, the reform of judicial institutions was one of the main aspects of the revision of the Constitution adopted in 2008. The Balladur Committee, formed just after Sarkozy's election to prepare the 2008 constitutional revision, made a number of recommendations concerning the constitutional reform of the judiciary. These proposals were both limited and important. They were limited because the new dispositions only changed some minor aspects in the rules of nominations to the judiciary. But they were important all the same: the President of the Republic would no longer chair the Council of the Magistrature, the body which makes the main judicial appointments. These new principles thus established a greater distance between the executive and the judiciary. Moreover, even if this revised article was short and simple, this revision put an end to an old debate: Article 65 of the Constitution having always been described as the symbol of the excessive power of political institutions over judicial actors. The fact remains, of course, that the executive branch still has a significant number of representatives in this peculiar authority, which serves as the body appointing and controlling judges.

Another major revision adopted at the beginning of Sarkozy presidency took the form of rationalizing various institutions and instruments. Important adjustments were made with the creation of a new institution, the so-called Defender of Rights (Défenseur des Droits) (Chevallier, 2011). The main purpose of this new institution, given constitutional protection, was to rationalize previous rules and institutions which had guaranteed basic rights in several domains. These preexisting institutions included the Ombudsman (Le Médiateur), the Children's Commissioner (Le Défenseur des Enfants), the High Authority against Discrimination (La Haute Autorité de Lutte Contre les Discriminations) and the National Commission of Deontology and Security (La Commission Nationale de Déontologie de la Sécurité). The Defender of Rights was created on recommendation of the Balladur Commission, but the new institution encountered significant resistance. As Olivier Renaudie showed in a recent study, the creation of this new Protection of Rights Body was the result of a complex process of conflict and cooperation between experts, members of Parliament and the government (Renaudie, 2011). Some other authors have also demon-

strated that its internal organization is still heterogeneous, characterized by the conditions under which the fusion of previous bodies oper-
ated (Cluzel-Métayer, 2011). But this rationalization might also be seen
as a sign of 'normalization' of the judicial system according to international standards: French citizens now benefit from a general protection
of their fundamental rights, which is a complement to more classical
and/or ordinary judicial procedures.

A last reform could be evoked here, since it was another initiative
described as a further step towards the normative judicialization of
the political system: the creation of a new procedure, the 'Priority
Issue of Constitutionality' (Question Prioritaire de Constitutionnalité
– QPC). This new disposition is sometimes described as one of the
main aspects of the constitutional reform adopted in 2008. Under
precise conditions, the QPC offers the opportunity for every citizen to
appeal to the Constitutional Council to control the constitutional conformity of a law. By the same token, the QPC puts an end to one of
the peculiarities of the French judicial system, the absence of 'a poste-
riori' constitutional controls. This new procedure was effectively
launched on 1 March 2010 and the Constitutional Council has
already made more than 230 rulings under the QPC. Some of these
decisions were quite important and abundantly discussed; this was
especially the case when the Council decided in May 2012 to annul a
law on sexual harassment because the original text had not been
written in sufficiently clear terms. It is too early to make a real evaluation of this new disposition. Interestingly, the QPC might reconcile
competing populist and constitutionalist dynamics: this new institutional procedure gives direct power to the citizen in judicial procedures, thereby potentially closing the gap between the expression of
populism and the rule of law.

In terms of the extensive definition of 'judicialization' that was
adopted at the beginning, one might consider that the first condition or
dimension has been achieved. A judicialization process is first and foremost the production, by constitutional or ordinary judges, of a formal
normative discourse that serves to clarify the rules governing the exercise of legislative power and those who guarantee fundamental rights.
We ought to recognize that the extension of the president's penal
responsibility – the transformation of important judicial institutions
such as the Council of the Magistrature, the extension and rationalization of fundamental rights with the creation of a Defender of Rights,
and the creation of the QPC – has signified the deepening and the
strengthening of the rule of law in France. This confirms that a judicialization process, partially independent of political pressures or shifts
in government, has progressively enhanced the role and power of judicial actors in the political system over the past 20 years (Commaille et
al., 2010).

Politics and justice under Sarkozy: an ever deeper conflict

However, if we take into account more informal evolutions and polit-ical strategies, the picture is more complicated. The period has also been characterized by a tense relationship between the political sphere and the judicial actors (Mouhanna, 2012). The second dimension we isolated in the definition of a judicialization process was probably not fully achieved during the Sarkozy presidency. If we go back to Stone's definition, this second dimension is mainly attached to the acceptance and reception of these norms and institutional arrangements by polit-ical actors. It means that there is no 'real' judicial power if a specific legitimacy is not recognized by the political sphere.

Therefore, if we go back to politics–justice relationships during the Sarkozy presidency, many observers would qualify those five years as a succession of conflicts, misunderstandings and crises between the execu-tive power and judicial actors. Several factors might indeed have nur-tured these bad relations. First, the period was characterized by a tight control of judicial actors by Sarkozy himself and/or by some of his closest collaborators. Second, Sarkozy's own conception of judicial powers and his political 'identity', closely related to security issues, led him to engage in a legal activism in sensitive domains, which imposed increasingly hard constraints on the ordinary functioning of the judicial institutions. It is probably in relation to this second aspect that the differ-ence between Sarkozy and his successor, François Hollande, will be the greatest, since the new president has constantly repeated that he would never interfere with the 'normal' course of judicial procedures. One good example occurred in November 2012, when the government did not hinder the extradition to Spain of Aurore Martin, a French citizen who was suspected to be a member of Basque terrorist organizations.

On the contrary, the first decisions taken by the newly elected President Sarkozy in 2007 were immediately criticized and interpreted as signifying a tight political control over judicial institutions. First and foremost, the nomination of Rachida Dati as justice minister in 2007 opened a long sequence of misunderstandings, ill-prepared reforms and controversial decision-making processes which largely determined the feeling that judicial powers were being degraded. Even though she was previously a judge, Dati was generally considered ill-suited to her task. Worse, the proximity she seemingly enjoyed with Sarkozy was widely interpreted as an example of the presidency exercising direct control over judicial actors. Just after her nomination, she was depicted as a close friend of the president and his wife, Cécilia Sarkozy, who then described Dati as 'more than a friend, she is my sister'. The composi-tion of her ministerial office (*cabinet*) was also seen as problematic: her advisors intervened to obtain several dismissals of high-ranking civil servants, who described the new minister as incompetent and only interested in her presence in the media. Analysts soon came to view Dati as a pure symbol, the real power being held by Sarkozy and some of his closest collaborators, such as Patrick Ouart. As in several other domains, the decision-making process was monopolized by the president and his administrative staff at the Elysée (De Maillard and Surel, 2012). After Dati's departure in 2009, the successive ministers of justice (Michèle Alliot-Marie and Michel Mercier) were not considered to be at all influential in the definition of judicial policies. The presence of second-rate political personalities after 2009 left a space for a more direct conflict between Sarkozy and judicial institutions and actors.

Some of the Sarkozy reforms had a deep impact on the structure of the judicial institutions and on some of their more important rules or practices. We will focus on two of these reforms: (i) the redefinition of the legal map of France (*carte judiciaire*) and (ii) the continuous debate on the role of investigating magistrates (*juges d'instruction*) and/or on the power of public prosecutors. The first one, the redefinition of the legal map, was engaged rapidly in October 2007 and its main objective was to rationalize the organization of the courts. This territorial network of judicial actors was first established under Napoleon and was conceived, already at that time, as one of the main aspects in the organization of the French state. The '*carte judiciaire*' is a generic term which covers all the principles and procedures which organize the meshing of judges and courts on French territory. One of the main criteria for its definition is related to the evolution of demography, but other elements might also apply, especially the relative importance of criminal practices in different regions. Since its creation, this judicial map had been reformed several times (Chauvaux and Yvorel, 1994), but many observers saw a new adaptation as necessary to allow a more equal and efficient functioning of the justice system (Commaille, 1996). Besides, the reform of the *carte judiciaire* was also part of the programme elaborated by the socialist candidate, Ségolène Royal, during the 2007 presidential campaign. The reform announced by Dati in 2007, then, was both anticipated and feared by judicial actors, especially because it entailed the suppression of several courts and the diminution in the number of judges and civil servants in the justice administration.

The formalization and the implementation of this reform were highly controversial. In a public announcement in January 2011, the minister announced that 401 courts would be closed down, whereas only 14 new ones were to be created. There are now 819 courts in France as opposed to 1,206 before this reform. In a recent report published by the Senate, senators Nicole Cohen-Seat and Yves Détraigne considered that the reform was undoubtedly necessary, but that it was launched without any real dialogue with judicial actors and implemented with precipitation and even brutality. One of the main consequences of the reform was the suppression of many positions in the judicial institutions: for the period 2009–12, the Senate report estimated that 76 judges were to be laid off each year (along with on average 447 positions in the administrative staff). Moreover, some of the initial objectives were far from achieved: the same report affirms that the delay for the examination of a legal case was on average 6.3 months over the period 2009–11, whereas it was only 5.7 months before (Cohen-Seat and Détraigne, 2012).

Another important and controversial reform had a deep impact on the functioning of judicial institutions and affected the investigating magistrates (*juges d'instruction*). In a speech made to the Court of Cassation on 7 January 2009, Nicolas Sarkozy interestingly exposed his own conception of the judiciary and announced some of the reforms he had then in mind. After reaffirming that France is governed by the rule of law ('without an independent and strong justice, there is no rule of law'), Sarkozy acknowledged that there might be conflicts between political actors and judicial institutions. Indeed, for Sarkozy, 'the relations between the political sphere and the judiciary are marked at best by a mutual distrust and at worse by a tradition of rivalry'. Making reference to the jurisprudence of the European Court of Human Rights (ECHR), the president then affirmed that a reform of criminal procedure was necessary in order to establish better the contradictory principles which are at the heart of a 'real' justice. The conclusion he drew from this was that 'the investigating magistrate (*le juge d'instruction*) ought to give way to a more arbitral judge (*un juge de l'instruction*), who will supervise criminal enquiries, but will no longer lead them'. This choice was closely related to the idea, shared by many political actors, that the investigating magistrate had become too powerful and was responsible for the discredit of political leaders since the 1990s.

Politicians of all complexions were fearful of legal inquiries that might endanger members of the current or former governments. Sarkozy himself was (and still is) threatened by the consequences of the 'Karachi affair'. He was Minister of the Budget in the Balladur government (1993–95) when a major defence contract for the sale of military ships between France and Pakistan was allegedly accompanied by dubious commissions. He always denied having anything to do with this affair, but doubts remain, and more generally Sarkozy and his entourage always considered that the (excessive) power of judges might be one of the reasons why the authority and legitimacy of political actors had been weakened. It came, then, as no surprise when the proposition to replace the *juge d'instruction* was immediately criticized by judicial actors.

This conflict between the political executive (and particularly the president) and the judges was replayed throughout the Sarkozy presidency. Relations were conflictual in part because Sarkozy had the tendency to (over)react to spectacular crimes or affairs. This was part of a more general communication strategy, which had been conceived by Sarkozy and his advisers to allow the president to occupy the political space as a whole. One of the most striking examples of this strategy in the field of justice is probably related to the 'Laetitia affair'. In January 2011, a young girl was savagely assassinated in Nantes, her corpse being discovered several weeks after. A former prisoner was rapidly suspected and some harsh criticism was made of the police and the judges, both accused of exercising insufficient control of criminals. One of the harshest criticisms came from President Sarkozy, who declared that this crime was probably due to 'grave dysfunctions' in the criminal process. The judges responded immediately with collective actions in several regions, especially with the organization of a 'work-to-rule' which blocked the normal functioning of several jurisdictions. Commenting on this, a representative for the magistrates declared that the President of the Republic had no monopoly of compassion for victims and that citizens were getting tired of such announcements.

Apart from these occasional conflicts, which could be understood in terms of electoral motives, Sarkozy's presidency was also characterized by a profusion of legal reforms which put the judges under further pressure. Sarkozy's speeches were not pure rhetoric, they also had legal implications with a view to the hardening of criminal provisions. As a former interior minister, Sarkozy's political identity and capital were closely related to security issues. According to some estimations (for example the analysis of Danet, 2008), more than 40 laws were adopted during the 2002–07 period which modified criminal procedure, and 30 laws affected the penal code. Mouhanna (2012) adds to this first estimation, demonstrating a continuity of this approach once Sarkozy became president. He shows that seven laws were adopted in 2010 and nine others during the first eight months of 2011. This strategy was not only used to illustrate the president's reactivity, but it was also designed to underline the contrast between the rapidity of the executive's actions and the slowness of the justice system. The problem lay, however, in the fact that these same laws were more often than not difficult to implement and that these rapid and constant shifts tended to weaken the legitimacy and the expertise of the judges.

To conclude this section, Sarkozy's presidency appeared rather paradoxical. Several improvements can be seen as positive factors in the judicialization of the French political system. Some important structural reforms were decided upon and implemented, and some important legal principles were reaffirmed. The first set of positive dynamics according to Stone's definition of the judicialization process, i.e. the idea that there is a growing normative and constitutional activity, was probably partly fulfilled under Sarkozy's presidency. But if we consider the second dimension, the explicit or passive acceptance of the rule of law by political actors, the picture is more complicated. This period saw a series of conflicts between the presidency and the judiciary, and the feeling was widespread that the independence of judges was no longer respected.

Supranational legal and judicial pressures

In contemporary democracies, the rule of law is no longer fully determined by domestic actors, institutions and/or dynamics. The supranationalization of modern societies and political systems means that decision-making processes and normative dynamics are defined at different levels of government. The rule of law is not only dependent on domestic institutions: it has become 'global', as have other economic, political and cultural processes (Held and McGrew, 2002; see also Cassese, 2003, for the specific domain of law). Domestic processes are in turn shaped by adaptive pressures coming from European and international judicial institutions and norms – though sometimes they are in competition with these norms. Therefore, even if judicialization appears threatened or hindered by domestic political actors, it might well be guaranteed by supranational institutions. For France, this relates mainly to the dynamics of Europeanization, but also to the growing role of international institutions and organizations.

The state of (legal) Europeanization processes

The notion of 'Europeanization', which can be defined in a broad sense as the effective consequences of the European integration process on domestic actors and institutions, has become an influential notion in political science (Caporaso et al., 2001; Featherstone and Radaelli, 2003; Palier and Surel, 2007). One of the best definitions has been given by Radaelli (2001, p. 30), who proposed the interpretation of 'Europeanization' as 'processes of (a) construction, (b) diffusion, and (c) institutionalization of formal and informal rules, procedures, policy paradigms, styles, "ways of doing things", and shared beliefs and norms which are first defined and consolidated in the making of EU public policy and politics and then incorporated in the logic of domestic discourse, identities, political structures, and public policies'. Inspired by the 'two-level game' developed by Robert Putnam (1988), this meaning of Europeanization encompasses several related processes amongst a great variety of actors and institutions placed at two (or more) levels of government. In the field of legal and judicial developments, making reference to Europeanization processes means to consider in parallel competitive and/or coordinative legal and judicial mechanisms, which define the actual evolution of the rule of law in a given country. As I have shown in a previous work (Surel, 2008), the impact of European norms and policies on several policy domains is now well established. This is the case for example in social policies (Palier, 2000), but also in policy fields such as education, where the direct effect of European laws or policies is not explicitly recognized (Ravinet, 2011).

One of the main aspects in this analysis of the Europeanization process is related to the quality and rapidity of domestic procedures in the transposition of European norms. The European Commission regularly publishes scoreboards in this respect, and it is quite striking to see that the overall performance of France in this regard has notably improved over the past few years. In fact, if we recall the evaluation made in 2006, France was ranked in eighteenth position out of 25 countries, but this is no longer the case as France is now one of the countries which transposes quite rapidly and efficiently European norms.

It is hard to find any real explanation for this improvement. It is probably necessary to consider more closely the effects of European norms in specific domains to gain a better picture of this evolution. But the fact remains that France might well not have been classified correctly in 'the world of neglect' identified by Falkner in her analyses of 'compliance' mechanisms. In several papers, Falkner and Treib (for example, 2008) have analysed the degree of compliance of EU member states and have identified several dominant categories (for a critique, see Thomson, 2009). In this classical typology, France is seen as one of the countries with the poorest performance in the transposition of EU directives. This seems no longer to be the case and, on the basis of this quantitative criteria, one might well consider that the judicialization of the French political system is also an effect of a much broader Europeanization of the French legal system.

This first finding has, however, to be complemented by other elements. In fact, judicialization is not only the product of an explicit, and sometimes, automatic dynamic of adjustment to the rule of law. It is also determined by the growing acceptance of judicial procedures and decisions by political actors. We saw earlier that, under the Sarkozy presidency, if domestic trends were apparently positive in institutional terms, there were constant conflicts between judicial actors and the government. A similar paradox is present here, since the improvement in the Europeanization performance has been accompanied by important conflicts between domestic and European institutions/actors over the last few years.

The most spectacular conflict probably broke out in 2010, when Viviane Reding, the European Commissioner for Justice, Fundamental Rights and Citizenship, compared the position held by the French government against Romany camps with the policies of the Third Reich during World War II. More precisely, in a public statement, Reding declared that she was 'appalled by a situation which gave the impression that people are being removed from a member state of the European Union just because they belong to a certain ethnic minority'. The reaction of the French government was immediate and quite brutal. Pierre Lellouche, who was then Minister for European Affairs, stated for example that the Commissioner was challenging French sovereignty and concluded with a provocation that 'the real upholder of European treaties is the French people'. And Sarkozy himself took advantage of a European summit to criticize the Commissioner and to recall his own conception of European integration, dominated by intergovernmental principles.

Another example of conflict between France and European institutions surfaced during the 2012 presidential election campaign when Nicolas Sarkozy threatened to withdraw France from the Schengen accords, arguing that the EU had to harden its immigration policy. In his Villepinte discourse, he stated that he wanted 'a political Europe that protects its citizens'. And to be clearer, he affirmed that 'at a time of economic crisis, if Europe doesn't pick those who can enter its borders, it won't be able to finance its welfare state any longer'. He then concluded that 'we need a common discipline in border controls ... We can't leave the management of migration flows to technocrats and tribunals'. These statements have to be situated in the peculiar context of this campaign. At that time, Sarkozy was still far behind his main opponent, Hollande, in all the published polls, and his strategy became quite clear: he saw his only opportunity of victory in the far-right electorate and developed a populist discourse to convince these people to vote for him on the second-round ballot. But this conflict also reveals that, according to the 'judicialization' analysis, there was a very limited acceptance of the norms defined by the European institutions over this period. In fact, the French government, even if this was not a new or original attitude, more often than not saw those norms and policies as constraints on its own action. This was not only 'a world of neglect', according to Falkner's typology, but 'a world of resistance' (Costa et al., 2008; Belot and Bouillaud, 2008) or even a 'world of reject', European law being an easy target in a blame avoidance strategy (Weaver, 1986). In the case of France over the past few years, it is quite clear that the government and political leaders have tended to use European decisions or initiatives as scapegoats.

The role of international norms and controls

But the pressures and relations between French political institutions and actors on the one hand and supranational institutions and organizations in the field of justice on the other are not limited to the European level. In fact, judicialization is also sometimes determined by pressures and decisions coming from private or public international organizations. These actions or dynamics are sometimes closely related to those exerted by European institutions. In the Romany controversy for example, Viviane Reding's statement was supported by the UN High Commissioner for Human Rights, who warned France, during this brief political crisis, that the decisions taken by the French government 'exacerbate the stigmatization of Romanies'. The tension between different rules of law attached to different levels of government is therefore not limited to the European integration process, but might well be determined by normative and judicial pressures exerted by international organizations. And the emergence of 'governance' dynamics in the field of justice signifies also that the judicialization process, be it objective or subjective, is determined by these international institutions and actors.

For France, several institutions play a decisive role in this respect. This is first of all the case with the Council of Europe and with the different organizations or committees which operate under its authority. The Council of Europe plays a decisive role in legal cooperation and in the harmonization of norms and procedures in the field of justice. And the decisions of the Council of Europe are not purely symbolic ones, since they determine directly or indirectly political responses and institutional reforms in its member states. The power of the Council of Europe can be ascertained by observing the influence exerted by some of its committees. One such committee, the European Commission for the Efficiency of Justice, evaluates the judicial systems of the Council of Europe's member states and publishes regular reports on legal and statistical data. According to its 2010 report, France appeared as one of the countries which committed the lowest proportion of its financial and human resources to the field of justice in two specific areas: the annual public budget allocated to the courts as a percentage of GDP per capita, and the number of courts provided per 100,000 inhabitants. This information was seized upon by several organizations in France, notably one of the main magistrates' unions (Union Syndicale des Magistrats – USM). As is the case with broader Europeanization dynamics, this example demonstrates that domestic actors attempt to gain new political resources from information and/or legal pressures coming from supranational institutions and organizations. From this perspective, the judicialization process, when different levels of government are taken into account, appears as a complex set of vertical and horizontal conflicts and forms of cooperation between private and public actors.

These relations and pressures are even sometimes more formal, as when we look at other institutions such as the European Court of

Human Rights (ECHR). This judicial institution, which is also related to the Council of Europe, was established by the European Convention on Human Rights and its main mission is to examine complaints in the case of violation by states of rights enshrined in the Convention and its protocols. In recent publications, the ECHR ranked France sixteenth in the overall statistics of the violations by article and by state over the period 1959–2011. France received 848 judgements against it in different matters during this period. ECHR rulings have created various conflicts between France and this supranational institution and have had an influence on domestic judicial procedures and policies. To take just one example, in a recent ruling (*Brusco v France*) adopted on 14 October 2010, the ECHR sentenced the French state to financial penalties for not having adopted a judicial regime which guaranteed the fundamental rights of a person placed under police custody. This ruling was confirmed and completed by several other decisions made by domestic judges (especially the Court of Cassation, the main judicial institution in France for private law). The French government was then obliged to reform these procedures and adopted a new law in 2011, which gives further guarantees for an arrested person (Law no. 2011-392, 14 April 2011). This affair is a good illustration of the complexity of judicialization processes. A domestic case might well be influenced by rulings made by supranational jurisdictions, rulings which are then mediated by domestic judicial procedures, which in turn cause new legal reforms to be elaborated by the government. Private and public actors, political and judicial institutions, and different levels of government interact in the definition and the evolution of the rule of law in a given country.

Conclusion

The judicialization process in France is difficult to characterize. In the period covered by this chapter, mainly that of the Sarkozy presidency, there were contrasting trends in evolution of the relations between judicial and political actors. If there were some major institutional improvements, the political discourse and the specific behaviour of the president sometimes gave the impression that the rule of law was not being fully respected. There were a number of signs of a decline of constitutionalist principles in favour of more 'populist' conceptions of the French political regime: the repeated reforms, the open conflicts between political actors and judges, and the redefinition of important institutional settings (such as the *carte judiciaire*) all went in this direction. Against this, one might argue that the redefinition of existing institutions (for example, the creation of the Défenseur des Droits), the emergence of new procedures (the QPC) and the successful adaptive pressures coming from the EU and/or from supranational organizations determined positive shifts in the relations between the political sphere and judicial actors.

What about the new political era opened with Hollande's election in May 2012? Can we observe any major, or anticipate any likely, future changes in this field? Hollande's campaign gives some indications. The very term 'justice' was interestingly one of the main arguments developed by the socialist candidate, even if this was in a very broad sense. For example, one of his slogans was attached to his promise to re-establish 'justice' for the French people, though this general objective encompassed fiscal reforms as well as new redistributive policies. Judicial institutions or matters were mainly developed in one of his 60 Commitments. Section 53 of his presidential platform announced more independence for judges, some additional reforms of the Higher Council of the Magistrature and some new initiatives for prisons. But, for the time being, there have been very few decisions. The justice minister nominated after Hollande's election, Christiane Taubira, was fairly non-committal in an interview published by *Le Monde* in September 2012. Overall, there will likely be a political discourse that is more attentive to the need of judicial actors and more sensitive to the symbolic respect of the rule of law. Taubira confirmed, in the same interview, that the existing very coercive conception of justice and its associated penal policy will be softened. If this proves to be the case, there might be a more explicit acceptance of the rule of law by political actors, which would complement the institutional reforms decided and implemented during the Sarkozy presidency. Such a move would add political legitimacy to the judicialization process that has been occurring over the past few years and further improve the rule of law in the French political system.

Chapter 5

Local and Regional Governance

ALISTAIR COLE AND ROMAIN PASQUIER

Based on vigorous cultural and political assimilationist policies (via the army, the education system and the national language), the Jacobin ideal of the 'nation state', according to which the nation is a product of the (democratic) state, has been seriously challenged in recent decades (Pasquier, 2012). The French state, like other European nation states, has been confronted for some years by the dual pressure of European integration and the growing desire for autonomy on the part of subnational political communities. As a result of the decentralization laws of 1982–83, the evolution of EU policies and, more generally, the increasing globalization of the overall economic context, the central administrative organs of the French state have lost their monopoly on political initiative (Le Galès, 1999). The state is increasingly exposed to new economic, social and cultural logics; and the growing power of local and regional authorities in the public policy process is one of the most striking features of the erosion of the Jacobin myth of the unity and indivisibility of the Republic. This is the main object of analysis in this chapter.

From territorial administration to the decentralized Republic

The French nation state is the product of centuries of state building and of the gradual development of national consciousness within recognized institutional and spatial boundaries (Rosanvallon, 2004). The French system of local administration that was defined by statute following the 1789 Revolution became the model on which local government systems were to be based throughout most of Western Europe. It resembled the Bourbon system that preceded it in its centralization of power and in being based on the same towns and villages. However, the Jacobin governments in 1789–90 codified this centralization process into a uniform structure of 83 *départements* and 44,000 *communes* headed by a central government official, the prefect. The prefects not only tended to dominate the proceedings of departmental councils (*conseils généraux*) but also exercised powers of supervision over decisions by the communes. This system of centralized direction stayed basically unchanged for over 180 years through two imperial, two royal and four republican regimes, though local powers gradually developed towards a form of local democracy. *Départements* were recognized as local authorities in the 1830s and they obtained full recognition as *collectivités territoriales* in 1871. In the *départements*, the prefects remained the chief executives until the law of March 1982. Mayors, at the head of the communes, became popularly elected in 1882 and were vested with budgetary responsibility, as well as a general competence provision, allowing municipal authorities to undertake policies in the interests of the locality.

The uniform politico-administrative structure in practice allowed some local innovation and discretion (Goldsmith and Page, 2010). The structure of incentives was centralized, however, and, as a by-product of centralization, a class of hybrid local/national politicians known as *notables* developed through the nineteenth and twentieth centuries. The more able and ambitious *notables* could acquire great prestige and authority, often through the accumulation of electoral offices which gave authority and influence (*le cumul des mandats*). They 'managed' relations with representatives of the state, including prefects, subprefects and sometimes members of central government, in order to advance their own interests and maintain political support for their localities. The system was described as one of 'tamed Jacobinism' by Pierre Grémion (1976), implying that the Lion of Jacobinism had been tamed by local interests. This system established interdependence between local leaders, central politicians and senior government officials. Political leaders pursued their interests by maintaining a deeply ambivalent attitude towards local autonomy.

The model of tamed Jacobinism was based around *notables*, central ministries, the prefects and local or departmental authorities. The main innovation of the post-war period was the development of the regional dimension in functional, political and finally institutional forms. Functional regionalization referred to the growing interest of the state in territorial policy. During the post-war 'thirty glorious years' (1945–74), the French state's territorial policy was expansionist, aimed at promoting growth in the regions and correcting the imbalances between Paris and the rest of France. In 1956, the central administration officially established a regional map of the country with 21 regions. This map has been modified only once since 1956 when, in 1971, Corsica was separated from Provences-Alpes-Côtes d'Azur. In 1964, 21 regional prefectures were created to spearhead the activities of the territorial state in coordinating economic planning. This 'functional regionalism' was temporarily halted with the failure of General de

Gaulle's referendum on regionalization in 1969, though it laid the basis for the later creation of the regional councils. France has now 22 metropolitan regions and four overseas regions (Guadeloupe, Martinique, French Guiana and Réunion).

The second dimension of a developing regionalism was more overtly political. From the 1960s, cultural and political claims were also raised in places such the Basque Country, Brittany, Corsica and Languedoc-Roussillon. Strong cultural, language and territorial defence movements have emerged since the 1970s. New forms of collective mobilization have raised the status of the Corsican, Breton, Occitan and Basque languages (Harguindéguy and Cole, 2009). There has been a revival of regional cultural traditions, languages and historic identities. There is a (small) electoral clientele for regionalism in Corsica, Alsace, Savoy, Brittany, Normandy, the Basque country and French Catalonia. Regionalist or autonomist parties have occasionally elected representatives to local and regional councils, though they have found it difficult to operate independently of the main parties (Pasquier, 2012). Some of the claims of these regionalist movements were adopted by the Socialist Party, which implemented the decentralization reform in 1982.

What about the politics of all this? A pro-decentralization coalition crystallized within the post-1971 Socialist Party and was comprised of two core elements. First, the leading representatives of municipal socialism – such as Interior Minister Gaston Defferre, author of the 1982 Act and mayor of Marseilles; or Pierre Mauroy, prime minister and mayor of Lille – sought to strengthen the powers of big city mayors and reduce the regulatory constraints on their action. Second, the revived Socialist Party in regions such as Brittany incorporated elements of the regionalist and environmental movements. Against this decentralizing coalition there was stout resistance from republican minded elements of the Socialist Party (for instance, those around Jean-Pierre Chevènement and the Centre d'Études, de Recherches et d'Éducation Socialiste (the Socialist Study, Research and Education Centre – CERES) for whom decentralization was synonymous with a challenge to traditional doctrines of republican equality and a threat to the pre-eminent role of the state. A similar degree of ideological diversity could be found on the right, divided between a Girondin liberal conservative and centrist wing, that looked favourably on restoring local liberties, and a republican Gaullist party deeply distrustful of all intermediary forces, including local government that had stubbornly resisted the Gaullist Party until the early 1980s. Though decentralization has been of vital importance for party politics, the centralization/decentralization cleavage cuts across any simple division between left and right, or even positions on a materialist/post-materialist axis.

Looking back at 30 years of decentralization

The year 2012 was the thirtieth anniversary of decentralization, which provided a standpoint from which to evaluate the longer term significance of this major reform. The socialist government's decentralization reform of 1982 established 22 elected regional councils and greatly enhanced the decision-making powers of the 96 (mainland) *départements* and larger communes. The 1982 reform transferred executive authority from the prefect to the elected heads of the 96 *départements* and 36,680 communes. The decision-making responsibilities of a range of local actors were increased, with the extension of their influence into policy sectors within which they had previously been marginal or excluded altogether, such as social affairs, economic development and education (Loughlin, 2007). A second act of decentralization (2003–04) then embedded the regions in the Constitution and transferred many new responsibilities to local, departmental and regional authorities. Reacting against the apparent lack of transparency of local government (the so-called *mille-feuille territorial*, whereby layers of subnational administration had loosely defined and overlapping competencies) President Sarkozy introduced a new reform in 2010 which claimed to rationalize and make more transparent and efficient the operation of local and regional authorities. Finally, the incoming Hollande administration of 2012 promised a new stage of decentralization for 2013; these plans will be referred to where appropriate.

We have argued elsewhere that there is no single interpretation of decentralization in France that allows an exhaustive understanding of the phenomenon (Cole, 2006; Pasquier, 2012). Understandings of the concept have varied since 1982. The earliest interpretations, produced during the 1982–92 period in particular, emphasized the continuity of practices with the pre-decentralization era. Organizational sociologists assumed continuity (Rondin's (1985) *Sacre des notables*, the continuing practice of *cumul des mandats*) and underplayed the significance of the 1982 reforms (except in terms of formally recognizing existing power structures). Lawyers centred their discussions around the ongoing battle over legal competencies. Political scientists identified the removal of constraints on existing actors, such as big city mayors or the presidents of departmental councils, rather than the emergence of new subnational institutions and practices (Mabileau, 1991).

The evolution of decentralization in the 1990s, on the other hand, was accompanied by the development of new conceptual frameworks, especially those of territorial governance (Le Galès, 1995) and capacity building (Pasquier, 2004). These analyses looked beyond formal competencies and emphasized new forms of public-private service delivery and the role played by non-public actors in local and regional governance. Emphasis was placed on the development of new institutions (especially the elected regions, far more significant actors than given credit for in early accounts), new spheres of policy intervention (economic development, transport, higher education, training, European networking) and new actors (a much broader community of local stakeholders, composed not only of local authorities, but also of private firms, public and semi-public agencies, state field services, consultancies, research institutes and associations). As well as describing a broad array of local actors, the governance perspective signifies that there is no single model of local power but patterns of variable geometry. The nature of power relationships depends on particular situations; no single actor appears as dominant in all situations. These analyses were most pertinent during what Cole (2011) labels as the period of 'networked institutionalism': from 1992 (the Territorial Administration of the Republic (ATR) reform) to 2002 (the return of the right).

Since 2002, but much more explicitly from 2007, efforts have been made by central government to reframe central–local relations in terms of a state productivity narrative (Cole, 2012). Analysts such as Epstein (2005) have emphasized the development of central government strategies of steering at a distance, whereby the state engages in a new interventionism via agencies of territorial management and attempts to control local government expenditure and the auditing of local authorities as part of the broader effort to control the public sector. Such activities have characterized one important dimension of central–local relations during the last decade, particularly during the Sarkozy period (2007–12). However, analysis of the Sarkozy and Hollande presidencies also demonstrates the weight of local and regional authorities (and their partisan and institutional supporters) as political actors in their own right. In the next section we endeavour to elucidate the complex world of French local and regional governance.

Actors and institutions of local and regional governance

The combined effects of the Jacobin heritage and the architecture of decentralization have created an institutional mosaic, the so-called '*mille-feuille territorial*'. The main local and regional authorities are presented in Table 5.1.

The communes and the communal bloc

With 40 per cent of the communes of the whole European Union, France's model of local government can legitimately be described as an

Table 5.1   *Sub-national authorities in France (2011)*

Type	Number	Functions
Communes	36,680	Varying services, including local plans, building permits, building and maintenance of primary schools, waste disposal, first port of administrative call, some welfare services.
Intercommunal Public Corporations (EPCI)*	2,599	Permanent organizsations in charge of inter-communal services such as fire-fighting, waste disposal, transport, economic development, some housing.
Departmental Councils	100	Social affairs, some secondary education (*collèges*), road building and maintenance, minimum income (RSA).
Regional Councils	26	Economic development, some transport, infrastructure, state--region plans, some secondary education (*lycées*), training, some health.

* Have their own tax-raising powers; there are 11,831 of these EPCI which rely on communal taxes.

Source: Ministère de l'intérieur (2011).

exception. Its 36,680 or so communes elect 550,000 local councillors, almost 500,000 of whom represent 34,000 rural or small town communes with less than 1,500 inhabitants. The commune is a symbol of civic identification; the next echelon, the canton, is a far more artificial institution, which often regroups communes with diverging interests and different socio-economic compositions. As measured in terms of budgets and staff, the communes remain by far the most important local authorities in France, but their situation varies dramatically and the governance capacity of the smallest communes is very limited.

If the communes deal with matters of immediate proximity (low-level social assistance, administrative port of first call, planning permission, primary education), most municipal services (such as housing) require the creation of intercommunal corporations or task specific agencies. The most important trend over the past two decades (in the Joxe law of 1992, the Chevènement law of 1999 and the Territorial Reform Act of 2010) has been the development of intercommunal corporations (EPCIs) as more cohesive local government structures. In French public law, the EPCI has the statute of a public corporation. It is not a fully constituted local authority – such as a commune, department or region – but it does have an indirectly elected executive, drawn from the participating communes which are represented on the council according to their size. EPCIs have some tax-raising powers and a pooled rate of local corporation tax across the participating communes. The 2010 Territorial Reform Act requires all communes to form part of an intercommunal public corporation by 2014, a decision confirmed by the new Hollande administration. As Table 5.1 illustrates, on 1 January 2010 there were already 2,599 EPCIs, which regrouped 36,680 communes (95 per cent of the total) and covered 92.2 per cent of the overall population. The EPCIs have been criticized from the basic democratic standpoint that these non-directly-elected bodies are responsible for the fastest growing part of local expenditure, yet they are subject to no real democratic scrutiny. Proposals for the direct election of the EPCIs were contained in early drafts of the 2010 Territorial Reform Act, but they were abandoned under pressure from the second chamber, the Senate, acting in the name of the interests of rural and small town mayors seeking to preserve their 'sovereignty'.

Since the failure of de Gaulle's referendum in 1969, the Senate has generally defended the communal and departmentalist position. Indeed, 95 per cent of the 150,000 electors who designate the 331 senators are councillors of small communes (less than 1,000 inhabitants). A large majority of senators are, at the same time, mayors of small rural municipalities or presidents of general councils (*départements*). Only two of them are presidents of regions. The Senate is the 'high council of the communes of France' and, indirectly, the 'high council of the departments of France' as well, preserving the structural basis and biases of French decentralization in favour of the pro-department coalition.

The *départements*

Since 1982 the president of the departmental council has been legally recognized as the fount of executive power within the department, replacing the centrally nominated prefect, and has become one of the coveted positions in French local government. The 96 elected departmental councils (the *départements*) are best conceived as major service delivery agencies of the welfare state (in social assistance, some intermediate education, social services, roads, minimal income (RSA), old-age care). Defenders of the departments point out that these basic services rarely occupy the limelight, but involve an extremely sophisticated financial and organizational infrastructure. The cost of social service provision has escalated dramatically, plunging several departmental councils into a severe financial crisis. Departments have also taken over responsibility for services they did not ask for: this is notably the case for the minimum income, created by the Rocard government in 1988, and the RSA, created in 2009. Above all, the departments have had financial difficulties in assuming the new service delivery responsibilities for the national road network, along with new responsibilities in social welfare, income support and intermediate education that were transferred to them in the law of 13 August 2004.

The regional councils

When the 22 regional councils were created as *collectivités territoriales* in 1982, they bore the imprint of the centralizing French republican tradition. Regions were imagined as institutions without a link to territory (Balme, 1999). They were created in a standardized form, including in areas where no regional tradition existed. With the partial exception of Brittany, Alsace and Corsica, France's historic regions and communities do not enjoy institutional expression. Unlike their counterparts in federal systems such as Germany or Belgium, they have no hierarchical control over other layers of local government. France remains a unitary state, albeit a 'decentralized' unitary one in terms of the 1958 Constitution as amended in 2003. There are no equivalents to the strong regions with fiscal and/or legislative powers, such as Scotland, the Belgian and Italian regions, the Spanish Autonomous Communities or the German *länder*. Attempts at introducing new forms of asymmetrical devolution in France have run up against serious obstacles, as is illustrated by the case of Corsica. The Matignon process undertaken by the socialist government in 2001, for example, envisaged transferring regulatory, then legislative, powers to the Corsican Assembly, until the Council of State objected and the Constitutional Council ruled the process unconstitutional.

Such a comparative appraisal ought not to lead us to dismiss French regions. By creating directly elected regional councils, the decentralization reforms of the early 1980s added a significant new player. France's 22 regions have a shared general competency, some with tax-varying powers and precise responsibilities in areas such as economic development, training, transport and secondary education, though their competencies are rarely exercised as stand-alone services. In 2004, the regions were further strengthened in matters deemed to be strategic: economic development, education, training, transport and some health. Regional institutions have built their legitimacy over three decades: first through investing in public policy delivery in new areas of service delivery such as education and transport; second, by demonstrating that they were viable partners of the state in the state-region plans since 1984; and third as active players in EU regional policy (Cole and Pasquier, 2012). From the early years of the French regions, empirical studies have uncovered institutionalized forms of interdependent relationships in areas as diverse as education (Dupuy, 2010), higher educa-tion (Aust and Crespy, 2009), employment and training (Berthet, 2010), transport (Barone, 2009), regional languages (Harguindéguy and Cole, 2009) and others. Early indications from the Hollande administration are that the regions are on the verge of discovering new roles: as managing authorities of EU structural funds for the 2014–20 period, as key partners in the new Public Investment Bank that was announced during the 2012 campaign, or as co-funders of the new programme of subsidized employment contracts (*contrats d'avenir*) for young people.

Central steering and the state

Whether led by governments under Gaullist, socialist or UMP control, the central state has been closely involved in local government reorgan-ization in the name of broader principles of territorial equity and eco-nomic efficiency. In the Jacobin tradition, the role of the locality, in Hayward's (1983) term, was to integrate the periphery into a highly centralized system. In the post-decentralization period, less direct methods of central steering were favoured: state-region plans from the mid-1980s onwards; state steering of EU structural funds from the late 1980s; sector-specific contractualized agreements; the creation of single task agencies (in the field of urban renovation, for example); the adop-tion of new budgetary rules having an indirect impact on local authori-ties; and the limited introduction of performance indicators. It lies beyond the limits of this chapter to engage in a full discussion of the varied tools and instruments whereby the French state attempts to control intergovernmental relations. However, the Sarkozy period offers a valuable insight into the difficulties of constructing holistic public policies that apply to the state and its territories.

There was a sustained political enterprise during the Sarkozy period (2007–12) to 'join up' questions of central and territorial state reor-ganization and local government reform. A state productivity discourse developed under Sarkozy that claimed to be macrolevel and holistic. This involved public organizations as a whole and purported to provide sets of coherent responses encompassing state, social security and local government organizations. The ensuing analysis focuses around the one key reform process of the Sarkozy period: namely the reform of the territorial state (RéATE) during 2008–10, which, along with the 2010 Territorial Reform Act, represented the heart of the ter-ritorial policy of the Fillon government (2007–12).

The RéATE refers to the package of decrees and circulars imple-mented from 2008–10 which addressed the complex issues of the reor-ganization of the regional and departmental levels of the state, as well as the relationship between the state and other public sector providers

(Cole, 2011). The Fillon government (read Sarkozy) sought to accelerate processes of modernizing territorial administration by clearly identifying the regional prefectures as the lead players within the territorial hierarchy of the state, as well as being the main interlocutors for interactions beyond the state (for example with local and regional authorities or the EU). Strengthening the regional state has, indeed, been one of the constant themes of French post-war territorial administration. The regional prefectures, created in 1964, have claimed to provide interministerial leadership of the state by way of coordinating the 'decentralized' services of government departments and, more recently, by contractualizing with local and regional authorities and the EU (ibid.). For the first time, the decree of 16 February 2010 affirmed that the regional prefect has 'authority' over the departmental prefects. Moreover, using the power of revocation ('evocation'), the regional prefect can exercise responsibilities normally reserved for the departmental prefectures for a limited period of time.

The departmental prefecture was confirmed by the 7 July 2008 circular in its traditional missions of law and order (control over police and, since 2007, gendarmerie). Prefectures gained several new functions in terms of immigration and asylum services, and the control of the legality of acts of local authorities. Overall, however, they complained (in interviews) of losing resources and functions, via the regionalization of back office and support services and the strengthening of the regional level. If more detailed consideration of this lies beyond the present exercise, we may however note that the overall logic of the reform of the territorial state was to strengthen the regional dimension (Cole, 2012). And yet, as will be demonstrated below, the regional level was *not* favoured in the 2010 local government reform; the fear of strengthening elected authorities controlled by political adversaries outweighed the logic of creating more cohesive, 'joined-up' relations between the state and the regional councils.

The incoming Ayrault government, inspired by François Hollande's campaign commitment to a new phase of it, also claimed that decentralization would need to be coupled with reform of the state. At the time of writing, the Hollande version of the relationship between decentralization and state reform was unclear in its contours. The call for more joined-up and accountable government was given symbolic weight by the creation of a unified ministry, under Maryse Lebranchu, entitled Civil Service, Decentralization and State Reform. But there are too many questions left unanswered at the time of writing to allow for any sustained judgement of the credibility of this new approach. Who would be in charge of a new decentralization reform: Prime Minister Ayrault, Local Government Minister Lebranchu or Interior Minister Valls? In the 2012 Ayrault government, the Directorate General for Local Government (DGCL) was answerable to three distinct ministers (interior, local government and housing). In the early months of the Hollande presidency, questions also remained unanswered in relation to the financing of local government, the ongoing debate about competencies and structures and the future consequences of the EU fiscal compact on governing public services in France.

Dimensions and dilemmas of local and regional governance

Reforming the *mille-feuille institutionel*

Decentralization has been the subject of considerable political and institutional struggles for several decades in France (Le Gales, 2006; Le Lidec, 2007). The main division is between regionalist and departmentalist coalitions, briefly mentioned above. The Defferre laws in 1982–83 had already opposed the pro-Mitterrand departmentalists (*départementalistes mitterandiens*) to the pro-Rocard regionalists (*regionalists rocardiens*) (Rondin, 1985, p. 67). But the decentralization reform driven by Jean-Pierre Raffarin, from the end of 2002, most clearly demonstrated the departmentalist veto of the rise of the regions. Prime Minister Raffarin announced in June 2003 that the 'reform must first strengthen the regions in France'. The constitutional law of 28 March 2003 recognized the decentralized organization of the Republic and included the regions in the constitution alongside the communes and departments. However, although he was a regionalist, Raffarin had to accommodate the departmentalist coalition, in particular in the Senate. Numerous, influential and taking advantage of gaps between the regions, the departments finally obtained a more significant transfer of competencies than the regions. Of a total of 11 billion transferred from the state to local and regional authorities, the departments obtained 8 billion. They were notably strengthened in their role as the implementers of social policy. Under the pressure of the Senate, several competencies claimed by the regions (for national roads, university buildings or the recognized leadership in the field of economic development and innovation) were not included in the law. Thus, even if the regionalist coalition seems to have won the battle of ideas at the highest summit of the state, the departmentalist coalition has always succeeded, in political and parliamentary battles, in preserving the broad contours of the territorial status quo.

The 2010 local government reform was intended in part to address the 'problem' of the institutional mosaic of overlapping structures. The reform was loosely based on the findings of the Balladur Commission of 2009, which advocated a radical overhaul of the structures, functions, legal principles and public finances of local and regional government, as well as a more joined-up approach to intergovernmental relations. The 2010 reform fell short of the ambitious recommendations of the Balladur Commission. Even before the report had been published a number of its key proposals were being challenged by interested stakeholders and potential losers. The ambition to create 15 regions of a 'European dimension' raised the objections of those – in Picardy and Poitou-Charentes notably – likely to be abolished under the new plans. The proposals to abolish the canton as an administrative unit provoked opposition from within the Commission itself. The proposed Grand Paris was discretely buried by President Sarkozy on the same day he received the report. Ultimately, the Balladur Commission was more remarkable for its absences than its precise proposals. Early rumours that the departments might be abolished were denied; the bicentennial structure would remain. Attempts to fuse regions forcibly were abandoned. Rather, as in 2004, in 2010 the idea of the lead authority (*chef de file*) was emptied of its substance. Strikingly, the decision *not* to proceed with a comprehensive overhaul of competencies was justified in interviews in terms of the complexity of the exercise; the government had neither the time nor the capacity to undertake this. The 2010 reform did not fundamentally resolve the problem of overlapping institutions.

The most controversial element of the 2010 local government reform was the new territorial councillor, a locally elected politician who would combine the existing roles of departmental and regional councillor from 2014 onwards. This institutional innovation was presented by the law's framers as a response to the calls for clarification between the roles of the regions and the departments. The argument in favour was that a single councillor would strengthen the cohesion of the 'department–region' couple, with a view to producing a harmonization between these two levels of local authority, hence addressing the problem of duplication. Two readings of this institutional innovation were expressed in interviews. One involved the expectation that the department would eventually wither away, with the regional councils gradually taking over the responsibilities of the departments. A more widespread sentiment took exactly the opposite position, namely that the regions would most likely be captured by departmental interests. As elections for the new councillors were due to take place on the basis of single member geographical constituencies, the territorial interests of the departments would prevail over the larger region. Ultimately, the 2010 Local Government Reform Act added still further to the institutional complexity that provided the *raison d'être* for the reform itself. One of the first acts of the new Ayrault government was to abolish the territorial councillor and push back the date of the regional election to 2015.

Consistent with the anti-Sarkozy tone of Hollande's campaign, the socialist candidate's promises in relation to decentralization were largely directed against the outgoing president and the local government reform of December 2010. In his Dijon speech of 3 March 2012, Hollande portrayed the vision of a neutral Republic and offered the prospect of a new phase of decentralization. Still a candidate, Hollande promised to amend a number of key elements of the law of 16 December 2010: the suppression of the territorial councillor (a formal proposal in the 60 engagements) and the granting of new regulatory powers to the 26 regions and placing local and regional authorities on a firmer financial basis by creating a publicly owned Public Investment Bank. The political language was one of change, of a resumption of the 30-year-long trend to decentralizing competencies and finances to local and regional authorities. On the other hand, Prime Minister Ayrault reportedly did not call into question the key feature of the 2010 Act: namely, the commitment to ensure that every French commune formed part of an intercommunal structure by 2014.

The local governance of penury

Over the past decade, the question of local government finance has been one of double edged pressures, mutual recriminations and central–local tensions. From the perspective of ambitious local and regional authorities, central government transferred new service delivery responsibilities in the 2004 decentralization act without adequate compensation in terms of financial transfers. From the perspective of an increasingly economy-minded central government, local government expenditure has increased in a disproportionate manner and well beyond its sustainable level. Since 2008, the focus has shifted to the consequences of the euro debt crisis, the legacy of toxic loans taken out by local authorities and the virtual insolvency of some councils.

In 2010, local public spending represented 20 per cent of the overall total public expenditure and nearly three-quarters of public investment, a proportion that is likely to increase further as the transfers of competencies decided in the 2003–04 decentralization reforms are fully implemented (see Table 5.2). There has also been a significant growth of local government employment over the past decade (see Table 5.3). The communal bloc is by far the main provider of local government employment. However, the transfer of competences in 2004, especially the transfer of technical employees of secondary and high schools, also largely increased the numbers of employees in the *départements* and regions. The regional councils have seen a five-fold increase in five years in the numbers of staff they employ, from 12,514 agents in 2002 to 73,843 in 2008.

The processes of territorial governance and capacity building presuppose that local and regional authorities control sufficient administrative and financial resources to exercise a degree of autonomy. So, how

Table 5.2   *Levels of public spending from 2003 to 2010 (By billons of euros)*

	2003	2005	2007	2010
Local and regional authorities	164.2	188.2	212.2	228.7
Central government	413.5	448.8.	446.9	473.6
Social security administrations	385.5	423.0	459.7	513.7

Source: Figures calculated from INSEE (2011).

are local and regional authorities financed? State financial transfers form an important part of the budgets of communal, departmental and regional councils (Loughlin, 2007). In addition to a general central government block grant (*dotation globale de fonctionnement*), regional and local authorities receive financial support from the decentralization grant (Dotation Générale de la Décentralization – DGD), a fund specifically designed to compensate for new policy responsibilities under decentralization. The regions and the *départements* also benefit from specific grants-in-aid in order to fulfil their responsibilities in education and to cover investment items. The remaining resources come from a variety of local taxes, charges and borrowing; as representatives of local government associations repeatedly point out, local authorities are legally bound to present balanced budgets, which is not (yet) the case for the French state.

The 2003 constitutional reform and the May 2004 law embedded the principle of the financial autonomy of local authorities. The constitution now affirms that the principle of 'free administration' requires local and regional authorities to be responsible for raising the 'preponderant part' of their 'local resources' by local taxation. There has been considerable controversy about how 'local resources' are defined; if we adopt a comparative approach, and if we take into account the struc-

Table 5.3   *Local government employment from 1996 to 2008*

	1996	2002	2007	2008
Communes	1,008,675	1,092,833	1,117,284	1,112,603
EPCIs	110,820	155, 789	225,868	233,245
Départements	160,514	187,199	245,966	281,717
Regions	8,657	12,514	47,513	73,843

Source: INSEE: Observatoire des finances locales (2010). Available at
http://www.insee.fr/fr/themes/document.asp?ref_id=T10F133; accessed 5 February 2013.

ture of public expenditure by type of administration in the world for 2009, France appears as a country where the circuits of public spending remain relatively highly centralized. Indeed, if we add the expenditure of central government to those of social security (mainly healthcare and pensions), 79.3 per cent of public expenditure is centralized as against 72.3 per cent in the UK, 68.9 per cent in Italy, 63.3 per cent in Germany and 50.6 per cent in Spain.

Controlling local government finance is one central feature of the state's close involvement in localities. Since 2004, the politicization of central–local relations has spilled over into disputes about local taxation. Largely run by the left throughout the first decade of the twenty-first century, local and regional authorities were accused by the UMP government of financial profligacy. In a move reminiscent of Margaret Thatcher in the UK in the 1980s, the Fillon government announced the abolition of the local collection and setting of business rates (*taxe professionnelle*) in January 2010 and its replacement by a more centralized formula-based method of tax collection, considerably limiting the fiscal autonomy of local authorities, especially the departments and regions. The effects of this radical move were immediate; from 2010 to 2012, the proportion of finances raised by local taxes declined from 50 to 20 per cent for departments and from 38 to 10 per cent for the regions. Though François Hollande promised to restore the financial autonomy of regions and departments during the 2012 presidential campaign, this looks unlikely in the current economic context.

Since 2008 in particular, a number of local and regional authorities have appeared as damaged collateral of the euro and sovereign debt crisis. In comparison with counterparts elsewhere is Europe, there has been no major calling into question of territorial equilibria as a result of downgrading of local or regional authorities, as has occurred notably in Spain. But the situation has reached crisis point in a number of local authorities, such as the departmental council of Seine St Denis, which is confronted with severe social problems as a result of the economic crisis. In a number of cases, social challenges have been made worse by the legacy of toxic loans agreed by (rather inexperienced) local and regional authorities earlier on in the 2000–10 decade. Whether local and regional authorities will manage to renegotiate the terms of these toxic loans will be one of the major challenges for the new Hollande administration. If the announced Public Investment Bank provides some vital short-term financial relief, the longer-term perspective is far less certain.

The politicization of central–local relations

Though the right won the three presidential elections of 1995, 2002 and 2007, the left has come to dominate the 'local state'. At the time of writing, after its victories in the 2008 municipal, the 2010 regional and the 2011 cantonal elections, the PS runs a majority of large cities, almost two-thirds of departments and virtually all (21 out of 22) of France's regional councils. Building on this electoral success, the left finally conquered the Senate in 2011 (see Chapter 3 for a fuller discussion). Until Hollande's 2012 election, this asymmetry complicated intergovernmental relations, as central government was extremely wary of transferring more competencies to the local level or allowing local and regional authorities full exercise over those responsibilities it formally controls. Partisan competition had a clear impact upon the outcomes of the 2004 reform: why strengthen the regions if they were to be controlled by the opposition parties? A similar calculation explained the refusal to engage in a far reaching overhaul of local government competencies in the 2010 Act.

The partisan dimension appears more powerful than ever under the Hollande presidency. Prime Minister Ayrault soon established a dialogue with the various local government associations that are all dominated by the governing PS. President Hollande himself received the presidents of the 22 regions (21 of them socialist) at the Elysée in September 2012, the first time ever that regional presidents as a group had been accorded such public attention. From these auspicious beginnings, local government policy under Hollande appears likely to be determined by the distinct territorial interests within the PS that, in 2012, dominated the elected regions, controlled a majority of departments (Hollande himself was previously president of the Corrèze department) and large cities, and had a small working majority in the Senate. The consensual style adopted and quasi-institutional involvement of the PS made it unlikely that any radical reform would be produced. The calendar of a new decentralization act, promised by candidate Hollande, was clarified by the Ayrault government in September 2012, with a new bill to be presented to Parliament in early 2013. If the content of this new act of decentralization remains vague, the debates and negotiations are likely to focus on three key dimensions of French decentralization: (1) the continuing rationalization of the communal bloc and the promotion of a new metropolitan statute; (2) the transfer of new competences to the regions with a regulatory power in some fields such as economic development and innovation (and the promise of co-management of the future Public Investment Bank and direct management of the European structural funds); and (3) the reform of the local tax system.

The European dimension

European integration presents a challenge for French local and regional authorities at several levels to limit public finances and to comply with restrictive European directives in areas such as public services and accessing the European institutions themselves. To start with the latter, France has traditionally had one of the tightest, most state-centric forms of interaction with Brussels. At an official intergovernmental level, all interactions are supposed to be cleared by the Secrétariat Genéral aux Affaires Européennes (SGAE), a bureaucratic unit attached to the prime minister's office. Another central state agency dependent upon the prime minister, the Délégation Interministérielle à l'Aménagement du Territoire et à l'Attractivité Régionale (DATAR), coordinates local and regional bids for funding, in close liaison with the regional prefectures, the Secrétariat Genéral aux Affaires Régionales (SGAR). In practice, French regions are not absent from this process. EU rules for the attribution of regional development and structural funds insist upon the involvement of local and regional authorities and voluntary associations. The Commission has clashed with the French government over the interpretation of these rules. The regional prefectures have associated the regions with the definition and the implementation of structural and cohesion funds. Since the passage of the 2004 decentralization law, French regions have been allowed to bid to exercise complete control over the management of structural funds on an experimental basis (the first contender being Alsace). The direction of change is clear, even though French administrative and political elites continue to resist, as in many other areas of decentralization.

Like their counterparts in other EU countries, French local and regional authorities adopt an ambivalent attitude towards the EU. On the one hand, the rhetoric of European integration includes references to a 'Europe of the regions'. The European level has been engaged as a resource, in spite of some formal opposition from the French state to this sort of activity. Writing on the European strategy of the Brittany region, for example, demonstrates how Breton leaders were able to bring pressure to bear on the European Commission to allow the French government to use European funds to part-finance the high speed rail route (LGV) between Le Mans and Rennes. But, on the other hand, in their day to day work, local and regional authorities also face a harsher edge of European integration, especially as structural and cohesion funds have dried up or been diverted to eastern and central European countries. Local authorities have had great difficulties in complying with public services legislation and the prevailing belief in the Commission (in DG Competition, if less in DG Regio) of the importance of competition as the basic principle of public service delivery. Local authorities have had to devise expensive means for tendering out such delivery and complying with the rules of public procurement. In particular, the specific rules for the provision of intercommunal services, whereby cross subsidies are considered as state aids, has created great practical difficulties for the smallest communes in providing basic public services. More broadly, the eurozone crisis has had an impact on the local and regional authorities. Since 2010, central governments across the zone have initiated policies of debt reduction which seriously limit the financial capacities of local and regional authorities. In 2011, for example, the Fillon government decided to freeze the local government block grant (Dotation Globale de Fonctionnement) for three years, a move confirmed by the Ayrault government in June 2012. President Hollande's pledge to eradicate the deficit by 2017 is likely to limit the magnitude of any new decentralization act.

Conclusion

The core question addressed in this chapter was presented in terms of whether the uneven and partially uncoordinated development of French local and regional government over the past three decades has produced a form of suboptimal institutional competition or, on the contrary, has improved public services as a result of local and regional innovation and investment. The two aspects of the question are less in opposition than might appear. On a positive reading, three decades of decentralization have reduced the tutelage of the centralized state, introduced genuine territorial checks and balances within the French political system, produced a degree of policy emulation across local authorities and, in some respects, improved local democracy. In specific sectors such as education, transport and economic development, French localities and regions have become the locomotives of public investment. A less positive interpretation might point to costly admin-istration, a confusion of service delivery responsibilities and an absence of genuine political accountability.

Local authorities are not blameless. The expansion of local govern-ment staff and expenditure over the past decade has been remarkable, involving, for instance, a 9 per cent spending increase in 2009 on the eve of the introduction of the 2010 Territorial Reform Bill. But neither is central government blameless. Notwithstanding Sarkozy's rhetoric in favour of more joined-up government, the reform of RéATE and the 2010 local government reform might have been implemented without reference to each other. The Balladur report (2009) proposed that, where state responsibilities have been transferred to local and regional authorities, the state field services ought to be cut, which would be a cost-cutting and potentially far-reaching measure. But there was no further reference to this in the bill.

If central–local relations have been more sanguine since Hollande's election, France's model of local and regional government faces new threats. The ratification of the Fiscal Compact Treaty, and the 'constitutional austerity' that some on the left fear is likely to ensue, might endanger some of the achievements of decentralization. Or, from a different perspective, the fiscal compact might act as a useful external constraint to enforce a much closer supervision of local and regional government activities than ever before, either by the French government or by the European authorities. The core challenge for local and regional authorities and their professional associations will be to negotiate a new compromise in a less favourable policy environment, one where performance indicators are likely to be determined by central government, where EU regulations will constrain what local authorities can do in service delivery terms, and where central government and the EU will continue to devise new instruments to steer policy in areas that affect local or regional government. Local and regional democracy thus appears caught between the rather contradictory pressures of 'institutional layering', as a result of three decades of decentralization reforms, and attempts by central governors to rein in local authority spending. Whatever the future holds, the incremental effects of years of reform and bottom-up innovation has been to increase the importance of local and regional authorities as major players in the French institutional landscape. It would take a radical change to challenge this state of affairs.

Chapter 6

Political Parties: The UMP and the Right

FLORENCE HAEGEL

In 2012, the Union for a Popular Movement (Union pour un Mouvement Populaire – UMP) celebrated its tenth anniversary. The movement was formed in 2002 as the latest attempt to unite the diverse families and groups on the French centre and right. In the summer of 2012, after Nicolas Sarkozy's defeat in the 2012 presidential election, the UMP appeared to be rediscovering the energy of its early years, when it had freely experimented with new forms of internal democracy, encouraged ideological pluralism and accommodated party factionalism. Since Sarkozy's defeat, UMP leaders have agreed on the need to copy the Socialist Party (PS) by introducing open primaries for the 2017 UMP presidential nomination. While awaiting this longer term challenge, UMP party managers and activists were primarily mobilized by the selection of a new leader, planned in November 2012. For the first time in the history of the party, the competition for the leadership was genuinely open and strongly contested. Jean-François Copé, the then general secretary (*secrétaire général*), was running for his re-election; François Fillon, the former prime minister, was challenging him. The party was thus confronted with the logic of a contest between an externally popular politician and an organizational strongman.

The democratic renewal of the party turned into a nightmare scenario. The election that took place on 18 November 2012 produced an extremely tight result, so narrow, in fact, that each candidate initially claimed victory. The strategy adopted by Copé to flatter the party activists showed itself to be more efficient than that of Fillon, who emphasized his record as former prime minister and primarily addressed UMP electors, rather than activists. Both candidates accused each other of electoral fraud, of lying and of misleading activists. Copé announced his victory first, by around 1,000 votes, followed shortly by Fillon, who claimed to be around 200 votes ahead of his rival. Copé's victory was confirmed by the official electoral commission, but at the time of writing it continues to be contested by Fillon, who has called into question the neutrality of the internal arbitration process. The violence of the exchanges between the two men shocked even seasoned political journalists and observers; neither of the two former UMP presidents – Alain Juppé and Nicolas Sarkozy – were able to bring the two rivals to an agreement.

In November 2012, the UMP not only elected a new leader but also voted on motions supported by internal party groups (called 'movements') which would structure party functioning for the next three years. The party appeared ideologically divided, as well as split over its future leader – and this almost evenly between various right-wing groups and others (such as the Humanists) who supported a more centre-right orientation. The most spectacular result, however, was that of the 'strong right' (*la droite forte*) motion, which attracted around 28 per cent of the activists' votes. Its success underlined how far the UMP had moved to the right.

Why was the UMP formed in the first place? Its creation in 2002 held out the promise of finally overcoming the fragmentation of the parties of the centre and the right, who were torn between a powerful Gaullist movement (the RPR from 1976) and a centre-right federation of various smaller parties (UDF from 1978). In contrast with other European countries, 'Christian democracy' never succeeded in becoming a pivotal force in the French right, although various attempts to set up Catholic parties had occurred during the Third Republic. After the Second World War, the Popular Republican Movement (Mouvement Républicain Populaire – MRP) did establish itself as a major centre-right party but its electoral fortunes waned during the post-war Fourth Republic and it was almost entirely supplanted by the resurgent Gaullist movement after 1958.

The Gaullist Party, under a confusing variety of names (Union pour la Nouvelle République – UNR, Union des Démocrats pour la République – UDR, Rassemblement pour la République – RPR), was the main (and sometimes dominant) party of the right for the period 1958–2002 (Knapp, 2004). But Gaullism never established a complete hegemony; it was challenged by non-Gaullist components on the centre and right, classically associated with the leadership of Valéry Giscard d'Estaing, who was elected president in 1974. In 1978, President Giscard d'Estaing created the Union for French Democracy (Union pour la Démocratie Française – UDF) as a centre-right party confederation to organize his own supporters against the more disciplined Gaullists. From 1978 to 2002, the right was thus divided in two main organizations, the RPR, the neo-Gaullist party refounded in December 1976 by Jacques Chirac, and the UDF. Though these parties joined forces for the legislative elections, they were in competition with each other in most presidential contests (1981, 1988, 1995). These two parties' genetic models were highly different: the RPR came close to Panebianco's (1988) 'charismatic model', while the UDF looked more like a loose confederation of provincial parliamentarians.

In this respect, 2002 was a major turning point since the UMP was created by a merger of various components of the right (Haegel, 2004), incorporating the former RPR and the main part of the UDF. The UMP was to be a unified party of the right, the unchallenged inheritor of the main Gaullist, liberal-conservative and Christian democratic traditions. Its creation was also intended to fend off the challenge of the radical right-wing National Front (Front National – FN).

From 2002 to 2012, the fortunes of the UMP were closely linked to those of Nicolas Sarkozy, who took control of the leadership in 2004, captured the presidency in 2007 and maintained a tight control over the party during his term as president from 2007 to 2012. In the aftermath of the 2012 presidential defeat, the party emerged as divided in relation to the legacy of the overwhelming figure of Sarkozy. The assessment of his record in office is controversial and his future place within the party remains an open question. Several former members of his governments criticized how the 2012 presidential campaign took place and the way it was led by a small presidential circle with very right-wing opinions.

How did Sarkozy influence the functioning of the UMP as an organization? Was he in any way responsible for the disarray of the UMP after he left office? Could the internal destabilization of the UMP, vividly illustrated in its 2012 leadership election, have been avoided? The main argument presented in this chapter is that the former president suspended or even froze the UMP's organization, while at the same time radicalizing its ideology. Two major organizational changes took place under Sarkozy's leadership regarding the selection of the party leader and the role of internal pluralism. In order to give an account of these organizational and ideological changes, I will analyse how Sarkozy 'froze' the party organization by controlling the leadership. I will then focus on internal party pluralism and analyse the operation of factionalism within the party and at its fringe. I will conclude by addressing the issue of the UMP's ideological radicalization and the impact it might have on the cohesion of the right in the longer term. These transformations strongly suggest that the form of the UMP as a party has dramatically changed depending upon the political cycle (electoral versus non-electoral sequences) and above all in relation to the power sequence: whether the UMP is the governing or presidential party, or whether it is in opposition. Weakly democratized and loosely institutionalized, the UMP was not prepared to confront a situation of hard internal competition; it was also deeply ideologically divided, which became crystallized during the 2012 leadership campaign.

The UMP: a frozen and controlled organization?

In many respects, arguing that the UMP is characterized by a shifting party form according to the political cycle is common sense. Winning or losing elections and being in or out of office will have a major impact on the internal life of all governmental parties. Nevertheless the UMP is an extreme case; the impact occurs to such an extent that party forms, rules and even statutes have changed significantly depending on political cycles. I argue that the party was purposely rendered docile during Sarkozy's presidential mandate. Two organizational changes deserve attention because they modified the party's internal life and had a major impact in terms of how leadership is shaped and internal party pluralism is exercised.

The first and major change dealt with leadership. The UMP used to be ruled by a president directly elected by members, but after the 2007 presidential victory, the party introduced a set of 'provisional' statutes that remained valid throughout the whole presidential term. From spring 2007 to autumn 2012, the post of UMP president disappeared on the grounds that 'morally, the UMP president remains Nicolas Sarkozy' (statement by Jean-Claude Gaudin, 25 June 2007). As a consequence, an overriding clause posited that the post of UMP president was to be replaced by an executive team when the party leader became President of the Republic: there can only be one president.

At the head of the executive team, the new party leader was called 'general secretary' (*secrétaire général*) and was no longer elected by members but appointed by Sarkozy and confirmed by the Bureau Politique, a collegial body including an executive team and ex officio and elected members. This arrangement applied to the whole presidential term and was to be suspended as soon as the party was no longer in office. This ad hoc change of party rules solemnly passed in 2002 characterizes the UMP as an organization that is weakly democratized and very loosely institutionalized.

In many respects the UMP during Sarkozy's presidential mandate departed from the common democratic rule shared by most western European parties, which affirms that the party leader should be selected by party members. UMP members were neither involved in the selection of mid-level executives (they are appointed by party headquarters) nor in internal debates on party orientations. In summary, UMP members are only weakly involved in internal party life except for the election of the leader. Deprived of this right to choose their leader, they were even more marginalized during Sarkozy's mandate. Therefore, whatever the indicators of internal party democracy one takes (the participation of members, the competitiveness of internal election or the extent of deliberation), the UMP appears to be weakly democratized. In addition, it also appears to be loosely institutionalized. If one measures the degree of institutionalization of an organization by the stability of rules and norms and the existence of sanctions framing interactions between actors, the UMP is indeed a weak institution in comparison to many other parties. Admittedly the traceability of some organizational rules (for instance the appointment and not election of party officials at the intermediary level of *fédérations*) shows an obvious historical continuity. But, to a large extent, the UMP has neither fostered stable rules nor imposed sanctions when these rules are broken. UMP leaders have been acting to form when they play with statutes, modifying them for their leader's stake and, according to the internal balance of power, by-passing them when necessary. Far from regarding statutes or even informal rules as sacred, the neo-Gaullist party has been adept at changing rules as quickly as it has needed to break them. This loose and instrumental relationship to formal rules makes the party rather similar to earlier neo-Gaullist organizations.

This suspension of the post of party presidency also gives us some clues about the balance of power during Sarkozy's presidential mandate. As expected, the party's centre of gravity shifted to the Elysée from 2007 to 2012. Sarkozy followed party matters, as all previous presidents had done, and, if anything, his interference in party life was more emphatic than those of his predecessors. Not only did he dispatch personal spin doctors in order to enhance the UMP's communication but he attended major party rallies and personally received UMP MPs at the Elysée and gathered the most generous party donors by way of gratitude for their financial support. In this respect, he differed dramatically from his predecessor Jacques Chirac who, once elected, did not publicly break the myth of 'a president above parties'. Chirac played the game according to the rules and did not physically attend party meetings. But even he used indirect means in order to intervene in the UMP's internal life: using the device of a statement read out by a messenger, a video address or sending his wife to sit in the front row of party meetings.

In the case of parties of the right, flexible rules go hand in hand with changing leaders. Without any president, the UMP was officially ruled from 2007 to 2012 by a general secretary who owed his legitimacy, ultimately, to President Sarkozy. The post of general secretary turned out not to be a particularly stable one. While Sarkozy kept his prime minister, Fillon, for the whole presidential term, the UMP changed its general secretaries three times during the same period. Xavier Bertrand, a former minister of labour in Fillon's government, replaced Patrick Devedjan (an elected representative in the Hauts-de-Seine, Sarkozy's stronghold) after only 16 months. Bertrand was followed by Copé, the former leader of the UMP deputies, after 22 months. Each time a new general secretary assumed control, there were some changes in the management team, including the posts of deputy general secretary. This evidence of turnover is quite consistent with longer standing traditions on the neo-Gaullist right, as demonstrated in the classic studies by W. R. Schonfeld (1980a, 1980b). Comparing changes in the leadership of the Neo-Gaullist party (UDR and RPR) and the PS from 1968 to 1979, Schonfeld concluded that the turnover of party elites was stronger in the UDR and the RPR than in the PS. According to Schonfeld, far from being due to a vivid internal democratic life, this large party renewal was characteristic of a 'monocratic party' in which top-down appointment was the rule. More than 30 years later, the UMP leader is still in a position to shape party recruitment, thanks to his power of appointment at national and intermediary levels. In this respect, Copé, after his nomination as UMP general secretary in February 2011, selected a very large national team in order to reward a maximum number of mid-rank leaders and local officials. Not only did such a move ensure the support of party managers for Sarkozy's presidential campaign, but it also created a legion of loyal cadres in support of Copé himself in the post-Sarkozy perspective. Cope's appointments to positions of influence within the UMP far exceeded those of his predecessors since 2007. In addition to the 21 members of the executive team, Copé appointed 48 'political advisors' and more than 190 national secretaries. In practice, the UMP was not ruled by this group of 200 particularly influential members, but by a small group supported by the party organization.

Two major positions deserve attention in order to understand how the UMP was ruled during this period. I have already mentioned the role of the general secretary who personifies the party's public and political face. Next to him there is a managing director (*directeur général*) who is in charge of administration. Nobody knows his name but he is the one who gets the UMP to work. None of these managing directors was elected by members or even by a large representative body. From 2002 to 2012, the managing directors were recruited through political networks, partly based on personal loyalties: two of them came from Jacques Chirac's Paris network or were connected to his presidential campaign team; the last one was a key member of Sarkozy's network based on his stronghold of the Hauts-de-Seine (France's richest *département*). Each managing director claimed to apply the so-called 'firm model' to the UMP on the grounds that management and marketing should be promoted and controlled by the party headquarters (Petitfils, 2007). Following the example of many European parties, the parties of the French right have promoted management and marketing tools thanks to the recruitment of party executives who are trained in business schools or are business consultants. Amongst them, the most famous is Eric Woerth, who recently faced criminal charges in relation to the illicit funding of the UMP (the

'Bettencourt Affair'). Woerth was trained at HEC (Haute École de Commerce), a leading French business school, and later on worked as a consultant for the accounting firm Arthur Andersen. He was previously in charge of party finances for the former RPR and the UMP (successively as administrative and financial director, then as treasurer of those parties) before becoming budget minister. Organizational changes to the UMP during Sarkozy's leadership echoed more general trends and appeared to validate the organizational form designated by the term 'professional electoral party' (Panebianco, 1988), characterized by the supremacy of electoral objectives, growing professionalization and the use of marketing and communication tools.

Sarkozy's presidential mandate corresponded also to a sequence of party freezing due to presidential control. This organizational freezing gives new evidence of the plasticity of this type of weakly institutionalized and highly adaptable party. But it also attests to the weak democratic demands of its members who accepted this reduction of their rights without voicing any protest. Other organizational changes also went in the same direction, since party internal pluralism was highly constrained during the period of Sarkozy's leadership.

The shifting pluralism of the UMP

There has been little extensive research undertaken on factionalism in Gaullist and post-Gaullist organizations, unlike the case of the PS which 'has been marked by its factional nature' (Cole, 1989, p. 79). This lack of scientific interest may be directly related to the fact that specialists share the assumption that 'groups within the French Gaullist Party, for example, are essentially cliques of national leaders and by and large have no capillary networks running down to the level of ordinary party members' (Hine, 1982, p. 39). This is characteristic of the so-called 'charismastic party' (Panebianco, 1988, ch. 8), founded on the authority of an exceptional personality and which does not allow fragmented loyalties or the personal allegiances of sub-leaders. In summary, scholars used to emphasize the basic contrast between the socialist organization on the one hand – based on pluralism with fractions fuelled by ideological debate and motivated by the allocation of posts and the promotion of sub-leaders and on the other hand the post-Gaullist organization working under the authority of a leader who leaves no room for the public expression of sub-groups and sub-leaders.

The respect of pluralism was inevitably at stake in the UMP due to the merging mentioned above and the fact that minor organizations argued strongly for keeping a form of autonomy or at least for a mode of expression of their specificity. Hence, the UMP's new party statutes of 2002 introduced a major change by institutionalizing factionalism so that party factions, or *mouvements* (movements), became even more formalized than 'currents' (*courants*) in the PS. To shape such a formal faction, party statutes stipulated that it was necessary to have the sponsorship of ten MPs and to express publicly a statement of principle supported by rank-and-file members voting in congress. The headquarters would then allocate resources, funding, offices and communication support to factions gathering more than 10 per cent of the votes at the party congress. Under Sarkozy's leadership the provisions for internal party factionalism remained registered in the UMP's party statutes and were regularly evoked by party actors, but these voices were too marginal to be seriously taken into account. The implementation of the new rules was postponed during Sarkozy's long leadership.

The reason for this failure to institutionalize factionalism is that many party leaders were reluctant to change the party's 'genetic model' which emphasized centralization and uniformity. Among the more vigorous opponents was Sarkozy himself, who advocated a return to a less binding arrangement when he took control of the UMP in November 2004. Since then, factionalism has been based on informal, centralized and even personal and private contracts with a myriad of organizations, clubs and think tanks which remain separate from internal competition. The so-called 'associated body corporate' ('*personnes morales associées*') has become the basic element of factionalism, at the expense of the 'movements'. These associations are more compatible with a centralized view of the neo-Gaullist organization than the more strongly structured movements.

Between 2004 (when he took over the party) and 2007 (when he won the presidential election), Sarkozy promoted strong central control of the UMP party sub-groups. The basic principle is that there should be contractualized agreements between the UMP central organization and its diverse sub-groups; as these contracts are private, however, the terms of negotiation are not at all transparent. There are several types of associated body which perform a range of distinctive functions. The most important is a financial one. The UMP has created a range of associations and small parties in order to be able to attract additional finance for the movement. In these circumstances, it is akin to a parent company that funds a large range of subsidiary companies, including smaller political organizations, associations, clubs or think tanks. Some of these associations are registered as genuine parties (able to contribute thereby to central UMP funds), while others are not.

The financial flows between the UMP organization and its groups are complex. Under Sarkozy's control beginning in 2004, the central organization considerably restricted the budget allocated to the management of party sub-groups. Since the 2012 presidential defeat, the financial pressure on the party has been even greater in so far as the shrinkage of the parliamentary group (down to 196 deputies since the June 2012 National Assembly election, compared with 314 deputies from 2007–12) has produced a steep reduction in its public funding. While it received €30 million per year from 2007 to 2012, since the 2012 general election, this has fallen to €20 million. It is unlikely that funding party factions will be a high priority in this new austere environment.

Creating affiliated groups allows the UMP to appeal for broader support to specific political organizations (for example the Radical Party) or in favour of broad political or philosophical positions. Notwithstanding the centralization under Sarkozy, the UMP has thus retained elements of a confederal structure, with more peripheral groups such as the Radicals or the Centrists retaining the option to exercise more independence at a later date.

What is the role of these associations in the functioning of the UMP? Do they really have a major impact upon party platforms and the choice of leader? A brief comparison of the 2007 and 2012 presidential election campaigns suggests that the role of the UMP as a whole depended on the context of specific elections. In 2007, the presidential platform was drawn up inside the party. Even though Emmanuelle Mignon, in charge of this task, had been originally recruited from non-partisan networks, she was appointed by the party, which played a central role in the 2007 campaign. In 2012, on the other hand, despite the attempts made by Copé to emphasize the place of clubs and think tanks in the setting up of the presidential platform, the party and its nebulous sub-groups were very clearly marginalized.

One key function assumed by some political parties in the Fifth Republic has been the selection of the party's presidential candidate. As Sawicki demonstrates in Chapter 7, the PS has had an increasingly important role in determining the party candidate, first as a result of internal party election (in 1995 and 2007), and much more recently through a successful process of primaries. In the neo-Gaullist tradition, leadership has not traditionally been assumed to flow from the mass consultation of party members. There was no open and contested competition for the 2007 or 2012 presidential nominations. As the selection of the candidate has not thus far been settled through genuine and open party competition, internal presidential contests have not relied on the competition between visible sub-groups within the party (though this might change if the UMP goes ahead with primaries from 2017). A culture of unanimity persists within the party, which, in this respect, must be considered as the inheritor of the neo-Gaullist party tradition, in spite of the much more diverse origins of the party. There remains a strong reluctance to institutionalize internal competition or to permit public pluralism.

There is a strong leadership tradition within the UMP, as there had been in previous Gaullist and neo-Gaullist parties. Since the birth of the UMP in 2002, leaders have emerged as a result of natural selection, rather than formal internal party competition. In formal terms, the selection of the party leader might involve a contest with several candidates, but these contests have always been very unequal ones. Since the creation of the UMP, the leaders Alain Juppé and Nicolas Sarkozy were both elected by rank and file members. And each time (in November 2002 and November 2004) minor candidates did challenge the party leaders, though they represented little threat to the front-runner, their presence serving mainly as a democratic guarantee. The leadership tradition favours selecting 'the best' by acclamation.

Throughout its existence, the UMP has housed a broad variety of principled or ideological factions representing clear divisions and positions. Leadership challengers in the past decade mainly sought to express their support for a particular ideological or policy position, in the belief that these orientations should steer the party. In the 2004 leadership election, for example, Christine Boutin stood in the name of the 'Christian and Democratic' group within the party. She took a stand on ethical and social issues, and argued that the UMP should be guided by the religious affiliation of its Christian members. Unable to secure much influence for this position, Boutin created her own small party, the Christian Democratic Party, lying partly within and partly without the UMP. Another leadership contender, Rachid Kaci, on the other hand, presented himself as a 'conservative and liberal' spokesman of the party's right wing and supported anti-Islamic, anti-multicultural, 'republican' and secular positions.

The most important, or least marginal, challenger to Sarkozy was Nicolas Dupont-Aignan, the candidate of the main Eurosceptic group within the UMP (Debout la République). Dupont-Aignan regularly challenged for the UMP leadership before finally deciding to quit the party in January 2007. Eventually, he ran in the 2012 presidential election on an anti-European ticket and polled 1.79 per cent of the votes. The anti-European positions espoused by him originally had an active constituency within the UMP; his bid for the leadership was supported by 14.91 per cent of the vote in the leadership elections of 2002 and 9.1 per cent in 2004. During Sarkozy's leadership the audience of the explicit Eurosceptics diminished greatly, and in 2012, no anti-European groups played an important role inside the party. In summary the UMP's Europeanization was completed during Sarkozy's leadership.

Under Sarkozy, after 2004, the central UMP organization became less tolerant of its internal diversity. The party was definitively not the arena for ideological opposition to express itself. Nevertheless, distinct ideological positions, sometimes in conflict with those of Sarkozy, were articulated within the UMP's parliamentary group. Unsurprisingly, the 2012 presidential defeat has changed this. In November 2012 the competition for the UMP leadership was based on a real contest between serious competitors. For the first time since 2002, moreover, the UMP applied the party statutes as they existed and gave the opportunity to sub-groups and factions to become more visible by competing for members' votes. These new 'factions' demonstrated how radical in ideological and policy terms the UMP had become.

The UMP, the FN and the radical right

Few scholars have addressed the tricky issue of how mainstream right-wing parties have reacted, or should react, to the success of the radical right. Strategic responses of mainstream parties towards radical newcomers vary from indifference to accommodation or opposition (Meguid, 2008). Scholars have endeavoured to measure the impact of these various strategies on the radical right's electoral success as well as on the ideology and policies both of the radical right and of the more mainstream parties (Van Spanje and Van Der Brug, 2007). Much work has been undertaken on the issue of immigration in particular and the agenda-setting role of radical right parties (Schain, 2006; Spanje and Brug, 2007). In broad terms, scholars have drawn two rather opposing sets of findings. Some have argued that isolation and ostracism keep the radical right focussed on radical stances, while inclusion leads it to a form of moderation or at least a trivialization, which leads to its weakening. Others (Arzheimer, 2009) have sustained the argument that ideological compromise leads to the legitimization of radical right stances and produces an increased audience for radical right parties. In summary, when the mainstream right parties copy the radical right by taking over its favourite issues, the so-called 'co-optation of policy positions' (Downs, 2001, p. 27), the radical right agenda is legitimized and their parties profit from this.

The French case echoes this debate directly in so far as the UMP's strategy towards the FN has combined ideological imitation with the co-optation of public policies, resulting in its electoral isolation. Indeed the borrowing of themes associated with the radical right was one of the driving forces during Sarkozy's presidential term. Under his leadership, the UMP was characterized by a form of radicalization (Haegel, 2011). Certainly, Chirac's strategy and ideology were not devoid of ambiguity. Faced with the emergence of the FN in the early 1980s, the right's reaction fluctuated: a policy of isolating the FN at the national level went alongside the early toleration of some regional alliances. In practice, the stance adopted towards the FN varied according to the type of election and the broader context. Hence, the distinction between Chirac and Sarkozy should not be overestimated, in so far as the RPR during Chirac's leadership was not totally hermetic to the issues or influence of the FN. In the 1993 legislative election, for example, Chirac's RPR directly borrowed some themes from the FN's platform, such as the 'national exception' and the stigmatization of polygamy.

Nevertheless, Sarkozy did make a break by calling for an ideological clarification and taking a strategic turn. He proclaimed himself to be a politician of the right and claimed one of his objectives as the reconquest of FN voters. In part, and as a consequence of this strategic objective, the French right has been radicalized, notably with regard to questions of immigration and national identity. This strategy, successfully applied in 2007, was consolidated after the defeat in the regional elections in March 2010. Taking a lead from Sarkozy, the UMP leadership then undertook a rightwards shift. Copé, first as head of the UMP parliamentary group, then as UMP general secretary, actively promoted this strategy by addressing the party's opposition to the wearing of headscarves and religious attire in public places. Interestingly, this initiative was first undertaken within the National Assembly when Copé was still head of the UMP group. Subsequently, as general secretary, he attempted to launch a debate about religious worship and the French secular tradition within the UMP. From 2010 in particular, the UMP went through a strategy of borrowing ideas from the FN while proclaiming opposition to any forms of collaboration with it, whether through electoral or governmental alliances. But there was a notable shift in attitudes towards the prospect of alliances with the FN from 2010 onwards. In the 2011 cantonal elections, where the FN performed particularly well (see Chapter 10), the UMP adopted the strategy of the so-called 'neither-nor', a stance repeated in the 2012 general election. In the case of second round contests where no UMP candidate was eligible to stand, the official party position was that electors should support neither the Socialist nor the FN candidate.

Such a strategy appeared to place the PS and the FN on the same footing, a stance that is being publicly challenged inside the party itself. On the one hand, some UMP politicians challenged the wisdom of appearing to label the FN and the 'republican' PS as the pest and the cholera. On the other hand, there was evidence that grass roots support for local alliances between the UMP and the FN was increasing. In August 2012, 52 per cent of UMP sympathizers were reported in one survey as being in favour of local agreements (*Le Journal du Dimanche*, 19 August 2012, p. 4).

Sarkozy's strategy towards the FN appeared to be successful in 2007 in so far as he 'managed to shrink the FN electorate' (Mayer, 2007). But this strategy was much less fruitful in 2012. If Jean-Marie Le Pen polled 3,800,000 votes in the first round of the 2007 presidential election, his daughter, Marine Le Pen, mobilized 6,400,000 voters five years later. In the meantime, the logistics of political demand and supply had changed. The economic crisis has had a major impact in

France, strengthening the radical right, as in a number of other countries in Europe, and, above all, destabilizing the existing political elite. There has been an important change within the FN, with it now being led by a strategically astute Marine Le Pen, daughter of Jean-Marie Le Pen. Part of the change was one of image: a young woman replacing an old man. But a more profound strategic shift was also afoot, as Marine Le Pen attempted to 'mainstream' the radical right and bring the FN closer to the exercise of power. Under her leadership since 2011, the FN has sought to recentre its appeal and campaign on social and economic difficulties, protectionism, the national 'priority' and challenging France's euro membership.

In the eyes of many popular working-class electors, Sarkozy could not compete with the harder line represented by Marine Le Pen. The FN candidate's campaign was further legitimized by the rightward shift of the Sarkozy administration after 2010 (the 'national identity' campaign, the expulsions of gypsies, the Grenoble speech of 2010 which promised an ever harder stance on law and order issues). This strategy of moving the FN towards the mainstream is far from being entirely new (Dézé, 2012; Shields, 2012). Since its creation, the FN has alternated sequences of demarcation with sequences of adaptation. More specifically, it has emphasized different messages depending upon which public (voters versus activists) it is addressing. As with any 'anti-system party', the FN is under pressure. On the one hand, its radical positions are electoral resources, popular stances that find a real echo amongst many electors. On the other hand, as with any party, the conquest of posts is crucial if the party is to be fully institutionalized and professionalized.

The radical right's influence on the UMP is apparent in relation to internal party dynamics. From 2007 to 2012, the core UMP factions focussed their activities in the parliamentary arena, rather than in the formal party organs. The role of the UMP parliamentary group from 2007–12 was of key importance in this respect, and the size of the group elected in 2007 was one reason for its emergence as a powerful actor, as was seen under Copé's leadership. It was also an institutional site where differences of opinion within the UMP could be expressed.

As the 2012 presidential campaign approached, there was a proliferation of parliamentary sub-groups, each organized around more or less subtle ideological divisions. UMP free marketeers had already set up a network and prompted coordination of their action within the parliamentary group (Haegel, 2007), but on the verge of the 2012 elections, several newcomers emerged, including the Popular Right (La Droite Populaire), the Rural Right (La Droite Rurale), the Social Right (La Droite Sociale) and the Humanists (Les Humanistes). After the presidential and parliamentary defeats of 2012, they were joined by new groups which lobbied strongly in advance of the 2012 internal elections, groups such as the Strong Right (La Droite Forte) and Gaullist Rally. Significantly the majority of these groups claim to belong to the right, despite this ideological label having been largely rejected some years ago.

Radicalization is indeed underway: in this respect, the Popular Right group played the role of a precursor and justifies the attention that will now be paid to it. The Popular Right parliamentary sub-group was created on the highly symbolic date of 14 July 2010 (14 July being a national holiday in memory of the French Revolution). It aimed to radicalize the party in the direction of a more explicitly right-wing message and to contribute ideas for Sarkozy's 2012 presidential platform and policies. It claimed to be against 'political correctness' and to challenge existing 'taboos', such as that which prevented dialogue with the FN. Its leader, Thierry Mariani, emphasized patriotism, the family, moral order and free-market economics. Led by deputies Mariani and Lionnel Luca, it rapidly became central to the UMP's internal ideological balance. Not only did it express itself in its own name in the media but it increasingly adopted positions within the party.

President Sarkozy demonstrated a high degree of tolerance towards groups such as the Popular Right, which, as he saw it, had been created in the spirit of the policies he had been following. He received them at the Elysée only a few months after their creation. Thierry Mariani used the Popular Right to rise up the echelons of power: he was *rapporteur* for the security bill in the summer of 2010, before being appointed as state secretary for transport.

The ideological universe of the Popular Right can be illustrated by looking at the numerous legislative bills they submitted or public stances they adopted during the 2007–12 legislature. UMP deputies belonging to the group tabled bills or amendments supporting many of the FN's favourite topics, such as: the limitation of immigrants' rights in both the social and legal fields (nationality becoming the main criterion in both fields); the limitation of the rights of dual-nationality citizens; issues of law and order (the partial reintroduction of the death penalty); tougher control of the legal system (more involvement of victims and the creation of popular juries in proceedings); the defence of the police and the army; traditionalist positions in relation to the familial, educational and sexual orders. Popular Right deputies are against civil rights for gays and lesbians, against any laws condemning homophobic statements or the discrimination of gays and lesbians, and hostile to gender theory. They place special importance on all symbolic and historical policies, especially those reasserting national and religious symbolisms. For instance, they are in favour introducing penalties when the national flag is not respected or in the case of blasphemy. Finally, its deputies argue that history should be closely monitored to 'tell the truth' about communism and colonization.

In the 2012 internal leadership election, the Popular Right group was challenged by a newer group, the Strong Right, led by two young men with even more markedly right-wing beliefs who claimed to be representatives of Sarkozy's generation (one of them, Guillaume Peltier, was a former member of the FN's youth organization). The Strong Right motion was largely supported by UMP members (28 per cent) while the Popular Right gathered no more than 11 per cent. The success of this latest right-wing ginger group within the party confirms that radicalization has become rooted in the UMP. The prospect of local alliances between it and the FN is more plausible than ever since UMP sympathizers increasingly support such a perspective. While around one-third of UMP sympathizers used to support local alliances with the FN, a majority of them were in favour of such a solution in 2012.

Conclusion

Created in 2002, the UMP has been in office for virtually the entire period since its foundation. How will it adapt to the new cycle opened by its 2012 electoral defeat and its move into opposition? This question follows logically from an overall evaluation of the Sarkozy period.

More or less directly led by Sarkozy from 2004 to 2012, the UMP was strongly influenced in manifold ways by him. The party came to look increasingly like an 'electoral professional party', driven by electoral objectives, shaped by electoral cycles and becoming a master of marketing tools. Under Sarkozy's leadership, party members were marginalized in the UMP's internal life and internal political pluralism was suspended. Internal party democracy was frozen in Sarkozy's UMP while professionalization was strengthened. In this respect, the UMP is not at all specific or exceptional as it complies with general party trends in Western Europe. In other respects, during Sarkozy's presidential mandate, it departed from a common model. From 2007 to 2012, for example, it suspended the common democratic rule, shared by most western European parties, stipulating that the party leader should be elected by rank and file members. It might be considered an extreme case in terms of weak institutionalization: party forms, rules and even statutes have changed significantly depending on political cycles. The confusion produced by the very tight result in the November 2012 leadership election provided a good example of the difficulties encountered by the UMP in playing the game of internal democracy and ensuring that all players have confidence in the fairness of internal rules.

But Sarkozy's impact on the UMP can not only be assessed by organizational changes: ideological changes are even more relevant. One such change concerned the radical right, which had been the object of ambivalence and fluctuation under Chirac. Under Sarkozy, the UMP's strategy towards the FN combined ideological imitation and the co-optation of public policies with an attempt to maintain the electoral isolation of the FN. Indeed the borrowing of themes associated with the radical right was one of the driving forces during most of Sarkozy's presidential term, a turn that was clearly reasserted during the 2012 presidential campaign. In summary, the UMP under Sarkozy was characterized by a form of ideological radicalization, in part driven by strategic calculations in relation to the broader pattern of party competition. But radicalization could not be disconnected from internal party dynamics, which were grounded in sociocultural and local milieus. These internal ideological divisions, that leading party personalities sought to stifle, emerged with a vengeance during the 2012 leadership campaign and are likely to structure the French right for years to come.

In opposition, the UMP will now have to face two major, possibly existential, challenges. The organizational challenge concerns not only the question of democratization and the introduction of institutionalized pluralism within the party, but, quite simply, the issue of the unity of a party deeply divided into two opposed teams. The ideological and strategic challenge raises the tricky issue of the relationship of the mainstream right-wing parties with the radical right.

Chapter 7

Political Parties: The Socialists and the Left

FRÉDÉRIC SAWICKI

The French Socialist Party (Parti Socialiste – PS) was returned to power in 2012 after a decade in opposition. How was it able to win an election again? How, previously, had it reacted to defeat in 2007? These two questions are the key ones that will be addressed in this chapter.

The left's victory in 2012 was explained in part by the unpopularity of the outgoing president, rather than by any inherent dynamics occurring in the left itself (Jaffré, 2012). But we must not forget that the right was also very unpopular in 2007, that the economic outlook was grim and that the left had won all the intermediary elections since 2004. A united PS, with a credible programme and led by a politician commanding broad respect, appeared to be a necessary, if not a sufficient, condition for victory in 2012. To make sense of current developments, I will begin by situating the PS within the broader context of left-wing party politics in France.

The Socialists within the left in France

In comparison with other European social-democratic parties, the French PS for a long time seemed to be a rather fragile party, cut off from any deep roots into the popular and working classes. From the end of the 1930s to the mid-1970s, the 'working class' was mainly represented in France by the French Communist Party (Parti Communiste Français – PCF) and by the General Labour Confederation (Confédération Générale du Travail – CGT), whose leaders and members were, in their large majority, also communists. The PS, on the other hand, was a party of public sector workers, teachers and civil servants, though in a few regions it managed to extend its appeal to farmers and small business as well. The PS owed its survival to its dense network of local councillors, as well as to its practice of forming alliances with centre-left and centre-right parties that, in principle, advocated policies opposed to the party's values.

The new rules of political competition in the Fifth Republic laid bare the party's weaknesses. The introduction of the second ballot electoral system in 1958 forced the PS to re-evaluate its traditional policy of electoral alliances with the centre-left and centre-right. After being almost wiped out in 1958, from 1962 onwards the party generally allied itself in parliamentary elections with the Communist Party in a series of electoral pacts whereby the best-placed candidate (Socialist or Communist) would represent the whole of the left on the second round. The introduction of the direct election of the French President in 1962 represented an additional challenge to a party that had traditionally defended a robust parliamentary tradition. Unable to present a candidate under its own colours, in 1965 the PS (along with the Communists) supported François Mitterrand as the candidate of the united left; Mitterrand won through to the second round and forced General de Gaulle to a run-off. The 1965 presidential election thus illustrated the strategic potential of the new semi-presidential institutions to support a realignment of the left around a powerful non-communist figure. In 1969, by contrast, the Socialist candidate standing alone obtained only 5.1 per cent on the first round of the presidential election, against 21 per cent for the PCF candidate.

These contrasting results demonstrated that the PS needed to renovate itself in order to survive and that it had to adapt its message and organization to the institutions. Recognition of these dual imperatives gradually transformed its fortunes and prospects. It avoided disappearing altogether because of the profound reconstruction that took place under the leadership of François Mitterrand. He took control of the party in 1971 on the basis of a firm commitment to an electoral and programmatic alliance with the PCF; he made the astute calculation that allying with the Communists provided the only means whereby a renovated PS could regain the leadership of the left by profoundly altering the structures and ideology of the party. One core feature of the post-1971 party was to authorize the existence of factions (*courants*), which would be represented at all levels of the organization by an internal electoral system based on proportional representation. These new rules of internal organization allowed various tendencies within the left to express their political and ideological identities: notably, neo-Marxists, reformists and Christian-socialists, as well as groups influenced by the ideas of May 1968.

Along with changes in internal organization, Mitterrand's PS also underwent a programmatic renewal. The party adopted an ambitious manifesto, entitled *A Changed Life* (*Changer la Vie*), which sought to harmonize the party's message with the preferences of the new salaried middle classes produced by post-war socio-economic change, as well as with the 'new proletariat' formed by first and second generation immigrants and new social movements based on feminism and political ecology. The PS benefited a great deal from the failure of the PCF to appeal to these new social movements and the Communists' deep distrust of May 1968. This strategy was a fruitful one. In 1981, after 23 years in opposition, the PS not only won the presidency, but also obtained an absolute majority of seats in the National Assembly.

Since 1981, the PS has been the dominant party on the left. It has benefited well from the institutional rules of the Fifth Republic, which favour left–right bipolarization around two dominant parties, one on the left, one on the right. It was also helped by the decline of the PCF following the decline or disappearance of large manufacturing industries, mines and steelworks, and the break-up of the former Soviet Union. At the same time, though, it has never succeeded in obtaining as broad an electoral base as a number of European social-democratic parties which are able to mobilize between 30 and 40 per cent in decisive national elections.

The second Mitterrand term (1988–95) created considerable disillusion amongst Socialist supporters, since it was marked by numerous scandals involving either the PS or President Mitterrand: of party finance, the illegal phone tapping of journalists and kickbacks from public tenders. Disillusion with the left in power was above all a function of the neo-liberal economic policy that Socialist governments implemented from 1983 onwards and which was justified using the argument of the need for France to participate fully in building the EU (Jobert, 1994). The macro-economic policies driven by Europe included the liberalization of financial markets, the signing of the Single European Act, the total or partial privatization of state-run firms, the lowering of taxation and the introducing of means-tested social policy. These policies were difficult to reconcile with Keynesian demand-management policies and the traditional discourse of national economic planning.

Though the PCF appeared to be in terminal decline, the Socialists had to contend with the emergence of a powerful Green Party and, from the mid-1990s, a revived far-left that developed in part in reaction to these neo-liberal policies. Most serious of all, from the late 1980s, the far-right National Front (Front National – FN) grew rapidly on the basis of a xenophobic, anti-European and protectionist programme. The FN attracted high levels of support from industrial and clerical workers, constituencies that had deserted the PS in 1993 and which the party seemed incapable of recapturing. The PS was humiliated in the 1993 legislative elections and its candidate Lionel Jospin was defeated in the second round against Chirac in the 1995 presidential contest. The left was, rather surprisingly, re-elected in 1997 after President Chirac's dissolution of the National Assembly badly backfired. After five years of plural left government, however, the left was comprehensively defeated in 2002, when its candidate, Jospin, did not manage to win through to the second round and suffered the humiliation of being outpolled by the FN leader, Jean-Marie Le Pen, who was easily defeated by Chirac. This defeat was particularly bitter, because the PS and its leading players were convinced that they had an excellent record in terms of socio-economic management and policy achievement.

The 2002 defeat proved traumatic for the left. It marked the beginning of a long period of doubt and instability that was only ended with the victory of François Hollande in the 2012 presidential election. The Socialists were convinced that they had led the most successful centre-left government in Europe from 1997–2002 – much more so than those led by Tony Blair in the UK or Gerhard Schroder in Germany – and yet they had suffered a humiliating defeat. Because they were proud of their record, the Socialists were unable to diagnose the causes of their defeat. In the mid-term elections held in 2004, the Socialists performed very well, strengthening the belief of many of them that 2002 had been an 'accident', an unexpected and unfortunate event that had been precipitated by the division of the left itself (which had no fewer than eight candidates, three of them Trotskyists) and by the poor campaign fought by Lionel Jospin.

The Socialists were brought back to earth by their divisions over the referendum on whether to approve or not the EU's draft constitutional treaty in 2005. Party leader François Hollande decided to hold an internal party referendum on the draft treaty; 42 per cent of party activists declared their opposition to its ratification. One might surmise that this internal result was less an anti-European stance than a refusal to see the principles of the market economy given constitutional status. Many Socialist actors and electors feared for the future of the French social model and criticized the neo-liberal instincts of the European Commission. But the policies proposed in the Constitution had been negotiated or agreed under Socialist governments from 1981–93 or 1997–2002. The PS itself was thus split into rival camps of Yes and No supporters. Party First Secretary Hollande campaigned for a Yes vote; the No camp was led by former Prime Minister Laurent Fabius. French electors – and a majority of PS voters – voted against ratifying the treaty, provoking a major period of uncertainty in Europe. The referendum result demonstrated the schism between PS leaders, on the one hand, who were largely favourable to the Treaty, and PS electors on the other, who voted against it by two-thirds. More fine-grained analysis demonstrated that the popular fraction of the PS electorate (workers, clerical staff, civil servants) were much more likely to oppose the Treaty than more affluent managers and professionals.

The 2005 referendum created a new line of fracture within the PS. The leading figure of the No campaign, Laurent Fabius, made known his intention to run as a presidential candidate. Another key voice in the No campaign, Jean-Luc Mélenchon, would later on quit the party (in 2008), create a new one (the Party of the Left) and stand as a credible presidential candidate in the 2012 election. In short, Europe almost split the PS asunder in 2005; that it was held together at all was due to the efforts of Party First Secretary Hollande, who dropped any idea of sanctions against those supporting the No vote in the referendum campaign. Furthermore, at the 2005 PS conference, Hollande manufactured a compromise between the Yes and the No camps that gave some satisfaction to everybody. Though Hollande demonstrated his capacities as a skilful party manager, his failure to unify the party over Europe led him to abandon plans to be its candidate in 2007. The uncertainty surrounding the party in 2005–07 provided a window of opportunity for the party to reform its own selection procedures for the presidential candidacy in 2007. In the internal PS 'primary' of 2006, three candidates competed for the support of party activists: former Prime Minister Fabius, former Finance Minister Dominique Strauss Kahn, and the eventual victor, Ségolène Royal. Though Royal had never structured her own faction within the PS, she surfed on her popularity in the opinion polls to cruise to victory. The 2006 PS primary demonstrated how important popular support had become: the Socialists wanted to pick a winner. Royal was assisted by a wave of new members joining the party and paying just one euro to be a member.

Royal's 2007 campaign revealed how important it was to mobilize the party organization fully behind the candidate. In practice, she fought a campaign that relied mainly on a network outside of the party – Désirs d'Avenir, based around a website – to mobilize support. There were numerous misunderstandings within the party leadership, and key personalities refused to campaign openly for Royal (Knapp and Sawicki, 2008). She campaigned on a programme that bore little relation to that formally endorsed by the party itself in 2006. She emphasized issues of national identity, security and citizenship that seemed to bear little relation to the party's formal programme; and her attempt to create another one that would connect with electors' concerns beyond the traditional boundaries of the left in part failed. She had to confront a combative and skilful Nicolas Sarkozy, who successfully blurred the traditional ideological battle lines and appealed to numerous electors whose support she would have needed to be elected. She was no match for Sarkozy, though both emphasized some similar themes such as identity and law and order. The right-wing media campaigned against Royal on the basis that she lacked competence and consistency; the very low proportion of older voters who supported her suggested strongly that these attacks had born fruit (Matonti, 2007). Royal was, in a real sense, a victim of negative gender framing.

The difficult renovation of the Socialist Party, 2007–12

Everything began very badly for the PS. Although the electoral defeat of 2007 was nowhere as severe as that of 2002, the party emerged from electoral defeat in a far more divided state. President Sarkozy's strategy of 'opening up' the majority was deliberately aimed at inciting a number of Socialists to cross the floor and join in the new presidential majority; his strategy was in part successful and increased divisions within PS ranks. Sarkozy undertook other initiatives that were partially aimed at dividing the left; notably the important environmental negotiations (*Grenelle de l'Environnement*) brought leading environmental associations into his orbit. But the main internal divisions were provoked by rival positions in relation to the party's alliance strategy. The strong performance of centre candidate François Bayrou in the 2007 presidential election, who came third with 18.6 per cent, followed by the creation of a new party, MoDem, placed the issue of electoral alliances onto the political agenda. Should the PS abandon its traditional alliance with a moribund Communist Party, whose candidate had obtained less than 2 per cent in 2007? Though weak in the presidential contest, the PCF kept control of important strongholds in local government and amongst the trade unions (Pudal, 2009). Or should the PS ally with the new MoDem and its leader François Bayrou, though the latter had been a member of several centre-right governments in the recent past? The PS candidate Royal openly came out in favour of an alliance with the centre in-between the two rounds of the presidential election. But this strategy backfired. Not only did Bayrou refuse to call upon his electors to support Royal on the second round, but the cause of allying with the MoDem was tainted by association with her failed candidacy.

How to position oneself in relation to Royal was a major issue of contention within the party, especially after her defeat. Unlike her predecessor Jospin in 2002, who announced that he would be retiring from politics on the evening of his first round defeat, Royal portrayed her own defeat as a partial victory, emphasizing that she had attracted over 17,000,000 voters on the second round. She made it clear that she blamed the party leadership for her defeat, with its refusal of her strategic bid for centre support and its dogmatic programme. She said she would attempt to stand again as a candidate in 2012, and that if this required to capture control of the PS, then so be it.

The Royal strategy increased tensions within the party. After the presidential defeat, the decision was taken to postpone the party's next congress until November 2008, to preserve the Socialists' chances in the municipal election of March 2008. In the event, the PS did well, capturing control of several new councils in large cities. But the period of almost 18 months between Royal's defeat in May 2007 and the PS congress of 2008 allowed the key factions within the PS to reorganize their forces for a showdown, which occurred against the backdrop of Hollande's announcement that he would stand down as First Secretary after the congress. The Reims congress of November 2008 was one of a number that have gone down in PS history as signifying a division (rather like the congress of Rennes 15 years ago, or that of Metz 30 years earlier). The main potential candidates – Fabius, Strauss-Kahn, Hollande, Aubry, Royal and Bertrand Delanöe (the popular mayor of Paris) – for the next PS nomination all presented motions at the Reims congress, notwithstanding their broad ideological proximity. All were determined to bar the route to Royal and prevent her capturing control of the party. Most of the main motions converged to support Martine Aubry as the new First Secretary of the party, though her motion only came third in terms of support. She was supported by an anti-Royal coalition and had all the requisite qualities to be an alternative contender to take control of the party. She was a woman, supported by two of the historic federations of the PS, the Nord and the Pas-de-Calais. She benefited from the reputation of being a social reformer, as the symbol of the 35 hour week reform made under the Jospin government; and she was not perceived to be a serious threat to the other potential presidential candidates. In spite of all of this, she was very narrowly elected on the second round against Royal, only 100 votes ahead of her rival out of a total of 134,800 voters. Suspicions of electoral fraud on both sides were manifold. Aubry became the leader of a party whose public image had been seriously damaged as a result of the in-fighting of the 2007–08 period. The PS paid a heavy price in the 2009 European elections, with the party obtaining only 16.8 per cent of the vote, narrowly ahead of the Greens (on 16.2 per cent).

The new leader Martine Aubry had to build her own legitimacy and improve the image of the party. To achieve these dual aims, she undertook an important programme of organizational renovation, the main novelty of which was to introduce a primary election procedure, open to all Socialist sympathizers, to select the party's next presidential candidate (Lefebvre, 2011). This step was intended to heal the party's wounds; thus far, all party leaders had refused such a process, which had only been supported by Royal. The adoption of primaries was approved in an internal referendum by 68 per cent of party members. The novelty of this initiative was that the primaries were intended to be open to left-wing sympathizers of all complexions *and* other parties of the left. Most Socialist politicians feared this new procedure would either favour Royal, or, as in 2007, another charismatic figure without a real base within the party. Under pressure, Aubry had to accept some strict conditions; to be able to stand for the nomination, PS candidates would need the support of 5 per cent of PS members of parliament, or 5 per cent of members of the party's national council, or 5 per cent support from the main local government councillors. Above all, the anti-Royal forces sought to make sure that there would be only one candidate in the primaries to oppose Royal. In this, a broad coalition emerged to support Dominique Strauss-Kahn (popularly known as DSK), head of the International Monetary Fund (IMF) and by far the most popular PS politician in the opinion polls. Strauss-Kahn would not only bar the route to Royal; he would be a candidate with immense political authority and an international reputation that would reassure international markets.

DSK was the most likely candidate to be able to defeat the then incumbent President Sarkozy. In order to facilitate DSK's task the leadership pushed back the date of the primaries to June 2011, as late as possible, with the idea that the primaries would allow the Socialists to plebiscite their candidate, in an analogous manner to the selection of Romano Prodi by the Italian left in 2005. Only Royal and Hollande refused to play the game. The latter was weakened by her double defeat, however, and Hollande seemed totally isolated. Hollande had never been a minister, and he was not supported by many *élus* (party officials). He appeared as a total outsider, and campaigned effectively in a vacuum.

The adoption of the primaries ought not to be interpreted simply as an adaptation to the systemic pressures of the presidential election. The decision to launch the primaries was at least as convincingly explained by internal party politics as it was by the relentless pressures of the institutional architecture (and notably the move to a five-year term, the *quinquennat*). The primaries saw the light of day because of the narrow nature of Aubry's victory and the need to reconcile the supporters of Royal and, to a degree, the left of the party as well. Once decided upon, however, the primaries represented a radical break with party tradition and specifically with the tendency since the 1980s to increase the role of party activists in the life of the party. By opening the choice of candidate to all sympathizers on the left, the PS agreed to accept the verdict of the primaries, even if this meant investing a candidate with shallow roots in the party itself, which took the risk of weakening its own organization and the role of its first secretary. Indeed, all candidates in the primaries were now determined to make sure that Aubry would not use the party organization to favour her own candidacy. The party also acknowledged that party candidates might attempt to distance themselves from party positions in order to attract interest in the media. This was a real break. For the first time, there was no expectation that the party secretary would probably be the party's candidate. The primaries were an institutional and organizational innovation. They were likely to accompany the personalization of political competition within the PS and to aggravate the process concerning whether a party candidate should define his or her specific programmes as distinct from that of the party.

Aubry was aware of the danger. She launched a process of defining a new programme in early 2010 and ensured the commitment of all contenders for the PS nomination to respect the party platform. The expectation being that the liberal Strauss-Kahn would obtain the nomination, party managers and activists were anxious to tie in the former IMF chief to a detailed programme of political reform. This programme was a compromise between the left and right wings of the party. In terms of the economy, it pledged to bring down the public deficit, yet make clear its intention to move the EU towards a more Keynesian, growth oriented, agenda. The programme specifically called for: the European Central Bank to be able to issue eurobonds (hence to mutualize eurozone debt) and to create an EU-wide tax on financial transactions; a Public Investment Bank; a division between the investment and retail arms of banks; and much stricter regulations limiting the right of firms to fire workers. The programme promised a tax reform that would lower taxes for small earners and small firms and create a more progressive tax system overall. In terms of social policy, a few reforms were proposed: notably, returning to the retirement age of 60 for employees who have paid 42 years of pension contributions, the creation of 300,000 state-assisted jobs aimed at young people, and the introduction of schooling from age three. Finally, the programme pledged to introduce some ambitious civil rights reforms, of which the two most symbolic were the recognition of gay marriage and the right for gay couples to adopt children, and the right of (extra-EU) foreigners to vote in local elections.

The miracle of the primaries: the unexpected consecration of a new leader

Strauss-Kahn's disqualification from the PS primary race after the events in the New York Sofitel Hotel of 19 May 2011 was totally unexpected and created a novel situation. It challenged the assumption that the primaries would be a celebratory confirmation of Strauss-Kahn's candidacy. With DSK out of contention, the primaries became a real contest. First, Manual Valls, representing the right wing of the PS, announced that he would stand as a candidate, followed closely by Aubry, the first secretary. Both Valls and Aubry had previously supported DSK. Others followed and in the end there were six candidates: five from the PS (Hollande, Royal, Aubry, Valls, Montebourg) and one from the Left Radical Party (Baylet). There were some fears that the primary election would encourage each candidate to distinguish him or herself, in order to attract the maximum attention from the media. However, the primary contenders exercised a good deal of self-restraint, conscious of the negative effects of the divisions in 2007 and that the real prospect of victory in 2012 required all candidates to acknowledge the fragile state of the domestic and world economy.

Two candidates clearly represented the left and right wings of the party, respectively Arnaud Montebourg and Manual Valls. Montebourg based his primary campaign on the calling into question of globalization and the adoption of protectionist measures at the EU level to protect Europe. Valls, on the other hand, declared his support for the 'golden rule' being advocated by Angela Merkel and to include the requirement for balanced budgets in the constitution. The three other candidates, Aubry, Hollande and Royal, all adopted fairly similar positions. Each declared their support for bringing down the deficit and the debt. The candidates sought to distinguish themselves in fairly minor ways. Hollande affirmed that he was the candidate of young people and put forward his 'generational contract' (whereby a person aged over 55 would mentor a young apprentice and both would be exonerated from social charges) as an efficient means of fighting unemployment. Hollande also called for the recruitment of 60,000 teachers over the course of the *quinquennat*. For her part, Aubry called for France to move away from its reliance on nuclear energy; she also advocated doubling the culture budget. Royal distinguished herself by her support for small and medium business, calling for the adoption of a 'Small Business Act' along the lines of that which exists in the USA. More than these small programmatic differences, however, the primary campaign was fought on the basis of the personal qualities of the various candidates.

Hollande was the one candidate who obviously benefited from the exclusion of DSK. He had been campaigning since 2010 and gaining ground on Strauss-Kahn even before the events of 19 May 2011. With the former head of the IMF prevented from standing, Hollande suddenly became transformed into the favourite, boosted by a strong lead in public opinion from August 2011. He was supported by most of the former Strauss-Kahn team, including heavyweights such as Pierre Moscovici (who would become finance minister). A positive dynamic was created in favour of his candidacy. He was presented in the media as the likely candidate to fight Nicolas Sarkozy in 2012, and he played on his good relations with the press to enhance his claims. He emerged as the clear victor after the first round of the primary, with 39.2 per cent of support, against only 30.4 per cent for Aubry. As the obvious favourite, he benefited from declarations of support from most waverers after the first ballot. He was easily elected on the second round with 56.6 per cent.

The Socialist primaries were an unexpected bonus for the party's candidate in 2012. The party was able to organize a genuine internal debate that captivated many electors; for example, 4.9 million people watched the debate between the three candidates on 11 September

2011. The party competition did not descend into internal squabbling, each candidate aware of the need not to challenge openly the Socialist programme that had been so difficult to negotiate in the first place. For a period of two months – September and October 2011 – the Socialist primaries almost entirely dominated the news headlines. The PS had privately expected around one million electors to participate in the primaries; the actual figure was much higher (2,600,000 for the first round, and 2,800,000 for the second). As the successful victor of the primaries, Hollande was invested with a strong personal mandate to carry the fight to Sarkozy.

The Socialist primaries did not fulfil some of the other functions that had been imagined. There was hardly any participation from the other parties of the left, with the exception of the small Left-radical Party. The PCF, the Greens, the Left Party (Parti de Gauche – PG) all refused to be drawn into the PS primaries. But this reinforced the sense that the PS would comprise the heart of a new governing coalition. Above all, the primaries gave the impression that the PS was a democratic party – and helped to obviate the negative publicity that had arisen as a result of the Strauss-Kahn affair. The primaries focussed attention onto the PS and its platform and made Hollande look like the best challenger to defeat Sarkozy.

The PS primaries also had an impact on the other potential challengers of the centre and the left. The Green candidate, Eva Joly, and the centrist François Bayrou were totally eclipsed during this critical period. The Greens had also engaged in a process of primaries for choosing their candidate. Unlike the PS, however, only party activists were entitled to vote and they preferred the former anti-corruption judge, Eva Joly, over the media presenter Nicolas Hulot. Joly proved to be a very inexperienced candidate, an unconvincing performer in the media and a poor public speaker. The former judge preferred to emphasize economic and European themes, rather than the core environmental causes that motivated many of her potential electors. Her first round score (2.31 per cent) was only marginally better than that of Dominque Voynet in 2007 (1.57 per cent).

The only real surprise of the 2012 campaign was the strong performance by the Left Front candidate Jean-Luc Mélenchon. This former Socialist Party politician took Oskar Lafontaine as his model, the former SPD (Sozialdemokratische Partei Deutschlands) man who formed Die Linke in Germany against social-democracy. Mélenchon was also deeply influenced by the radical South American left, notably the Venezuelan President Hugo Chávez. Mélenchon came to public prominence in 2005, as one of the leaders of the No campaign in the French referendum on the draft constitutional treaty, a campaign that brought him close to the PCF. In 2009, the Left Front was created as an alliance to fight that year's regional and European elections. It presented joint lists of candidates from the PCF, the Left Party (created in February 2009) and a minority of Trotskyist activists having quit the Revolutionary Communist League. The same strategic choice was made for the 2012 presidential election, though this time there was some Communist opposition to Mélenchon, who was finally approved by 59 per cent of PCF activists as their candidate in an internal primary election. Mélenchon proved himself to be an excellent public speaker and a powerful debater. His mastery of a radical left register and language created real difficulties for Hollande at moments during the 2012 campaign. For the first time since 1981, Mélenchon polled more than 10 per cent in the name of the Communists, the Left Party and their allies.

The 2012 presidential election campaign

François Hollande began his campaign for the 2012 elections in the position of favourite. By the end of October 2011, certain polls were giving him a very comfortable advance of 58 per cent compared with 42 per cent for Sarkozy in the second round. At this time, more than 60 per cent of electors believed that Hollande would win the election. This position of favourite had its own disadvantages, the danger being that Hollande would be the focus of attacks from across the political spectrum and would be bound by the Socialist programme. He was particularly susceptible to two lines of attack that had been used against him in the Socialist primaries: that he was politically inexperienced, having never held high ministerial office, and that he was indecisive. These arguments were potentially very powerful, given the state of economic crisis the country faced. Arguments about his perceived lack of weight were used to most effect by Mélenchon. In November 2011, Mélenchon quipped that Hollande was the 'pedal boat captain' in a season of storms, casting doubt on his qualities for the top job and implying he would be swept aside by the economic crisis. The UMP and Sarkozy consistently attempted to use this argument to undermine Hollande. While Sarkozy was the captain of the ship, an international statesman steering France through stormy weather, Hollande was presented as politically inexperienced and indecisive. But Hollande was able to turn this argument on its head; his whole campaign was based on the self-image of a 'normal' president, calm, reflexive and anxious to take advice, the exact contrast to the agitated and authoritarian Sarkozy.

The CEVIPOF research centre at Sciences Po, Paris, carried out a very full and extensive panel survey into changing attitudes towards the presidential candidates from October 2011 to May 2012. With a panel of 5,415, the survey provides a rich database of the 2012 elections and highlights several movements as a result of the campaign (CEVIPOF, 2012). The survey confirmed that the images of Hollande as inexperienced and indecisive were largely shared amongst electors and that Sarkozy's strategy aimed at discrediting Hollande was an effective one. The proportion of electors considering that Sarkozy had more of a presidential stature than Hollande steadily increased throughout the campaign. If Sarkozy's lead over Hollande in terms of presidential stature was initially rather narrow (57 against 53 per cent in October 2011), by the eve of the first round a large gap had opened in favour of Sarkozy (65 against 46 per cent). Hollande led Sarkozy, on the other hand, in terms of sincerity, honesty and empathy, but these personal qualities also diminished in the course of the campaign. Hollande's strong showing owed more to his ability to defend public services and social justice than it did to his personal qualities as a future president. The focus on public services and social justice allowed Hollande to rally the broad support of left-wing electors, though his promises were, in fact, rather limited. Hence, the promise to create 60,000 jobs in the teaching sector over five years was counterbalanced by cuts in other areas of public sector employment. The restoration of the right to retire at 60 only concerned a relatively small number of workers who had started work early and had already paid 42 years of pension contributions. Once into the campaign Hollande played down the promise to create state-assisted jobs for young people, reducing their number from 300,000 to 150,000. The core proposal repeated by him was the promise to bring down the current account deficit to 3 per cent in 2013 and 0 per cent by the end of 2017. Social spending would only rise if it could be financed by economic growth.

Hollande's prudent positioning was essential in order to build a broad-based coalition for the second round. But it allowed space for the Left Front candidate, Mélenchon, who fought a very skilful campaign based on a left-wing, anti-globalization rhetoric and a strategy of mass mobilization through large rallies. His strong performance forced Hollande to give more of a left-wing flavour to his campaign. Hence, Hollande opened his campaign with a powerful speech at Le Bourget in January 2012 with the declaration that 'my only real enemy is the world of finance'. This was followed shortly after by him announcing the creation of a top rate of taxation of 75 per cent for those earning over €1 million per annum. This measure was a highly symbolic one; it would concern at most 3,000 fiscal households and would raise at most €2 million. But it was a clear left-wing message, designed to rally support for Hollande from those tempted to support Mélenchon or one of the other left-wing candidates. It allowed Hollande to distance himself clearly from Nicolas Sarkozy, portrayed as the president of the rich and powerful. Hollande also took steps to limit the likelihood that the Green candidate Eva Joly would be able to mount a credible post-materialist and anti-nuclear challenge. One of Hollande's first acts as candidate was to conclude an electoral pact with the Greens (Europe Écologie les Verts (Europe Ecology) – EELV), whereby they were guaranteed 20–30 winnable seats in return for the modest commitment by Hollande to close (only) one nuclear reactor (that of Flamanville, the oldest and most dangerous). The Greens played the game in return for the assurance that they would be well-represented in a future PS–Green majority. This strategy paid off.

Thus, Hollande's campaign was marked by a strong dose of economic realism, together with a strategy designed to avoid too many criticisms from the other candidates of the left. He spared no effort in repeating his attachment to the values of the left and the Republic: social justice, equality, *laïcité*. But his substantive reform proposals were fairly limited; even those in the Socialist project were watered down, with Hollande using the argument of economic necessity produced by the crisis. As a result of this clever positioning (rallying the left, while not falling into the trap of economic irresponsibility laid by Sarkozy), Hollande managed to hold onto his opinion lead and arrive narrowly ahead of Sarkozy on the first round (28.6 against 27.1 per cent). Rather like Royal in 2007, Hollande attracted the support from the first round of around one-quarter of extreme-left sympathizers and one-third of self-identified ecologists, making effective use of the argument that he alone could defeat Sarkozy on the second ballot. Yet he managed to maintain his electoral capital intact in relation to many (around one-third) first-round centre voters, those supporters of Bayrou on 22 April, who eventually transferred to Hollande on 6 May. Hollande benefited from a powerful reaction on behalf of centre-right voters against the nationalist, rather xenophobic and security focussed, campaign fought by Sarkozy, especially in the second round. The counterpart to Hollande's cautious approach was, according to the CEVIPOF survey, a lack of enthusiasm for the left's first successful presidential candidate since 1988. The survey revealed that in April 2012 a majority of electors were unconvinced that either Hollande (57 per cent) or Sarkozy (65 per cent) would honour their engagements. Few believed, moreover, that the economic situation would improve should Hollande be elected president (31 per cent, against 42 per cent for those who believed the situation would become worse, and 27 per cent that nothing would change). Carried to power on the wave of a powerful anti-Sarkozy sentiment and the general tendency for incumbent governments to lose elections following the onset of the financial crisis in 2008, Hollande did not exactly exemplify confidence in the future. Only one person in three (33 per cent) expressed 'their confidence in the left to govern the country' (23 per cent for the right), while 44 per cent declared that they had confidence neither in the left, nor in the right, to govern France.

With Hollande elected as a Socialist president, what role could be performed by the Socialist Party? If the new president was anxious not to be seen to exercise a direct steering of the party from the Elysée – there would be no repeat of the party breakfasts under Mitterrand or Sarkozy, for example – Hollande has maintained his influence over the PS. This was demonstrated when he imposed his choice of Harlem Désir as the new PS leader at the Toulouse congress of October 2012 (against Jean-Pierre Cambedelis) and by the signing of a joint motion between Prime Minister Ayrault and the outgoing First Secretary Aubry.

Almost from the inception of the Ayrault government, a good deal of soul-searching has gone on, not least in the context of the turn to budgetary restraint and European competitiveness. Should the party be conceptualized as an avant-garde, illuminating the road to be followed by the government? Or should it be a loyal supporter of the government? As in previous episodes of the left in power, the party's voice has been most vocal in the context of the PS parliamentary groups. Opposition from around 20 deputies to the fiscal compact treaty in October 2012 demonstrated the emergence of a left opposition from within the PS, a move then reflected in the high score obtained at the October 2012 PS Toulouse congress by two left-wing alternative motions to the composite leadership list signed by Prime Minister Ayrault and the outgoing party secretary Aubry. For the moment, this left opposition has been limited in its effectiveness but, at the time of writing, there were increasing signs of dissension from amongst PS deputies on issues of budgetary policy and the competitiveness pact, announced in November 2012, which introduced €20 billion of tax credits for employers (ostensibly to reduce labour costs) but raised VAT to offset the cost.

Conclusion

On a purely formal level, the PS victory in 2012 bore many similarities with that of Mitterrand and the Socialists in 1981. Like Mitterrand before him, Hollande had obtained just under 52 per cent of the vote and managed to obtain the election of an overall Socialist majority in the parliamentary elections following the presidential contest. In contrast with 1981, after 2011 the left even had a majority in the Senate, the second chamber. The PS also controls nearly all regional councils, a majority of departmental councils and most large cities. But the similarities with Mitterrand in 1981 must not be exaggerated. Then, the left was carried to power on a wave of enthusiasm as part of a broader societal and cultural shift. It advocated a radical transformation of society and implemented a programme of far-reaching reform from 1981–83. There was little evidence of such a cultural shift in 2012: Hollande's campaign was deliberately moderate, designed at reassuring global financial markets and EU partners. He won because of a strong rejection of outgoing President Nicolas Sarkozy. This shift might be explained in part by the context of the economic crisis, but only in part. Since 1981, the PS itself has undergone a fundamental transformation. By becoming a party of government in 1981, the party accepted, de facto, the market economy that its ideology had strongly contested – and which continues to be viewed with suspicion by many activists and left factions within the party. In practice, the PS adapted itself to the international economy without too many difficulties. It abandoned its programme of nationalization and its preferences for a planned economy, using European integration as a justification for this shift. But it never really engaged in a doctrinal renewal, certainly not of the type experienced by the British Labour Party or the German Social Democrats.

On the other hand, the party's electoral constituency has also varied considerably over the period. Back in 1978, its electorate was a popular one, composed of industrial and clerical workers and public sector professionals (Capdevielle, 1981). In 2012 its electorate had become much less popular: in part because of the declining importance of workers in the population as a whole, but also because it had attracted new electors following its long experience in government. The contemporary PS is much more a party of the salaried middle classes and managers than it is of industrial or clerical workers (the latter strongly attracted by the FN and its national populist message) (Fourquet, 2012). In fact, in 2012, industrial and office workers did move back to Hollande in substantial numbers, though they were even more attracted by the FN (for industrial workers) or abstention. The left no longer bears the burden of the hopes of the working classes on its shoulders (Michelat and Tiberj, 2007).

The new Ayrault government seems likely to disappoint the very limited hopes placed in it by the popular classes. Unlike in 1981, there is no talk of relaunching the economy by boosting popular consumption or of distributing wealth. The easiest way to reconnect with the fragile popular classes would be to adopt a discourse based on insecurity, national protection and a strict limitation of immigration; the survey evidence reveals that these themes are powerful ones for a proportion of the working-class electorate. But the PS must resist this easy temptation. It needs to use its return to power to engage in a long-term reflection on the meaning of socialism in an economically open society which is part of a broader European space. This is vital for the future. Without a serious attempt to reconnect with the popular classes, the most likely future scenario will be that of a return to opposition after five years and of a France governed by an economically neo-liberal right in alliance with a tough, security-minded and anti-immigrant FN.

Chapter 8

The Media

RAYMOND KUHN

The news media of press, radio, television and the internet function as providers of information for citizens and as communication platforms for a range of political actors in France. While their power is open to debate, the media contribute to the construction of political and policy agendas, frame issues in a way that is more (or less) helpful according to sources and influence the salience of topics for public discussion. The media are, therefore, central actors in the representative democratic politics of the Fifth Republic.

This chapter focuses on selected political aspects of the structures and functioning of the media during the presidency of Nicolas Sarkozy and the early months of François Hollande's tenure at the Elysée.

The contemporary media landscape

The contemporary media landscape is characterized by abundance and diversity, with old and new media both competing with and complementing each other in an increasingly converged digital system. In the press sector French newspapers suffer from low circulation figures by the standards of many other western European democracies, with the absence of mass-selling tabloids a particularly notable feature. In recent years the business model of many newspapers has virtually collapsed in the face of competition from online information sources and a corresponding change in consumer habits of accessing news. In contrast, the sales of weekly news magazines such as *L'Express* are reasonably healthy.

The radio sector contains a wide range of public, commercial, national, local and community stations, differentiated by content specialism and target audience, competing for listeners and revenue. The early morning news programmes on the main national networks (France Inter, RTL, RMC and Europe 1) attract high listening figures and are prime slots for interviews with leading politicians. In television there is a mix of national and local, public and commercial, free-to-air and pay TV channels accessible via a variety of digital platforms, with most households receiving content via the terrestrial platform. The main generalist channels are TF1, M6 and Canal+ (all privately owned) and France 2 and France 3 (both part of the public service France Télévisions). In addition, rolling news channels, such as LCI, BFM TV and i>TELE, have established themselves as an integral part of the digital media landscape, playing an important informational role in the 2012 presidential campaign (Kuhn, 2013). Television has long been the main source of political information for most citizens: at the start of 2012 it was the primary source of national and international news for 56 per cent of the public, followed a long way behind by radio (19 per cent), the press (12 per cent) and the internet (12 per cent) (TNS-La Croix, 2012).

Finally, the online media sector has burgeoned. It includes websites of government ministries, political parties and pressure groups, of mainstream print and broadcast media and of free-standing independent news outlets such as Mediapart and Arrêt sur images, which have become important sites for critical journalism and alternative voices as well as useful sources for the mainstream media. Social media such as Facebook, YouTube, Dailymotion and Twitter have become part of what some regard as a change from a top-down, professional model of public information provision to a more horizontal, interactive communications environment in which citizens can generate their own content. The growth of online media has also sparked changes in news consumption patterns: in 2012 among the 18–24 age group the internet (25 per cent) was the second most important source of national and international news after television (58 per cent) (ibid.), although it should be noted that much internet access to political information is via the websites of mainstream media such as lemonde.fr and lefigaro.fr.

The state and the media

The state has long enjoyed close links with the media, notably in the role of owner, regulator, financial provider and policy-maker. While much of the functioning of the French media is now driven by market forces, France is far from being a US-style economically liberal media system. For instance, during the Sarkozy presidency the state's financial support of the press was strengthened, an important reform of public broadcasting was enacted and legislation designed to counter illegal internet downloading was introduced. These policy initiatives fully conformed to the post-war tradition of state involvement in the media.

Up until 1982 there was a state monopoly in the provision of broadcast services, particularly strongly enforced in television. While the state no longer enjoys monopoly ownership in what has become a highly competitive broadcasting system, there still exist publicly owned outlets in radio (Radio France) and television (France Télévisions), with both companies funded mainly from a licence fee which is fixed by government and imposed on all households possessing a television set. In addition, the state imposes rules on maximum ownership shares in radio and television that can be held by any single media group. The state also regulates broadcast content, with quotas designed to protect the indigenous music and film industries from foreign competition and to defend French cultural values. Rules also govern pluralism in broadcast political and election coverage to ensure fairness between different political parties and candidates. All of these regulations are governed by a regulatory authority, the High Council for the Audiovisual Media (Conseil Supérieur de l'Audiovisuel – CSA), which is supposed to act as a barrier between the executive and the broadcast media, although in practice it still enjoys close links with the former.

In the press sector, newspapers and magazines have long been in private ownership. Unlike broadcasting, there are no rules regarding political pluralism in newspaper coverage and no regulatory authority exists for the press. Newspapers are thus free to be as partisan in their political coverage as they wish. National dailies tend to be associated with certain political values: *Le Figaro* is conservative and was so strongly supportive of Sarkozy throughout his presidency that in a break with standard practice Hollande refused to be interviewed by the newspaper during the 2012 campaign; *Libération* is ideologically on the left and supported Hollande in 2012; and the quality daily, *Le Monde*, was also critical of President Sarkozy, but did not formally endorse Hollande or any other candidate. Regional newspapers, several of which (such as *Ouest France*) enjoy large circulations in their geographical fiefdoms, tend to eschew overt partisanship for fear of alienating readers.

An important linkage between the state and the press is that of financial subsidy to supplement income from advertising and sales. The idea that the state has a legitimate role to play as a patron for the press has long been accepted by governments of both right and left as well as by many in the newspaper business. This system of state aid to the press has the avowed objective of fostering pluralism across the range of newspaper titles. In the eyes of some critics, however, a dependency culture has been built up, whereby newspapers look to the state to help resolve their difficulties rather than fostering a culture of commercial independence. In addition, the system tends to favour already existing newspaper titles rather than encouraging new start-ups. It has been estimated that prior to the Sarkozy reforms state aid already accounted for around 10 per cent of the total turnover of French newspapers (Albert, 2008, p. 59) and more in the case of some titles. In this respect the French press enjoys a closer relationship with the state than is to be found in many other western European democracies, including Germany and the UK.

The ongoing economic crisis in the press elicited a policy response from Sarkozy early in his presidency. The state agreed to commit about €200 million of extra aid per year for three years on top of the significant financial assistance already provided. A large proportion of the extra subsidy was allocated to improving distribution networks. To avoid discrimination between online and print journalism, electronic newspapers would also benefit from state assistance. It was also agreed to give every French youngster on their eighteenth birthday a year's free subscription to a newspaper of their choice for one day per week: newspapers cover the cost of the free copies, while the state finances their delivery.

By the standards of other advanced democracies this policy response of the French government to the problems of the newspaper industry was both wide-ranging and financially generous. However, this does not necessarily mean that the response is properly focused or guaranteed to succeed. First, some aspects of the old post-war model in publishing and distribution, including chronic overstaffing, have not been satisfactorily addressed for fear of the industrial unrest that might ensue. Second, some aspects of the initiative, such as improvements in the home delivery system, look out of date in an age when many citizens access news online. Finally, as newspapers haemorrhage revenue, even large amounts of state aid will not necessarily guarantee the vitality of the press as a whole, far less the survival of any particular title. More still needs to be done on how to save professional journalism (a particular information function) rather than simply protect the newspaper industry (a particular set of structures and practices).

Why did Sarkozy not make a break with the practice of state intervention and allow market forces to determine the fate of newspapers? One reason lies in the complexity of the president's ideological value system. Although sometimes presented as a politician steeped in a neo-liberal mindset, Sarkozy was in fact an ideological chameleon, capable of changing his discourse to suit the prevailing conditions (Marlière, 2009). Second, the president enjoyed a close interdependent relationship with several media proprietors, some of whom, such as Serge Dassault (*Le Figaro*) and Bernard Arnault (*Les Échos*), are owners of major newspaper titles. Third, Sarkozy wanted to build up powerful national media groups that could compete in transnational markets. Finally, there was the fear that if French newspaper titles went under then the 'news gap' might well be filled by media companies such as Google over which the state had potentially less control.

Prior to his policy initiatives in the press, the president had intervened spectacularly at his first press conference in January 2008 to announce a wide-sweeping reform of public television – the biggest policy shake-up in broadcasting since the 1980s – that was to have an impact well beyond that of France Télévisions. The three main provisions of the new legislation passed in 2009 were:

- The establishment of a single organizational entity to manage the digital channels and online services of public television.
- The withdrawal of commercial advertising from France Télévisions in the period between 8 p.m. and 6 a.m. It was originally planned to extend this to the rest of the schedules after full digital switchover in 2011, but this is now unlikely to be carried out by President Hollande.
- The appointment of the chief executive of France Télévisions directly by the president.

Although defended by its proponents as a forward-looking piece of legislation, in these three key aspects the reform actually returned public television to an earlier age of French broadcasting. First, the establishment of a single company re-established the institutional arrangements that existed prior to the 1974 Giscardian reform and completed a process of moving towards the reconstruction of a unitary public television organization that had begun in 1989. The argument in favour of this change was that in a more competitive and fragmented media landscape the provision of public television required better coordination to ensure a strong public service presence against an expanding array of generalist and niche-oriented commercial channels and new content providers.

Second, the withdrawal of commercial advertising from France Télévisions took public television back towards the financial arrangements of the 1960s when the state broadcasting organization had been funded almost exclusively from licence-fee revenue. In stark contrast to the BBC's domestic television services, public television in France had been part-funded from commercial advertising since 1968. In 2007 advertising represented about 30 per cent of total revenue for France Télévisions and its withdrawal represented a major financial challenge for the company. This was particularly the case as the level of the licence fee in France (€125 in 2012) is low compared to that of most other European broadcasting systems. The 2009 reform initially introduced new taxes on internet service providers, phone operators and private television channels to plug the financial hole. However, since it proved legally impossible to allocate the revenue from these taxes directly to France Télévisions, this component of company revenue is now directly allocated out of general state funds. As a result, public television is now funded in part from licence revenue, in part directly from the state budget and in part from advertising.

This central aspect of the reform was defended by President Sarkozy on the grounds that, because of their dependence on advertising revenue for an important part of their income stream, the programme output of the public channels was insufficiently differentiated from that of their commercial rivals, with the tyranny of the ratings influencing both the substantive content of programming and the allocation of programmes to particular time slots. This allegation was fiercely contested by the management of France Télévisions, whose argument that their output was substantially different from that of their commercial competitors was supported by the CSA.

The withdrawal of advertising predictably caused uproar when it was first announced. Yet in political terms the initiative was shrewdly calculated since the opposition parties of the left had long campaigned against the perverse impact of advertising on programming without ever going so far as to legislate for its abandonment. The broadcasting trade unions were similarly put on the back foot – opposed to advertising on public television in principle, but fearful of the consequences of its withdrawal in practice, notably on levels of employment within the industry. Some television professionals welcomed the change, arguing that it would remove the pressure of the ratings system and open up new possibilities for cultural creativity. The problem in the eyes of those opposed to this aspect of Sarkozy's reform was not the principle of the initiative – there is clearly nothing unacceptable in having an advertising-free public service provider of television content – but rather the government's reluctance to raise the level of the licence fee and the problematic nature of the proposed additional revenue streams.

Finally, the president regained direct responsibility for the appointment of the chief executives of the two public broadcasting companies, France Télévisions and Radio France, with the regulatory authority reduced to exercising a purely consultative role. This direct mode of appointment returned public broadcasting to the era prior to President Mitterrand's 1982 reform that first established a regulatory authority for broadcasting (Dagnaud, 2000). Successive reforms of broadcasting, introduced by governments of both right and left, had maintained the role of the regulatory authority as the source of appointment to the top managerial posts in public broadcasting.

Sarkozy defended the policy shift on two grounds. First, he argued that since the president enjoys the power of appointment of the chief executive in other spheres of the public sector, it was logically coherent that this should also apply in the case of public broadcasting. Second, the Elysée alleged that the system of appointment by the CSA was essentially hypocritical in that, while it appeared to transfer power away from the political realm and so depoliticize the process, in reality the regulatory authority had with one notable exception always bowed to the wishes of the political executive with regard to those selected (Cotta, 2008). Reassigning responsibility for the appointment of the heads of the public broadcasting companies directly to the president would, it was claimed, simply make the process more transparent. One of Hollande's campaign pledges was to return this power of appointment to a revamped CSA as part of a new broadcasting reform scheduled to be introduced in 2014.

The 2009 reorganization of public television was motivated above all by political concerns. In 2007 Sarkozy had campaigned on a platform of 'quiet change' and sought after his election to give expression to this desire for change across a range of policy areas. Yet the reform was also a manifestation of continuity. Both Valéry Giscard d'Estaing and François Mitterrand had introduced major broadcasting legislation near the start of their presidential terms and so in paying attention to reform in this area Sarkozy was maintaining a Fifth Republic tradition of presidential interventionism.

There was also an element of revanchism in the president's concern to reform France Télévisions. Before becoming president, Sarkozy had frequently complained about the supposed inefficiencies of the public broadcasting organization and the allegedly discourteous attitude shown to him by some of its journalists, notably on the regional channel France 3. As president he did not seek to develop a fruitful working relationship with the chief executive, Patrick de Carolis, who was not consulted or even briefed in advance about the controversial reform measures. In contrast, Sarkozy enjoyed close relations with several media bosses in the private sector, including Martin Bouygues, the owner of TF1. In the run-up to the 2008 presidential press conference TF1 actively lobbied the president and his immediate entourage in favour of the type of reform that Sarkozy subsequently announced (Musso, 2009, pp. 97–100). This led to charges in the press that the reform of public television had been motivated primarily by a desire to help the large established private channels prosper in the more competitive digital environment.

The final initiative in media policy under Sarkozy concerned the internet, with legislation introduced in 2009 to tackle the thorny issue of internet piracy. The law established a public regulatory agency, the High Authority for the Distribution of Works and the Protection of Rights on the Internet (HADOPI), with the specific objective of targeting the sharing of peer-to-peer files where this constituted a breach of the author's intellectual property rights. The legislation was not only controversial with many internet users, but also proved impossible to enforce. President Hollande has set up a commission to investigate how best to reconcile the rights of cultural content producers (film, music) with the practices of consumers who have become accustomed to accessing internet content for free.

The executive and news management

This section focuses on the news management activities of the French executive as an official source. The aim is to show how executive actors, especially the president, seek to influence the construction of the media's news agenda and the framing of issues. The central argument is that the executive cannot impose its version of events in a top-down fashion. It has a range of resources that frequently allow it to function as a primary definer in news management; but at the same time the executive is often fragmented, while the media may criticize or even reject the executive's preferred version of events.

Sarkozy's attempts to manage the news media could be seen as simply part of the tradition of presidential rule in the Fifth Republic. There is in particular a long history of political intervention in the news output of the broadcasting media that stretches back over 50 years to the start of General de Gaulle's presidency. Yet executive news management has altered immeasurably in the intervening period. The task has become much more complicated because of the huge expansion of broadcast and online media and the transition to a 24/7 rolling news culture. There are not just more outlets than in the 1960s, but the processes of news gathering, production and distribution have been revolutionized with the advent of digital media and the internet to include the reporting of events in (almost) real time. These developments make it considerably more difficult for the executive to exert effective management over the news media than in the days of a single state monopoly television channel with one main evening news programme. The strategic response of the executive to this more complex news media environment of necessity needs to be more multi-faceted than in the past. Aspects of top-down Gaullist-style control were still evident under Sarkozy, notably in the case of public broadcasting; however, he also incorporated into his approach to news management elements of exchange and 'story-telling'.

The election of Sarkozy in 2007 had striking consequences for the executive's relationship with the media. His professional approach to political communication in his capacity as a minister, party leader and presidential candidate was applied to news management after he acceded to the supreme office. The resources for primary definition structurally embedded in the office of the presidency – institutional centrality, political authority and electoral legitimacy – were fully mobilized as he used (some would say abused) the primacy of his position in a strategic approach to news management. He dominated media coverage not just of domestic politics, but also of those European and international political issues, such as the global financial crisis, in which France was closely involved as a policy actor and which tended to be covered by the French media through a predominantly national prism that focused on the key leadership role of the president.

Sarkozy's mediated omnipresence was channelled through five hierarchically distinct but in practice interrelated and overlapping types of media content. As it moved down this categorical hierarchy, the less control the executive could effectively exert over the mediation of its message in the public sphere and the more problems it potentially encountered in ensuring that its desired framing dominated news coverage. The different modes of interaction were:

- Top-down political communication that was overt and wholly under the control of the president and his advisers, such as formal, set-piece speeches, televised addresses to the nation, the official Elysée website and the president's own Facebook page;
- Informal off-the-record briefings and covert leaks to news reporters and political commentators;
- Two-way public communication between the president and journalists or the president and members of the public, including television news interviews, press conferences and broadcast debate programmes with audience participation;
- Professional journalistic reportage and commentary about the president available via a range of traditional outlets in the press, radio and television, as well as on the websites of these established mainstream media;
- A range of alternative, participatory and social media content on the internet, including independent news websites, political blogs, citizen journalism and user-generated content.

Sarkozy took many initiatives designed to maintain a prominent news profile, including two trips per week to provincial locations to secure coverage in the regional media (a standard that President Hollande also adopted in September 2012). Sarkozy's attention to a proactive approach to news management was particularly important given the way that he shaped his exercise of the presidential function. In dominating the political and policy terrains the president also occupied media space, going further than any of his predecessors at the Elysée in his efforts to manage the news agenda on a daily basis. Particularly in the early years of his presidency, Sarkozy thrust himself into the public spotlight at every possible opportunity: not only was he the object of more news stories than any other national politician, but to a significant extent he also influenced the framing of his presidential tenure – for good and ill. This televisual blitzkrieg stood in marked contrast to the experience of his two immediate predecessors, François Mitterrand and Jacques Chirac, who on the advice of their communication adviser, Jacques Pilhan, believed that appearing relatively infrequently on television amplified the impact of their message when they did speak (Bazin, 2009).

As in the early months of the Blair premiership in the UK, Sarkozy also kept the news agenda moving on a fast rolling basis in a way that left journalists little time to follow up presidential initiatives in a sustained critical fashion. Moreover, in a break with the tradition that presidential advisers maintain a low public profile, leading officials appeared on the broadcast media in the early years of the presidency to explain and defend policy proposals (Joffrin, 2008, p. 45). Sarkozy later put a stop to this practice and it will certainly not be re-established under Hollande.

Under Sarkozy, news management served various functions: to educate voters regarding the necessity of reform measures, to explain the substance of the proposed reforms and to counter any objections from political opponents – in short, to use the technique of 'story telling' to construct a coherent holistic narrative around the theme of reform (Salmon, 2007). Furthermore, for Sarkozy mediated presidential communication was not simply an explanatory support for policy action, but could play an important role in setting the policy agenda – a shock tactic to kick start the policy process – as, for example, in the presidential announcement that advertising would be withdrawn as a revenue stream for France Télévisions. In this respect Sarkozy was not just a news manager, but a news maker: he was a master at creating events specifically to grab media headlines.

In his relations with commercial media outlets Sarkozy emphasized an exchange style of relationship with owners, senior management and news editors. Well before becoming president, he had fostered privileged links with owners of mainstream commercial media outlets in both the press and broadcasting. These highly personal relationships with media proprietors and senior news managers were designed to give him an inbuilt advantage in the form of privileged access to define the news agenda and influence issue framing. Some qualifications are, however, important in this context. First, it should be remembered that by no means do all media proprietors wish to intervene in editorial decision-making. Second, even when owners try to interfere their intervention frequently comes up against newsroom resistance, as Dassault discovered at *Le Figaro*. Finally, deterministic explanations of news production that focus primarily on the dimension of proprietorial control oversimplify the way in which news agendas are formed and issues framed on a day-to-day basis. Evidence from across Western democracies shows that the routine operationalization of news values may result in critical news reporting of politicians even in those outlets where owners (and top management) are favourably predisposed towards them.

In the early part of his presidency Sarkozy benefited from the prevalent journalistic culture in France, whereby the media, especially television news, tend to be followers rather than leaders in the process of agenda construction – they are secondary rather than primary definers. Yet as his term in office evolved and the 2012 presidential contest came closer, not even the best efforts of the Elysée could prevent the news media from highlighting the president's electoral unpopularity as registered in regular opinion polls, the various movements of industrial unrest that continued to plague France and the increasing sense of unease within the ranks of his party. As a result, the Elysée lost a significant degree of control over the mediatized framing of his presidential performance. The overwhelmingly critical media coverage in late 2009 of the president's attempt to have his son Jean elected as head of the public body responsible for the development of the business district to the west of Paris was a good example of early 'Sarko bashing', with even those media outlets generally supportive of the president reflecting the widespread indignation among his conservative electorate at the perception of nepotism.

After becoming president, Sarkozy tried to address the structural defects in the organization of the political executive so as to improve its efficacy in news management. For instance, the government information service, traditionally a source of non-partisan public information, became part of the presidential communication toolkit. Sarkozy concentrated decision-making at the Elysée, sought to limit the contribution of Prime Minister François Fillon and other government ministers to that of a largely supporting role and in effect maintained his former position as leader of the majority parliamentary party, the UMP. While in terms of political power he may not have been a 'hyperpresident', he certainly rendered the presidency 'hypervisible' (Duhamel, 2009).

Yet despite this dominant leadership role, fragmentation within the executive and in its relations with the governing majority in Parliament persisted, including conflicting messages in the news media from president and prime minister on key issues such as the reduction of France's budgetary deficit (Bouilhaguet, 2010). Like its predecessors the Sarkozy presidency also saw its fair share of ministerial divisions played out in the media. While sometimes this was simply the result of a lack of coordination of executive communication, frequently ministers and their officials used the news media to brief against each other. At its worst this even involved senior and junior ministers from the same department falling out in public.

Sarkozy clearly believed in the agenda setting power of the media to shape public perceptions and therefore devoted more time and greater attention to news management than any of his predecessors at the Elysée. This reflected his own conception of mediatized executive leadership and the importance he attached to public communication, especially via television. It was often commented that he was the first president of the Fifth Republic whose whole life had been lived during the television age. There was therefore a strong personal element underpinning his news management activities; a different incumbent of the presidential office might well have behaved differently.

Yet it is also clear that in terms of news management any incumbent of the Elysée is now to a significant extent influenced, even constrained, by certain structural factors. Some of these are national – such as the institutional arrangements of the political system, the configuration of the media landscape and the specificities of the journalistic culture. Others are transnational in scope, including the growing importance of the leadership dimension in both presidential and parliamentary systems across Western democracies, the transfer of news management practices across democratic political executives and the highly competitive nature of contemporary media markets. From this perspective the attention paid to news management by Sarkozy may be seen as largely driven by factors outside of not just his control, but that of any president.

While some aspects of news management will be different from his predecessor, Hollande will be at pains to ensure that in terms of news coverage the executive at least conveys the impression of being in control of events. Early indications were not encouraging: the honeymoon period usually enjoyed by incoming presidents was remarkably short in Hollande's case. As voter confidence in the new president's ability to solve France's economic problems waned, some print media engaged in 'Hollande bashing' as early as the autumn of 2012 in an attempt to boost sales.

The media and celebrity politics

This section concentrates on symbolic image construction in an era of mediatized politics. As well as focusing on Sarkozy, I will also make some general points about contemporary French media coverage of the private/public dimensions of elite political figures within the context of an apparently growing 'celebritization' of political personalities.

Sarkozy's concern with image projection long pre-dated the 2007 presidential campaign. Between 2002 and 2007 he actively fostered a positive relationship with the news media, particularly television. For instance, his 'coronation' in 2004 as leader of the UMP was stage-managed for the benefit of the television audience, with the party providing its own controlled pictures for use by the news media, a ploy repeated by the campaign teams of both Sarkozy and Hollande during the 2012 presidential campaign. During his ministerial career Sarkozy projected an image as a man of order and authority. As part of the preparation for his presidential candidacy, he sought to soften this authoritarian image by presenting himself as an ordinary family man, loving husband and dutiful father. Promotion of a spouse and family – especially in the case of male politicians – can help provide a more rounded, human image to the public.

Sarkozy experienced no reluctance in constantly using aspects of his private life for the purpose of political marketing. Until their marital problems became the big news story of the summer of 2005, the close relationship between Sarkozy and his wife Cécilia had been mediatized at length by the government minister. The extent to which Sarkozy exploited his spouse and family for political self-promotion through controlled media exposure was ground-breaking in the French context, especially in its focus on the intimate aspects of the private sphere. It was not surprising, therefore, that when the official transfer of presidential power from Chirac to Sarkozy took place at the Elysée in May 2007, the mediatization of the event on television included a mix of public and private as the formal aspects of the official ceremony meshed with the ongoing story of Sarkozy's marital relationship.

The high point of this marketing of the personal by Sarkozy came after his 2007 election victory and involved the early months of his new relationship with Carla Bruni. Staged photo opportunities were arranged at Euro Disneyland, in Egypt and in Jordan, while at a presidential press conference Sarkozy was at pains to remark that his new relationship was not a light-hearted fling. In short, for a few months in late 2007/early 2008 the president unashamedly played up his new romantic relationship. As constructed for and presented by the media, this phase of the Nicolas/Carla romance had all the elements of a soap opera, with the president not just a principal character in the drama but the author and narrator of its unfolding romantic plot.

Mediatization of the private sphere can, however, be dangerous territory with considerable rebound potential from both the media and public opinion. By using his spouse and family for the purposes of electoral self-promotion, Sarkozy had in the eyes of many journalists given up his right to protection from media intrusion. When in 2005 the photo magazine *Paris Match* published a front page photo of Cécilia with her new partner, Sarkozy secured the removal of the editor from his post (Genestar, 2008). When their marriage finally disintegrated, the president had to engage in a reactive, damage limitation strategy in his public communication. The media had a field day in covering first the insider gossip and then the public revelation of the couple's divorce – the first time that a president had divorced in office. In this context it might be noted that, while an overwhelming majority of French voters considered that the Sarkozy divorce had no political significance, there was still huge public interest in the story, stimulating the appetite of the media for more information.

Even when there is cooperation between politicians and the media in the construction of a story – as in the early coverage of Sarkozy's romance with Carla Bruni – there is always the risk of a critical public response. The mediated image of a contemporary French president is necessarily complex and multi-faceted. It is particularly important, for example, for the incumbent to project an image consonant with the function of head of state. Even if the sacerdotal presidency of the Gaullian era is no longer in vogue, there is still an expectation among French voters that the president should behave in a manner appropriate to the supreme office and maintain certain high standards of protocol – which Sarkozy belatedly achieved during the 2012 campaign when he symbolically represented the nation at the funeral of three soldiers killed by the gunman, Mohammed Merah. In several of his previous public appearances, however, he frequently deviated from this ideal, most memorably when in early 2008, in response to a member of the public who refused to shake hands with him, he lost his cool: '*Casse-toi, pauv' con!*' ('Get lost, asshole!'). Footage of this incident was quickly made available on the web, exemplifying the way in which public and semi-public utterances of the president, that in the past would not have been distributed by the mainstream media, are now standard fare on online video sites such as Dailymotion and YouTube.

This mediatization of intimacy backfired in terms of media coverage and electoral response. The president's opinion poll ratings plummeted at the start of 2008, humiliatingly overtaken by those of his prime minister who had largely abstained from mediated self-promotion. In addition to voter disillusionment with the president's economic policy, one of the reasons for the decline in Sarkozy's popularity, especially among traditional Catholic and older voters, was the perception that their 'bling-bling' president had become too focused on his private life at the expense of his public responsibilities. Sarkozy's advisers urged him to readjust the thrust of his public utterances away from his personal life and towards more conventional political issues. As a result, he pulled back from the full-blown mediatization of the personal (note, for instance, the way in which news of Carla Bruni's pregnancy and the birth of their daughter Giulia in 2011 was managed in a relatively understated fashion), culminating in his attempt to 'representidentialize' his incumbency in the run-up to the 2012 contest.

What evaluative conclusions can be drawn regarding the contribution of the media to the 'celebritization' of politics? First, it is clear that a well-delineated boundary between public and private spheres is less well maintained than previously, whether in the controlled communication of politicians or in political journalism. It is not just that, as a result of changing political practices, media behaviour and social mores, the line between the private and public spheres has shifted over the years. It is rather that a simple bipolar antithesis of public versus private fails to convey the complexity of contemporary political communication and journalism with its open secrets, private revelations, non-attributable leaks, on and off-the-record briefings, gossip, hearsay, rumour and spin (Stanyer, 2013).

The example of Cécilia is interesting in this context, because it is clear that she did play a political role alongside her husband, promoting the career development of some advisers and politicians (such as Rachida Dati) and blocking that of others. When their marriage broke down irretrievably in 2007, some of Sarkozy's closest advisers who had been frozen out of the inner circle by Cécilia returned to positions of influence. The state of the relationship between Sarkozy and Cécilia was therefore a legitimate matter of public interest in that it had political ramifications, even if this was not the aspect highlighted in the media coverage of their marital breakdown.

Revelations about the sexual life of Dominique Strauss-Kahn, following his arrest on a charge of sexual assault in a New York hotel in May 2011, also exposed the fine line between public and private. As lurid tales of his sexual behaviour emerged into the public sphere, questions were asked of and by the media as to whether they could and should have revealed more about the private life of the man who for a long time was widely regarded as the favourite not just to win the Socialist party's nomination for the 2012 presidential contest, but also to be elected as head of state.

The second conclusion, concerning the phenomenon of the mediatization of the private lives of French politicians, both under controlled conditions and through journalistic commentary, is not as novel as one might imagine. It certainly did not begin with Sarkozy. In 1954, for instance, René Coty's wife was photographed by *Paris Match* performing a variety of domestic tasks at the Elysée following her husband's accession to the presidency (Delporte, 2007, pp. 54–5). Nonetheless, there undoubtedly has been a qualitative shift in the extent to which in image projection the personal has become political, and at least some of the responsibility for this can be attributed to Sarkozy. In seeking to mediatize his personal life for electoral gain, first as presidential candidate and then as president, he went further than any previous political figure in France in changing the rules of behaviour that govern the mediatization of elite politicians.

What is striking is the reduction in the degree of control that a top political figure can now exert over what becomes public when compared to only a few years ago, notwithstanding apparently tough privacy legislation. The younger generation of French politicians has learnt to embrace these developments, aware that there is little chance of the clock being turned back. In contrast, by no means all contemporary politicians have been happy to mediatize aspects of their private lives for electoral purposes. For example, during his premiership Fillon kept his wife and children largely out of the public spotlight.

Similarly, in the run-up to the 2012 election Hollande sought to differentiate himself from the incumbent by campaigning as an 'ordinary candidate' ('*candidat normal*'), not exposing his private life for the purposes of political marketing and condemning Sarkozy for blurring the line between private life and public office. However, this apparently principled stance soon rebounded against the new president when his partner, the journalist Valérie Trierweiler, sent a supportive tweet to a dissident Socialist candidate during the parliamentary election campaign. The Socialist Party's official candidate, who had received the president's endorsement, happened to be Hollande's former partner, the mother of their four children and the party's defeated candidate in the 2007 presidential election, Ségolène Royal. Social and mainstream media had a field day in covering the impact of the tweet, with lively debates on the role of the 'first lady', the political function of Twitter, the enmity between Trierweiler and Royal and the embarrassing position that Hollande now found himself in.

Conclusion

Whether one focuses on media policy and regulation, news management or symbolic image construction, the executive's relationship with the French media needs to be understood with reference to three inter-related levels: the personal, national and transnational. For example, on the issue of public service media reform the president has a certain freedom of manoeuvre in deciding how much financial support should be provided by the state. In this respect Sarkozy's reform of France Télévisions in 2009 was to a large extent driven by the president's own views; Hollande would have acted differently. At the same time there are national paths of dependency regarding the desirability of state intervention that would make it difficult, if not impossible, for any president to do away with public service media entirely. Most French voters would simply not accept such a policy outcome. Finally, the French media cannot remain isolated from transnational changes, which have made national borders more porous or even wholly ineffective. In an increasingly global media environment, policy debates on the future role of national public service media are taking place across individual Western nation states as well as at the supranational EU level. In short, while the structures and functioning of the French media are influenced by presidential choices and national factors, more than ever before they are also affected by decisions and developments that take place at the global level.

Chapter 9

Interests and Collective Action

ARTHUR GOLDHAMMER

The neo-Jacobin model of the French state, featuring a strong central government facing an atomized society in which the collective representation of societal interests is delegitimized, if not actually forbidden, never accurately described reality, as Pierre Rosanvallon showed in *Le Modèle Politique Français* (Rosanvallon, 2004). In recent years, however, several scholars have proposed one version or another of a veritable anti- or post-Jacobin model, in which the influence of societal actors rivals or even subordinates the role of the state. Rosanvallon (2007, 2008, 2010, 2012), working at the level of political theory, attributes the rise of what he calls 'counterpowers' to a crisis of democracy, which in his view has compelled the state to adopt new strategies: no longer able to count on the electoral and legislative processes as adequate sources of legitimacy, it must, in order to maintain its authority, establish quasi-independent organizations in which societal interests are more or less adequately represented and which must negotiate the implementation of laws with affected interest groups. Levy (1999, 2006), building on Grémion (1976), similarly portrays a state that cannot act unless it enlists societal instruments in support of its initiatives. And Moravcsik (1998, 2000) depicts societal interests as effective checks on the independence of state action even in circumstances relatively favourable to executive autonomy.

To judge by the rhetoric that accompanied Nicolas Sarkozy's accession to the presidency in 2007, his conception of the office partook of both neo-Jacobin and post-Jacobin views of the state. On the one hand, he stressed a quite voluntaristic vision of state action, in which the executive would 'search for growth with his teeth' with the implication that the private sector was incapable of generating such growth on its own and that he would bring 'security' to a society allegedly plagued by crime, rampant illegal immigration and employment instability – scourges against which, he implied, atomized individuals could not defend themselves, hence necessitating and justifying state action. On the other hand, his frequent vows to confront and overcome all sorts of conservatism (*'tous les conservatismes'*) suggested a post-

Jacobin view of society as composed of a range of well-organized special-interest groups bent on defending acquired privileges and, in the absence of a strong executive, being effective in impeding or thwarting governmental action. Indeed, in 2012 he proposed a referendum aimed at 'intermediary bodies' (Public Sénat, 2012) and denied that he was the candidate of a 'tiny elite' (*Journal du Dimanche*, 2012). Yet to many opponents of the former president, his entire programme, including especially tax reduction for the wealthy, limitations on the right to strike, reduced job protections and reductions in payroll taxes, reflected the capture of government by certain societal interests at the expense of others. At the same time, Sarkozy frequently insisted that the state itself had become the seat of any number of vested interests, including organizations of its own agents such as the High Council of the Magistrature (Conseil Supérieur de la Magistrature, representing agents of the judicial system), the hospital administration and the education bureaucracy, which both absorbed too much of the public exchequer and hindered essential adaptations to a radically and rapidly changing global environment. To combat *these* special interests – which, even though lodged within the heart of the state, retain a partial or corporatist character – he proposed a Comprehensive Policy Review (Révision Générale des Politiques Publiques – RGPP), which encompassed not only a broad reduction in the number of government employees but also a fundamental restructuring of the provision of certain services such as education, justice, and employment protection and assistance.

Given the intrinsic complexity and internal contradictions of Sarkozy, any attempt to describe state–society relations must begin with a simplifying schema designed to impose a certain order, however artificial. I therefore propose the following typology, which combines four 'interest types' (employer, employee, citizen and civil servant) with three 'action types' (coordination, negotiation and representation, which can include direct confrontation) to form a 4 x 3 matrix of interest–action pairs as shown in Table 9.1. Examples of each pair type are indicated in the appropriate boxes. This typology will form the basis of the discussion that follows. Space will not allow me to discuss all the examples in the table, which is by no means exhaustive of all forms of collective action in the Sarkozy years. Those indicated in boldface will be examined in greater detail below.

Throughout the remainder of the chapter, the reader should bear in mind not only this organizing schema but also the fact – of capital importance – that the Sarkozy presidency was broken in two – figuratively as well as literally – by the deep economic crisis that began in 2008 and slowly developed over the next several years. As we shall see, the consequences of this crisis halted and in some cases reversed the reforms that Sarkozy had initially hoped would define his presidency.

Table 9.1   *Interest types and action types: a framework for analysis*

	Coordination	Negotiation	Representation
Employer	Medef (*mouvement des entreprises de France*) formulation of common views regarding tax reform, **retirement reform**, overtime, economic stimulus, etc.	Medef negotiations in **retirement reform**.	Medef-sponsored polls, op-eds, etc.
Employee	Trade union efforts to reach consensus on **retirement reform**, minimum service, etc.	Trade union negotiations with social partners over **retirement reform**.	Trade-union initiated protests, work stoppages. Wildcat strikes and 'bossnappings' to protest against outsourcing/offshoring.
Citizen	Formation of social movements around issues such as genetically modified organisms (**GMO**), **housing for homeless**, immigrant rights, mobile phone towers, HADOPI, Raffarin law reform, Attali commission.	Negotiations with Ministry of the Environment, the Senate, etc. over **GMO regulation**.	Anti-GMO agitation; rights of homeless (*Enfants de Don Quichotte*).
Civil servant	**Magistrates** deliberate over proper response to criticism of their work from Elysée; **faculties discuss the University Autonomy Law** (*Loi Relative aux Libertés et Responsabilités des Universités* – LRU).	**Magistrates** negotiate with ministry over court reform; **university presidents negotiate** with ministry over terms of LRU.	**Faculty and student protests against LRU**; hospital worker protests against RTT and rural hospital closures; RATP protests against asbestos in tunnels.

More than that, the crisis also deeply affected the social movements that opposed those reforms, weakening them in some cases, strengthening them in others, in still others rendering them moot. In what follows, I will examine in greater detail several loci of state–society confrontation during Sarkozy's presidency: pension reform, the regulation of genetically modified organisms (GMO), university reform and the reform of the justice system. Where appropriate I will integrate findings from the early Hollande presidency.

Pension reform

Pension reform exemplifies the complexities and ambiguities of state–society relations in the Sarkozy era. It was arguably the most important of all the reform initiatives of the Fillon government and probably, along with university reform, the only major Sarkozy policy that will survive the era of conservative rule, despite a likely whittling away of some of its central provisions by the new Socialist government under Hollande. The pension initiative also aroused the most public and sustained protest against Sarkozy's policies, including, as we shall see, some street violence, as well as counter-threats to use military force to break pickets. In the end, however, the government largely had its way on the key issues, albeit not without significant concessions to well-organized societal interests, which received side payments in exchange for their acquiescence.

The reasons for pension reform's centrality and success are not far to seek. For more than 20 years pension costs had accounted for a large and growing share of persistent state budget deficits. Efforts to rein in those costs had been at the top of successive government agendas for that entire period. France's employment-to-population ratio in the 55–64 age group was among the lowest in Europe (thanks in part to Mitterrand's reduction of the retirement age to 60 in 1982), making it difficult to finance the pension system despite a relatively favourable dependency ratio. Consequently, an elite consensus about the broad outlines of reform had formed long before Sarkozy came to power.

To restore the pension system to a sound fiscal basis, most informed observers agreed that some combination of an increased retirement age, reduced benefits and higher contributions would be needed. In 1993, Édouard Balladur had taken a first step in that direction, instituting changes in the 'retirement regime' applicable to private-sector workers, one of three such regimes in France (although, in practice, the public, private and special regimes were supplemented by a host of minor regimes applicable to only a small number of individuals). Jacques Chirac and his Prime Minister Alain Juppé proposed a similar reform for public-sector pensions in 1995, shortly after Chirac's election to the presidency, only to have their well-laid plans upset by massive and wholly unanticipated public protests across France, which paralysed the country for three weeks. The virulence of this reaction imposed caution on subsequent reformers. In 2003, François Fillon, then minister of labour and social affairs, essentially effected the Juppé reform but spared certain public-sector workers, mainly those employed in public transportation and utilities and covered by so-called 'special regimes'. These groups had spearheaded the opposition to the Juppé initiative, and Fillon's tactical prudence in avoiding another direct confrontation with them contributed to the success of this second major step in welfare-state retrenchment a decade after the Balladur reform of 1993.

The Fillon Law of 2003 set the stage for the initial phase of Sarkozy's retirement reform strategy. In his campaign for the presidency, Sarkozy had promised to eliminate the 'special regimes' that Fillon had left untouched. Opposition was concentrated, naturally enough, in the affected groups, especially railway workers. The right's strategy of divide and conquer, spread across many years ('politics,' said Max Weber, 'is the long, slow boring of hard, dry boards'), ultimately proved successful. In 2008, unlike in 1995, the vast majority of public-sector employees had already been assimilated into the general regime, so the remainder covered by the special regimes looked increasingly to be a privileged group clinging to generous benefits no longer justified in many cases by especially arduous working conditions. Labour groups were consulted and did press for certain changes in the government's reform proposal (CFDT, 2008). But the unions, and especially the CGT, were themselves internally divided. Many of the more militant railway workers in the CGT, and especially in the splinter group SUD-Rail, were covered by the special regime and had in any case long been restive under the leadership of Bernard Thibault, whose attitude towards the government was judged too conciliatory by many (Groux, 2009). The membership of the other major French union, the Confédération Française Démocratique du Travail (French Democratic Labour Confederation – CFDT), had for the most part already gone over to the general regime established by the Fillon Law of 2003 and therefore had little to gain by opposing the 2008 reform. Its primary interest was in slowing another Sarkozy initiative, aimed at reducing the size of the government bureaucracy, where many CFDT members were employed, as well as introducing more flexible rules governing job assignments.

The government therefore had leverage on both major unions. There was nonetheless considerable residual public sympathy for those who were threatened with loss of *acquis sociaux*, special benefits deemed to have been won in hard social struggle. Currents of sympathy shifted back and forth during the protracted discussions leading up to ultimate passage of the reform in 2008. There were a number of strikes (Gold-hammer, 2009c), some of which disrupted public transportation and tended to dampen public sympathy. The government also played its hand shrewdly in dealing with one of its most persistent opponents, the train drivers union (Goldhammer, 2007c). In separate talks with this group, an amelioration of terms was worked out: even in ending the special regime, there would be maintained another special regime granting a lengthier transition period and more generous benefits to this key group.

Throughout this first round of pension reform under Sarkozy, most societal actors were convinced that there would be a second act and therefore chose to keep their powder dry, as it were, for the battle to come. Although Sarkozy had not campaigned explicitly on an increase in the age of early and full retirement under the general regime, the unions reasonably assumed that such a move would occur eventually, not least because Germany had increased its age of full retirement to 67 – and this contributed to pressures on the French government to make its industry more competitive, especially in view of the steadily deteriorating current account position after 2001. The financial crisis, which intensified pressure on the government to demonstrate tighter budgetary discipline, undoubtedly accelerated the timetable, but the Woerth reform of 2010, which ultimately increased the age of early retirement to 62 and full retirement to 67, would eventually have come anyway. Since this change affected the entire work force and not just a relatively small and privileged group, tougher opposition was expected; and expectations were not disappointed. Even the CFDT, which had been generally supportive of earlier reform efforts including the abortive Juppé reform of 1995, found much to dislike in the Woerth proposal. The unions called for and received broad support from the public in a series of demonstrations of escalating size and intensity, beginning with a day of strikes and marches in March 2010 and culminating in a wave of strikes in October and November of the same year.

Despite these manifestations of broad opposition to the reform, the government remained firm, and key actors among the opposition seemed unwilling to push the confrontation to an ultimate test of strength. When blockages at oil refineries around the country led to severe gasoline shortages, public transport strikes in major cities prevented many people from getting to work, and strikes by garbage collectors in Marseille and other cities left streets covered with filth, it became clear that the anti-reform movement could soon provoke a backlash. The government threatened to use the military to clear the refineries and get the gas flowing again, at which point the unions withdrew their pickets from refinery gates. This effectively ended the protest, and opponents of reform were obliged to pin any further hopes on vague promises from the PS candidate that he would revisit the issue if elected.

The foregoing narrative of the successful two-stage reform of the pension system under Sarkozy shows clearly that reports of the demise of the neo-Jacobin state have been greatly exaggerated. To be sure, welfare-state retrenchment is not the first policy area to which one would look for vibrant 'counter-democratic institutions' in Rosanvallon's sense. Retrenchment being inherently unpopular, no government would undertake it unless compelled by serious fiscal challenges. Despite innumerable 'consultations' with societal actors, the initiative for the reform, and the general philosophy that shaped its provisions, remained with the state.

François Hollande, Sarkozy's successor, has made marginal changes in Sarkozy's reforms, allowing early retirement (at age 60) for workers who had paid into the social security system every quarter for 42 years. The number of workers covered by this modification is small, however, and on the whole Hollande, faced with serious budgetary challenges, has allowed the heart of Sarkozy's reform to stand.

Genetically modified organisms

By contrast, the tortured path of legislation to restrict the use of genetically modified organisms (GMO) in France (prompted by an EU directive authorizing such use) was at least in part a consequence of the vigorous surveillance of state action in this area by societal actors on both sides of the question: this might seem, at first glance, to be a case of post-Jacobinism in action, even if the state remained the ultimate arbiter. As we shall see, however, the influence of anti-GMO societal actors depended in large part on the president's determination to seek outside support in a battle with elements of his own party, allied with pro-GMO interests, including the powerful agribusiness lobby the Fédération Nationale des Syndicats d'Exploitants Agricoles (National Federation of Farming Unions – FNSEA), which favoured an expansive interpretation of the EU directive and a very liberal policy regarding GMO, including authorization of Monsanto 810, a genetically modified high-yield corn.

There were two reasons for the president's decision to back a policy that ultimately alienated the FNSEA. Scientific opinion about the alleged dangers of GMO had little to do with it, despite the frequent invocation of the 'precautionary principle' in the course of the debate. First, Sarkozy wanted to woo the ecological movement. To that end, he created a new 'superministry of the environment', which was given a high profile, with the nomination first of former Prime Minister Alain Juppé (who had to resign when he failed to win election to the National Assembly) and then of centrist Jean-Louis Borloo. Borloo was given responsibility for organizing a so-called 'Grenelle of the Environment' (in allusion to the broad-spectrum state–society consultations that ended the May '68 uprisings, culminating in the Grenelle Accords), which was to set a new course for French environmental policy in the decades ahead. The discussions covered all aspects of environmental policy, including a carbon tax, a 'bonus-malus' system of automobile pricing according to pollution potential, French reliance on nuclear power, and many other issues. Societal actors of all stripes were invited to participate, and the general public was urged to join in the consultations via a website created for the purpose – a concrete instance of the 'citizen juries' envisioned by Rosanvallon in his theory of the 'counter-democratic state' and touted by Ségolène Royal in her unsuccessful campaign for the presidency against Sarkozy. Longstanding opposition to GMO by organizations such as Greenpeace found renewed expression here (Greenpeace, 2012).

Second, within the core of Sarkozy's electorate, there were many voters, particularly among older retired people living in rural and semi-rural areas, who were sceptical of industry claims that GMO were safe. There was substantial sympathy on the right for José Bové and the so-called *faucheurs volontaires* (volunteer harvesters) who invaded corn fields sown with Monsanto seeds to cut down the feared stalks (Monde solidaire, 2012). The government wanted to spare the sensibilities of this group (and prevent defections to the FN or Greens) by slowing implementation of the EU directive.

The ruling party was therefore divided. Jean-François Le Grand, a UMP senator who also chaired a scientific committee charged with investigating the safety of Monsanto 810, declared that there were 'serious doubts' about the product; but 14 members of the committee, including 12 scientists, then publicly protested that he had misrepresented the tenor of their report and implied that he had succumbed to governmental pressure to change its wording (Goldhammer, 2008). Ecology secretary Nathalie Kosciusko-Morizet, the bill's floor manager in the Assembly, did not block passage of an amendment introduced by Communist deputy André Chassaigne, which severely limited the areas open to GMO planting, with several UMP deputies joining the left in the vote. This aroused a storm of protest from pro-GMO elements in the UMP. The ecology secretary then accused party leaders of 'vying with one another in cowardice' on the issue (*Le Figaro*, 9 April 2008). The confused handling of the affair attested to the deep ambivalence of the ruling party.

Despite the parliamentary vote to restrict the use of GMO, the European Court of Justice ruled that France had no legal basis for banning Monsanto 810, and in November of 2011 the law was invalidated by the Council of State on the grounds that the minister of agriculture had failed to demonstrate any scientific basis for the restrictions. The government established a High Council for Biotechnology to deal with GMO and related matters, but on 1 February 2012 the FNSEA resigned its seat on that council, alleging that it was 'ineffective' and 'useless': 'our representatives [on this body] are at best impotent spectators, at worst alibis for the state's delaying tactics in regard to vegetal biotechnologies' (France Agricole, 2012).

How are we to interpret this extended episode? Societal interest groups did exert real influence on the government, but that influence had as much to do with the president's broader political aims as it did with the goals of the collective actors who sought to shape the legislation. The furious reaction of UMP parliamentary leader Jean-François

Copé and, to a lesser extent, of Prime Minister Fillon to the ecology secretary's accusation that they did not fully support the 'government' position suggests that the government – or, more precisely, the secretary herself, with implicit presidential backing, but without the support of the prime minister or UMP parliamentary group leader – deliberately amplified the protests of outsiders in order to outmanoeuvre powerful inside players. This tactical mobilization of outside interests contrasted sharply with the unified front the government presented in the fight over retirement reform. The fact that the initial impetus for this issue came from an EU directive stiffened the resistance of sovereignist elements within the presidential majority.

Ultimately, however, it was the president's larger strategy of political repositioning and coalition building that determined the outcome. In the early years of the Sarkozy presidency especially, the president entertained hopes of shoring up his support in the centre of the political spectrum by demonstrating flexibility on certain environmental issues such as the carbon tax and GMO restrictions. Although his staunch defence of nuclear power clearly precluded actual co-optation of the green movement, which remained implacably opposed to French dependence on nuclear energy, initiatives such as the Grenelle of the Environment and the anti-GMO legislation offered opportunities to present a different face to centrist, environmentally sensitive voters. Borloo and Kosciusko-Morizet, both popular figures with established credentials on environmental issues, were ideal pawns in this gambit, and Sarkozy no doubt felt that by building up Borloo, he could minimize the threat of a challenge in the centre from François Bayrou, who had taken a substantial number of votes from him in 2007. The president was also keen to retain the support of the Chasse, Peche, Nature et Tradition (CPNT), a small party of hunters, fishermen and naturelovers, which backed him in 2007 and steadfastly opposed GMOs. In this respect, the GMO episode illustrates not so much the strength of societal actors as the exploitation of a peripheral issue domain in the service of what the president hoped would be a recomposition of the electorate. In the end, that strategy came to naught and the anti-GMO legislation was invalidated, although no GMO are currently being cultivated in France – a victory of sorts for anti-GMO interests. But for Sarkozy himself, the goal was never actually to limit the use of GMO but rather to signal his sympathy with environmentalists and their concerns.

University reform

The comprehensive reform of the French university system (in law by 10 August 2007, often referred to as the LRU), impinged directly on the interests of any number of well-organized societal groups: university students, faculties, administrators, staff employees, associations of *Grande École* graduates, academic researchers, industry groups concerned with the supply of educated workers and the organization of research and development activities, educational reformers, and mayors of cities faced with the problem of housing large numbers of students, to name a few. Add to that the fact that students are a notoriously volatile group, especially likely to manifest their displeasure by public demonstration, and you have the ingredients of a particularly fraught policy-making sequence.

The date of the law – just a few months into the Sarkozy presidency – in itself showed that this was a top priority of the new president. Many factors contributed to the sense of urgency. French universities accept large numbers of students (anyone who passes the *baccalauréat* is eligible for admission), but they also eliminate many students at the end of the second year. Many observers believed that university curricula were ill-adapted to the requirements of the job market, thus contributing to high youth unemployment rates. Although the 84 universities in the system were equal in theory, in practice far more resources went to a few select institutions. In addition, the segregation of the more prestigious *Grandes Écoles* from the remainder of the higher educational system compounded the inequalities in a system that prided itself on nominal egalitarianism. Furthermore, the separation of teaching from research, which was entrusted to institutions such as the National Centre for Scientific Research (Centre National de Recherche Scientifique – CNRS), was deemed problematic and perceived as contributing to the relatively low placement of French universities in international surveys such as the Shanghai ranking. Dilapidated buildings, lack of staff support in faculties, ill-equipped laboratories and libraries, and a shortage of student housing depressed morale and hindered teaching. Despite the complexity of the new law, its guiding philosophy is easily summarized:

- Transfer decision-making authority from the Ministry of Education to university presidents, to be elected by governing boards representing faculty, staff, students and outside interests.
- Increase competition among universities for students and resources, a move that would presumably reduce complacency and provide incentives for innovation.
- Group formerly separate institutions into 'poles of excellence' in order to create economies of scale, promote variety and flexibility, and integrate teaching and research.
- Permit universities to seek funds from private, non-state sources (a major and controversial innovation in the state-centred French educational landscape).

- Ultimately, especially after the *Grand Emprunt* of 2010 – a public loan facility whereby the French government sold bonds to finance the expansion of higher education) funnel additional resources into the higher education system. (Goldhammer, 2009b)

How did interested societal groups react to these proposals? Although university presidents stood to gain a good deal in power and autonomy, they were at first wary of the law and sought clarifications from the ministry, forcing President Sarkozy to intervene in the discussions. The Conference of University Presidents rejected the initial proposal by a vote of 19 to 12, with three abstentions (Goldhammer, 2007b). When their concerns were met, however, most of these same university presidents became staunch supporters of the change, particularly as student and faculty opposition turned militant. In 2009, however, several of them published an open letter to President Sarkozy expressing concern about several aspects of the reform process, including the lack of funds to support autonomy. These objections were alleviated after the *Grand Emprunt* increased the credits available to implement the reform.

Faculty responses to the LRU varied widely. The most vociferous opponents challenged the reform on a variety of grounds and in a variety of forums, sometimes through organized interest groups, other times through innumerable articles, speeches and other public interventions. One of the more interesting responses was a manifesto published in the journal *MAUSS*, which not only attacked the reform but deplored what its authors, Alain Caillé and François Vatin, saw as a fragmentation of the entire system of higher education. The LRU, in their view, was a subterfuge. Its true intention was not to strengthen the university system, as it claimed, but to develop a few universities to the rank of international competitors while relegating the rest to serve as 'low-level professional schools' (Caillé and Vatin, 2009). The Syndicat National de l'Enseignement Supérieur (SNESup), the principal organization of university teachers and researchers, prepared a brief against the law to be used by local chapters in organizing protests (SNESup, 2009). Other teachers' unions, such as SUD Éducation and CNT-SR, demanded abrogation of the law pure and simple.

Meanwhile, student opposition was widespread, with a number of organizations vying for leadership during a chaotic period of strikes and demonstrations that lasted for several months. One should be wary, however, of confusing the visibility of the anti-LRU movement with the true extent of its support. *Le Point* reported that only 45 of France's 84 universities had suffered any disruption at all by student strikes. Pécresse noted that opposition seemed to be concentrated in social science faculties (*Le Point*, 2009). On the other hand, in the six-teenth week of the strike movement of 2009, following the implementation of budgetary autonomy in 18 universities, *Les Échos* retorted that the student-led opposition to the reform had animated the most impressive social movement in France since May '68. Six universities remained totally shut down, although support for the strikers seemed to be waning as the scheduled examination period approached.

One key sticking point in the opposition between faculty and administrators was the issue of evaluation of academic performance. Harvard sociologist Michèle Lamont, interviewed by *nonfiction.fr*, observed that 'the primary problem is that the system has become hyperpoliticized, partly because of the persistent lack of resources ... It seems that the government wants to replace the current system with a managerial approach' (Lamont, 2009) under the decentralized control of university presidents. In her view, this ran the risk of increasing an already marked tendency to 'localism', that is, recruitment of doctoral students from an institution to fill teaching posts in that same institution, which led to 'mediocrity' (Goldhammer, 2009a). This view was echoed by Patrick Weil, a French political scientist, who, like Lamont, has spent considerable time observing American universities (*Marianne*, 2009). The 'managerial approach' identified by Lamont particularly offended academics, who doubted that the 'objective' evaluation criteria favoured by the government could do justice to academic teaching and research, endeavours in which simply totting up output can be a highly misleading indicator of 'productivity'. Everyone agrees that evaluation is necessary, but who does the evaluation, and how it is performed, are the real issues. In the universities, trust had apparently broken down completely. The 'managers' of the system do not trust academics to do peer review because 'mandarins' take care of their own, entrenched local coteries do the same, and the result, in the managers' eyes, is stagnation. The academics do not trust the managers and their 'international business consultants' because these outsiders have no understanding of what academics do. Hence the result is stalemate, bitterness and endless recrimination, as reflected in the angry words of the demonstrators.

Even within the student movement, there were divisions. The principal student organization in France, the National Union of Students in France (Union Nationale des Étudiants de France – UNEF), led initially by Bruno Julliard, found itself challenged and outmanoeuvred by an ad hoc anti-LRU group called the Group against University Autonomy (Collectif contre l'Autonomie des Universités), which was heavily influenced by elements of the extreme left. Julliard himself was criticized for succumbing to the 'seductions of Sarkozy' (the two had lunch together at one point), and indeed Julliard eventually concluded that the government would not back down from its reform initiative and that the best course was therefore to exert pressure on budgetary issues and work towards concessions on student housing (Goldhammer, 2007a).

As for the political parties of the opposition, attitudes varied. The PS expressed support for the principle of autonomy but worried about insufficient financing (*Nouvel Observateur*, 2007). Other parties called for repeal.

As in the case of pension reform, the other defining initiative of the Sarkozy presidency, the government scarcely wavered in its adherence to the central principles. For tactical reasons, however, it did show readiness to compromise with societal actors on details of implementation. To be sure, such compromise was essential to its strategy of divide-and-conquer, but the government may also have had more fundamental reasons for its conciliatory tactics, because input from outside sources revealed problems with its initial plans. The faction with which the ministry seemed least inclined to compromise was the faculty. The students had the numbers and the will to disrupt business as usual, while the university presidents figured as key players in the government plan and had to be brought on board if it was to have a chance of working. The professors, on the other hand, had neither the numbers nor the institutional centrality to block the programme. It was therefore left to the university presidents to deal with their opposition as proxies (and shields) for the ministry. In terms of our overall analytic schema, the decentralizing character of the reform might be characterized as a step towards a more post-Jacobin model of state action, though the reform itself was classically Jacobin: prepared in advance by the central administration, opened to consultation with societal actors only in the final phases of elaboration, and modified only to the extent necessary to divide opponents and win the adherence of essential allies.

Reform of the justice system

In the three cases examined thus far – retirement reform, GMO restriction and university reform – the key societal actors were situated outside the government: employer associations, trade unions, university presidents, teachers, students and environmental organizations. Rachida Dati's actions as justice minister aroused a different kind of opposition. Although some of it came from outside the government, the principal obstacles to several of her major reform efforts came from civil servants.

Dati's mandate as justice minister was twofold: she was charged with implementing President Sarkozy's promises to punish lawbreakers more severely while at the same time reducing the administrative costs of the justice system. In pursuit of the first goal she took steps such as imposing minimum sentencing requirements that many magistrates felt interfered improperly with their prerogatives. In pursuit of the second, she closed tribunals across the country, consolidating judicial operations in larger cities. The ensuing staff reductions impinged directly on the interests of many state employees, who reacted angrily to her initiatives.

A more adroit minister of justice might have avoided pushing magistrates, normally reluctant to voice their grievances in the public square, onto the streets. But Dati seemed to relish confrontation. Within months of taking office, her chief of staff and three subordinates resigned in protest at what they regarded as her high-handed methods and refusal to respect judicial traditions. In this she may have been faithfully reflecting the attitude of the head of state, who made no secret of the fact that he regarded the lower-level judges (*les petits juges*) as the very embodiment of one of the many 'conservatisms' he had vowed to overcome. Indeed, the prickly insistence on independence of the magistracy rankled many politicians, who believed that investigating magistrates (*juges d'instruction*) had begun to think of themselves as one of the 'counter-powers' charged with checking abuses of power by elected officials, as theorized by students of the post-Jacobin state (see also Chapter 4).

Hence the stage was set for open confrontation, which was not long in coming. On 23 October 2008, magistrates and other judicial system personnel demonstrated in front of courthouses across France (*Libération*, 2008a). Their complaints included new minimum sentencing guidelines as well as what one protester described as the 'increasing inhumanity of the judicial machine' owing to a speed-up imposed by the economy-minded justice ministry: 'when you judge 35 people in a morning, you can't really say that you're judging people'. They also complained about budget cuts that made it difficult to comply with more 'security-minded' directives regarding pre-trial detention, for example.

By this point, however, Dati's star had begun to fade. The president had cooled towards her, partly for personal reasons but more importantly because she stirred up so much opposition, even among justice system personnel generally favourable to his policies. Once again he tried to divide the organized opposition by receiving one association of magistrates, the Union syndicale des magistrats (USM), deemed to be more moderate than the left-leaning Syndicat de la Magistrature (the Magistrates' Union – SM) (*Libération*, 2008b). Sarkozy's animus towards the latter group dated from his time as minister of the interior, when he charged the SM with having been too lenient with suburban rioters after the 2005 disturbances. Nevertheless, the two groups presented a united front against Dati's reforms (*Libération*, 2008c).

The two groups of civil servants were joined by lawyers who were not civil servants but who found themselves targeted by another Dati economy initiative. The minister had proposed that divorce proceedings be handled privately by notaries rather than 'judicialized' in family law tribunals. Lawyers objected to this attack on their livelihoods (*Le Figaro*, 2008b).

The success of these collective actions was mixed. Although the justice minister succeeded in her effort to close numerous courthouses, if the ultimate goal was to limit the independence of magistrates and restrain the 'counter-power' they had begun to assert against the state, the ministerial reform fell well short of achieving its aim. One major proposal in this direction, to replace the venerable *juge d'instruction* with a new and more subservient *juge de l'instruction*, went nowhere (see p. 61). Indeed, *les petits juges* may have savoured the irony that followed Sarkozy's defeat in the 2012 presidential election: shortly after leaving office, the former president suffered the indignity of having his home searched on orders of a *juge d'instruction* investigating the possibility of illegal financing of his 2007 campaign.

Summarizing the above cases, in conclusion, it would be a mistake to read Sarkozy's presidency as evidence of a 're-Jacobinization' of the French state. In many ways he was sui generis as a president of the Fifth Republic. Without deep roots in *la France profonde* or strong ties to the elite administrative culture, he tried to dispose of societal actors as he had always dealt with obstacles to his political ascendancy: by precipitating crises, dramatizing oppositions, mobilizing the media, dividing enemies and disciplining supporters. Because he personalized the presidency, protest focused on his person even more than on his policies. He availed himself of the plebiscitary legitimacy of presidential election by universal suffrage but failed to recognize that, in an age of constant polling, a steadily declining approval rating would be interpreted as disavowal prior to the expiration of his term. He could have the legislation he wanted but not the consensus that his policies were setting France on a new and better course. If he seemed to exhibit a preference for the Jacobin model, it was because he had none of the instincts of the old-style Fourth-Republican politician. Chirac, one ally tried to warn him, had benefited greatly from his deep roots in the Corrèze, whereas Sarkozy's only roots were in Neuilly: 'And what's Neuilly? A rich suburb? A bedroom community? A broad avenue ... Surely not a place where you go in search of the people of France' (Giesbert, 2012, p. 126). Negotiating with actors at the grass roots was simply not his style. Hence collective action in the Sarkozy years was doomed to mirror his own style: it dramatized positions, as he did, but largely failed to advance towards a useful compromise. A polarizing president, he liked to portray himself as leading the charge against defenders of the status quo. He was not a man to lead a post-Jacobin state, because societal actors had no real existence for him, except as enemies. Nor was he much of a Jacobin, because his values were rooted in the real rather than the ideal. Hence state–society relations had something of the quality of shadow boxing in the years 2007–12.

The Hollande presidency and future perspectives

Will this approach to governance change under President Hollande? Although it is very early in his presidency, he gives every indication of wishing to engage with rather than circumvent societal actors. During his first six months in office, for example, he held important consultations with the 'social partners' (representatives of business and labour) and with environmental interest groups. But as we have seen, Sarkozy did the same thing, with initially warm reviews, only to arouse even more intense opposition when the hopes he had raised were later disappointed. In some respects, Hollande seems to be attempting to tame future opposition by offering larger initial prizes to groups at best lukewarm to his presidency than many observers expected. This process might be observed on the question of fracking, a technique for extracting gas from shale, which many environmental groups strenuously oppose but which many business interests equally fervently support in the hope that it will reduce energy costs and ease balance-of-payment deficits. Hollande might have deferred any major decision by referring the issue to a commission for further study and allowing experimental pilot projects to proceed. Instead, he issued a summary ban on further exploration, which has every appearance of being a definitive decision. Environmental groups were cheered by this decision, which opponents consider premature.

Hollande also offered a symbolic prize of sorts to trade unions, by proposing a 75 per cent marginal income tax rate on individuals earning more than €1 million per year. But the proposal has already been weakened by making the tax applicable to individuals rather than families, excluding capital gains, and limiting its duration to two years (it is billed as a 'temporary effort of solidarity' rather than a permanent new tax). He has also surprised many observers by continuing his predecessor's policy of dismantling Romany camps, and he has beefed up police presence in a number of designated 'security zones' around the country. Finally, he has proposed a revision of the way in which the social security system is financed. The burden will be shifted away from payrolls and onto a broader base of taxpayers through the Contribution Sociale Généralisée, a move much-desired by business interests as a boost to French competitiveness.

Hollande also upset many supporters on the left by abandoning his opposition to the Treaty on Stability, Growth and Governance (TSCG), which he had promised as a candidate to 'renegotiate'. As president, however, he insisted on parliamentary approval despite Germany's refusal to change so much as a single comma of the treaty. Hollande has thus committed his government to a programme of austerity and budget-balancing through a combination of tax increases and reduced expenditures, which is likely to prove contractionary in the near future.

In short, Hollande has inaugurated his presidency by granting unanticipated gifts to left, right, centre and greens, perhaps because he expects strong opposition from all of these quarters later this year, when he and Frau Merkel will discuss a possible revision of EU institutions as a permanent solution to the euro crisis. It is doubtful that the recipients of these gifts will consider them sufficient quid pro quo to support any subordination of French sovereignty of which they do not approve. Behind the scenes, however, Hollande may be engaging in discussions with key societal actors in each of these quarters, whose scope is difficult to discern from the visible policy fruits harvested to date.

A final word

As this book goes to press, in the tenth month after Hollande's election, it is clear that his presidency and Sarkozy's have followed similar trajectories. Both leaders began their terms with remarkably high approval ratings only to witness a rapid decline in their first year. In both cases, rejection by the electorate was compounded by a deteriorating economic climate that forced major policy reversals. Hollande had presented himself to voters as the anti-Sarkozy, but before his first year was out he had fully embraced the Sarkozy–Merkel argument that austerity was the only way to save the euro. He was forced to propose yet another pension reform that would raise the early retirement age even higher than Sarkozy had done. And his repeal of the tax rebate on overtime hours has met with stiff opposition from the beneficiaries of that Sarkozy reform, misguided and ineffective though it was.

The lesson of these two presidencies is therefore that in the twenty-first century, it is neither the state nor civil society that predominates in the making of French policy. The advent of the European Union has profoundly reshaped the old problem of the Jacobin state. Economically, France has become an open economy which must respond to the challenges of the global marketplace and to the constraints of international finance. The state no longer has a free hand in defining the contours of its welfare regime, yet societal actors continue to hold it responsible for every failure to defend local interests. The vulnerability of the French presidency is a prominent symptom of this new malady of the centralized state. The presidency of the Fifth Republic was conceived as the ultimate sovereign, the supreme arbiter of the general interest above particular interests. It can no longer effectively play that role, however, because key power resources lie beyond French borders. The high hopes that accompanied the elections of the past two French presidents were therefore matched only by the depths of depression occasioned by the rapid collapse of presidential popularity and authority.

Chapter 10

Elections in France: Electoral Disorder in a Realignment Era

FLORENT GOUGOU AND SIMON LABOURET

Confronted with a major and lasting global economic crisis, Nicolas Sarkozy did not win re-election in May 2012 as President of the French Republic. Elected in 2007 on the promise of building a new era of prosperity, he quickly became unpopular, finishing his term with a rising rate of unemployment and an enormous amount of public debt. Trailing Socialist Party (PS) candidate François Hollande in the first round (27.2 against 28.6 per cent), Sarkozy managed nevertheless to resist the recovery of the National Front (FN) led by Marine Le Pen (17.9 per cent), before losing by only a rather small margin in the runoff (48.6 per cent). This conservative resistance was quite unexpected. However, it did not outlive Sarkozy's defeat, as the PS benefited from a presidential push in the June legislative elections and secured a comfortable hold on the National Assembly.

In a way, the presidential and legislative elections of 2012 simply brought the final touch to the impressive series of defeats undergone by the right-wing UMP in the second-order elections held since 2007. However, the recent story of French elections has not just been one of repetitive 'sanction votes' against the government. Central to this chapter is the idea that the economic crisis disrupted a political system that was already undergoing change. Our point is that the presidential and legislative polls of 2007, held more than one year before the bankruptcy of Lehman Brothers, were not ordinary elections as they marked the collapse of the electoral order that had been in place since the realignment era of the 1980s (Martin, 2000, 2007a). The re-election of the incumbent majority, a first since 1978, the spectacular decline of the FN, as well as the emergence of a genuine independent centre with the breakthrough of François Bayrou and the creation of the MoDem, represented a 'moment of rupture' which initiated a period of electoral disorder. In this perspective, each party has struggled since 2007 not only for power, but also for its own position or survival in the system. What has been at stake is the shape of the next stable electoral order.

This chapter shows how both the repetitive 'sanction votes' against the government and the 'rupture' of 2007 influenced French electoral politics during President Sarkozy's term. Regarding methodology, the chapter uses data relating to metropolitan France in order to compare first-order and second-order elections. Overseas territories and regions, as well as Nationals living abroad, do not vote in all elections.

The presidential and legislative elections of 2007: a new moment of rupture

The election of Nicolas Sarkozy in 2007 did not only coincide with the first re-election of an incumbent majority in the National Assembly in 29 years. It also revealed a new political landscape, at odds with the electoral order that had been in place since the 1980s.

The main features of the old electoral order

French politics, as we knew it throughout the 1990s and most of the 2000s, came into being in the early 1980s. Until 1981, the Communist Party (PCF) was the keystone of the party system, making alternation in power between the Right and the Left next to impossible, as a majority of voters did not want a leftist government granting a large role for the PCF. That locked electoral order suddenly collapsed in 1981 when the PCF experienced a significant decline in the first round of the presidential election, as a result of the degradation of the Soviet Union's image (the workers' strikes in Poland, the invasion of Afghanistan), at a time when generational replacement had undermined PCF identification (Duhamel and Parodi, 1982). Unable to deal with the problem of mass unemployment and weakened by the long-term decline in church attendance, incumbent President Valéry Giscard d'Estaing lost his most effective rallying cry. Thanks to the fall of the Communist scarecrow, the Socialist leader François Mitterrand was elected president, and his party won an absolute majority in the National Assembly. Producing the first real alternation of power since the beginning of the Fifth Republic in 1958, the presidential and legislative elections of 1981 constituted a 'moment of rupture' (Martin, 2000).

The collapse of the established electoral order opened a window of opportunity for polarization on new issues. Immigration and law and order, that were only secondary issues before 1981, gained saliency. This transformation of the political agenda benefited the extreme-right FN, which made a breakthrough in the 1984 European elections and managed to receive between 10 to 15 percent of the valid votes in almost every election until 2007. In the meantime, the PCF continued to decline.

The rise of the FN came along with a spectacular shift of French electoral politics to the right: from 1984 to 2007, the Right (including the FN) gathered more than 50 per cent of the votes at almost all elections. Anti-immigration feelings and 'hard on crime' demands, as well as the Socialists' U-turn on economic policies in 1983, led to this lasting rightward shift. There was also a geographical redistribution of the votes, reflecting the differential impact of the new cultural issues, especially immigration: from 1984 onwards, departments with a high proportion of foreigners from North Africa and Turkey voted more towards the Right (Martin, 2000).

Though being second-order elections, the European elections of 1984 constituted a 'moment of realignment', introducing a new stable electoral order based on the high salience of immigration and law and order issues, as well as on the imposition of neo-liberalism as the dominant economic ideology for the major parties (Jobert and Théret, 1994). Ending the realignment era initiated in 1981, these elections were also marked by the new commitment of both the PS and the Gaullist RPR towards more European integration.

Before 1981, the French party system could be described as a 'bipolar quadrille' (PCF–PS versus UDF–RPR). After 1984, while the two coalitions remained intact, a new significant but *isolated* force emerged at the far-right of the political landscape. Moreover, both the PS and the RPR consolidated themselves as dominant parties on their respective side. Finally, the national elections of 1986 and 1988 confirmed the new electoral order and introduced an additional feature, as alternations in power and power-sharing (*cohabitation*) became the 'normal rule'.

This electoral order remained in place until 2007, although some minor modifications did occur. On the left of the political spectrum, there were the rise of the Trotskyist extreme left and the creation of a new PCF–PS–Greens governmental coalition in 1997. Formerly claiming to be 'neither left nor right', the Greens competed with the PCF to be the second largest party of the Left, though they remained a minor party that was heavily dependent on the PS for obtaining legislative seats. On the right of the party system, the successes of Eurosceptic parties were short term and limited to European elections. More significant was the creation of the UMP in 2002 which grouped the moderate Right into one party and crowned the increasing domination of the RPR over the UDF (see Chapter 6). However, this party change did not undermine the electoral order, since the UDF managed to survive under the leadership of François Bayrou.

Besides these changes, three kinds of electoral modification occurred from 1984 to 2007. First, short term variations were produced by the economic conjuncture and the images of the candidates. Second, more lasting changes could be attributed to the delayed impact of the new realigning issues which had continued to infuse the parties and the electorate after the 'moment of realignment'. Third, independent long-term demographic, economic, social and cultural evolutions changed the face of the electorate. In the end, the most significant dynamics were (1) the trend towards lower voter turnout (Bréchon, 2009, pp. 25–62); (2) the shift to the right of the working class and the increasing edge of the FN among this realigned electorate (Gougou, 2012); (3) the rise of the Left among urban voters with a high level of education or a foreign background (Gougou and Tiberj, forthcoming 2013).

The collapse of the old electoral order

The victory of Nicolas Sarkozy and his party in the 2007 elections broke key features of the established electoral order. The most spectacular change was the sudden decline of the FN. Jean-Marie Le Pen got only 10.7 per cent of the votes in the first round of the presidential election, losing considerable ground compared with the 2002 election (17.2 per cent), all the more so as FN dissident Bruno Mégret (2.4 per cent in 2002) had endorsed his candidacy at that time. After almost two decades of steady increase, the FN achieved its worst result in a presidential election since its breakthrough in the 1980s (14.6 per cent in 1988, 15.3 per cent in 1995). Two months later, the legislative elections amplified the setback, as the FN polled only 4.4 per cent.

The spectacular decline of the FN benefited Sarkozy. Traditional voters of the FN were seduced by his politically incorrect style, his record as a hardline minister of the interior, as well as his platform stressing immigration controls, the defence of national identity and repressive law enforcement (Tiberj, 2008). Attacked by the Left as a dangerous extremist, he was a credible 'republican' alternative to Jean-Marie Le Pen, whose inability to conquer power had been demonstrated in 2002. The UMP candidate also emphasized a set of moral values based on hard work, merit and individual responsibility. Denouncing egalitarianism and public assistance as a way of life, he caught the attention of those who believe that welfare has become an unfair and ineffective system that discourages hard work.

Sarkozy's race to the Right resulted in a decisive lead in the first round of the presidential contest. With 31 per cent, he outran Socialist Ségolène Royal (25.4 per cent) and gathered a larger share of the votes than the combined scores of Jacques Chirac, Alain Madelin and Christine Boutin in 2002 (24.6 per cent). His performance was all the more impressive as UDF leader François Bayrou received 18.8 per cent against only 6.9 per cent in 2002. Sarkozy's support among FN sympathizers produced a shift in the electoral map (Fourquet, 2007; Martin, 2007b), with a surge in the east, on the Mediterranean border, and in the suburban areas surrounding Greater Paris. Sarkozy was particularly successful in attracting xenophobic middle-class, self-employed and retired voters. With the exception of the conservative blue-collars living in Alsace or Rhône-Alpes, his foray into the traditional working class proved to be limited (Gougou, 2012). Transfers from the traditional FN electorate increased in the runoff and in the legislative elections, providing a large victory for Sarkozy (53.3 per cent) and an absolute majority of seats for the UMP. For the first time since 1978, the incumbent majority was not rejected at the polls, testament to the confidence inspired by Sarkozy in a broad coalition of electors.

However, the 'Sarkozy revolution' also created a space in the centre of the political spectrum as many moderate centre-right voters felt uneasy with the radicalization of the UMP. Bayrou benefited from this reluctance, as well as from the doubts of many centre-left voters regarding the candidacy of Royal (Bréchon, 2008). Although the UDF had been closely allied with the Gaullist Right since the 1970s, Bayrou opposed both the Left and the Right, and positioned himself as a genuine independent anti-establishment centrist candidate. He therefore refused to endorse either candidate in the runoff, and even declared that he would not vote for Sarkozy, while most of his troops decided to jump on the bandwagon of the UMP candidate.

Bayrou finally decided to transform the UDF into a new party, the MoDem, before the legislative elections. With 7.7 per cent of the votes in the first round, it lost half of its electoral basis in comparison with the presidential poll, and elected only three deputies (including Bayrou). However, the MoDem's failure should be nuanced: despite its lack of candidates with deep political roots (almost all the incumbent UDF deputies left for the UMP), the party's share of the votes was the third largest. Further, the strength of the MoDem was actually one of the key variables explaining the seat losses experienced by the UMP on the second round of the 2007 parliamentary election, as many MoDem voters chose to support the Left in order to limit the scope of the victory of the Right (Martin, 2007c).

The breakthrough of Bayrou and the very low level of the Left in the 2007 presidential election (36.1 per cent) forced the PS to consider new alliances. Despite the opposition of almost all the Socialist leaders, Royal tried to engage negotiations with Bayrou before the second round. In the end, such a profound and rapid strategic reorientation did not occur as Bayrou declined any alliances. However, the fact that Royal offered him the post of prime minister meant that old rules and old axioms no longer applied, since an alliance between the PS and the UDF would have been unthinkable previously. Finally, the strategy of 'opening up' decided by Nicolas Sarkozy after his accession to the presidency (three former Socialists became ministers) increased the blurred distinctions between Left and Right.

Continuity and change

To be sure, all the features of the old electoral order were not erased. The stranglehold of the PS and the UMP on French politics was confirmed and even amplified (Grunberg and Haegel, 2007; Grunberg, 2008), while the PCF could not halt its decline. After being the revelation of the 2002 presidential contest, the Revolutionary Communist League (Ligue Communiste Révolutionnaire – LCR) spokesman Olivier Besancenot imposed himself as the leader of the radical left, despite having received only 4.2 per cent of the vote. The rise of the Right in suburban and rural areas continued, as well as the surge of the Left in the large cities (Guilluy, 2010). Finally the massive decline in voter turnout between the 2007 presidential contest and the legislative elections confirmed the trend towards lower participation, the sensitivity of turnout to short term factors and the presidential dynamic whereby legislative elections tend to be viewed as secondary elections.

In any case, the whole party system was under stress. Although the main changes had occurred on the right side of the political spectrum, the Left was also undergoing turmoil. Despite a rather favourable context, it suffered its third consecutive defeat in a presidential poll. Furthermore, the changing balance of power within the Right, especially the collapse of the extreme Right, constituted a new challenge for it. As the keystone of the old 'tri-polar' party system, the FN was not only a factor of division for the Right, but also a very convenient enemy against whom the left-wing parties could easily define themselves and mobilize the electorate.

Second-order elections since 2007: transitional elections in a realignment era

President Sarkozy's term was characterized by an overloaded electoral calendar, with second-order elections every year. Sarkozy had raised great hopes in the electorate. Yet, the honeymoon period was short as his popularity experienced an almost uninterrupted drop-off starting in autumn 2007. According to the TNS-Sofres barometer, the president's confidence rating was 37 per cent in March 2008, before the municipal and cantonal elections; it rose somewhat to 41 per cent in June 2009 before the European elections, but declined to 31 per cent in March 2010 for the regional elections and only 22 per cent in March 2011 for the cantonal elections. There was only one short period of recovery in the second half of 2008, at the height of the global financial crisis, due to his activism as President of the Council of the EU (Martin and Labouret, 2009).

Such an enduring unpopularity produced a repetitive 'sanction vote' in all second-order elections held between 2008 and 2011.

The dynamics of sanction

Organized less than one year after the 2007 presidential and legislative eletions, the 2008 municipal elections revealed first signs of a strong 'sanction vote' against President Sarkozy and his government (Gougou, 2008).

Understanding the dynamics of the municipal elections is not an easy exercise, as more than 36,000 municipal councils are renewed at the same time. Drawing national conclusions involves restricting the analysis to a limited number of cities. Only cities with over 30,000 inhabitants are connected to the national party system, with the contests in the smaller communes being more local in character. Even though the analysis here concerns only 235 cities, it deals with about 25 per cent of the electorate. The first round showed a clear domination of the Left: for the first time since the 1977 municipal elections, it gathered a greater share of the vote in urban France than the Right (49.8 against 43.3 per cent). The reversal of the balance of power following the victory of Nicolas Sarkozy was impressive, as right-wing candidates had received 41.8 per cent of the votes in cities with more than 30,000 people in the first round of the 2007 presidential election, while left-wing candidates had settled for 38.9 per cent. The second round confirmed the 'sanction vote' against the government and led to a clear defeat of the Right in urban France. There were 34 cities with more than 30,000 people that moved towards the Left (including five in the first round), whereas only three moved in the opposite direction. Such an anti-government tide had not occurred since the 1983 municipal elections: a model case of a sanction vote (Parodi, 1983).

Despite votes holding up thanks to the electoral system and localism in rural counties, the right-wing governing coalition also suffered losses in the cantonal elections that were organized at the same time as the municipal elections (cantonal elections only concern one half of the cantons in each department at a time). The Left gained eight presidencies of general councils over the Right and lost only one, so it led 54 out of 95 departments in metropolitan France (Paris excluded).

At first glance, the 2009 European elections looked like a success for Sarkozy. With 27.8 per cent of the valid votes, the lists of the right-wing governing coalition were in the lead in the seven metropolitan constituencies, and took a clear advantage over the Socialist lists, which received only 16.4 per cent. In elections that usually display fragmentation, the score of the UMP proved to be a remarkable performance. However, its victory was only relative, and its lead could not hide the fact that the combined vote for the Left was almost the same as in 2004 (45.2 per cent in 2009 against 45.9 per cent in 2004), while the vote for the Right as a whole dramatically fell (41.7 per cent in 2009 against 50.5 per cent in 2004). Moreover, the UMP lists (27.8 per cent), which grouped all the parties supporting the government, did not match the aggregated score of the UMP and UDF lists in 2004 (28.4 per cent). The performance of the MoDem (8.4 per cent) took the gloss off the UMP's score.

The governing coalition did not have a lot to lose in the 2010 regional elections: since the disaster of 2004, it controlled only two regions out of 22 in metropolitan France, Alsace and Corsica. Yet, with 26.2 per cent of the votes on the first round (against 35.6 per cent in 2004) and 35.4 per cent on the second round (against 37.0 per cent in 2004), it suffered another severe defeat. Meanwhile, the Left obtained an impressive surge in the first round (from 44.9 per cent in 2004 to 53.7 per cent in 2010) and reached in the second round its highest level since the 1981 legislative elections (from 50.2 per cent in 2004 to 54.1 per cent in 2010). The sanction vote against the government was hence more powerful in 2010 than in 2004 (Gougou and Labouret, 2010). However, this was not enough to ensure a 'Grand Slam' since the Right kept control of Alsace. The poor result of the right-wing governing coalition was particularly striking at the departmental level: the lists of the UMP and its allies were in the lead in only six departments out of 96. And for the first time ever in French politics, the conservative stronghold of Vendée produced a majority for the Left.

As in the previous second-order elections, the right-wing governing coalition suffered a voter sanction in the 2011 cantonal elections. Its candidates won only 22.5 per cent of the valid votes in the first round, whereas the UMP and the UDF secured 25.8 per cent in 2004. With 49.3 per cent of the votes, the Left did slightly better than in 2004 (48.3 per cent). As in the 2010 regional elections, the blow was more powerful than in the 2004 elections.

In the end, the 2011 cantonal elections, despite a lower nationalization of the vote, as they were not coupled with regional elections, replicated most of the outcome of 2004 which had been terrible for the Right. The net gain in seats for the Left was small (only ten) while the re-election rate of incumbent candidates – whether they belonged to the Left or the Right – reached a massive 87.2 per cent (Gougou and

Labouret, 2011a). Winning the majority in two additional departments and losing it in one, the Left secured 55 out of 95 presidencies of general councils in metropolitan France.

The dynamics of disorder

Besides displaying voter sanctions, the second-order elections held under President Sarkozy's five-year term were also marked by new record low levels of voter turnout (Gougou and Labouret, 2011b). Admittedly, a trend towards lower turnout had been at work since the end of the 1970s. However, the impressive drop that occurred in the first round of the 2010 regional elections (a 16-point decline in comparison with the 2004 elections) could not be explained by the long-term changes of the electorate. Such a decline in turnout was all the more puzzling in that it happened only three years after the unexpectedly high participation in the 2007 presidential election (Escalona et al., 2013).

Among the factors put forward to explain such a sudden fall, the fact that the regional elections were not held together with other elections was intensively discussed (Fauvelle-Aymar, 2011). In our view, a more robust explanation would emphasize: (1) the pessimism and the resignation of the electorate towards the inability of the government to deal with the economic crisis; (2) the exceptional circumstances of the 2004 regional elections, which had produced a strong left voter turnout as a reaction to the Socialist's failure to win through to the second round of the 2002 presidential election; (3) the weariness of the electorate after the repetition of second-order elections after 2007 (Gougou and Labouret, 2010, 2011b). In any case, the heavy variations in voter turnout that occurred since 2007 have added to the impression that French politics had been going through a critical juncture.

The Left reached historic levels in the second-order elections held after 2007. Achieving an unprecedented dominant position in local politics, it even took control of the indirectly elected Senate in September 2011. Yet, the most impressive change was the drop of the Right (including the FN), which gathered only 41.9 per cent in the European elections of 2009 and fell to its lowest level since 1945 in the first round of the 2010 regional elections with no more than 40.1 per cent. Such a historical decline even occurred in the cantonal elections, with 46.1 per cent in 2008 and 47.5 per cent in 2011, against 49.9 per cent in 2004 and more than 52 per cent from 1985 to 2001.

A shift towards the opposition is a usual feature of second-order elections. In a way, it can be argued that the exceptional left-leaning balance of power since the 2007 elections has just been the consequence of the unpopularity of the government. Yet, the enduring decline of the Right was already visible in the first round of the 2007 presidential election, where it had gathered no more than 44 per cent, due to the breakthrough of Bayrou. Hence, it suggests that some structural evolutions are occurring within the French party system.

Whereas the Right used to be a majority between 1984 and 2007, it has heavily suffered from the creation of an independent centre. Unable to match the score of Bayrou in the presidential poll, the MoDem nevertheless received around 8 per cent of the valid votes in urban France in the 2008 municipal elections (Gougou, 2008), and then 8.4 per cent in the 2009 European elections. Two years after its creation, the MoDem continued to occupy a new pivotal centrist position in the party system, with the support of a heterogeneous electorate composed of independent middle-class voters attached to liberal principles and reluctant to support the PS or the UMP (Sauger, 2007). However, the MoDem began to suffer from the competition of the ecologists in the European elections of 2009, before losing considerable ground in the regional elections of 2010 with only 4.3 per cent of the valid votes. In other words, the elections of 2009 and 2010 showed that the Left could take advantage of the separation of the centre from the Right (Gougou and Labouret, 2010).

In order to limit the damage due to voter disappointment, Sarkozy encouraged a union of the governing coalition. At first, this strategy led to a victory in the 2009 European elections, as there was only one round. But in the regional and the cantonal elections, the two-ballot system transformed the record low level reached by the Right into a landslide for the Left. Finally, the revival enjoyed by the FN increased the pressure on the UMP.

In great financial difficulties after its poor results in the 2007 legislative elections, the FN almost folded in 2008. Yet, the outcome of the 2009 European elections indicated a partial recovery, which was amplified in the 2010 regional elections, and above all in the 2011 cantonal elections with a historical breakthrough. The FN obtained 15.6 per cent of the valid votes in those very local elections against 12.5 per cent in 2004, with a surge of 6.4 points in the constituencies where it could actually field a candidate (Gougou and Labouret, 2011a). For the first time since the sudden collapse of Jean-Marie Le Pen in the 2007 presidential contest, the FN enjoyed a better score than the previous election of the same kind.

The historic momentum of the Left was accompanied by significant changes in the balance of power within it. After a large victory in the municipal and cantonal elections of 2008, the PS paid the price of a calamitous party conference in Reims and endured a severe defeat in the European elections of 2009. With 16.4 per cent of the valid votes, it was heavily challenged by Europe Ecology (a new coalition gathering gogether the Greens, various ecological movements and some well-known personalities from civil society), which received 16.3 per cent and led the Left in two constituencies out of seven in metropolitan France. However, the PS managed to regain its dominant position in the regional elections of 2010 and the cantonal elections of 2010 thanks to the local anchorage of its candidates, especially its incumbents (Gougou and Labouret, 2010, 2011a). For its part, Europe Ecology managed to resist the recovery of the PS by gaining votes from the collapse of the MoDem in both elections (12.5 per cent in the regional elections, 8.4 per cent in the cantonal elections, with a candidate in 60 per cent of the counties). Despite a decline, it confirmed its new status acquired in 2009 and replaced the PCF as the main partner of the PS. Europe Ecology transformed itself into a genuine party, named Europe Ecology – The Greens (Europe Écologie les Verts – EELV), after the 2010 regional elections.

Towards alternation without alternative

The victories of the Left in the second-order elections held between 2007 and 2012 were above all a consequence of voters' sanctions against the government. The right-wing coalition in power since 2007 consistently suffered from an extremely unfavourable economic environment and the controversies surrounding Nicolas Sarkozy's leadership and personality. The historical levels reached by the Left were early signs of an alternation in 2012 – but an alternation without a real alternative.

As the very low turnout showed, there was no real enthusiasm for the Left, most notably the PS. Furthermore, the surge of the Greens at the expense of the PS or the MoDem, as well as the success of the third-party lists, including those of the FN, in the second round of the 2010 regional elections, was fostered by the continuing reluctance of many voters to vote either for the traditional Left or the moderate Right. Scepticism towards an alternative from the Left was also perceptible in the fact that the radical Left was not able to take advantage of the economic crisis. The Left Front (Front de Gauche – FG), grouping the PCF, dissidents from the PS and other small left-wing parties, failed to make a breakthrough, though it dominated the far left (especially the LCR which changed its name to the Nouveau Parti Anticapitaliste (New anti-Capitalist Party) – NPA) in the European elections of 2009 (6.2 against 5.0 per cent) and increased its lead in the 2010 and 2011 polls.

The presidential and legislative elections of 2012: change and uncertainty

In the wake of its surge in second-order elections, the Left regained national power in 2012. Hollande's defeat of Sarkozy was nevertheless fairly narrow (51.3 per cent in metropolitan France), as the incumbent president managed to mobilize not only the voters who wanted him to be president, but also those, especially among the electorate of Marine Le Pen, who *did not want* a Socialist as the head of the state (Labouret, 2012a).

In the legislative elections held a few weeks later, the 'stop the pro-immigration Left' argument lost relevance as most voters thought that the game was up (Labouret, 2012b). Moreover, some Sarkozy voters were reluctant to return to *cohabitation* and wanted to give the new executive a chance, while others, who had backed the incumbent president because of his leadership, had no reason to vote for the leaderless UMP. This allowed the PS to enjoy an absolute majority of seats without the Greens. As in 2007, voter turnout reached a high level in the presidential poll (over 81 per cent in the two rounds) before breaking a new low record in the legislative elections (58.7 per cent in the first round).

The confirmation of the rupture of 2007

While a quick overview of the 2012 elections may lead the casual observer to conclude that the old electoral order had been rebuilt, a closer look confirms that 2007 was a 'moment of rupture' (Gougou and Martin, 2013). Arguments in favour of the re-establishment of the old electoral order are threefold: (1) the FN enjoyed a strong revival; (2) the MoDem almost disappeared; (3) there was an alternation in power. However, such a view does not take into consideration the fact that the landscape at the left and right sides of the political spectrum has become very different from the one that existed before 2007.

Certainly, the good showing of Marine Le Pen (18.3 per cent) extended the dynamic enjoyed by the FN in the 2011 cantonal elections. Compared to the score of her father in 2007 – whom she succeeded as president of the FN in January 2011 – her result was a 7.6 point increase. While being the best result ever received by the FN, this performance should nevertheless be relativized since the cumulative score of Jean-Marie Le Pen and Bruno Mégret in 2002 was greater (19.6 per cent). Moreover, Marine Le Pen was heavily overtaken by Nicolas Sarkozy who received 27 per cent, whereas they were head to head in the polls in January.

While being the first incumbent president to trail on the first round, Sarkozy lost only 4 points in comparison with 2007. Such a remarkable resistance could be imputed to his incumbency and charisma, but also to his rightist campaign which focused – more than ever – on immigration, security and national identity (Labouret, 2012a). Yet, contrary to 2007, his strategy was not to seduce the far-right sympathizers but to appear as the only bulwark against the allegedly pro-immigration and soft-on-crime Left, especially in the second round. In the end, Sarkozy managed to neutralize a major part of the 'sanction vote' by stressing those issues that were favourable to him.

Sarkozy's electoral map in the two rounds showed both a great stability in comparison with the 2007 presidential contest and a great divergence in comparison with the presidential elections held before 2007. This means that Sarkozy suffered a rather uniform swing, leaving the shape of his voter coalition fairly untouched. Despite his decline and the revival of the FN, he retained most of the authoritarian and anti-immigrant voters who had supported him in 2007. The sharp divide that existed in the old electoral order between the moderate-right electorate and the extreme-right electorate (Grunberg and Schweisguth, 1997, 2003) broke down in 2007 and did not reappear in 2012. As in 2007, most of Sarkozy's voters shared the concerns of the electorate of Le Pen about immigration (Martin, 2012). And in the meantime, surveys showed that UMP sympathizers had become favourable to an alliance with the FN. According to an Ipsos survey conducted on 7–9 June 2012, 66 per cent of the UMP sympathizers were favourable to an electoral alliance between the UMP and the FN.

With 14 per cent of the votes in the legislative elections, the FN obtained its second best result in such a contest (15.2 per cent in 1997), but declined in comparison with the presidential election. Only two far-right deputies were elected, whereas Marine Le Pen narrowly failed to win a seat. This demobilization of the FN electorate, which had occurred in the previous post-presidential legislative elections as well (–4.3 points in 2012 against –6.3 in 2007, –5.9 in 2002 and –4.9 in 1988 – these figures being the difference between the FN score in the presidential election and the ensuing parliamentary contest), helped the moderate Right to resist (Labouret, 2012b). Besides the electoral calendar, the UMP was favoured by a high number of incumbents and by the electoral system, as most of the FN candidates could not reach the threshold required to pass through the first round. To recap, candidates have to poll more than 12.5 per cent of the registered voters to go through to the second round. As a result of the low turnout, there were only 59 constituencies featuring a FN candidate in the second round (including 28 Left/moderate Right/FN contests), against 132 in 1997 (including 76 three-way contests). In the end, the FN failed really to challenge the UMP or to force it to enter into an alliance. As Sarkozy's defeat had been narrower than expected, the moderate wing of the UMP felt unable to criticize his campaign and his ambivalence towards the FN. Hence, the UMP maintained its unity, the only change being the creation of a minor parliamentary group gathering 28 centre-right deputies from the New Centre (created in 2007 by the incumbent UDF deputies who supported Nicolas Sarkozy in the second round of the presidential election) and the Radical Party (one of France's oldest parties and that was an associate party of the UMP between 2002 and 2011).

With only 9.2 per cent of the votes, Bayrou lost half of his 2007 electorate and could not derive any benefit from the unpopularity of Sarkozy. The separation of the Centre from the Right since 2007 has had its counterpart, namely the unification of the Right. Because of his moderate-to-liberal positions on immigration and law and order, the MoDem leader did not represent an acceptable option for most of the right-wing voters. The 'culture war', started by Sarkozy in 2007, resulted in the isolation of Bayrou. Suffering from a lack of credibility since the fall of the MoDem in second-order elections, and confronted with two very strong candidates, Bayrou could only retain the genuine anti-system centrist component of his 2007 electorate.

The *raison d'être* of the MoDem was to break up the PS–UMP duopoly. Bayrou's third presidential candidacy was like going 'all-in' at poker. And he failed. From there, the MoDem was doomed, all the more so since Bayrou refused to join the new presidential majority, despite his personal vote for Hollande in reaction to Sarkozy's race to the Right. In the end, the MoDem won less than 2 per cent in the legislative elections and disappeared from the political landscape, with Bayrou himself defeated by the PS in a three-way contest with the UMP.

Thanks to Jean-Luc Mélenchon's candidacy, the Left Front had a strong showing in the first round of the presidential election (11.3 per cent) and increased its edge over left-wing rivals, Workers' Struggle (Lutte Ouvrière – LO) and the NPA, whose candidates in 2012 were far less well-known than the charismatic Arlette Laguiller (LO) and Olivier Besancenot (NPA) of earlier elections. For the first time since 1981, a presidential candidate supported by the PCF got a double digit result. That said, the total of the scores of Jean-Luc Mélenchon, Philippe Poutou and Nathalie Arthaud (13 per cent) did not match the aggregate result of the PCF and the Trotskyist Far Left in 2002 (14.1 per cent) or 1995 (14.1 per cent). Furthermore, the FG declined in the legislative elections (7.1 per cent), as a result of the Socialist momentum in the wake of the victory of Hollande. Half of the 21 incumbent FG deputies lost their seats, while Mélenchon, who stood in the same constituency as Marine Le Pen, was eliminated in the first round. In the end, the FG did not manage to challenge the PS, but its performance in the presidential poll may have signalled a potential to radicalize the left-wing electorate that could ultimately represent an important piece of the current realignment era.

EELV had an opposite dynamic as it managed to elect 18 deputies after having endured a terrible performance in the presidential election (2.3 per cent). The key of this trend reversal was the backing of the PS in 66 constituencies, as EELV only received 5.5 per cent of the valid votes. Despite the challenge of many Socialist dissidents, EELV capitalized on its deal with the PS, which had been signed in November 2011 in the wake of its good performances in the second-order elections. Besides having its own parliamentary group for the first time, EELV also obtained two ministries, including the housing department. Ultimately, the 2012 elections confirmed that EELV has become the main partner of the PS, instead of the PCF. That said, the PS, which got an absolute majority of deputies, appeared to be more dominant than ever, while EELV remained unable to get legislative seats without its support.

Towards a new electoral order?

There is little chance that the elections of 2012 will finally constitute a 'moment of realignment' introducing a new electoral order. Admittedly, identifying durable realigning changes necessitates waiting for the next first-order elections. Nevertheless, the seriousness of the global recession and the endless euro crisis suggest that the current reshaping of the French party system is just at the beginning. To put it another way, it is hard to imagine the establishment of a new stable electoral order in such a period of economic turmoil. In this context, the policies implemented by the new left-wing governing coalition will play a major role. Whether Hollande fails or succeeds in stopping the degradation of the economy will make a big difference. At this time, no scenario can be ruled out, all the more since the issues on the political agenda have been evolving.

A realignment era is basically a period of instability and disorder. The collapse of an old electoral order opens a window of opportunity to introduce lasting changes in the nature of party competition. In concrete terms, political parties try to displace the main lines of conflict to an arena where they have the advantage. In such a perspective, issue evolutions are a key aspect for assessing the features of a possible new electoral order.

The first significant evolution concerns immigration. From the 1980s to the 2000s, immigration was primarily discussed as an external threat in a context of growing mass unemployment and rising insecurity. The main debates related to migration flows and access to French citizenship. However, such a framing that opposes French nationals against foreigners has lost much of its saliency as most of the young 'arabs' and 'blacks' living in France today are not foreigners, but French nationals. From this point of view, the 2007 campaign was a turning point. Sarkozy continued to use the old framing (with the so-called 'chosen immigration'), but he added a new one opposing cultural assimilation and multiculturalism. Contrary to Jean-Marie Le Pen, who had always been hostile to assimilation, Sarkozy articulated the fears of those xenophobic voters who do not believe in the 'send them back home' solution. For those voters, who have – reluctantly – accepted that France is not a white country anymore, the most important concern is that populations with a foreign background accept traditional French cultural codes. This new framing was at the root of the creation of a Ministry for National Identity and Immigration in 2007, which then made its way with the law banning the burqa and more generally with the debate about the place of Islam in French society. In his 2012 campaign, Sarkozy was strongly challenged by Marine Le Pen, who broke with the FN's traditional positions by taking a strong pro-assimilation stance (particularly stunning was her move towards a pro-secularism position in order to attack the Muslims). In this way, the new framing of the immigration issue contributed to the transformation of the Right by moving the UMP and the FN closer together.

On the other hand, significant changes in the political agenda have been produced by the international context. The doubts about the future of the eurozone and the imposition of austerity by the EU have made the European issue particularly salient and revived divisions that were previously limited to European elections and referenda on European integration. In this respect, the 2005 referendum on the Constitutional Treaty had already suggested that Europe could introduce a new conflict dimension into French politics and produce major shifts in voter coalitions. Moreover, this issue is closely connected to important economic issues, especially the control of public debt. The opponents of austerity are likely to shout louder and louder, should the troubles continue in the eurozone, all the more so since Hollande was swept to power on the back of a platform advocating growth instead of austerity. Such a debate on economic policies, in relation to the debate on the EU's democratic deficit, would have a high potential for realignment in the French party system.

Future perspectives

As expected, after the defeats of the UMP and its allies in all second-order elections since 2007, a change in power took place in the presidential and legislative elections of 2012. Yet, the French party system is still under stress. The 'rupture' initiated by Sarkozy in 2007 was confirmed in 2012, but the global recession and the instability in Europe cast doubts about the future direction of French electoral politics. After a few months in office, Hollande has already experienced a drop-off in the polls, whereas the rise of unemployment and the enduring crisis in the eurozone do not augur a quick recovery of the economy. On the right side of the political spectrum, changes continue with the battle for the leadership of the UMP, whereas Jean-Louis Borloo seeks to revive the former UDF. The next second-order elections should bring new developments in the reshaping of the French political universe, but electoral disorder will probably last until the 2017 presidential and legislative elections.

Chapter 11

The Evolution of Political Attitudes and Policy Preferences in France

JAMES STIMSON, VINCENT TIBERJ AND
CYRILLE THIÉBAUT

The approach adopted in this chapter places developments in French politics in a new context. French political history is well known for being *eventful* and political developments are often narrated in relation to key events. But contemporary politics also requires an understanding of the longer-term evolution of social attitudes and preferences. Political attitudes today, as expressed in surveys or electoral choices, make more sense when we are able to use suitable longitudinal indexes of opinion preferences. Beyond the antipathy towards particular political figures (or to their style or appeal), beyond a purely event-based understanding of politics, in this chapter we argue that electoral victories and defeats have their roots in the evolution of the public's demands over the medium to long term and their preferences for certain policies. It is because French voters, like their American, Canadian or British equivalents, react to the public policies implemented by those in power that these governments endure, are sanctioned or even dismissed at subsequent elections. This is not to say that all governments are defeated in the polls, but clearly part of their unpopularity comes from changes in the electorate's preferences in the short term (in relation to any given election). Our study drills down deeper than any particular election, however. We develop the concept of the public policy mood as an aggregate measure of evolving attitudes on the two core dimensions of socio-economic and cultural values. Taking a longer-term historical view, we argue that there has been an evolution of French attitudes towards a demand for more welfare and equality (on the socio-economic axis) and for more tolerance towards migrants or minorities (the cultural axis). These longer term trends do not always combine with shorter-term incentives to ensure any particular election result: otherwise, Lionel Jospin would have won in 2002 and Ségolène Royal in 2007. But understanding the

170

public policy *mood* is one important indicator of electoral outcomes, as well as being a weathervane of the more general evolution of French politics.

The public policy mood

The mood as an instrument allows us to understand better the impact of public policy on the evolution of public opinion over time. From the election of François Mitterrand in 1981 to that of François Hollande in 2012, almost every government was rejected in the elections following its victory. The year 1986 saw the return of the right, 1988 the return of the left, which was then defeated in 1993 before returning to power in 1997, losing it again in 2002 and finally winning it back in 2012. The only two exceptions in these three decades of tumultuous political history are Jacques Chirac in 1995 and Nicolas Sarkozy in 2007. In order to win, these two presidents clearly distanced themselves from the then government's record, even though they had supported it and even participated in it in the case of Nicolas Sarkozy between 2002 and 2007.

How can this instability be explained? Why does the 'will of the people' change so radically and sometimes also so rapidly? Is the 2012 election just another manifestation of the curse of incumbency or are there other explanations? Was Sarkozy's defeat only a matter of personality? Did he simply pay for the economic crisis, as did a number of his fellow European leaders? Or were the roots of his defeat explained by more profound phenomena?

Electoral sociology generally struggles to explain evolutions and alternations in power because its models are developed on the basis of long-term variables. For example, sociological models, and their French equivalent known as 'heavy variables' (Boy and Mayer, 1997), emphasize the fact that individuals vote according to their social characteristics (particularly their class and religion). Psycho-social models emphasize electors' long-term attachments to a party (or to the left or the right in the French case); an attachment that is manifest in attitudes towards information but also in the ability to mobilize and even more to vote. Other political models still (political in the sense that they include the logic of partisan agendas in their analysis) tend to focus on explanations of stability rather than evolution. Thus the realignment school (Key, 1955; Sundquist, 1973; Martin, 2000; see also Chapter 10 in this volume) recognizes evolutions, though these are seen as transition phases between two electoral orders marked by political and partisan permanence. Although elections may deviate from expected results, the 'normal vote' (Converse, 1966), remains the electoral behaviour that is expected.

There is another research tradition that appears to be more fruitful in attempting to explain alternations in French political power. If we turn to the American literature on presidential popularity, several explanatory mechanisms (Gerstlé and François, 2011) may be relevant. First, there may be a 'wear and tear effect' essentially due to the fact that the government will necessarily progressively disappoint some of the groups that support it (Mueller, 1973; Stimson, 1976). Second, the popularity of the executive body may depend on dominant political issues, particularly economic crises (Fiorina, 1981; Monroe, 1984; Lewis-Beck, 1988) and international crises. Third, communication strategies might cause popularity levels to increase or decline (Kernell, 1986). This analytical framework works in fruitful dialogue with certain analyses of French electoral evolutions. Some scholars explain alternation in power in the 1980s and 1990s by the differential mobilization of electorates (Jadot, 2000). With this logic we can see the effect of electoral cycles with a systematic erosion of the electoral weight of governing parties (Parodi, 1983).

At the basis of this US literature we find the economic approach to voting, which links the fate of governments to their results in terms of growth or unemployment, and in its most simplified version reduces voters to their role as an economic actor negotiating costs and benefits (Downs, 1957). Its adherents refer to this as the 'fundamentals' school. In fact, the succession of changes of power between left and right governments occurred mainly during the 'thirty woeful years' that France experienced after the 1973 oil crisis; it stands to reason that, faced with unfavourable economic conditions and the failure of successive governments to resolve the problems of unemployment, electors penalized each of them in turn at the voting booth. However, economic modelling of elections in France has not been very successful (Foucault and Nadeau, 2012). The Iowa model applied to France predicted victory for Jospin in 2002 (Jérôme and Jérôme, 2004) and for Ségolène Royal in 2007 (Lewis-Beck et al., 2008). In other words, 'it's [not only] the economy stupid!'.

Thus the scientific enigma remains unsolved, unless we take a different perspective. What if the preferences of electors evolved depending on which side is in power and which policies they implement? Of course this would mean explaining politics by politics but this approach has the merit of putting public policy back at the centre of the game rather than considering that it is just an extension of the economy and its current state. This theory accords pride of place to change, both from the perspective of electors and those they elect.

Here we follow on from studies that have brought to light the dynamics of representation in the United States. James Stimson (1991, 2004) created an index, the 'public policy mood', based on opinion data collected between the 1950s and the early 2000s. He demonstrated that American electors evolve in their demand for more or less liberalism in the United States (that is to say more welfare state or redistribution) depending on who occupies the White House. Christopher Wlezien (1995) has explained these evolutions according to the idea of the 'thermostat': electors react with either more or less demand for left-wing policies depending on whether they have been increased or decreased. Above all, Wlezien, along with Soroka (Soroka and Wlezien, 2010), showed, based on a study of the United States, Canada and the United Kingdom, that not only do electors react to the policies being implemented (public responsiveness) but politicians modify their propositions in accordance with the evolutions in the electorate (policy representation).

Is such a theory verifiable and applicable to France? After all, Americans are often considered to be 'innocent of ideology'. This idea dates back to the founding studies of the Michigan School (Campbell et al., 1960) and is a conception of a public that does not have a stable and structured value system that has been verified in subsequent studies (Kinder and Sears, 1985; Smith, 1989). In light of this, might we not suppose that if their demands for public policy evolve, it is above all because they do not have persistent and durable normative preferences? In other words, public policy demands would be a matter of context on the other side of the Atlantic, whereas in France – a country known to be more polarized and more ideological that the United States – electors would be more resistant to the winds of change and therefore more stable in terms of what they expect from a government. We may thus wonder about the evolutions of the French public and their demands, the size and reasons for these evolutions, but also their links between these changes and the electoral results. Do the French 'move' in terms of their demand for public action? Are these evolutions purely social and economic, or are they related to other issues such as immigration or social customs? If there is evolution, is it marginal or substantial in size? Is it based on conjuncture, economics or politics, or does it follow other determining factors? Above all, does it allow us to understand the electoral results of the last three decades?

We will present here the two prevalent French public policy moods, which are based on the compilation of the results of more than three decades of public opinion polls, comparable to the ones developed in the US (Stimson, 1991) and in the Canada and the UK (Soroka and Wlezien, 2010). Our moods will cover the evolution of preferences of the French voters from the end of the 1970s until 2012. These preferences have been sorted into two dimensions corresponding to the issues and values of the 'old politics' and the 'new politics' (Houtman et al., 2008) as investigated by various scholars of French politics since the end of the 1980s (Grunberg and Schweisguth, 1990, 1997; Chiche et al., 2000; Schweisguth, 2007). The first dimension emphasizes socio-economical cleavages (questions relating to the size and role of the state, the attitude towards the welfare state and income distribution). The second dimension concerns controversies and debates regarding gender role, gay rights, law and order and immigration, an approach that captures the debates about 'modernity' which have occupied a growing place in European political life since the 1970s.

The longitudinal index of *social preferences* is based on the aggregation of 125 series of French questions posed in surveys at least twice in strictly identical terms since 1978. Among these questions 13 were asked ten times or more in these surveys and 51 at least five times. Our measure is based on a file that records 554 measures of public opinion overall. The index of *cultural preferences* is based on an even larger group of measures: 134 series are available for the 1978–2012 period, of which 80 have been asked at least 5 times, 19 at least 10 times, and 4 at least 20 times. This is based on 830 measures of public opinion. These question series are the elementary bricks on which the public policy mood algorithm can provide a unique measure of the preferences of the electorate and which are comparable over time. The algorithm proceeds by analysing the correlations between items and construct. When the latent dimension (the mood) is based on the way part of the 'elementary bricks' have moved across time, it can assess the ups and downs of the mood. The strength of this algorithm is that it is not necessary to have all the elementary bricks in place so as to assess the evolutions (for a presentation of the method, see Stimson, 1991; Stimson et al., 2011). The mood is based on a very simple 0 to 100 metric. A score of 50 means that the conservative positions are as strong as the progressive positions; a score of 100 means that the French have all voiced a progressive position; a score of 0 means they have all advocated a conservative position.

Along with shedding a new light on elections, charting public policy moods will also provide readers with an insight into the way that France has evolved in both social and cultural matters. It is often said that France remains attached to a strong state and adopts an egalitarian view regarding incomes and wealth. Others have stressed its (reluctant) adaptation to the globalized economy and an acceptance of less public intervention in the private market (see Chapter 15). Evaluating the public policy mood allows us to measure whether socio-economic attitudes have evolved at the level of the electorate and it is also invaluable for understanding our second cultural axis. The rise of the FN and the anti-immigrant posture adopted by the UMP, following the lead of Nicolas Sarkozy and now Jean-François Copé, might leave the impression that the level of intolerance is on the rise. Recent debates regarding the place of Islam in France (the headscarf affair, the cartoons of Muhammad, the bombing of the satirical newspaper *Charlie Hebdo*) or the crisis in the suburbs of 2005 reinforce this impression of a society that is more and more divided across ethnic and religious communities. On the other hand, tolerance within French society also seems to be making progress in relation to issues such as the acceptance of gay rights (such as adoption rights or marriage) and the country has adopted various laws against gender and ethnic discrimination. So the situation is more complex than it seems. Once again the public policy mood will provide a clear evolution of the way the French public has evolved.

How and why do French voters evolve?

How are the curves in Figure 11.1 to be interpreted? First, we observe that social demands are not stable over time. Instead they have evolved from a low of 46 in 1985 to a high of 59 in 2009. This means that a significant part of the French population has changed its opinion, demanding either more or less state intervention. In this, they appear to be sensitive to the effects of the period in much the same way as the Americans (studied by James Stimson) or the Canadians and the English (studied by Soroka and Wlezien) are. The French are thus not exceptional in this and neither more nor less ideological (and thus theoretically immunized against change) than the electors in these other countries.

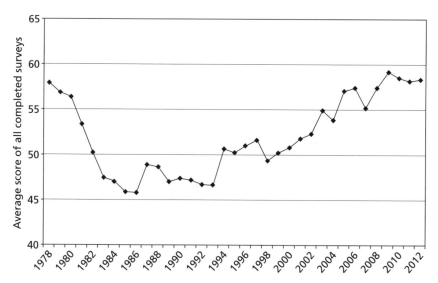

Note: Completed surveys were ranked on a scale between 0 and 100, where 0 means all the answers given were right-inclining and 100 means all the answers given were left-inclining.

Figure 11.1 *The longitudinal index of social preferences*

Second, French voters' preferences for social values were strong on the eve of the 2012 presidential election. The index even attained levels that had not been reached since the end of the 1970s. Thus, in the lead-up to François Mitterrand's election, the index was 56.5 whereas in 2011 it stood at 58.0. This result is all the more remarkable in that it is very close to the maximum point recorded in 2009. By way of comparison, in 2006, one year before Nicolas Sarkozy's victory, the level of social demand was at 57.0, and in 2001, one year before the re-election of Jacques Chirac, it was 51.5.

These evolutions can be summarized as follows. After the election of Mitterrand, the decline in social demand was particularly strong (–7.5 points over four years), and, even if it subsequently increased between 1986 and 1987, it remained relatively low until the middle of the 1990s, at between 46 and 48. Since then, the tendency has been towards a steady rise. Thus between 1993 and 2011, social demand has progressed by 11.5 points, between 2002 and 2011 by 6 points and between 2007 and 2011 by 3 points. It is also noteworthy that the economic crisis that began in 2008 has only marginally affected social demand.

This is a remarkable result from both a scientific and political perspective. Whereas partisan elites on the right and to a lesser extent on the left suggest that French voters are increasingly less attached to the welfare state, it is in fact the opposite. There seems to be a gap here between electoral demands and public policy proposals from major parties, as though the latter are reluctant to integrate certain signs from below. This is paradoxical to say the least in an 'opinion democracy' where surveys are supposed to enable us to gauge the will of the people in real time. Could this be proof of a certain ideological inertia among party elites? It seems that it is, and this inertia can also be found in the response to the cultural preferences of voters.

Often commentators give the impression that France and the French rarely change, particularly in terms of tolerance. This is clearly not the case. Like social preferences, cultural preferences have evolved, from a minimum of 48 in 1985 to a maximum of 64 in 2009, an evolution of some 16 points above the level of the other mood (see Figure 11.2). This is all the more remarkable given that we are dealing here with values that are supposedly stable. Opposition to immigrants is generally not considered to be something that evolves, nor something that is fundamentally sensitive to the economic situation of the country. Instead, it is supposed to reflect prejudice and thought patterns often constructed in childhood (Adorno, 1950; Allport, 1954; Tajfel, 1978). The same is true for opinions relating to homosexuality, the role of women, authority and the death penalty which are embedded in traditions transmitted and maintained by institutions such as the family or the Catholic Church. Yet French voters do evolve in their opinions and

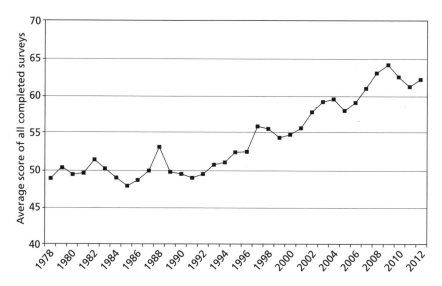

Note: Completed surveys were ranked on a scale between 0 and 100, where 0 means all the answers given were conservative and 100 means they were tolerant.

Figure 11.2   *The longitudinal index of cultural preferences*

this is visible in some of the more emblematic series of questions behind this index. In 1981 only 33 per cent of interviewees would not have been shocked if their son was a homosexual, whereas 60 per cent would have been 'deeply' shocked and would have 'done everything to change him'. In 2006 the proportions were 83 and 16 per cent respectively. In 1992, only 44.5 per cent of French people considered that immigration was a source of cultural enrichment, compared with 66 per cent in March 2012. In 1984 barely 21 per cent of French people supported the right to vote for foreigners, compared with 57 per cent in March 2012. As for the death penalty, 64 per cent of French respondents supported its reintroduction in 1984, compared with only 33 per cent in March 2012.

Preferences of French voters are evolving but we must distinguish between two periods. Firstly the variations between 1978 and the beginning of the 1990s were significant but not very large; they were also stable over the medium term. Secondly, from 1992/1993 the trend in the medium term was towards an increase in tolerance with bigger variations, as though the issues relating to this index were more sensitive to their context. Also in this second period, the overall progression of the cultural index is remarkable, even taking into account phases of temporary decline. When tolerance declines, in other words, the level remains higher than the baseline of the previous minimum. In 1999 the decline brought the index down to a level of 54.5, 2 points more than in 1996. Likewise in 2005 the decline left the index at 58.0, 3 points more than in 1999. In 2011 the drop in the cultural index to 61.0 was still 3 points higher than the previous 2005 low.

In the medium term there has been both a progression and a decline in tolerance. These paradoxical findings are consistent with Kellstedt's (2003) theory of prejudice according to which both tolerant and intolerant opinions coexist in any citizen's mind, particularly towards immigrants; the dominance of the former over the latter or vice versa is a matter of context and the way debates are framed. It is therefore no accident that 2005 corresponds to a decline, given that the riots in the suburbs provoked a surge in anti-immigrant sentiment in that year (Tiberj, 2008). It was not until the end of 2007 that tolerance attained and then exceeded its 2004 level.

The causes of these evolutions

Different explanations can be proposed for these evolutions in social and cultural preferences, the first and foremost being the economic situation of the country. Other theories tend to assume changes in values and normative preferences over the medium or even the long term, such as the theory of generational renewal (Inglehart, 1977). Last but not least, others suppose that the political process takes its share in the ups and downs: who is in power will weight on values, as well as the main debates and the way they are framed. We will come back to these other explanations shortly, but first, is it all about economics?

All about economics?

Among classical theories of voting behaviour, there is a strong tradition of emphasizing the importance of the economic vote. In this tradition, the vote and the popularity of the government depend on macro-economic data (particularly inflation and unemployment; Lewis-Beck, 2000). It seems reasonable to infer that inflation and unemployment rates will also weigh heavily on demands for more or less redistribution of wealth, or more or less welfare state. The higher the unemployment rate, for example, the lower the support for redistributive policies. But in fact there is little evidence to support such clear relationships. The socio-economic mood seems to be correlated with unemployment (the more the unemployment rate increases, the more the demands for left-wing policies decrease; $R = -0.44$: R is a correlation measure varying from -1 (perfect negative association) to $+1$ (perfect positive association), O meaning no association between the two variables); but this strong negative correlation is primarily based on the 1978–83 period during which unemployment remained at a low level (a maximum of 7.3 per cent). After this period it fluctuated between 8.1 and 10.3 per cent. If we exclude the years prior to the election of Mitterrand the correlation drops to −0.07. The evidence for a strong link between the social preference index and the level of unemployment and inflation is thus limited and temporally variable.

The link between the economy and the cultural preferences index has not been hypothesized as rigorously as that concerning the economic vote, but some researchers consider that if the economic situation of a country deteriorates, then prejudices against migrants will increase (Sheriff, 1996). A strong correlation has been found between the level of inflation and the cultural mood, but most of the relationship is again dependent on the period at which the index starts. After 1984, the relationship between inflation and cultural preferences was not significant. Clearly it is difficult to distinguish here between an inflation effect and a period effect. The years where cultural preferences were at their lowest were also the years in which inflation was at its highest; and they are all to be found in the first period of study. In a nutshell, the economic situation alone is not responsible for the evolution of French attitudes, whether or not its social or cultural dimensions are considered.

A question of generation?

When we work on long periods, we must take into account the fact that the electorate is not always made up of the same people. Thus 53 per cent of electors in 2012 were not yet old enough to vote in 1978 (and 21 per cent were not yet born). These new cohorts have replaced older ones. Although electors born in or before 1930 comprised 39 per cent of the electoral body in 1978, they only counted for 4 per cent in 2012. Of course this is only of interest if the values of new voters differ from those of older voters. This is the case only in terms of cultural values. If we analyse the impact of different sociological values (such as education, birth cohort, profession (or former profession) and relationship to religion) on socio-economic and cultural values during the presidential elections held between 1988 and 2007, all other things being equal, we see several patterns – but two are particularly important here (Tiberj, 2012). Birth cohort does not have an independent impact on the socio-economic values of individuals. Instead, new voters primarily demonstrate the values of their professional or religious group(s). On the other hand, different cohorts, regardless of their religion, class, gender or level of education, can be distinguished according to their cultural values during these presidential elections. The oldest cohorts can be identified by their conservatism and the more recent ones by their openness. Generational renewal can thus clearly play on this cultural index, even if it does not explain 'all' of the movement towards openness demonstrated by French public opinion.

Constituting moods by group is possible but challenging. It is difficult to find enough data at a global level. It is even more complex to obtain proper information at the level of each socio-political group; and this is even more true for age cohorts. In order to reconstitute these evolutions, it is necessary to have the detailed data itself and not only reports by survey institutes, because cohorts are not part of their routine analysis. The indexes that are constructed here are based on data that is available from the CNCDH's barometer of racism and deal solely with the issue of xenophobia and prejudice towards minorities. It is impossible to reconstitute the whole longitudinal index of cultural preferences at the level of cohorts but all the series that are used here are part of it. We can thus reasonably transpose these trends to the whole of the index.

For each year of the study, the more a cohort is recent, the higher its level of tolerance. For example, individuals born in or before 1940 obtained an index of 39 in 1999, compared to 52 for individuals born in 1977 or after. Given that the former will be replaced by the latter, this mechanism is indeed behind the increase in the index, though it is not sufficient to explain the whole movement.

All of the indexes are on the rise. In other words, people do not become more racist as they get older but rather the opposite. Let's take a cohort in the prime of life in 1999: those born between 1956 and 1966, who were between 33 and 43 years old at the time. Their index was then at 48. A decade later, when they were between 43 and 53 years old, their index was 63 – at a higher level of tolerance than any other cohort in 1999. Overall, the medium-term trend towards tolerance that the index of cultural preferences reveals is partly explained by generational renewal, but only partly.

The thermostat explanation

Part of the evolution of the indexes is clarified by generational renewal, but only for one index – nothing for the moment sheds light on the social index – and we still cannot account for the short-term highs and lows. One final possible explanation puts politics, and particularly the policy proposals of the government, at the centre of the issue. It is inspired by the 'thermostat theory' of Christopher Wlezien (1995). According to this theory, mood would depend on the policies implemented by the current government. Public policy would thus have a direct impact on voters' higher or lower social demands. These evolutions would run counter to the policies actually being implemented, however: a left-wing government leading to right-wing demands and vice versa. This relationship has been verified for socio-economic indexes in the US, Canada and the UK (see Table 11.1).

We can see that this relationship is also present for the French case, for both longitudinal indexes. The highs and lows also evolve

Table 11.1   *The ups and downs of moods: the thermostat explanation*

Period	Social preference index	Cultural preference index
1981–85	−7.533	−1.637
1986–87	3.085	1.280
1988–92	−1.957	−3.616
1993–96	4.327	1.742
1997–2001	0.160	−0.227
2002–11	5.796	3.408

depending on which party is in government, whereas in the United States, the rhythm is more reliant on the political affiliation of the president. Thus when the PS is in government, the two indexes tend to decline, and when the right is in power the two indexes increase. Sometimes these evolutions do not occur or are very weak, such as during the Jospin government, and sometimes they are very significant in size, such as during the first Mitterrand mandate (between 1981 and 1985), during the Balladur and Juppé governments (1993–97), or after the re-election of Chirac in 2002. The speed with which public opinion reacts is quite striking. After barely two years of Chirac government during the first cohabitation, the social preference index had regained almost half the points lost during the Fabius and Mauroy governments. Above all, these evolutions are also reflected in the cultural values of voters, even though for a long time they were not a major political issue. This was particularly true after the re-election of Mitterrand. Moreover, if these values had not been affected by specific crises like the riots in 2005, the evolutions of the last decade would have been the same size as those on the social index. Thus, between 2002 and 2004 the social index progressed by 1.5 and the cultural index by 1.7, and between 2002 and 2009 the respective evolutions were 6.8 and 6.2. But the crisis in the suburbs and the particularly xenophobic context of the 2010–11 period (the Arab revolutions, President Sarkozy's speech in Grenoble) led to moments of tension in French public opinion (Mayer et al., 2012).

Another interesting result is that French voters 'move' on average at a comparable pace to their American counterparts on the socio-economic dimension. Thus, during the Eisenhower administration social demands progressed by 2 points per year. This rhythm can be observed, inversely, during the Mauroy and Fabius governments in France. In other words, French electors are not more resistant to evolutions, be they high or low, than their American counterparts. This is reflected in their cultural values too, notably since the year 2000. Thus between 2007–09 they progressed by 4 points. The size of these variations cannot simply be explained by generational renewal: the time lapse is too short. Instead they can be explained by the immigration and security policies that were put into place by the Fillon government. On the other hand, the weak variation in cultural and socio-economic preferences during the Jospin government might be surprising. Is it because voters did not perceive the policies implemented during this period as being particularly left wing?

Moods and elections

Voters evolve and these evolutions follow particular patterns. Beyond generational renewal and the medium-term progression of tolerance for cultural preferences, the driving force behind decreases and increases in the index remains the public policies implemented by the government. One question remains however: are these evolutions linked to electoral results?

The absolute level of preferences for the Left is insufficient to predict a socialist victory. For example, the Left won in 1981, 1988 and 1997 with levels of cultural preferences significantly lower than those measured in 2002 and 2007. Likewise, it won in 1988 with a level of socio-economic preferences of 48; but they lost in 1995 with a level of 50, in 2002 with a level of 52 and in 2007 with a level of 55. And this is only the level of social preferences.

Yet there is a link and thus a relationship between longitudinal preference indexes and elections, but it is a very specific one. Firstly, what matters is not the absolute value of these indexes but the way they have evolved since the last handover of power, in other words the size of the increase or decrease of social and/or cultural demands since a particular majority was in place. Above all, we can only understand the success or defeat of the Left and Right by taking into account the fact that voting patterns have changed in France. To test the proposition that policy moods matter, we now present three variants of a 'moods' model: the social (Model 1), the social and cultural (Model 2) and the social and progressively social and cultural (Model 3) (see Table 11.2). These models were tested using data from the two major elections in French political life since 1981: the presidential (P) and the legislative (L) elections. In order to consolidate our findings, we added the regional elections (R) from 1992. The models were tested using logistic regression analysis, the dependent variable being the success of the Left.

We tested the capacity of the indexes to predict a victory for the Left, according to three different variants which reflect different ways of understanding what determines the choice between the Left and the

Table 11.2   *Moods and elections: three explanatory models*

Characteristics of the model	Model 1 (social only)	Model 2 (social and cultural)	Model 3 (social and progressively social and cultural)
Correct predictions	1981PL, 1986L, 1988PL, 1992R, 1993L, 1997L, 1998R, 2002PL, 2004R, 2010R	1986L, 1988PL, 1992R, 1993L, 1998R, 2002PL, 2004R, 2010R	1981PL, 1986L, 1988PL, 1992R, 1993L, 1995P, 1998R, 2002PL, 2004R, 2007PL, 2010R
False predictions	1995P, 2007PL	1981PL, 1995P, 1997L, 2007PL	1997L
Probability of a victory for the Left in 2012	0.98	1.00	1.00

Note: P = presidential election ; L = legislative election; R = regional election.

Right. The first model postulates that the Left and Right are only differentiated along social and economic lines, in other words the 'old politics' that dominated in the 1970s and 1980s and which still dominated in the 2000s when voters had to choose between only the Left and the Right. The second model postulates that electoral failure or victory is both the result of evolutions in social *and* cultural preferences. In other words, a vote for Mitterrand rather than Giscard d'Estaing or for Royal rather than Sarkozy was as much to do with classical issues such as wealth redistribution as 'new politics' issues such as the death penalty or immigration.

Model 1 indeed allows us to explain all the changes of power between 1981 and 2002, but it fails to explain 2007. In other words, we could consider that the election of Sarkozy was an election that ran 'against the tide', because he was able to play against the social demands of public opinion structures. Alternatively, social demands may have weighed less in this election than cultural demands, as other researchers have suggested (Schweisguth, 2007; Tiberj, 2008). Model 2 tests the hypothesis that the cultural is as important as the social in determining the choice between the Left and the Right. In fact, this model allows us to predict certain victories for the Left and the Right; but not only does it again fail to explain the 2007 election, but it also fails to explain the legislative election of 1997 and especially Mitterrand's election in 1981.

Model 3 appears to offer a solution, differing from the others in two main ways. Firstly, it postulates the progressive introduction of cultural preferences into voting strategies (not playing a role until the 1990s, and then progressively becoming important). Secondly, even at its high point towards 2010, cultural preferences remain secondary to the variations of the social index. These specifications seem to reflect better the evolutions of French politics overall, including the election of Sarkozy in 2007. The only notable error in prediction concerns the legislative elections of 1997. This seems to be only explained by the social-only model, most likely proof that at the end of the 1990s the cultural dimension was not yet fully established as part of voting strategy. On the other hand, after 2000 it had clearly become a deciding factor in whether to vote for the Left or Right.

The moods also tell a story about how French voters have evolved since the 1970s. Firstly, the world has changed, but the French are still very attached (or as attached as before) to a strong state that is able to cope with social inequalities. In this respect, the discrepancy between the French public mindset and the possibility of such a state in the globalized economy is getting wider. This can explain the Eurocritical discourse which advocates a different EU. Secondly, tolerance has never been so strong in France as today which contrasts markedly with the way that immigration and multiculturalism are addressed in contemporary French politics. Politicians such as Sarkozy, or more recently Jean-François Copé, the former UMP General Secretary, have courted controversy by raising societal issues relating to French identity and the ostensible threat posed by the Islamization of the country. During the UMP leadership campaign of November 2012, for example, Copé claimed that children had had their chocolate breads snatched from them during the Ramadan period. By raising such emotive issues, the UMP is targeting the conservative hardcore of the electorate. Our findings suggest that this hardcore is losing ground, however, and that the difference between a hardcore conservative electorate and the rest of the population is getting bigger. This is obvious regarding the debate about gay marriage, one of the chief cultural policies promoted by the Hollande administration; only the Catholic organizations are in opposition, while a large majority of the French support this measure.

Conclusion

The approach adopted in this chapter thus places developments in French politics in a new context. The fate of governments is not totally dependent on the economy and the unemployment rate. Otherwise, Lionel Jospin would have won in 2002, and Ségolène Royal in 2007. The mood as an instrument allows us to understand better the impact of public policy on the evolution of public opinion over time, but it also opens new avenues for research. For example, how can we explain the reactive nature of voters to public policy, given that we know that they generally do not follow political news on a daily basis? One key question needs to be answered in relation to the Hollande presidency: will the French adjust their preferences in reaction to the policies of the new administration, as they did with the various governments since the 1980s? If so, we would expect there to be a move towards a decline in both indexes, which would constitute a move towards less tolerance and less state. This question presupposes that the Hollande/Ayrault team will enact a different economic policy from that of Sarkozy; given the nature of the responses to the economic crisis during the first six months (the 2012 austerity budget, or the competitiveness pact of November 2012 in particular), such a prognosis would be hazardous. On the other hand, the liberal stance adopted by the Left on societal issues (on gay marriage, for example) might well provoke a temporary downturn in the cultural index. This new constellation of an economically responsible, culturally permissive Left charts unknown territories for the evolving policy mood.

Chapter 12

France in Crisis? Economic and Welfare Policy Reform

TIMOTHY B. SMITH

The riots and protests that took place in late 2005 in and around France's public housing estates caused many French people to rethink the merits of their social model. The nation that gave birth to the ideal of 'solidarity' was exposed as a troubled place: racially segregated, rife with job discrimination and racked by high levels of chronic, long-term unemployment. As in a few other European nations, including Italy, Spain and Greece, for 20 years those under the age of 30 had suffered high unemployment, low wages, delayed access to career-path jobs, delayed marriages, low home ownership rates, as well as poor chances of becoming as wealthy as their parents. Many second and third- generation French citizens were still called 'immigrants' by their compatriots and in 2010 over 50 per cent of them said they had been the victims of racial discrimination (Brinbaum, 2010). France's unemployment rate had hovered around 10 per cent since the 1980s, sometimes reaching 12 per cent, sometimes dipping to 8 per cent. France has not seen full employment since the early 1970s. The country's social and economic problems were shared by a handful of other rich European nations, but in no other was the gap between political ideals and social realities so pronounced.

Politically speaking, the key beneficiary of the 2005 riots was Nicolas Sarkozy. In the midst of the collective soul-searching that followed, he launched a sustained critique of the French social model, calling for a 'rupture' with past practices. He was elected in 2007 to reform that model. In this chapter I seek to explain why he had limited success. Sarkozy was able to convince a certain portion of those who voted for him (he won 53 per cent of the vote) of the *idea* of reform; but a significant portion of the public resisted when they learned the details. At no point in his mandate did a majority of labour union leaders give their support.

Sarkozy implemented some bold reforms. But in the key areas under examination in this chapter, his proposals were generally more timid than his election platform suggested they would be, and they were usually watered down during negotiations. By 2012, there was no 'rupture' with past practice, except perhaps in two areas which did not figure at the centre of Sarkozy's electoral mandate: foreign policy and policy towards the universities.

In 1980, the French enjoyed the world's eighth highest per capita GDP. By January 2008, before the economic crisis had hit, the country had fallen to nineteenth position. New wealth was not translated into net private sector job creation. During the 1980s and 1990s, the public sector witnessed annual job growth rates of 3.0 per cent (the second highest rate in a group of 18 major European, North American and Asian OECD nations) but the private sector experienced growth of just 0.8 per cent – the second lowest rate (Pontusson, 2006, p. 85). The national debt almost tripled from 1980 to 2007. By the late 2000s, France spent 57 per cent of its GDP versus an OECD average of 43 per cent (Attali, 2008, p. 15). But high spending had not led to a stable polity, a harmonious labour force or a generally content population. Levels of trust in politicians (just 30 per cent) and in other citizens were at historic lows. Pessimism and unhappiness were at recorded highs, and higher than in almost every other rich nation (*The Guardian*, 25 March 2011). With the average bout of unemployment lasting 14 months, there was much to fear (Cahuc and Zylberberg, 2009).

Most people believed that their children would be poorer than themselves. Instead of creating the conditions for bipartisan reform, the opposite happened, as people clung tenaciously to their *'acquis'* (their 'social rights'). A large portion of the French signalled to Sarkozy to scale back his reforms. He did. This was understandable: despite the strong job protections for full-time workers, chronic unemployment meant that half of all workers feared losing their jobs. Three-quarters of the population feared falling victim to *déclassement* (downward social mobility). To many people 'reform' seemed to point in the direction of rising inequality in the American or British style, hence the remedy seemed worse than the problem. Yet major reforms of pensions, taxes, labour market policy and the civil service had also taken place since the 1980s and 1990s in the Netherlands, Sweden, Denmark, Finland, Germany and Canada.

Amidst all this malaise and misery, many people had never had it so good. Life was bad for millions of people, but for many more France was and is, for the time being, one of the best places in the world in which to live. According to Pontusson's study of 18 rich nations, employment protection for existing workers was strongest in France (Pontusson, 2006, p. 120). Since 1980, social spending growth has also been among the highest in the rich world: in 1980, France spent 21.1 per cent of GDP on things social, and by 2001 it was 27.2 per cent, as against Sweden's 27.5 per cent in 2001. Less than 7 per cent of

France's social spending was means-tested, or targeted at the poor. The lion's share went to the gainfully employed, to the middle class, to the wealthy. A middle-class welfare state garnered strong middle-class support. Millions of workers were seeing their monthly income supplemented by state programmes to the tune of hundreds of euros, or even more. Why fix what was, for them, not broken?

Here was one problem for the unemployed, and here was a key obstacle to reform. Most social spending went to middle-class 'insiders' (full-time workers, retirees), significantly improving their standard of living. To the majority of citizens, change seemed like more of a threat than a promise of a new day. Roughly two-thirds of the adult population was either employed with ironclad job security and generous social benefits, or retired. During the 2000s, retirees were 10 to 15 per cent *richer* than the workers funding their pay-as-you-go pensions, and retirees were also wealthier in relation to their rich country counterparts (Peillon, 2010a). But with one of the world's costliest welfare states, 15 million people were struggling every month to pay the bills (Chrisafis, 2012a).

Those who called for a realignment of spending with resources, a matching of wage increases with productivity increases, a reshuffling of resources away from insiders towards the poor, an alignment of retirement ages with other rich nations, or a loosening of labour laws in the direction of Germany or Scandinavia, were often denounced as enemies of the French social model, enemies of French 'civilization'. The welfare state figured at the core of the national identity, the last rampart to defend the nation from globalization. As long as France was deemed 'too big to fail' by the bond rating agencies, and as long as France was able to continue to borrow at very low rates (unlike Greece, Italy and Spain, who fell like dominoes between 2008 and 2011 in the face of foreign bond rating agencies and bond buyers alike), the country could continue to avoid the day of reckoning with its economic model. Whoever won the election in 2007 would have to convince the 'insiders' and the 'veto players' (unions, lobby groups) that in calling for change their intentions were good, in the long-term interests of all French citizens. This was a tall order, to say the least.

And yet, there had been a glimmer of hope from late 2005, when the riots jolted the nation, until 2008 when the US bubble economy burst and the idea of reform was dealt a severe blow, guilty by association with the US model. Prior to 2008, critics received a degree of attention unthinkable a few years earlier; Nicolas Sarkozy found an audience receptive to his reform agenda as he campaigned for the presidency. He charged that the public sector was inefficient and overstaffed; he would set that right with a policy of attrition. (In the end he would eliminate just 150,000 public sector jobs in a nation with almost 5 million such jobs.) The 'special pension regimes' in the public sector, with their low contribution rates and early retirement ages, would be brought in line with the general public system. The retirement age must rise to reflect demographic reality. Taxes must fall below 50 per cent. Sarkozy argued that France was in the grips of 'corporatist' bodies like labour unions, occupation-based interest groups and certain sections of the civil service. The idea of 'work' had been devalued; Sarkozy promised to 'rehabilitate' it. He observed before the start of the global economic crisis that:

> Reforming our famous social system will certainly be one of the hardest taboos to break. But let's hope we're able to do so before it collapses like a house of cards ... Since 1984, a generation ago, the unemployment rate has hovered around 10 percent. This is not an inevitability linked to the European economy – many of our European partners have returned to full employment. The best social model is one that creates jobs for everyone, and this is obviously not ours, since our unemployment level is twice as high as that of our main partners. (Sarkozy, 2007d, pp. 82, 83–4)

Millions of people seemed to agree. Sarkozy was given a clear mandate to reform France. By 2012, however, there were one million more unemployed than in 2007 and over 350,000 manufacturing jobs had been lost. The national debt had increased by €600 billion, rising from 64 to 85 per cent of GDP. The Court of Accounts (national audit office) concluded that one-fifth of this massive sum, or €120 billion, was unrelated to Sarkozy's measures to address the financial crisis (Chrisafis, 2012b). Payroll taxes had increased from 43.4 per cent of GDP to over 44 per cent by 2012, among the highest in the world, added on top of relatively high wage costs to begin with. Some 600,000 additional people were below the low-income line of 60 per cent of median income (€964 per month), bringing the total to 8.6 million people. About 4.5 million people lived in official poverty, on less than €781 per month. The low-income rate of the unemployed was 36.4 per cent. The increase in child poverty accounted for over two-thirds of the total increase in poverty since 2007. The poverty rate of children was twice as high as that of retirees and it was approaching North American levels (Burricand et al., 2012).

Clearly Sarkozy did not deliver what he promised. What went wrong? Were his personal failings and fall in popularity to blame? Was the general public's opposition to reform, once they saw the details, the key? Did vested interests put up too strong an opposition? Was reform rendered unlikely by the global financial crisis? These are questions that cannot be answered with any precision, but surely all four factors came into play to varying degrees. Through a discussion of some key dossiers, such as the reform of the 35-hour law, pension reform, the promise to boost purchasing power, and the introduction of the active solidarity income (*revenu de solidarité active* – RSA), I argue that there was no obvious 'rupture' with past practices.

Many believe that Sarkozy switched course in response to the global economic crisis. His speeches would support such a view. He declared in late 2008 that the crisis had 're-legitimized the French model' – the very model against which he had campaigned. When he told the French Parliament 'the crisis has put the French model back in fashion' (*The Economist*, 2009) how much did he undercut his authority when he negotiated future reforms? Despite this rhetoric, there was no U-turn (Szarka, 2009). Half-measures emerged from negotiations with the 'social partners' as one-quarter measures. Because Sarkozy attempted so many reforms, he was prone to compromise and to lose focus on what was crucial and what could be bargained away (Le Boucher, 2011). Existing laws were *modified* with additional laws, resulting in additional costs and red tape (*Le Point*, 2010). And there was always the American counter-model to hold up in order to justify inaction on the most sensitive files (Meunier, 2010). The implosion of the American way of bubble and debt-fuelled capitalism should not necessarily have relegitimized the French model, but it did. People who had never been keen on reform had their doubts vindicated. The man who denounced the big state in 2007 embraced it in 2008.

Since the 1980s, France has lacked a universal discourse stressing common goals. Instead of rallying the population in the face of new challenges, politicians have stressed the things that divide the French, from class politics (the Left) to the politics of immigration (the Right). Instead of presenting globalization as a challenge to harness, politicians across the political spectrum have presented it as a threat to be 'mastered', or for which the French are owed 'protection', which is to say they have promised what they cannot deliver (Hall, 2006). This 'protection' came at quite a cost: France was spending 57 per cent of GDP as against an OECD average of 43 per cent in 2011 (Jarreau, 2012).

The politics of over-promise: labour law

To see just how ineffective French labour law was in 'protecting' people, consider that, in any given year, between 20 to 25 per cent of any given rich nation's workforce will change jobs. They will leave on their own accord in search of greener pastures, or they will be fired for cause (incompetence, failure to show up to work or malfeasance), or they will be 'downsized' in the name of 'efficiency' (profits) or to avert bankruptcy. In Canada, the USA, the UK, Denmark and Sweden, this 'churn' of the labour force is spread across age groups and occupational categories. In a two-track labour market such as exists in France (and in Italy, Greece and Spain), most job losses are suffered by the young and by those without a full-time position. During the 2000s, every workday saw roughly 30,000 French workers change jobs. Roughly 6,000 left voluntarily and 4,000 retired each day. Only 2 per cent (in a nation of 61 million) were 'downsized' in the name of averting bankruptcy (Cahuc and Zylberberg, 2004, p. 133). Over 15,000 people were terminated at the end of their short-term contract every day. The rest, or about 4,000, were fired for cause or were placed on disability leave or died.

Large-scale layoffs are subjected to unusually high levels of government scrutiny. High profile cases (like Michelin, Danone, Lipton, Peugeot and Marks & Spencer) attract the attention of the Ministry of Labour, which in turn might refuse to accept layoffs, or, more commonly, it will review and delay them. This ritual serves not to protect workers' job security but rather to erode it. The politicization and bureaucratization of layoffs results in fewer full-time jobs being created in the first place. Instead of firing workers to cut costs after the 2008 economic crisis, companies stopped hiring. People on short-term contracts were not renewed. New temporary contracts fell by 20 per cent; these positions constitute almost three-quarters of job offers in France (OECD, 2011). The 'adjustment' was indeed happening, on a large scale, and it was borne by the least protected members of society.

Employment policy under Sarkozy consisted of spending an extra €13 billion per year on various 'exonerations' of payroll taxes and on tax breaks for 'overtime' work. For years, companies had complained that the biggest obstacle to hiring was the Labour Code (Code du Travail), a 3,200-page tome that decrees everything from job classifications to the ability to dismiss workers. Sarkozy, like all presidents since the 1960s, added to the Code's complexity. In any given year, 20 to 25 per cent of job dismissals are contested in the labour courts. It can take six months to adjudicate these cases, at considerable cost to companies. The high cost of firing and the uncertainty regarding future legislative restrictions leads most firms to avoid hiring full-time workers (Kramarz and Michaud, 2004).

The Fraser Institute, a conservative Canadian think tank, publishes a widely cited survey of 'economic freedom' around the world. The 2011 survey (for 2009) concluded that Canada was the fifth most business and employment-friendly nation in the world. The UK was ranked 8, the USA was 10 and Finland was 11. Denmark was ranked 15, Germany 21, but France was 42, down from 24 in 1980. Spain came in at 54 and Italy at 70. France's labour market regulations were ranked 88 in the world and its overall 'regulation' score was 71. Denmark's business regulation score was 6 (Sweden's was 14, France's 46). A certain portion of France's unemployment is explained by these statistics. Changing this situation would have required taking a leap of faith and creating uncertainty for French workers and aspiring workers in the midst of a global economic crisis. Small wonder Sarkozy's plans to thoroughly overhaul labour law were shelved. Had France undergone a swift reversal of fortune which demonstrated the obvious domestic roots of the crisis (like the Dutch in the 1980s or the Swedes and Canadians in the early 1990s) then the solutions might have been more visible. But the *global* nature of the 2008 crisis served, in some intangible way, to render the home-grown nature of France's problems less visible. Didn't the whole mess start in the USA anyway?

This type of reasoning ignored the well-documented, long-standing rigidities of France's job market. Sarkozy had argued in his political memoirs published before the 2007 election that 'labour market reform is critical' to boost employment (Sarkozy, 2007d, p. xi). But the licensing and zoning restrictions in the retail sector that slowed job growth and led to high prices for basic consumer goods and groceries in 2007 remained in 2012. French youth had been shut out of good jobs for a quarter of a century. A rigid labour market, in which companies have the upper hand and can be extraordinarily choosy, allows them to offer most new jobs in the form of temporary contracts. The labour market is a buyer's market: in 1993 just 8 per cent of French workers earned the minimum wage but by 2004 16 per cent did. Educational 'credentials' became more and more crucial to success, further marginalizing those who did not possess them. This, in turn, is partially related to low social mobility levels. French parents determine the success or failure of their children to a greater extent than in most rich nations. In 2007, roughly 41 per cent of the relative difference in parental earnings was transmitted to children, as against 15 to 19 per cent in Australia, Denmark, Finland, Norway and Canada, and compared with 27 to 31 per cent in Sweden, Germany and Spain. The figures for Italy, the UK and the USA were between 48 and 50 per cent (OECD, 2008, pp. 205–6).

No effort was made to recruit significant numbers of students from disadvantaged homes or districts to university. Only 15 per cent of the general university student body hailed from the working class; in some of the elite *grandes écoles*, it was under 5 per cent. In the wake of the 2005 riots, journalists and social scientists exposed the endemic racism that exists in France at the hiring line. The French are very protective of their privacy in most matters, but they accept the custom that job applicants submit a photograph with their CV, which enables firms to eliminate visible minorities from consideration. Youth unemployment in several urban districts, where visible minorities live in disproportionate numbers, can reach 25 to 50 per cent. Initially Sarkozy went to unprecedented lengths to recruit visible minorities to his government. He tried to sell the idea of affirmative action in a nation that generally views it as a threat to republican unity, to the equality of individuals.

His first cabinet was the most diverse in French history, but by 2012 all of his ministers hailing from African or Middle Eastern immigrant families had resigned or been fired. His Janus-faced attitude and policies towards immigration and racial discrimination makes an examination vexing – one never knew which side of Sarkozy would present itself.

In any case, the public's concern with racial discrimination and the economic exclusion of visible minorities was short-lived. By 2007, the wages of those already employed took precedence over the lack of wages of millions of people. By the end of President Sarkozy's term in office, France had 10 per cent unemployment and the euro area's second-highest unit cost of labour after Belgium, according to an April 2012 Eurostat report. France was only the twelfth richest nation in Europe, yet pay levels did not reflect this: the average hourly wage figure of €34.20 ($42) compared unfavourably with Germany's €30.10, Italy's €26.80 and Spain's €20.60. According to the Bank of France, between 2000 and 2012, French wages per unit of labour rose by 20 per cent in relation to Germany (*Los Angeles Times*, 2012). France's exports suffered a 3 per cent drop in market share between 2000 and 2007, setting the nation apart from other eurozone nations, which traded with the same currency (OECD, 2009, p. 8).

'Je veux être le Président du pouvoir d'achat' [I want to be the president of purchasing power]

These trends were visible in 2007. It was a mistake, then, for Sarkozy to promise to boost the average French worker's purchasing power. He was vilified as a right-wing ideologue, but he was always firmly rooted in the French interventionist tradition. He bailed out struggling corporations as a minister during the Chirac presidency. As president he took the lead of the G-20 in denouncing 'Anglo-Saxon' financial capitalism and in proposing an international tax on financial transactions. He presided over a 4.9 per cent increase in social spending in 2009 in an effort to boost purchasing power (Libération, 2010). His promises regarding wages and purchasing power stemmed from his statist instincts.

Scarcely 14 months after the riots of unemployed youth of November–December 2005, the presidential candidate made a remarkably open-ended promise, one he had no power to deliver. The French could only 'work more to earn more' if all other things remained equal: housing, food and fuel prices, the inflation rate, interest rates, the bargaining position of workers in the labour market, the state of the global economy and so on. There were too many variables beyond his control; only a weak grasp of economics (and a firm grasp of electoral politics) can explain Sarkozy's promise. If incomes were stagnating in the run-up to the 2007 election, it was because *they should have*, because they had outstripped productivity growth rates. As the Nobel laureate Edmund Phelps noted, 'in Italy and France, productivity growth virtually stopped around 1998, without wealth slowing as much'. 'If France had its own currency,' wrote Phelps, 'it could devalue and suffer the resulting loss of wealth, as imports, oil and many consumer goods would rise in price. Lacking this option, France has had no choice but to suffer from wage stagnation in recent years, as labour costs become better aligned with productivity rates' (Phelps, 2012).

These trends were no secret to officials in 2006–07; Sarkozy's injunction to 'work more to earn more' therefore seems misguided. He promised that a higher standard of living was within reach before the end of his five-year mandate. The unemployment rate could fall to 5 per cent in five years. No other leader of a rich nation made such bold promises; no other leader believed he or she could boost disposable income (except through broad tax cuts, which were never considered). 'Working longer' really meant 'working as much as we used to work, before the 35-hour law'. Sarkozy's promise to boost purchasing power came back to haunt him in 2012; voters did not forget it. The politicization of wages has increased expectations and demands on the state, which has in turn eroded trust in politicians and helped to sever the link between wage policy and productivity levels in the minds of many French people.

Another crucial error concerned taxes: many people saw their payroll taxes rise a bit and everyone saw the sales tax rise between 2007 and 2012, but Sarkozy began his mandate by giving substantial tax breaks to the wealthy. Did Lillian Bettencourt, the richest woman in France, need a tax cut of €30 million? Sarkozy did a partial back step and reversed some of the more egregiously pro-wealthy tax cuts, but the political damage was done. How could he ask the unemployed to accept a job that a few years earlier they would have been free to refuse by citing a skill mismatch? How could he ask people to work longer before their retirement when he seemed to offer gifts to the wealthy?

Sarkozy's promise to boost purchasing power put the spotlight on the travails of the middle class, or those who *already had jobs*. The unemployed faded to a faint blip on the political radar screen. The downward mobility of middle-class youth was an important problem, but in the context of a labour market hostile to under-privileged youth from the suburban housing estates, the public discourse seemed tipped in favour of the children of 'insiders'.

This leads us to the question of what the public wanted in voting for Nicolas Sarkozy. Was the public willing to accept a more dynamic labour market that would spread the risk of job loss around the table but create more jobs as well, including jobs for under-employed middle-class youth? No. Did the French signal that they would in future work as much as the average citizen of the average rich nation, and retire at the same age? Absolutely not. To what extent, then, were French politicians held back from introducing reforms by the public's fear that their '*acquis*' were in jeopardy? Opinion polls in 2010 revealed that between half and two-thirds of French people accepted that pension reform was necessary but that two-thirds to three-quarters of the population was opposed to Sarkozy's reform that called for retirement at age 62.

The end of retirement at 60

Sarkozy began the reform of the welfare state with the special pension regimes in the public sector. It was a symbolic move, intended to show that he meant business. Some 500,000 workers at EDF-GDF, SNCF, RATP and various others were involved (there were also 1.1 million retirees benefitting from these special pension funds). The special regimes were portrayed as the epitome of corporatist excess, with some people retiring in their early fifties on a full pension, worth 85 per cent of their salary during their final six months of employment, thanks to taxpayer subsidies.

Between the idea of reform and the reality of union resistance, fell the shadow of May '68 and November–December 1995, when the country was brought to a standstill by strikes. The transit systems of Paris and other large cities were shut down for a dozen days. But this time was different, with just 150,000 to 300,000 people participating in Paris, and with two-thirds of the French in favour of Sarkozy's reform (*Le Monde*, 2010). With a strong mandate for reform, Sarkozy agreed to a murky deal that, on the surface, seemed to align the special regimes with the general public one, requiring 40 years of contributions instead of 37.5 by 2016 (Glad, 2010).

The government refused to provide an accounting of the cost savings, requested by fellow UMP deputies. It fell to an individual UMP Senator, Dominique Leclerc, to determine that after 2020 all savings from this reform would evaporate and thenceforth would constitute a drain on state finances (ibid.). Fathers who had had three children were allowed to retire early; various bonuses and credits related to seniority were used for the same purpose. To his critics on the right, what counted for Sarkozy was the *appearance* of change. He could claim victory – the beneficiaries of the special regimes would, after all, have to work longer before receiving their pension. Except they didn't all have to do so, and they were rewarded with financial bonuses to sweeten the deal, negating the savings that might have accrued from the requirement to work 2.5 additional years.

With this reform and a law mandating a minimum level of service in the public sector in the event of strikes under his belt, Sarkozy turned in 2010 to what he called 'the mother of all reforms', the general pension system for private sector workers. As one UMP parliamentarian admitted to the *Financial Times* three years into Sarkozy's mandate: 'he was elected to do reforms but they have not been done. He has three to four months to do something that will restore his credibility' (Hollinger, 2010). In 2009 there were just 1.43 contributors to every 1.0 pensioner in the general regime; during the 1960s, the ratio of contributors to pensioners was four times higher. The typical person who lived to age 60 in the year 2010 could expect to live another 24 years, on one of the world's most generous pensions (Sénat, 2010, pp. 38–9). The typical Frenchman retired in 2010 at the age of 58.7; the OECD average was 63.5. The annual deficit of the main regime was €32 billion and rising (Lichfield, 2010). The overall state deficit in 2010 was projected to be around 8 per cent. Even with these figures at his disposal, Sarkozy could not garner public support.

Sarkozy made an effort to negotiate with union leaders but, seeing no hope of compromise, he imposed his reform against their will. The unions' publications and public statements indicate that they were never going to get on board. Bernard Thibault, the leader of the CGT union, argued that Sarkozy aimed to please the 'private militias' of the 'bond rating agencies' (Lhaïk, 2010). The Socialist Party (PS) printed 10 million copies of a pamphlet distributed to the public explaining its opposition. The PS charged that the retirement age was being raised out of 'ideology' (Guiral, 2010). This episode was a sad commentary on the public's awareness of an issue that had been dealt with in pragmatic fashion in most other rich nations, where recent reforms had pushed or would eventually push ages for full pensions up to 67 from 65 (as in Germany, Denmark, the USA and Canada) and even to 68 (in Ireland and Britain).

Some 73 per cent of left voters wished to maintain retirement at 60 and some 42 per cent of right voters did too (Peillon, 2010b). Up to 3 million people marched in the streets in protest at an 'unjust' reform, to which Eric Woerth, the Labour Minister, retorted: 'leaving deficits to future generations is unjust'. Woerth presented the reform as a pragmatic *demographic* response to a *demographic* problem (Huret, 2010a). Sarkozy felt compelled to heed the Left's proposal to add a small surtax on the 500,000 top incomes and on financial wealth to help pay for the reform. Was the raising of the retirement age to 62 an important step? Sarkozy's supporters would argue that this was no small feat in light of the strong institutional and political opposition. In any case, had the age been pushed to 63, it would have raised just *one half* of the funds needed to achieve solvency by 2030 (Hollinger, 2010; Auguste, 2010).

The 35-hour working week (RTT)

> When you destroy thousands of jobs with this ridiculously inflex-
> ible policy of a thirty-five hour workweek, and when you prevent
> France's modernization by refusing to see the world as it is ... you
> can at least take responsibility for what you have done. (Sarkozy,
> 2007d, p. 59)

Nicolas Sarkozy campaigned against the Socialists' landmark 35-hour
law. He retained it once in power. The new TEPA law (*travail, emploi,
pouvoir d'achat*) was intended to 'rehabilitate' the value of work, to
revive the economy. But it did so by subsidizing what millions of
people had done before for no extra benefit. The law allowed individuals to work four extra hours per week (the 36–39 hours) tax-free.
Surely if work were a value worthy of rehabilitation, the state had no
business subsidizing 'overtime' in a nation which already worked less
than most of its competitors? Unsurprisingly, the amount of *claimed*
overtime work increased by 10 per cent (Landré, 2010). The number
of hours *actually worked* in France did not increase commensurately.
Claims for 'overtime' rose substantially 'among professionals, managers, technicians', but not among low-income workers. The price to
the treasury was between €4 and 5 billion per year. President Hollande
eliminated these tax breaks in 2012.

The 'reforms' to the 35-hour law resulted essentially in a few million
people working the same amount of time in order to earn more. In one
critic's view, the message was: 'you will work more in order to earn
more right away, here and now. Everyone must and will find an immediate gain from reform. Who will pay for this miracle? The state, of
course' (Peyrelevade, 2008, p. 122). The message ought to have been:
we must return to the 39-hour working week if we wish to regain our
former standard of living.

Supporters of the 35-hour law were inclined to point to France's
high per capita, per hour-worked, productivity rate during the 1990s.
In the 2000s, however, the country's productivity was falling and its
chief competitors were working 100 to 300 additional hours per
person per year, so it was, without acknowledging it, producing less
wealth. If France measured its success in relation to other rich
nations – and it did – then it would become poorer. Economic growth
from 2000 to 2007 was just 1.7 per cent per year, too low to sustain
the costs of the 35-hour week. What did it matter if the official
French productivity rate was equal to or 5 to 10 per cent higher than
its chief competitors, when the French worked 5 to 20 per cent fewer
hours per person than its competitors? If France had higher state
spending levels than its competitors (the nation spent 57 per cent of
GDP versus the 43 per cent OECD average), and if France had higher

debt levels and higher taxes (again, France did) then a smaller pie of private wealth was being asked to fund a growing list of public wants.

The precise costs of the transition from an official 39-hour work week to a 35-hour week will never be known, but all other things being equal, it should have led to an 11 per cent increase in the cost of salaried labour. In practice, it did so in some firms, though not in others, as many employers used the law to justify the slowing down of wage growth. Millions of labour-hours were lost in the firm-specific negotiations required to transition to the new order. Labour relations were in tumult. Business confidence dropped. Some workers paid by the hour in low-wage sectors saw a direct decline in take-home pay. Employer–employee relations were poisoned as high expectations foundered on the shoals of fiscal reality. In many sectors the pace of work sped up, even as people worked fewer hours. The key beneficiaries were salaried professionals, paid by the month, not by the hour. Indeed, France's relatively low level of part-time work masked the degree to which full-time employees worked less than their counterparts in the rich world. Just 14 per cent of the workforce was considered part-time in 2011 versus 25 per cent in Germany and Britain and 37 per cent in the Netherlands (OECD, 2012).

Finally, France's unusually low employment rate exaggerates its productivity rate, since the unemployed are, disproportionately, the least skilled and least productive. If this group worked at the same rate as their American counterparts, France's productivity rate would have been roughly 7 per cent inferior to the American (Cette, 2004). French statistics would suffer a similar downgrade in any comparison with Germany or Canada.

The Revenu de Solidarité Active (RSA)

There were a few bright spots. The value of the monthly disability allowance for the handicapped was increased substantially, a reform for which Sarkozy's opponents had little positive to say. A portion of the working poor benefitted from the Active Solidarity Income (Revenu de Solidarité Active – RSA), which replaced the Minimum Income (Revenu Minimum d'Insertion – RMI) and the allocation to single parents. Sarkozy presented the RMI as a welfare trap. Only a third of those on it had ever been registered job-seekers at unemployment offices. This reform seemed rooted in pragmatism: it was inspired by the British Labour Party's measures to 'make work pay'.

The RSA went into full swing in 2009. It was provided to 1.8 million people in 2010. Recipients were now required to look for work or to enrol in a training programme. Roughly 30 per cent of the RSA's recipients were employed, as it was a top-up for low pay. For the rest, the RSA was very much like the old RMI: a social minimum of the last resort. The RSA amounted to €475 per month for a single person without work; €418 if such a recipient lived in public housing. The benefits rose to over €850 to €980 for those with two children and were calibrated to ensure that those taking up work would be better off financially than had they remained on welfare. It was financed by a new tax on financial profits (*Le Monde*, 2009c). The programme cost just €1.5 billion in 2010. Two-thirds of those eligible for the RSA's top-up component for the low-paid did not claim it.

The RSA's creator, Martin Hirsch, never intended the programme to reduce the overall poverty rate by more than one-tenth (Hirsch, 2008). It proved very popular with many beneficiaries (Huret, 2010b). But it was a limited success: these measures reached fewer than two million people. Its overall impact on the labour market has been neutral: there has been no net creation of jobs, no increase in the participation rate of the low-skilled. This is because the labour market itself was not reformed. The underlying assumption behind the RSA was that people could be coaxed into employment because jobs were available. But where were those on welfare to go if there were not more service sector jobs on offer?

France's welfare state was more or less the same in 2012 as it had been in 2007. It was a case of *rupture manquée*. Given the dire economic situation of the world economy, given Sarkozy's wish to be re-elected, and given the fact that France had not yet hit rock bottom and had not been put on probation by those who hold the nation's growing debt, this is understandable.

The 2012 election

With the exception of the centrist François Bayrou, the presidential candidates failed to be frank about the coming challenges. The PS promised to bring back retirement at 60 for those who started work at the age of 18, and it honoured this promise in 2012. No candidate proposed further reforms to the pension system. Four candidates proposed substantial hikes to the minimum wage; President Hollande raised it by 2 per cent, or 0.6 per cent above the inflation rate (Carnegy, 2012).

Six candidates, including the four major ones, were in favour of protectionist measures. All candidates except Sarkozy were in favour of higher taxes on the rich. The focus on the obligations of the rich served to absolve the average citizen of responsibility for France's finances. No candidate proposed a significant reform of labour law. The PS had its generational contracts (*contrats de génération*) designed to create and/or protect 500,000 jobs for youth and older workers, but no plan to boost private sector job creation.

At the time of writing, President Hollande is going ahead with his promise to raise taxes to 75 per cent on incomes above €1 million per year. New taxes on finance, dividends and inherited wealth were introduced during the summer of 2012. Hollande said in 2012, 'does anyone really believe that liberalism, privatisation, deregulation which led us to where we are today in the financial crisis will help us get out of this crisis?' (ibid.). This was deflecting from the main issue. France was in crisis before the USA sent the world into a global recession. It was shoddy regulation of the mortgage and banking industries as well as an asset bubble fuelled by low interest rates that created the crisis. The deregulation of labour markets was not responsible. France has been in deficit since 1974. Countries like Canada, Denmark and Sweden, which were in budget surplus or very close to it in 2008, and which had already reformed their labour markets and pensions, had ample wiggle room to engage in deficit spending when the crash occurred in 2008.

On page 3 of his election manifesto, Hollande put the blame for France's problems solely on the shoulders of Nicolas Sarkozy and 'finance'. The truth was that France was living beyond its means. Greece, Ireland and Spain were reducing the minimum wage and several other social benefits. These reforms were no cause to jump for joy, but they were rooted in a desire to realign spending with actual levels of wealth. In 2012, several nations were increasing the age of eligibility for pensions, but not France. Over the past 20 years Germany cut its overall pension costs but France's had risen by 2.5 points of GDP. Three-quarters of the revenues needed to balance the French budget were to come from tax increases on businesses and a small slice of the population. It is difficult to see how this will prepare the general public for the more significant reforms that must surely come. All the evidence we have suggests that in tough times, cutting spending is less damaging to growth than raising taxes.

It was unclear how Hollande might honour his promise to balance the budget by 2017. In late October 2012 he admitted that France had a 'competitiveness problem' but he made no mention of this during the election. By November, his approval rating had dropped to 36 per cent.

Gerhard Schroeder, the Social Democratic author of Germany's job-generating (and inequality-generating) labour market reforms, questioned Hollande's credibility when he told a Paris audience: 'the election promises of the French president are going to shatter on the walls of economic reality'. Schroeder was referring to the return to retirement at age 60 for those who began work young, the raising of the minimum wage and the lack of attention to competitiveness. He went on: 'reality will catch up with our French friends' (Leparmentier, 2012). Schroeder presided over a loosening of the German labour market, rendering low-wage, part-time 'mini-jobs' possible. He also tacitly supported a business sector campaign to suppress wage growth in the name of job retention and creation. Whereas Schroeder and his successor Merkel lowered business taxes, Hollande initially raised them.

In 2012 business confidence dropped by 22 points. The capital gains tax was now 62 per cent versus 28 and 26 percent in Britain and Germany, respectively. As during the early 1980s, France seemed to be going against the grain, operating as if the general rules of its competitors did not matter. Hollande embraced a mild form of austerity (planning to balance the budget over five years) but not labour market reform.

Hollande could procrastinate during 2012 because France was seen as 'too big to fail'. But perceptions change, and markets are not rational. Italy and Spain were once seen as too big to fail; now the bond raters have them in the sights of their guns and these nations are also under the gaze of the IMF and the EU and are under pressure to reform.

Conclusion

In conclusion, this chapter has demonstrated that there is no consensus in favour of reform in France, unlike the Netherlands during the 1980s, Sweden and Canada during the 1990s, or Germany during the early 2000s. For thirty years, France has been paralysed by its pursuit of perfection, looking in vain for a pain-free path to reform. Even when the political will has been strong, the voices of opposition to reform have been even stronger. President Hollande faces his own specific dilemmas in this respect. The Socialist President raised taxes on the rich in the early months of his presidential term, but then adopted a competitiveness pact designed to lower costs on business. The inconsistencies of the first nine months raise a number of legitimate questions. Is Hollande stuck in the early 1980s, determined to soak the rich and direct industry? Or is he poised to become France's great reformer? His early symbolic measures in favour of more social justice might be interpreted as providing the political cover he needs in order to ask the average person, not just the rich, to pay higher taxes, to accept freer labour markets, and to expect reduced services. Perhaps this had been his intention, all along.

Contested Citizenship in France: The Republican Politics of Identity and Integration

PATRICK SIMON

The 2012 French presidential campaign, which ended with the election of a Socialist president in May, put immigration – once again – at the heart of debate and societal choices. While the politicization of immigration issues did not begin in the 2000s, the sequence of events opened by the appointment of Nicolas Sarkozy in 2002 as interior minister in the Raffarin government made immigration a core issue before it was eclipsed – for only a few months – by the impact of the financial and subsequent economic crisis that hit Europe. Even more than his predecessors, Sarkozy addressed immigration in its three increasingly intermingled aspects: the management of migration flows; the processes of integration; and the fight against discrimination and the promotion of diversity. Indeed, he went so far as to make it one of the *core identity themes* of his political discourse. In this field, as in others, Sarkozy took a proactive stance that sought to break with earlier policies. However, this did not prevent a string of reversals and failures to meet the stated goals.

The creation of the Ministry for Immigration, Integration, National Identity, and Supportive Development in 2007 and the unexpected launch of a 'national conversation on national identity' in December 2009 constituted a major revision of – if not a challenge to – the 'grand bargain' (Hollifield, 1994) that had shaped immigration and integration policies since the late 1980s, transcending changes in political majorities. That bargain consisted in restricting immigration flows in exchange for opening French society to diversity. The will to reassert the pre-eminent role of national identity in fostering social cohesion marked a toughening of the 'immigrants' duty' clause in the 'republican contract' and the instrumentalization of national identity for exclusionary purposes (Noiriel, 2007). The debate on national identity thus gave prominence to the question of loyalty, which weighs constantly on immigrants and their descendants. While the debate did not lead to spectacular reforms of nationality law, it was a further step in the nationalist reaction that tends to converge towards the 'closed, xenophobic, and even racist nationalism' (Taguieff, 1995, p. 14). National identity is indeed a Janus-like concept that generates cohesion by incorporating individuals through citizenship, while at the same time excluding other individuals by creating and reproducing hierarchies among members of the *polis*. The main divide between citizens and non-citizens is seconded by the hierarchical statuses based on gender, ethnicity and race. The 'Sarkozy period' is characterized by a racialization of immigration policies and social issues, which Bancel (2011) describes as a 'nationalist retraction'.

In this chapter I revisit the developments in French immigration and integration policies of the past decade, placing them in the longer history of the construction of the integration model. I assess the legacy of the Sarkozy period (2002–12) in the fields of immigration, integration and national belongings.

Immigration policies: discourses and reversals

Immigration was the first area in which Nicolas Sarkozy implemented his break-with-the-past policy. On his appointment as interior minister in 2002, he introduced a series of laws to reform entry and residence conditions for foreigners, while adopting a policy that linked immigration and integration in a clearly coercive spirit. But when we screen out the bills passed and the administrative, legal and police practices, can we truly characterize the immigration policies since 2002 as a departure from the past? Judging from the controversies and clashes triggered by these policies, there seems little doubt that the republican consensus over immigration management was transgressed. Yet it is hard to separate the real changes introduced by the four laws voted in over eight years from the hyper-proactive and aggressive communication tone adopted by Sarkozy as well as his successors at the Interior Ministry. In this field, the impact of announcements is as significant as concrete achievements. Beyond the dissuasive effects on would-be immigrants, the rhetoric of the hard stick against immigration is targeting public opinion. So leaving aside the rhetorical effects, we can try to evaluate how successful the new immigration policy was in meeting its own goals.

First, the laws. Rather than a break with the past, Danièle Lochak coins the suggestive image of a dreadful path-dependency to describe the common inspiration behind the laws enacted since 1974 (Lochak, 2011). The replacement of the *ordonnance* of 1945 by the The Asylum and Foreign Residency Code (Code d'Entrée et de Séjour des Étrangers et des Demandeurs d'Asile – CESEDA) in March 2005 can serve as the marker for the policy switch towards a mainly coercive management of immigration flows (Slama, 2006). This entailed an unprecedented administrative integration of services involved in immigration management under the authority of the Ministry for Immigration, Integration, National Identity and Supportive Development: visa delivery, naturalization, asylum and integration policy. In addition, prerogatives were transferred from the judiciary to administrative authorities (particularly for decisions regarding illegal residence and expulsion procedures) and powers previously held by central government were devolved to prefects.

The four immigration laws passed in 2002–12 do not, strictly speaking, represent a decisive break with the previous legal-political framework. They did entail the following changes: a longer waiting period for obtaining residence permits; their replacement by 'long-stay visas'; broader use of short-term permits to be renewed several times before issuance of a permanent permit; and more complicated conditions for family reunification and entry of French nationals' spouses. However, this tightening should be viewed as a significant narrowing of opportunities for migrating to France, not as a radical change of course. In a sense, the red line was not crossed – but not for lack of trying.

The first significant turning point came with the new framing of the *immigration choisie* (chosen immigration). By stressing the need to open the doors to highly skilled migrants, the 2003 Immigration Act marked a departure from the zero-immigration model theorized by Charles Pasqua, then interior minister, in 1993. The concept gained strength with the second 'Sarkozy Act' in 2006 which 'creates new legal instruments to regulate better immigration, combat misuse of procedures, and promote chosen immigration and successful integration'. The *immigration choisie* cannot be understood without its corollary of *immigration subie* (unwanted immigration), which designates the forms of immigration, mostly of family members, blamed for the integration difficulties encountered by immigrants to France.

Labour immigration was thus officially reopened for the first time since 1974. The government published a list of occupations facing labour shortages, for which the hiring of foreign workers was not only authorized but desirable. In 2007, the new immigration minister, Brice Hortefeux, announced the government's goal of raising labour immigration from 10 to 50 per cent of total annual flows. The easing of conditions for residence permits to highly skilled migrants was supposed to boost the economically motivated share of immigration, while the additional constraints on family reunification and spouses of French nationals would reduce the proportion of 'undesirable' immigration. Five years later, this policy has clearly failed. Between 2006 and 2010, economic immigration rose from 6 to 9 per cent of entries, whereas family immigration declined modestly from 54 to 44 per cent. Ultimately, the inertia of immigration flows underscores the limits of the political management of immigration, already identified since their inception in 1946–50 (Tapinos, 1975). In this field, nothing has ever turned out the way the authorities had expected.

Indeed, the tools for achieving a qualitative transformation of immigration seem ineffective. An estimate done by the Mazeaud Commission (2008) indicated that only 5 per cent of annual inflows could be controlled 'at the government's discretion'. An explanation of the government's relative powerlessness to enforce its policy orientations resides in the legal supervision of the Constitutional Council and the Council of State (Hollifield, 1994) and the EU directives that frame the immigration policies of member states. The EU has adopted several directives to (1) establish a common legal framework defining conditions for migrants' entry and residence, and (2) promote a coordination of national policies and harmonize the governance of migration flows. The directives concern an action plan against illegal migration (2002), a 'return' directive (2008) and a 'European blue card' directive (2009). A further step in this harmonization process was the signing of the European Pact on Immigration and Asylum in 2008 (Guiraudon, 2010). This dual framework – domestic and external – forces national immigration policies to respect immigrants' basic rights and avoids crossing the red line into state racism.

The many restrictions on family migration delay immigrants' plans to live together as a family, but cannot permanently stop such plans from being fulfilled. Family migration is no longer an induced migration as in the 1970s and 1980s. Family reunification does persist, but it is declining and has been largely replaced by the arrival of family members of French nationals, mainly their spouses. The number of marriages of French nationals abroad reached 47,000 in 2010 and is expected to stay at that level because of the globalization of marriage markets. A decrease in family migration seems unlikely to happen in the short term.

The government contemplated introducing 'restrictive migration quotas' based on migrants' skills and/or nationality. The notion in itself is not new and echoes the point system implemented in Germany or Canada, even though the criteria of nationality has not been explicitly mentioned by any other immigration countries for a long time. The resurgence of ethnic selection challenges the 'republican synthesis' (Weil, 2008a). This attempt to control immigration failed as well. When asked for its opinion, the Constitutional Council confirmed that annual quotas on immigrants would be unconstitutional. The Mazeaud commission set up to challenge this opinion concluded that quotas are 'unachievable and worthless' – a verdict that closed the case.

Having failed to enact quotas, the government set quantitative targets for the number of deportations of undocumented migrants. Expulsions rose to nearly 30,000 in 2008, including almost 10,000 'voluntary returns' of Romanian and Bulgarian citizens. This highly controversial 'quantitative' policy relied on a limitation of foreigners' right of appeal, an increase in the capacity of detention centres in the number of expedited procedures condemned by human-rights and immigrant-defence NGOs. The gains achieved in carrying out procedures did not, however, reduce the social visibility of undocumented migrants (Martinez, 2011).

If immigration policy has failed to alter significantly the composition of migration flows, has it at least impacted on their intensity? Although still very imperfect, migration statistics show that the suspension enacted in 1974 led to a steep drop in entries from 130,000 that year to 80,000 in 1975. Entries of foreigners then settled at around 60,000 until the early 1980s, bottoming out at roughly 40,000 after the 1982 regularizations. The number started to rise again in the early 1990s to over 100,000 before levelling off at slightly over 200,000 in 2002–05, then easing to around 190,000 after 2006. In the years in which the four successive immigration laws were enacted, the variations were weak and incommensurate with the degree of political publicity over the issue. In fact, these swings seem largely due to economic conditions, international geopolitical dynamics and the inertia generated by the composition and intensity of earlier flows.

If the voluntarism showed during Nicolas Sarkozy's presidency did not substantially alter the intensity and composition of migration flows, the living conditions of immigrants – whether legal or illegal – were heavily affected by the tightening of controls and the erosion of their legal status. The *immigration choisie* was soon thwarted by the economic crisis, which shut the door that had been timidly opened, and the concurrent stigmatization campaign against immigrants suspected of resisting integration. Despite studies showing the net positive contribution of immigration not only to the economy but also to the welfare accounts (Monso, 2008; Chojnicki and Ragot, 2011), the image of immigrants as a burden on French society has come to prevail.

Failures of the French integration model

The linkage between new immigration and the integration of immigrants already settled in France began in the late 1980s but gained momentum in the 2000s. Previously, the connection had been one of the rhetorical arguments to justify closing the borders – i.e. restricting entries to secure the residence of immigrants already in France. The key argument was that the continuous inflow of new immigrants – the 'invasion', as former President Valéry Giscard d'Estaing put it – triggers xenophobic and racist reactions, and worsens the status of existing immigrants. While one of the most widespread clichés on immigration, it has never been demonstrated. In the 2000s, what was essentially rhetoric has turned into the new immigration Acts.

The 2003 Act required immigrants to demonstrate their 'republican integration' in order to be granted their right of residence. This perceptible shift was confirmed by the 2006 and 2007 Acts. Integration was no longer a goal to be reached in one or more generations, but a prerequisite for obtaining a residence permit (with minimal but explicit criteria). A 'reception and integration contract', which became compulsory in 2006, is signed when the first residence permit is issued. It includes a commitment to abide by the laws and values of the Republic, a civic-education training day and a language test. In this context, the integration criteria proved to act as an indirect method for selecting on the basis of ethnic origin, since these criteria tend to favour – on a cultural basis – certain profiles of immigrants deemed easier to assimilate than others. Moreover, the assessment of the civic and linguistic skills of applicants largely relies on the subjectivity of consular staff or (in France) *préfecture* officials.

The integration framing has thus opened a large space of subjective and discretionary practices (Lochak, 2006). It assumes that immigration applicants have already adjusted or can be adjusted to the destination society, and that they possess sufficient financial and cognitive resources to settle without placing an additional burden on the country. The imposition of 'civic integration' criteria not only for naturalization applicants, but also for immigrants applying for residence in several European countries (the Netherlands, the United Kingdom, Germany and France), signals a coercive reaction to the deep changes triggered by cultural diversity (Joppke, 2007; Goodman, 2010).

The insistence on the immigrants' acceptance of the norms and values of the destination society is not, strictly speaking, a novelty in France, whose model is essentially assimilationist (Simon and Sala-Pala, 2009). Although the term 'national model' is strongly criticized in comparative studies (Bertossi, 2009), we can make the case that France's 'republican' approach to integration is far more assimilationist than that of the United Kingdom or, until recently, the Netherlands. Even if integration policies have been increasingly Europeanized with the Tampere Summit in 1999, the Basic Common Principles for Immigrant Integration Policy in 2004 and the Common Agenda for Integration of 2005, national idiosyncrasies do persist. What does 'assimilationist' mean in the French context? The High Council for Integration (HCI) has formalized the official definition of integration:

Integration consists in fostering the active participation, in the society as a whole, of all women and men who will be living permanently on our soil, by accepting without ulterior motives the persistence of specificities, particularly of a cultural nature, but emphasizing the similarities and convergences in the equality of rights and duties, in order to ensure the cohesion of our social fabric ... It postulates the participation of differences in a common project and not, like assimilation, their elimination, or on the contrary, as with inclusion [French: *insertion*], the guarantee that will ensure their long-term survival. (HCI, 1993)

The HCI has remained deliberately vague about the balance between the rights and duties of 'women and men who will be living permanently on our soil', and especially about the changes needed in French society to accommodate newcomers and the degree of tolerance for the public expression of differences. The means to achieve integration are described as: proficiency in French; the dispersion of the immigrant population across residential areas; the gradual weakening of community ties and their replacement by an individualized relationship with the state; and, above all, the acquisition of French nationality in two generations. According to this vision, once they have become French, immigrants and – even more so – their children born in France will no longer stand apart as distinct elements in society. In exchange, they will obtain equal access to all spheres of social life.

The discourse underlying integration policy rests on an ambivalent vision of the ever more visible signs of the multicultural character of French society. The concrete signs of belonging to ethno-cultural or religious minorities in the public arena are rapidly stigmatized as an expression of 'communitarianism' and such minorities receive injunctions to return to the collective norm. Concentrations of ethnic minorities in deprived neighbourhoods –portrayed as ethnic ghettos – are interpreted not only as the consequence of segregation processes, but also as a threat to national cohesion. The 'ghetto' is treated as a source of 'identitarian closure'. This vision feeds on fantasies of 'parallel societies' – as in the United Kingdom and Germany – where dominant social and cultural norms, as well as the language and religious practices, tend to be those of the designated group: immigrants, or sub-Saharan Africans and North Africans, or Muslims, as the case may be.

Yet such visibility is the outcome of a lasting change in the composition of the large urban metropolitan areas, which have become more ethnically diverse than ever. The resumption of immigration flows in the second half of the 1990s and the transition to adulthood of the second generation of immigrants who arrived in the 1960s and 1970s translate into an unprecedented demographic presence of groups of immigrant origin. Over two generations, persons of immigrant origin accounted for an average 25 per cent of the total population in metropolitan France (including Corsica), but for up to 56 per cent in the Paris region and 75 per cent in the Seine-Saint-Denis *département* just north and east of Paris. Their visibility is accentuated by the deep shift in immigrant geographical background. Until 1975, Europeans formed the majority of the immigrant stock: 63 per cent were European, versus 27 per cent North and sub-Saharan African. Over the past ten years, the overwhelming majority of newcomers have arrived from North and sub-Saharan Africa and Asia. In 2008, 42 per cent of immigrants residing in France were born in an African country and 10 per cent in an Asian country. In 2010, 54 per cent of foreigners admitted as residents came from Africa and 25 per cent from Asia. These trends are reproduced, with lags, in the second generation. In 2008, the second generation was still mainly of European origin among adults, but mostly of North and sub-Saharan African origin among the under-18s. The demographic data merely hint at what a basic observer in large urban centres – and especially their suburbs – would feel immediately: cities and neighbourhoods are organized and stratified around ethno-racial and religious diversity.

The 'immigrants' referred to in the debates over integration are thus largely of North and sub-Saharan African origin, more rarely of Asian or Turkish origin. They stem from a 'post-colonial' immigration that is not only more visible but vulnerable to longer-lasting discriminations than those once directed at European immigrants (Simon, 2010). Their visibility challenges the main purpose of the integration model which is to assimilate outsiders into the national body politic by making them similar. The pivotal notion of the model is that institutions of integration – foremost among them, the school system – ensure the convergence of minority groups towards the majority population, into which they will ultimately melt and dissolve. The persistence of minority practices is tolerated, but only as a residue expected to fade away. The framework of the integration model is then clearly averse to the need for more plasticity being required for multicultural societies. The constant revision of norms and values that constitutes the core process of adjustment between minorities and the majority calls for an update of national identity. But the republican consensus that emerged in the 1990s has in fact reasserted the supremacy of the majority over minorities. While emphasizing the reciprocity of exchanges, it organizes and justifies the immutability of national identity. By promoting uniformity against diversity, the republican model of integration is organizing the clash of norms and thus the subordination of minorities to the majority.

Among the various aspects that crystallize tensions around the definition of norms, Islam and its expressions have come to the forefront. Conflict over the role of Islam has underpinned the legislation on the headscarf (1989, 2004) and the burka (2009–10); the street prayers denounced by Marine Le Pen of the FN (December 2010) and debated by the then majority party, the UMP (May 2011); halal slaughter and the availability of halal food in school canteens (March 2012); adjustments to working hours to meet religious obligations; the financing of mosques; the reservation of time slots at swimming pools for Muslim (or Jewish) women. The media response to the survey coordinated by G. Kepel in Clichy-sous-Bois and Montfermeil (two cities in the Seine-Saint-Denis *département*) for the Institut Montaigne is symptomatic in this respect (Kepel et al., 2011). Conducted in 2010–11, the local monograph published in 2011 shows how social and institutional life develops in a deprived and immigrant neighbourhood. Most media commentary focused on the section of the report devoted to Islam's role in the structuring of the social bond. Coming as a revelation, the role played by religious-based community groups and networks was interpreted not as the mundane and expected reflection of the population composition in the neighbourhoods studied, but as the sign of a failure of the integration model. As the title of the weekly *Le Point* on 1 November 2012 put it – 'L'islam sans gêne' ('Uninhibited Islam') – the issue of accommodation is perceived as excessive and ultimately *unreasonable*.

National identity and dual nationality: tilting at windmills

A final recurrent theme in the poisoned debates on immigration is the questioning of nationality law. Since the late nineteenth century, the nationality code has combined the right of birthplace (*jus soli*) and right of blood (*jus sanguinis*) by guaranteeing the automatic acquisition of nationality after reaching the age of majority for children of foreigners born in France. A foreigner can also acquire nationality through marriage or naturalization. These provisions have been regularly challenged, and after an initial failure in 1986, a reform of the nationality code was eventually enacted in 1993 when the Right recaptured a parliamentary majority. The key concept behind the attacks against the nationality code is that citizenship should reflect and foster national sentiment. However, just as minorities are accused of not abiding by the rules of integration, French citizens of first or second-generation immigrant origin are also suspected of having a flawed national identity and of lacking loyalty to their homeland. They have been described as 'French on paper' (*des Français de papier*) by the FN – an expression taken up by a section of the mainstream conservative parties. Alternatively, they have been called the 'involuntary French' (*Français malgré eux*), a status deplored by the advocates of the 1993 reform, which introduced the need to 'demonstrate a voluntary choice' for young people born in France to foreign parents as a substitute for their automatic acquisition of French nationality on coming of age.

These doubts on the national sentiment of French people of immigrant origin were fed by various incidents, notably the trauma caused by the jeering of the French national anthem (and not the Algerian anthem) during the friendly France–Algeria soccer game in Marseille on 6 October 2001 (Gastaut, 2008). The event is still referred to today, so much so that it is mentioned in the introduction to the report submitted in June 2011 by the Parliamentary Information Mission on Nationality Law, chaired by Manuel Valls (the current minister of the interior). The suspicions about the authenticity of national sentiment among French citizens of immigrant origin are directed at descendants of North and sub-Saharan Africans and almost never at descendants of European or Asian immigrants. This focus reveals a racialization of national identity that disrupts the traditional construct based on legally defined citizenship.

In autumn 2010 and spring 2011, an exacerbated nationalist reaction prompted the FN and members of Parliament of the 'popular Right' ('*droite populaire*'; an authoritarian faction close to the far right-wing of the UMP) to challenge the right to dual nationality. A bill was introduced to abolish dual nationality on the grounds that it generated (or reflected) a deterioration of national sentiment and threatened national cohesion. Beyond the issue of national sentiment, it was argued that a choice was needed in regard to voting rights. The bill was eventually rejected in Parliament, but the attacks against the nationality code – deemed too loose – were extended by a tightening of naturalization procedures in February 2012.

The crystallization of controversies on the nationality code needs to be understood in the context of the historical formation of the French nation state. Countries that have adopted multiculturalism more or less officially (Canada, the United States, Australia, the United Kingdom) promote multiple national and/or ethnic identities as positive signs of a diverse heritage. By contrast, assimilationist countries tend to promote exclusive choices and to regard the preservation of an ethnic identity as the sign of incomplete assimilation. Public assertions of a 'hyphenated identity' combining references to a foreign culture or country and France are perceived negatively. This hostility against hyphenation reveals a vision of identities as a 'finite stock'. In other words, the feeling of belonging to a country should automatically result in a correlative weakness of the feeling of being French and thus a lack of stickiness of the national identity. This assumption is contradicted by the reality of multiple identities that individuals express by combining citizenships, belongings and ethnicities according to the contexts.

For evidence of this we can turn to the findings of the Trajectories and Origins (TeO) Survey, which was conducted by INED (Institut National d'Études Démographiques) and INSEE (Institut National de la Statistique et des Études Économiques) in 2008–09 on a sample of 22,000 immigrants, children of immigrants and persons whose families have been French for two generations (Beauchemin et al., 2010). First, the range of citizenships varies across generations of migration and countries of origin. As we know, acquisition of French nationality is almost automatic for children of immigrants born in France, and 95 per cent of them are effectively French. The same is true of 28 per cent of immigrants who arrived as adults and 59 per cent of those who arrived as children ('generation 1.5' in the rest of this chapter). It is observed that there are major variations by country of origin, reflecting the time span of migration flows, the age of arrival in France and the role of nationality in the relationships with the country of origin. The naturalization procedure itself adds a filter to the process. Despite its 'openness', access to nationality is regulated by several selections including an 'assimilation report' prepared by a *préfecture* official.

The document comprises three parts: (1) details on migration, training and occupational status (age at migration, educational attainment and current employment); (2) proficiency in French; and (3) 'inclusion in the French community'. The third part records details on participation in local life and the applicant's links with the country of origin. The official must assess whether the applicant 'seems to have assimilated our practices and customs'. The philosophy of this procedure and its practical implementation have been well analysed by Hajjat (2012).

These criteria are informed by a culturalist approach that does not match the vision of the political bond that (so it is argued) forms the basis of French citizenship. The decoding of the underlying criteria implemented in the naturalization procedure and citizenship induction ceremonies shows that the political context and social debates strongly influence the content assigned to citizenship and thus steer decision-making (Fassin and Mazzouz, 2007). The pressure exerted by the context of the debate on national identity and the official circulars are aimed at making the procedures more selective. The number of naturalizations fell from 91,000 in 2010 to 66,200 in 2011. This steep drop was due to a spectacular rise in rejections and delays based on language or cultural criteria. These criteria signal the emergence of a selection based on a 'naturalization of naturalization', to coin the expression of Sayad (1993). In other words, the newly naturalized must embody an ideal citizen who has incorporated the history, values, personality and physical attributes of the Frenchman or Frenchwoman. The new French must 'perform the nation'.

The rise of multiple identities and belongings can be seen in the development of bi-nationality among immigrants and second generations. French law allows dual nationality and does not require naturalized foreigners to renounce their former nationality. The same applies to children of foreigners born in France who may keep the nationality of their parents when becoming French. According to the TeO Survey, nearly half of the immigrants who acquire French nationality keep their former nationality. Fewer than 10 per cent of immigrants from

South East Asia are bi-national, but more than two-thirds of North African immigrants, 55 per cent of Turkish immigrants and 43 per cent of Portuguese immigrants combine French nationality with that of their country of origin. The proportions of bi-nationals recorded in the 2008 TeO Survey greatly exceed those observed in 1992 in the Geographic Mobility and Social Integration Survey (Mobilité Géographique et Insertion Sociale – MGIS). The percentage of bi-nationals rose from 7 per cent (1992) to 67 per cent (MGIS) among Algerian immigrants, and from 18 to 43 per cent among Portuguese immigrants (Beauchemin et al., 2010). Without any significant legislative change since 1992, we can only conclude that immigrants' practices in regard to dual nationality have changed considerably. Immigrants' children also preserve a bond with their parents' nationality of origin. Nearly one-third of children of two immigrant parents still declare dual nationality. The proportion drops to 12 per cent for second generations of mixed parentage.

Beyond citizenship, the TeO Survey covers the topic of national sentiment with separate questions on respondents' identification with their country(ies) of origin (or French overseas territory if they are from one of those or are a descendant of their inhabitants). For the second generations, the question is duplicated for each parent and refers to the country(ies) of origin of the immigrant mother and father. National sentiment runs relatively high among the majority population – of whom 98 per cent say they feel French, indicating the absence of a significant crisis of national affiliation. The proportions are comparable for second generations of mixed parentage and are only slightly lower for children of immigrants (89 per cent) and for generation 1.5 (84 per cent). French national sentiment is obviously far less widespread among immigrants (52 per cent), although one does observe a significant affiliation among naturalized citizens (79 per cent). If 21 per cent of immigrants who have become French show no national sentiment, more than half of foreign residents feel French – reaching as many as two-thirds of North African immigrants. If there is a result worth noting here, it is not the lack of affiliation with national identity among immigrants and their children, but – on the contrary – the powerful attraction of that identity.

The complementary side of French national sentiment is affiliation with the country of origin. Routinely described as antithetical in public speeches, these allegiances and feelings of closeness towards several national entities are not necessarily perceived as contradictory by immigrants and their offspring. But to what extent does the commitment to one country erode the commitment to the other, as if in a zero-sum game? In practice, we do observe the persistence of a tie with the country(ies) of origin (or that/those of the parents) across generations for 84 per cent of immigrants who arrived as adults and three-quarters of immigrants' children. However, that is not contradictory with the fact of feeling French. The combination of allegiances increases from the immigrants who arrived as adults (45 per cent describe two feelings of affiliation) to the 1.5 generation (56 per cent) and peaks in the second generation (66 per cent). It then declines sharply among descendants with mixed parentage, of whom 58 per cent report an exclusively French national sentiment. In fact, there is only a moderate correlation between the intensity of national sentiment for France and for the country of origin. The fear of dual loyalty as an obstacle to national cohesion therefore seems largely unfounded.

The TeO Survey results offer scant evidence to substantiate the accusations directed against dual nationals, as FN leader Marine Le Pen wrote in a message to members of Parliament: 'Today, the multiplicity of affiliations with other nations is helping ... to undermine our compatriots' acceptance of a common destiny'. The data, however, show a feeble impact of dual nationality on French national sentiment. Binational immigrants feel just as French as those who have dropped their former nationality (82 per cent in both categories). In contrast, dual nationality is significantly linked with a stronger sentiment of affiliation with the country of origin (one's own country or that of one's parents). In other words, being bi-national is a sign of attachment to one's origins, but is not incompatible with a strong French national identity. The French dilemma thus resides in the respect for, and recognition of, the pluralism of identities rather than a weakness of national sentiment among the newly naturalized.

The mismatch between ethno-cultural origin and citizenship can be assessed through the acceptance of citizens with a 'visible minority background' as 'one of us' by the majority group. A question in the TeO Survey records this acceptance from the standpoint of French citizens with an immigrant background. Respondents were asked to state whether they felt that they were perceived as French or not. Strikingly, while only 3 per cent of members of the majority population give a negative answer, the proportion reaches 36 per cent among respondents from French overseas *départements*, over 50 per cent for immigrants from North Africa and South East Asia, and 65 per cent for immigrants from sub-Saharan Africa. European immigrants are shielded from this a priori exclusion from the national community. Even more significantly, the exclusion from Frenchness persists for the North African, Asian and sub-Saharan African second generations, despite a substantial decline with respect to the experience reported by first-generation immigrants from those regions. These findings tally with the results of the survey by Brouard and Tiberj (2005), who found that citizens of North African, sub-Saharan African and Turkish origin are indeed 'French like the others' in terms of their participation and affiliation, but are not perceived as such.

The legal citizenship of the members of visible minorities does not give them full assimilation to the national community, while European immigrants and their descendants avoid this negative othering. They *are* French, they *feel* French, but they don't *look* French. This gap tells a lot about the current status of the model of integration. The crisis of the model stems from two closely linked trends: first, the social and political visibility of post-colonial immigration, notably the descendants of North African and sub-Saharan immigrants; second, ethno-racial discrimination which target immigrants as French citizens of immigrant origin. Discrimination deeply challenges the integration model and its promises of equality. It contradicts the fiction of a community of citizens united in a shared national identity. In the late 1990s, the consensus view of integration came under challenge when the fight against discrimination was put on the political agenda (Simon, 2009). The implementation of an effective anti-discrimination policy has quickly reached its limits. Today, instead, the contradictions surrounding the tools and equipments to implement a proactive equality policy have eroded the progress achieved. The opposition to 'positive discrimination' (the French equivalent of 'affirmative action') and the refusal to compile ethnic statistics that could be used to monitor equality have shown the difficulty – if not the impossibility – of linking the philosophy of anti-discrimination with that of integration. The French version of 'colour-blindness' deepens the ethno-racial divisions that it claims to circumvent. This French dilemma revives the dark side of national identity, the one that theorizes the unassimilable character of certain origins to justify an ethno-racial hierarchy which regulates access to power and privilege. Will the nationalist one-upmanship initiated by the previous government be halted by the socialist government elected in 2012?

Conclusion

In conclusion, the 'Sarkozy period' was characterized by a racialization of immigration policies and social issues, which Bancel (2011) describes as a 'nationalist retraction'. The creation of the Ministry for Immigration, Integration, National Identity and Supportive Development in 2007 and the unexpected launch of a 'national conversation on national identity' in December 2009 constituted a major revision of – if not a challenge to – the 'grand bargain' (Hollifield, 1994) that had shaped immigration and integration policies since the late 1980s, transcending changes in political majorities. That bargain consisted in restricting immigration flows in exchange for opening French society to diversity. The will to reassert the pre-eminent role of national identity in fostering social cohesion marked a toughening of the 'immigrants' duty' clause in the 'republican contract' and the instrumental-ization of national identity for exclusionary purposes (Noirel, 2007). The debate on national identity thus gave prominence to the question of loyalty, which weighs constantly on immigrants and their descen-dants. While the debate did not lead to spectacular reforms of nation-ality law, it was a further step in the nationalist reaction that tends to converge towards the 'closed, xenophobic, and even racist nationalism' (Taguieff, 1995, p. 14). National identity is indeed a Janus-like concept that generates cohesion by incorporating individuals through citizen-ship, while at the same time excluding other individuals by creating and reproducing hierarchies among members of the polis. The main divide between citizens and non-citizens is seconded by the hierarchical statuses based on gender, ethnicity and race.

The first decisions taken by the new interior minister, Manuel Valls, do not constitute a decisive break: a bill granting foreigners the right to vote in local elections has been postponed if not shelved; the adminis-trative organization for managing immigration, integration and natu-ralization has been preserved; and the demolition of Romany camps and shanty-towns has been vigorously pursued. The main initiative to counteract the previous policy has focused on naturalizations, which are projected to return to their 2009 level of around 100,000 per year. These decisions (or lack of) demonstrate continuity with the Sarkozy period, albeit a slight return to the open version of the nationality code. It testifies that, beyond political shift, the republican model of integration still frames and curtails the expression of ethnic diversity in France.

Chapter 14

France and the European Union

HELEN DRAKE

On the evening of 6 May 2007, in a hoarse voice and to a crowd of youthful supporters chanting 'Nicolas! Nicolas! Nicolas!', the freshly elected President Sarkozy delivered a speech barely 13 minutes long. Half-way through he turned, rhetorically speaking, to address France's European Union (EU) partners with whom, he declared, France's destiny was 'profoundly conjoined'. He reassured these partners that all his life he had been European, that he 'profoundly and sincerely' believed in *la construction européenne* and that '*ce soir, la France est de retour en Europe*': tonight, he pronounced, projecting his persona to imagined audiences well beyond la Salle Gaveau in Paris, 'France is back in Europe'.

Even setting aside the hyperbole characteristic of such a unique occasion, the message was startling: from where was France to return? At one level, the comment referred to former President Jacques Chirac's failure to ratify the EU's Constitutional Treaty (CT) in the referendum he had called on 29 May 2005. That loss had blighted the remainder of Chirac's presidency and damaged France's reputation and, going on Sarkozy's analysis, had created a void in European diplomacy where once France had been centre-stage. Here, as we will see below, Sarkozy swiftly and effectively repaired the harm, as he perceived it, by successfully negotiating and then ratifying the CT's successor, the Lisbon Treaty (LT), as early as January 2008. The comment can also be interpreted more as a nostalgic reference to France's historical record in building up the EU. During those 50 years, Presidents of the Fifth French Republic had become accustomed to leading their European partners by means of tangible influence on policies, structures and strategy; yet the EU enlargements of the post-Cold War era had gradually eroded French claims to lead the continent, and the lost referendum had dealt a serious blow to French claims to leadership. In this respect too, President Sarkozy set out to put France back in the driving seat, and the EU Council Presidency which fell to Paris in the second half of 2008 provided a perfect opportunity to do so. This was an occasion for France to set out its European policy in clear terms and build a dynamic for future action – and the French executive judged its own Council presidency in very positive terms indeed. In particular, those six months were marked by a sudden and precipitous collapse of market confidence in the economies of the USA and most of the EU's member states, and that pervasive sense of economic crisis dominated Sarkozy's European diplomacy for the remainder of his term in office and, during the 2008 French EU Council Presidency (FPEU08), provided a stage for the French president to portray France as the leader of *'une Europe qui protège'* ('a protective Europe').

In this specific context, France's European diplomacy was facing major challenges. The EU was struggling to reach agreement on short-term fixes for the eurozone's most ailing economies; the EU institutions themselves were in a situation dominated by an ongoing race to shore up the eurozone and its weaker member states, especially Greece, from debt default and market attacks; and immigration into the EU, swelled by the turbulence of the Arab Spring, coincided with an ever tightening security discourse in France that increasingly targeted official perceptions of non-Frenchness of various kinds.

By December 2011, just two years after the ratification of the LT France had put its name to what became known as a new 'fiscal compact' for the EU (minus the UK and the Czech Republic): the Treaty on Stability, Coordination and Governance in the Economic and Monetary Union. This agreement potentially represented a step further towards the federal governance of national economic policy. Later I will examine this interplay between, on the one hand, the domestic and EU levels of governance – this 'Europeanization' – whereby France lies somewhere between a 'transnational polity, which means that it operates in a European system of shared governance that is no longer entirely national nor fully federal' (Gueldry, 2001, p. 189), and, on the other hand, the 'realities of nations' and national sovereignty, as professed by Sarkozy. This was a relationship which Sarkozy challenged – as his predecessors had before him – and he entered the 2012 presidential elections with a campaign that explicitly challenged the EU to be more effective in 'protecting' its member states and their peoples. This was a serious contradiction in his discourse on the EU: both expecting it to act as if it were a state in its own right, and preferring 'intergovernmental co-operation [which] has been the theme linking all of Sarkozy's initiatives' (Dimitrakopoulos et al., 2009, p. 451).

Lisbon Mark II: a dynamic of change

In 2008 Hussein Kassim (2008, p. 276) noted that Nicolas Sarkozy, in his first months in office in 2007, had shown 'activism' towards 'Europe's ills', as well as positive engagement 'with France's European partners'. Nowhere was this more evident that in the speed with which Sarkozy set about rectifying the impact of that 'no' vote two years earlier: not for nothing has Cole (2012) dubbed the 2007–12 years the 'fast presidency'. Sarkozy's election in May 2007 coincided with the closing months of the German EU Council Presidency. Progress (on a revised Treaty) under that presidency had been conditional on the outcome of the French presidential election, and newly elected President Sarkozy lost no time in turning to his German counterparts with proposals for a 'reform' treaty to replace the CT (for a fuller discussion, see Drake and Lequesne, 2010).

The CT had itself by and large reflected French priorities, particularly in its institutional provisions for new leadership posts, EU foreign policy and a reduced Commission size, for example, and those gains had themselves emanated from a strong Franco-German tandem at the Convention. Accordingly, the task in 2007 was not to fritter away these advantages, while making overtures to those domestic French constituencies who had rejected what they saw as the CT's overly 'liberal' (or what President Chirac himself called 'Anglo-Saxon') dimensions; these were the Eurosceptics identified by Rozenberg (2011, p. 6) by their 'denunciation of the pro laissez-faire features of European policies and the regret of the lack of *Europe sociale*' – in 2005 they were not all on the political Left. Sarkozy's own analysis of the 2005 'non' was, indeed, that the EU had disappointed in failing to 'protect' workers and citizens, and that it lacked the political will to act in this regard. He also considered that 'the failures of the French and Dutch referendums were in part provoked by a hostility to a Europe without frontiers' (Sarkozy, 2006) – a barely coded reference to the prospect of Turkish EU accession.

The June 2007 European Council summit that brought the German EU Council presidency to a close was a pivotal moment for what would become the LT. Sarkozy himself acknowledged that the victories negotiated there were primarily symbolic in kind, but argued that they had the virtue of opening up debate on difficult issues (Dimitrakopoulos et al., 2009, p. 455). By way of example, the mention, in the CT's Article I-3 on 'The Union's Objectives', that 'the Union shall offer its citizens ... an internal market where competition is free and *undistorted*' (my emphasis) was removed and in its place was inserted the Protocol on the Internal Market and Competition which states that 'the internal market ... includes a system ensuring that *competition is not distorted*'. The Preamble to the LT, additionally, refers to 'balanced trade and fair competition' only. Furthermore, the LT's Protocol on Services of General Interest refers, in its Article 1, to 'the shared values of the Union in respect of *services of general economic interest*', including 'the essential role and the wide discretion of national, regional and local authorities in providing, commissioning and organising services of general economic interest as closely as possible to the needs of the users' (*Official Journal of the European Union*, 2007). What had been Part III of the CT ('The Policies and Functioning of the Union'), moreover, was removed completely from the revised version, excising at a swoop much of the content that had been offensive to the CT's opponents in France.

Thus did Sarkozy allow himself to take credit for the LT on which the member states agreed at the October 2007 European Council summit. His efforts now turned to domestic ratification of the deal. He had been explicit in his election campaign in 2007 that he would seek ratification by parliamentary approval, not referendum, unlike his opponent, Ségolène Royal, and he stuck to this course of action in the face of audible but muted political opposition at home: it was hard for his domestic opponents, divided amongst themselves, to claim that parliamentary ratification was undemocratic, although reversing a decision previously made by referendum is an uncomfortable position for a French president.

Within one year of taking office, therefore, a significant thorn in the side of French–EU relations had been removed, and the opportunity to build on this presented itself in the form of France's six-month 'turn' in the EU Council chair. The first 12 months were not without their warning signs, nonetheless, in particular Sarkozy's 'government's decision to postpone honouring France's commitment under the Stability and Growth Pact to return the budget to equilibrium by 2010' (Dimitrakopoulos et al., 2009, p. 455): unsurprising given the state of French public finances which, in January 2008, had warranted unfavourable comment from the European Commission which called on France (and Italy) to be more 'ambitious' in reducing the size of the public deficit.

France back in the chair? The French EU Council Presidency, June–December 2008

The French EU Council Presidency got off to a somewhat rocky start on 1 July 2008: in June 2008, the Irish electorate rejected the LT in a referendum; and what was to be a flagship initiative of the French Presidency – a Union for the Mediterranean (UPM), officially launched in mid-July in Paris to coincide with the 14 July Bastille Day military parade – met with serious opposition from other member states, principally Germany, as well as from within Sarkozy's own presidency team itself. The result here was that what had originally been intended as a Schuman Plan-type community of states bordering the Mediterranean or with interests there was diluted into no more than an additional dimension of the existing Barcelona process.

The presidency work programme proper, however, indicated three priority areas: to make Europe a model of sustainable development; to make Europe more 'attentive' to the rights, security and aspirations of citizens; and to confirm Europe's role on the international scene (UE2008.fr, 2008). These objectives, clearly, revolved around strengthening the EU's external identity and capacity. In particular, they prioritized the building of a more substantial European Security and Defence Policy (ESDP), the fight against climate change, the quest for energy security, a review of the Common Agricultural Policy (CAP), and further moves towards a common EU policy on immigration and asylum. These were goals that reflected the risks and concerns posed to the EU by its openness to international forces and flows of all kinds; and indeed the motto agreed for FPEU08 before it began was 'a Europe that protects' ('*une Europe qui protège*'), as already mentioned. In the event, further crises erupted to derail potentially the Council Presidency. First, on 7 August 2008, President Mikheil Saakashvili of Georgia ordered the invasion of the separatist region, South Ossetia, triggering an all-out and protracted conflict between the former Soviet state and Moscow, which intervened to support South Ossetia. In mid-August, Sarkozy visited both Moscow and Tbilisi, and at the extraordinary European Council convened on 1 September 2008, the EU's member states pronounced themselves unanimous in their concern for the ramifications of the Georgian conflict and in their condemnation for Russia's unilateral recognition of the independence of South Ossetia and Abkhazia.

Similarly, when faced with the severe crisis of the world's financial markets in early October 2008, President Sarkozy and his diplomatic team led the EU27 into shows of unity despite the scrambling by national capitals for national solutions to failing banks and plummeting markets, and notwithstanding the significant differences between member state positions. Jabko (2011, p. 7) describes, for example, the 'acute tensions that surfaced between [Sarkozy] and the German chancellor on the issue of economic stimulus during France's six-month presidency of the EU in 2008'. A six-week period beginning in early October saw intense activity at numerous EU levels – the European Council, the eurozone and the Presidency – as well as transatlantically, during which the cooperation between the Presidency and Commission was remarkable, particularly given France's history of public disdain for the EU's supranational body.

Franco-British cooperation was also to the fore, despite differing views on market regulations, and was in favour of a new 'Bretton Woods' settlement for global financial trade. These efforts peaked on 15 November 2008 in an international summit of the G20 held in Washington DC on financial markets and the world economy, and which culminated, at the Presidency's concluding summit on 11–12 December, in the approval of the Commission's 'European Economic Recovery Plan' which would cost approximately 1.5 per cent of the EU27's GDP and lay out a 'common framework' for the member states' ongoing responses to international financial instability and its ramifications for national economies and labour markets. These were developments and compromises for which Sarkozy's brinksmanship and energy have to take some credit, although the role that France realistically could play was limited; indeed, argues Jabko (2011, p. 10), 'Germany has been the pivotal player', whereas, he argues, 'France has played a significant role in mediating the dialogue between Germany and other Eurozone member states, but can hardly be described as the agenda-setter': the official rhetoric was overblown.

The EU Council Presidency itself received broadly positive evaluations, in that it stayed the course and achieved results in all of its priority areas, although its critics, inevitably, found its achievements limited: there had been little concrete progress in 'protecting' Europe, it lacked vision and there was a strong overtone of securitization (Jamet, 2008; Terra Nova, 2012). Significantly, it generated a language of success that provided an important dynamic and rationale for French EU policy throughout the remaining years of the Sarkozy Presidency, including its twin Presidency of the G8 and G20 groups of industrialized nations in 2011. In the 2009 European Parliament elections, most notably, the UMP's campaign literature specifically linked the ongoing French pursuit of a 'political Europe' to the achievements of FPEU08; and its slogan – '*quand l'Europe veut, l'Europe peut*' ('when Europe wants to [act], it can [act]') – directly echoed the intent that Sarkozy had declared at the start of the 2008 EU Council Presidency to 'put politics back in Europe' (Sarkozy, 2008a). He had already argued, in his maiden speech to the European Parliament on 13 November 2007, for a 'political' Europe, as opposed to the EU being a 'machine ... for issuing rules, regulations, directives' (Sarkozy, 2007e); and he repeated the message in his rallying speech to the UMP in Nîmes, on 5 May 2009.

On 1 December 2009, the LT finally came into effect and this – alongside FPEU08 itself, and the outcome of the 2009 European Parliament elections, at which the president's party did relatively well, winning 27.8 per cent of the total votes, and 29 of the 72 French seats in the European Parliament – could be tallied as credits to the Sarkozy regime. But again, there were warnings: the year had been marked by considerable domestic unrest around Sarkozy's socio-economic and fiscal policy, and the French economy was both structurally weak and being derailed in its plans to address the situation by the eurozone crisis which deepened and worsened in the following years.

2010–12: conflict, crisis and cooperation

These were years marked by a serious struggle (which is not over yet, at the time of writing in late 2012) to hold the eurozone together, and this necessitated Franco-German cooperation, bilaterally and via a succession of European Council and eurozone group summits, on precisely those subjects where they had the deepest differences, namely, economic governance – specifically regarding the balance of responsibility between the national, EU and global levels of government – and fiscal policy more broadly. Many of the skirmishes did not go France's way, in particular regarding immediate and short-term measures to stem the fall out from the Greek situation. There was also disagreement over the successor to Jean-Claude Trichet at the head of the European Central Bank. In late 2011, the triple-A credit rating of the French economy was put under surveillance by two of the international ratings agencies, undermining French credibility in the rescue talks. Furthermore, the 3–4 November Cannes summit to close the French Presidency of G20 was overshadowed by the surprise decision of the Greek Prime Minister George Papandreou to hold a referendum on the painfully negotiated rescue packages, and, although he was subsequently persuaded to change his mind, it underlined the precariousness of the situation and distracted France's partners from fully praising the French turn in the G20 chair.

On longer term matters of EU economic governance, however, there was, eventually, agreement. In August 2011, for example, 'France and Germany ... set out plans to create the first "true economic government" headed by a single appointed leader as part of a major move to synchronize tax and spending and save the failing eurozone' (*The Guardian*, 2011b). By the end of the year, moreover, France was at the forefront of the negotiations that culminated in the TSCG, signed by 25 of the EU's 27 member states as an intergovernmental pact. This was a significant document that created a 'new legal framework' for eurozone member states which, crucially, was to be integrated into national law 'at constitutional level or equivalent', and offer scope to the Commission and the Court of Justice for oversight and enforcement (European Council, 2012).

How did this affect national sovereignty, Sarkozy was asked? Was it a further transfer of powers? No, he argued:

> we will not delegate our economic sovereignty to others. It will be an exercise in shared sovereignty undertaken by democratically elected governments. By exercising sovereignty with friends, allies and partners, our sovereignty and independence are strengthened [*on conforte sa souveraineté et son indépendance*]. And I may add that not one new domain of competences will be transferred to any supranational authority. (*Le Monde*, 12 December 2011)

French Prime Minister François Fillon took a similar line, calling for 'enlightened patriotism lifted up to the European level' (*Le Monde*, 4 December 2011); and both declarations are reminiscent of the French Constitution, which, in Article 88-1, states that 'the Republic shall participate in the European Union constituted by States which have freely chosen to exercise some of their powers in common by virtue of the Treaty on European Union and of the Treaty on the Functioning of the European Union, as they result from the treaty signed in Lisbon on 13 December, 2007'.

Other developments occurred in this period to test French commitment to its EU engagements, and none were more newsworthy than the ongoing securitization of immigration and integration policy in France, and the clashes that this generated with EU policy on free movement and migrants' rights. Matters came to a head over the summer of 2010. The issue was not so much that, following an attack on a French gendarmerie on 18 July, purportedly carried out by travellers (*gens de voyage*) following the death of a traveller at a police road-block, the authorities accelerated an ongoing programme of destroying illegal encampments and deporting illegal migrants, including EU citizens from Romania and Bulgaria. More serious was that the government was discovered to have specifically targetted an ethnic group – Romanians – for deportation, contrary to EU law, and that President Sarkozy himself, in a now infamous speech on 30 July 2011, linked not only travellers, but also gypsies, and even French citizens of foreign origin, to the criminal behaviour that he had long fought (or constructed) since his role as interior minister in the early to mid-2000s. The evidence of discrimination (in the form of a government circular) took the French government into direct confrontation with the European Commission which threatened France with legal action and provoked the European Parliament into voting a resolution which urged France to suspend its deportations. Ultimately, in October 2011, the European Commission decided against referring France to the Court of Justice and the French government revised its instructions on the clearing of gypsy camps to bring it back into line with its EU commitments in this regard.

But France showed itself to be similarly cavalier – or clumsy – regarding its EU commitments with regard to the rules of the Schengen passport-free zone in the face of the humanitarian crisis caused by refugees fleeing the upheavals of the Arab Spring in Tunisia and then Libya. Here, France argued that it should have the right to suspend its participation in the Schengen zone in such emergency situations, as it saw them. Brady (2012, pp. 1, 2) has pointed out that this 'scepticism of the Schengen project goes right back to its inception in 1995', since 'the French feel trapped inside a club in which they claim higher standards than others while having little faith that fellow members can be kept even to the minimalist rules to which they have signed up'. Indeed, in 2011, France argued that border controls should be re-established within Schengen under a third condition: 'large-scale illegal immigration' (ibid.); and the Commission has, subsequently, overseen such discussions at the EU level.

Thus, in both eurozone politics and the matter of immigration, the tensions between France's EU commitments on the one hand, and its domestic margin of manoeuvre on the other hand, were brought into stark relief as it became evident as to just how open France and its neighbours were to global forces and movements, which laid bare contradictions in the French discourse on Europe. By way of additional example, and as we saw above, a key objective of the French 2008 EU Council Presidency had been to strengthen the EU's common provisions for foreign and security policy; yet the military support lent to Libyan rebel fighters in early 2011 turned not only on a Franco-British 'island of cooperation', rather than a collective EU response (Valasek, 2012), but it also necessitated the (rather more grudging) acceptance of a NATO umbrella – Sarkozy having overseen France's 'return' to NATO's integrated command in April 2009, against vocal but institutionally powerless domestic opposition (see Chapter 16). Gérard Longuet, French defence minister at the time of the Libyan operation, recounted how much he had 'suffered', as a politician who counted himself as 'very European', to acknowledge that Germany had not been willing to join the operation (*Libération*, 26 March 2011) and that the result was to have 'buried' French dreams of *l'Europe-puissance*: Europe as a military actor in its own right. It is also the case that France had unilaterally recognized the Libyan National Transitional Council rather than seek an EU-level position on the situation.

The Europeanization of the Fifth French Republic: the end of an era?

By the end of 2011, the 2012 election campaigns were underway in all but name, and this shaped much of Sarkozy's policy towards Europe in the closing months of his first term. On 11 March 2012, Sarkozy delivered a speech that emphatically marked his transition from president to candidate and, in due course, to former President Sarkozy. The campaign slogan was unequivocal: *la France forte* (a strong France). The setting was a vast hangar-type conference centre at Villepinte outside Paris. The cast comprised a front row of family members, assorted celebrities (including actor Gérard Dépardieu), a line of rather soberly suited government ministers and former politicians (such as Édouard Balladur), and an allegedly 70,000-strong, full hall of flag-waving supporters. The president was just as hoarse as in May 2007, and the sheer size of the venue itself – combined with the scale of the event, the tricolour light show and the bright, white dais on which the president-candidate stood, alone – only served to accentuate his small physical stature. Perhaps this was intentional, since he began the speech with references to the weight of the responsibilities that he had had to shoulder during his presidential term.

His speech, in heroic style, was unmistakeably Gaullist in its cadences and expressions ('*Aidez-moi!*'), although, alongside *le Général*, he invoked Robert Schuman and Jean Monnet, the Fourth Republic architects of today's EU, and cast shame on those politicians in France who had voted against the LT. He also portrayed himself, as in 2007, as a life-long supporter of European integration, now disappointed by a Europe on the brink of failing to respond adequately to its ongoing crises. In a lengthy passage halfway through the speech, he issued a challenge to the EU itself, which in the light of what we have discussed above should not have come as much of a surprise: either the EU became more effective at policy-making within the coming year or France would suspend its participation in core EU policies, specifically the Schengen zone and the EU's common competition (*libre échange*) policy.

His threats, if carried through, would ostensibly have wiped out much of his legacy – and image – as chief builder of *la construction européenne* for the previous five years. But these were rhetorical flourishes, designed of course to rally his party supporters, and also purpose-written for the media to broadcast to France's EU partners and to the EU's global competitors in a context in which: the EU *did* have a problem in securing its external borders with regard to all of its four freedoms, and especially the 'freedom' of people to migrate away from trouble spots towards the relative safety of the EU's member states; the ongoing eurozone crisis *had* exposed the gaps in EU-level governance of the single currency; the EU *was* struggling to maintain global market share in many sectors in the face of emerging countries and regions, at the risk of damaging private companies and public services alike.

Sarkozy had not so much transgressed in this speech, as converted complex governance issues into populist promises of a France that would ensure that Europe protected its peoples by taking 'political' decisions and not abdicating responsibility to technocratic bodies: a Gaullist language par excellence. Far from seeking to wipe out his and France's legacy as protagonists of *la construction européenne*, Sarkozy sought to convey the idea that he had been and still was responsible for salvaging Europe's future ('We had to save the euro and save France'; 'If France doesn't take these decisions, nothing happens. And if nothing happens, Europe loses its place in the world. Let's give Europe back control over its future, and France control of its destiny'; 'Help me!,' he pleaded, 'to build a strong France that is battling to change the world, to change Europe.')

For Sarkozy, the future of France and Europe was both 'more Europe' – and more nation state 'reality'. Was this simply a restatement of the 'traditional tension between European ambitions and national objectives' (Dimitrakopoulos et al., 2009, p. 452) or something genuinely bolder, particularly given the commitments contained in the EU's new 'fiscal compact'? From one perspective, these pronouncements could be read as an attempt to revive Charles de Gaulle's 1960s 'Fouchet' plans for a 'European Union of States' that would have framed highly developed transnational cooperation on defence, foreign affairs, culture and the economy, with diminished supranational institutions, and would have included only those member states prepared to go the extra mile – so without the UK, then as now, for example. In 2012, the institutional vision was arguably bolder still – a permanent, *Strasbourg-based* secretariat for the Eurogroup, and a eurozone parliament-type chamber – and, unlike the 1960s, support for such a move from France's EU partners was likely to be more forthcoming: only two (the UK and the Czech Republic) had not signed the fiscal compact.

At the same time, such a direction would not automatically equate to a federal future, in which the Commission president, for example, would be elected by universal suffrage, giving the EU executive 'direct democratic legitimacy' (Ferrand, 2009, p. 33), as has been suggested by Germany on several occasions in the past 25 years. France has come close to taking federal leaps in the past to try to create a 'political' Union to accompany European Monetary Union, such as in 1954, to create a European Defence Community, and in 1991, in the Maastricht Treaty's provisions for European citizenship, to create a common Foreign and Security Policy. And we have seen that a dominant strain in Sarkozy's language on Europe was his persistent call for a 'political' Europe. It has been argued that France is edging ever closer to the sort of 'integrated governance at EU and global level' (Darnis, 2012) that would see 'Europeanization' take France a further stage away from the 'cultural automatism' that makes it so difficult to consider that 'the current transformation of the French nation-state into a transnational polity is just another moment in a series of historical metamorphoses' (Gueldry, 2001, p. 198). Indeed, in 2012, both outgoing President Sarkozy and incoming President François Hollande clearly stated how integrated the EU level of governance was in the politics of the nation. Sarkozy, in his Villepinte speech, declared that:

> as president of the Republic, I learned that the destiny of France plays out at one and the same time inside and outside France [*à l'intérieur et à l'extérieur*]; that between the world, European and

national stages [*scènes*], there is no longer a screen [*cloison*]. I came up against this reality: it is one and the same policy that must be conducted inside and outside, with different means, but with the same objectives and the same determination.

For François Hollande, barely two months into his presidency, on Bastille Day 2012, he had already had time to discover that 'I no longer make the distinction between foreign policy [*politique extérieure*], European policy and domestic [*national*] policy. It's the same idea [*conception*], the same method and the same objectives: growth, justice and employment' (Elysée, 2012).

President Hollande: the constrained European?

François Hollande's successful 2012 presidential campaign was primarily built on a strong anti-Sarkozy message and a skilful attempt to synthesize the centrifugal forces of the French Left, while remaining attractive to undecided electors in the second round. Nowhere was such ambivalence more marked than in the field of European policy. Still a candidate, Hollande made a firm pledge to 'renegotiate' the Fiscal Compact Treaty negotiated by Sarkozy and Merkel in December 2011. Candidate Hollande argued strongly that the new treaty would undermine French budgetary sovereignty and institutionalize economic austerity. While accepting the need for more supervision over budgets in the eurozone, Hollande held forth the promise of a renegotiation of the Fiscal Compact Treaty and publicly affirmed that France would not change its constitution to allow ratification of it. Then, once elected president, he appeared to link eventual ratification of the new treaty with the adoption by the EU of a Growth Pact to counter-balance the deflationary effects of the Fiscal Compact. By October 2012, however, the new treaty had been approved by the French Parliament, albeit against the opposition of the Communists, Greens and some Socialist deputies and senators.

This Sphinx-like position becomes more comprehensible when the range of contradictory domestic, European and international forces are taken into account. First, Hollande emerged as a compromise candidate. Personally strongly pro-European and social democratic, he was deeply conscious of the need to reach out to the *France du Non* that had captured a majority of PS voters in the 2005 referendum. The Socialist candidate's ambivalence over the new European treaty was in part intended to strike a balance between contrasting positions over Europe within the PS and electorate; he had to accommodate tensions between traditional pro-European Social Democrats in the Delors tradition (amongst which he counted himself) and the harder opposition to a neo-liberal Europe that had expressed itself in the rejection of the draft constitutional treaty in the 2005 referendum. These Yes and No positions coexisted within the PS electorate; opposition to neo-liberal integration and budgetary austerity was even more pronounced on the Left, embodied in the 2012 election by the Left Front candidate Jean-Luc Mélenchon.

Elected on a domestic policy agenda, Hollande's agenda immediately following his election was dominated by European and international affairs. He visited Berlin in his first week, as is customary for a newly elected French president. The G8 and NATO summits occurred in his first fortnight in power, both in the US (see Chapter 15 for a more thoroughgoing discussion of President Hollande and foreign affairs more generally). Hollande's real European baptism of fire occurred in his first major rendezvous, the EU European Council summit of 28–29 June 2012. At that summit, he formulated and submitted to the EU's institutions and France's EU partners a memorandum on a 'Pact for Responsibility, Governance and Growth'. This initiative was intended to trigger a movement towards what he called a 'renegotiation' of the EU's 'fiscal compact' in his presidential campaign. He was partially successful, at least insofar as the European Council confirmed in its conclusions that it would formulate a Growth and Employment Pact (Drake, 2013, pp. 138–9). Tying the adoption of the new treaty with the approval of a Growth Pact allowed Hollande to call on the French Parliament to ratify the TSCG in the Economic and Monetary Union. This ratification instead was achieved in Parliament by 11 October 2012 when the Senate voted 307 in favour, 32 against, although the government needed opposition votes to carry the motion – the National Assembly had voted earlier the same week, also in favour with 490 votes, 34 against and 18 abstentions.

Tensions between France and Germany did not disappear with the ratification of the EU treaty, however. These were apparent in the regular EU summit of October 2012 and the Brussels Summit on the EU budget of November 2012. The October summit featured the first big clash in the three-year crisis between Germany and France, high-lighting how the troubles over the single currency and sovereign debt have moved to the very heart of the EU. Hollande's key aim was to speed up the establishment of the new banking regime, conferring upon the European Central Bank the overall regulatory authority of the eurozone's banks and allowing it to support threatened banks (that might include French ones in due course). Chancellor Merkel, for her part, was far more concerned with lobbying support for the German proposal to create a 'Budget Tsar', a super European Commissioner with the power to intervene *ex ante* in the national budgets, a step too far for Hollande. Merkel and Hollande also clashed over the German soundings about a Federal Europe (*The Guardian*, 20 October 2012).

The federal reference remains an awkward one for French politicians and Hollande will certainly not be hurrying France into a more federal EU direction. The first six months of his presidency suggested that the Franco-German relationship would be just as challenging under him as under his predecessors, and that France and Germany would continue to support competing paradigms for eurozone governance. But it is equally probable that any lasting solution to the problems of this governance, or, indeed, to the institutional architecture of the EU, will depend upon a broad agreement between France and Germany.

Conclusions

In December 2011, the Economist Intelligence Unit's 'democracy index' pointed to the 'erosion of sovereignty and democratic accountability associated with the effects of and responses to the eurozone crisis' (EIU, 2011) that had contributed to a 'decline' in France's democracy score (along with six other EU countries); this compounded its 2010 downgrading of France from a 'full' to a 'flawed' democracy. Rozenberg (2011) and others have argued, furthermore, that the ability of the French president to take decisions without the formal approval of other bodies such as the Parliament, or even coalition partners in government, as is the case in current-day Germany, is a source of democratic weakness in French EU policy-making. We saw above, indeed, in the 2005 referendum on the CT, how President Chirac had failed to build securely a political or social consensus on Europe's next step, and also how, on balance, Sarkozy concentrated power even more absolutely around his office than had any of his predecessors. Yet we also saw that by the end of 2011, in the form of the EU's Fiscal Compact alone, France, thanks to Sarkozy's EU actions in extremely constrained circumstances, was poised to take just such a step towards the further integration of the national and EU levels of governance, although the French Constitutional Council did rule, in 2012, that the compact's 'golden rule' (that member states must balance their budgets) did not require prior constitutional amendment, thus sparing President Hollande the prospect of a possible parliamentary defeat on such a critical issue.

Gueldry (2001, p. 201) may have been exaggerating when he wrote that 'the European Union epitomizes de Gaulle's second death and with it, France slowly lurches towards the Sixth Republic'. Under President Sarkozy, the language of nations, sovereignty, borders and identity was as strong as ever; in candidate Sarkozy's 'Letter to the French People', sent just before the 2012 presidential elections, he reinforced that message in ever more emphatic style: 'Europe is an open continent. It must not be like a sieve [*continent passoire*] ... A society without borders is a society without respect. A country without borders is a country without identity. A continent without borders is a continent that will end up building walls to protect itself. Help me to build a strong France' (Sarkozy, 2012b).

Sarkozy's defeat at the hands of François Hollande on 7 May 2012 opened a new era in France's relations with the EU, but short of a Sixth Republic in all but name in which, argues Thomas Klau, 'if the euro is to survive … France's next head of state must redefine the office and learn to share control over economic policy' (Klau, 2011, p. 8), it is hard to foresee a substantially altered direction for France's engagement with the EU. Unlike the United Kingdom, semi-detachment, let alone withdrawal, does not appear anywhere in the picture unless, that is, we widen our field of vision to include the also-rans in the 2012 French presidential election – Marine le Pen and Jean-Luc Mélenchon, who between them polled 29 per cent of the popular vote and who campaigned to 'recover' France's national sovereignty from the EU treaties and to 'disobey EU directives' respectively.

Chapter 15

France and the Global Economic Order

SOPHIE MEUNIER

Introduction: globalization's comeback in French politics

Globalization has never been popular in France. This is, after all, the country that had given birth to anti-McDonald's hero José Bové, the policy of 'cultural exception' and the anti-globalization organization ATTAC (Association pour la Taxation des Transactions pour l'Aide aux Citoyens (Association for Taxing Transactions for the Benefit of Citizens)). As a result, French policy-makers and big companies have long had to tread carefully, globalizing by stealth while pretending not to – never mind that France is the fifth largest commercial power in the world, one of the world's most attractive destinations for foreign investment and one of the largest holders of real assets in other countries.

Nicolas Sarkozy was elected president after the apex of the '*alterglobalisation*' movement, which occurred in the early 2000s. A decade ago, the French were collectively obsessed with globalization, which politicians vilified all across the political spectrum. Today, France is less exceptional in its relation to globalization, not because the French grew tired of their obsession, but because the rest of the developed world rallied around the same fears, disillusions and identity crises (Meunier, 2012).

The Sarkozy presidency started off in an appeased international economic climate, leaving the centre stage to domestic issues, from law and order to university reform, and international affairs, from freeing the Bulgarian nurses held in Libya to settling the Georgia conflict. Yet Sarkozy and his government were quickly confronted with a succession of economic crises that indeed demanded global management – first the financial crisis that erupted in the United States in September 2008, then the 2010 Greek crisis which subsequently degenerated into a crisis of the eurozone and culminated in January 2012 with the degradation of France's AAA debt rating, a '*coup dur*' for national prestige. As a result, the theme of globalization made a central comeback in the 2012 electoral season.

In this chapter I review French perceptions of globalization at the dawn of the Sarkozy era, explore how the Sarkozy presidency initially made a priority of managing the global economic order, analyse why and in what direction French perceptions of the nature of globalization evolved in recent years, and explain how and to what effect the themes of '*démondialisation*' and protection played a role in the presidential campaign and beyond. What is unique about the French rapport with globalization is that they seem to ignore their own place in the global economic order – they both underestimate the real size and assets of the national economy, while they overestimate their national capacity to order and master globalization. This was true of the Sarkozy administration, as it was true of Chirac's before him, and it seems to be true again of the Hollande presidency, at least in its first six months.

French perceptions of globalization at the dawn of the Sarkozy era

The singular French reluctance towards globalization in the early 2000s had been tamed in the ensuing years through promises by successive politicians that globalization could actually be 'managed' ('*maîtrisée*') thanks to a combination of European and international policy initiatives. It therefore became less of an issue in political rhetoric. Yet even though Sarkozy's 2007 platform, characterized by many in France and abroad as triumphant neo-liberal capitalism, was not a hindrance to his election, his initial stance on globalization was prudent, reflecting the general French uneasiness with the phenomenon.

Judging by numbers alone, France should not have been one of the countries in the world most uneasy and fearful about globalization, nor most pessimistic about its own national future in the global economic order. The French economy is highly integrated in, and highly dependent on, the global economy. It is one of the world's largest traders: in 2010, the country was the sixth largest exporter of goods and the fifth largest exporter of services, while at the same time it was the fifth largest importer of goods and the sixth largest importer of services. It was also the fourth largest destination for foreign direct investment in the world. French workers are among the world's most productive, and overall competitiveness rankings put France among the top 20 worldwide. In 2012 it boasted 32 companies among the *Global Fortune 500* ranking of the world's biggest companies, the largest number in Europe, and many of these are world leaders in their sector (Fortune, 2012). Overall, globalization has benefited France and enabled it to conserve both its status as one of the world's largest economies and its high standard of living.

And yet the country turned out in the late 1990s to be one of the hotbeds and epicentres of the anti-globalization movement. Why has resistance to globalization been more intense, more widespread across the political spectrum, and more forcefully articulated publicly in France than among its European and Western partners? Globalization represents a particular challenge for France for a variety of reasons (Gordon and Meunier, 2001).

The first reason is the individual and decentralized nature of globalization. By increasing the power of private, individual actors over that of the state, globalization seemed to weaken the foundations of modern France, which has relied on a highly centralized state for entrepreneurship, redistribution and economic support. The French do not fault the state for doing too much and meddling in the private sphere, like Americans do. On the contrary, everything is expected from the state, which is constantly accused of not doing enough.

Second, 'Anglo-Saxon neo-liberal' globalization was initially equated with Americanization. Its most potent symbols were the English language, American corporate logos and cultural icons. As a result, globalization was also accused of threatening French identity, with the potential for American mass culture, from Hollywood to Google books, to send French culture into oblivion. In defence against these perceived attacks against national identity, France passed in 1994 the Loi Toubon, which mandated the exclusive use of the French language in all government and commercial publications and subjected radio and television broadcasts to a minimum quota of works in French. Other countries, whose national identity was less tied to its language and cultural production, did not exhibit a similar collective resistance to globalization.

Third, France's proud special role in international affairs seemed menaced by a world in which money had replaced ideas as the main determinant of foreign policy. The disproportionate international role of the country, reached through centuries of imperialism and careful cultivation of a universalist message, was under threat by a world under which consumerism had replaced values and English had become the new lingua franca.

Finally, France has a well-documented collective penchant for being the most pessimistic nation in the world, and one understands better why the French were so wary of globalization. Therefore, the country became a hotbed of contestation against globalization with the launch of the anti-globalization movement ATTAC in 1998 (which spread out to 40 countries), a dynamic intellectual activity backing '*altermondialisme*' and a generalized anti-globalization discourse which politicians left and right tried to appropriate (Ancelovici, 2002; Fougier, 2003).

The theme of globalization was centrally present in the 2002 election, though more as a bogeyman and rhetorical focal point than as a cause of division. Incumbent conservative president Jacques Chirac talked about the need to 'humanize' globalization, while his socialist challenger Lionel Jospin claimed that it ought to be 'tamed' and 'civilized'. As for FN candidate Jean-Marie Le Pen, who faced Chirac in the run-off second round, he did include the denunciation of globalization alongside his repudiation of immigration and European integration as one of the central components of his far-right platform.

By the next electoral cycle in 2007, however, the issue had lost considerable political salience. On one hand, resistance to globalization had morphed into resistance to the process of European integration. The divisive referendum on the project of European constitution, which a majority of the French ended up rejecting in May 2005, had focussed the arguments against the downsides of neo-liberalism and its deleterious effects on employment, welfare and the general standard of living in France. On the other hand, some of the fears about globalization had been temporarily assuaged because they did not materialize. Unemployment was relatively stable, with the rate falling to a 24-year low of 7.4 per cent in March 2008. After two years of a sluggish 0.9 per cent GDP growth rate in 2002 and 2003, the economy grew more than 2 per cent on average over the next four years. Some French analysts, such as Alain Minc, saw in this evidence of '*la mondialisation heureuse*' ('happy globalization'). As a result, the 2007 presidential election was fought on a different terrain, that of law and order, immigration and European integration.

Sarkozy was portrayed in the media at the time of his election as an unabashed neo-liberal capitalist – a compliment in the Anglo-Saxon press, a criticism in the left-wing French press. Yet even before his election he gave clear signs that he conceived of globalization in ambiguous terms, much like his predecessor. In his first major speech on globalization, delivered in November 2006 in Saint Etienne, Sarkozy insisted on the need for management and protection against a phenomenon that cannot be curtailed but that does have real negative effects. And indeed, as soon as he took office, Sarkozy appointed Hubert Védrine, the former foreign minister under socialist president François Mitterrand, to write a major report on the role of France in the globalized world (Védrine, 2007).

Sarkozy and the management of the global economic order

Globalization came back with a vengeance to the political centre stage in the autumn of 2008. This gave France an opportunity both to try to fashion the global economic order at the international level and to resurrect the collective demonization of globalization at home. In this section I analyse Sarkozy's attempts to manage the global economic order in the immediate aftermath of the outburst of the American financial crisis and throughout the rest of his presidency, as the crisis of the euro progressed.

The 2008 financial crisis

The bankruptcy of Lehman Brothers in September 2008, which precipitated much of the advanced industrialized world into the biggest economic crisis since the Great Depression in 1929, was in many respects a crisis of globalization. The causes of the crisis did lie in the excesses of globalization: a combination of neo-liberalism run amok and intense international interconnectedness that acted as a multiplier effect. The crisis also had an impact on globalization, at least temporarily, with an immediate contraction of world trade and a drying up of the private flow of credit and investment, which worsened the situation.

The financial crisis provided a chance for Nicolas Sarkozy to shine and for France to reclaim some control over the global economic order. Personal factors meshed opportunistically with political and institutional factors for France to step forward.

As he has proven throughout his political career, Sarkozy is a man who thrives on crises. When a crisis occurs, he is omnipresent, hyperactive and deploys great energy in order to bring about a resolution. That is how he treated the outbreak of the financial crisis in September 2008: as an emergency situation to which he would devote his entire attention.

The international context was also propitious for this take-charge approach by Sarkozy. US politicians were not in a position to articulate ambitious responses because the American electoral context was heated and divisive and the Bush administration was on the way out. As for the EU, France was actually holding the rotating presidency in the second half of 2008, so Sarkozy was speaking not only on behalf of France but also on behalf of the whole EU 27 when articulating a response to the crisis (see pp. 221–3).

French initiatives were ambitious, both in form and substance. In form, Sarkozy pushed for a multilateral response to the crisis, which concretely became the G20. Indeed, Sarkozy claims that one of his biggest accomplishments is the invention of the G20 in its contemporary incarnation. The G20 includes 19 of the world's largest economies plus the EU, as well as representatives from the International Monetary Fund (IMF), the World Bank and some invited countries, representing 85 per cent of the world's GDP.[1] Initially created in 1999 in response to

---

1 Members of the G20 are Argentina, Australia, Brazil, Canada, China, France, Germany, India, Indonesia, Italy, Japan, Mexico, Russia, Saudi Arabia, South Africa, South Korea, Turkey, the United Kingdom, the United States and the EU.

the Asian financial crisis, the G20 was first a low-profile gathering of finance ministers and central bank governors who met annually to discuss international financial stability. When meeting with American president George Bush in September 2008, in the midst of the financial crisis, Sarkozy suggested that a broad multilateral forum be convened as a meeting of heads of state in emergency. The format of the G20 was agreed upon because, conveniently, it already existed, even if its nature changed dramatically once it became a forum for heads of state.

The pioneering heads of state 'G20 Summit on Financial Markets and the World Economy' took place in Washington in November 2008. Since then, it has met bi-annually and has overcome the G8 in stature due to its more accurate representation of the world's population and economy. It is an informal institution whose secretariat is assured by the country holding the presidency. It convened in London in April 2009. At the September 2009 Pittsburgh summit, it was decided that, starting in 2011, the heads of state G20 would meet annually and that France, which was already scheduled to hold the rotating presidency of the G8, would preside over the G20 as well.

In substance, the initiatives led by Sarkozy to manage the global economic order were ambitious as well. The crisis was interpreted as a vindication against the dangers of jungle capitalism. Given the traditional Gallic unease vis-à-vis globalization and Sarkozy's own prior admonition to protect the country from its damaging effects, the French made, in the heat of the crisis, a series of bold proposals to overhaul radically the international financial architecture and regulate neo-liberal economics. Speaking both on France's behalf and on behalf of the EU, Sarkozy called for a 'rethinking of the financial system from scratch, as at Bretton Woods' and made proposals concerning regulation, transparency, supervision and integrity. Over the course of the following two years, France continued to push for restoring the moral dimension of capitalism against deregulated globalization.

The G8/G20 presidency

The highlight of Sarkozy's attempt to manage and reform the global economic order was the twin French presidency of the G8 and the G20, the world's premier international economic fora, in 2011. With the G8 summit in May in Deauville and the G20 summit in November in Cannes, the French president had much to gain both internationally and domestically, or so it initially seemed, from this opportunity to showcase France as the first country ever to head the two groupings simultaneously. Internationally, Sarkozy could acquire world stature, which might help him domestically ahead of the 2012 electoral contest – especially since that contest was expected to involve Dominique Strauss-Kahn, then the managing director of the IMF and recognized as one of the world's leading experts on the management of the global economic order.

The main objective of the G20 is to tackle the root causes of the 2008 financial and economic crisis and to improve global stability and prosperity in order to prevent the recurrence of such a crisis. The country holding the presidency inherits the agenda left over from previous summits. However, it also has some latitude in determining the rest of the agenda which finance ministers, central bankers, heads of state and countless working groups will be labouring on. The objectives stated by France for its G20 presidency were ambitious:

1. reforming the international monetary system;
2. strengthening financial regulation;
3. combating commodity price volatility;
4. supporting employment and strengthening the social dimension of globalization;
5. fighting corruption;
6. working on behalf of development.

As Sarkozy stated, 'we live in a new world, so we need new ideas'.

In addition to being ambitious (some international observers characterized them as 'grandiose'), these priorities were also somewhat unrealistic. Coordination and goodwill were possible at the apex of the crisis in 2008 when there was a shared sense of urgency, but now that most G20 members were seeing the end of the recession tunnel and the new crisis of the day was the future of the euro, national interest and immediate domestic political considerations came clashing against ambitious rhetoric. The international and European economic situation was no longer particularly propitious for the ambitious regulatory agenda and overhaul of financial governance proposed by France.

As the months went by, the French presidency fizzled, both for internal and external reasons. Internally, lofty ambitions progressively gave way to petty disagreements, such as on current account definitions, and the order of the day evolved from rethinking the international system to extinguishing immediate fires. Externally, the European sovereign debt crisis of the euro, with its potential for triggering a collapse of the euro with unpredictable economic consequences, became the most pressing order of business, relegating ambitions to manage the global economic order to the background. What was supposed to be the highlight of Sarkozy's presidency of the G20, the Cannes summit in November 2011, was overshadowed by the simultaneous crisis of the euro – its initial sweeping agenda eventually replaced by a quasi-exclusive focus on bolstering the euro bailout agreement to ensure that the euro crisis would not spread to the rest of the world.

Did France change the global economic order?

Sarkozy's attempts to manage the global economic order during his five-year tenure reflect France's dual underestimation and overestimation of its role in globalization. By denouncing Anglo-Saxon capitalism and calling for a radical overhaul of the international financial system, Sarkozy confirmed deeply held national suspicions that France had been a victim of globalization, underestimating its nature as a major actor of globalization instead. At the same time, by planning to use its presidency of the G20 to reform fundamentally the international monetary system and drastically strengthen financial regulation, Sarkozy overestimated the power of France, and of French public actors, to alter the course of global finance and reorganize it with a purpose against the will of its central players.

For a short window of time, the crisis seemed like a vindication of the French model of capitalism, with its peculiar balance of state and market. In March 2009, the usually French-bashing *The Economist* even put a big Sarkozy next to a little Merkel (and a quasi-disappearing Gordon Brown) on its cover with the title 'Europe's New Pecking Order' to accompany a laudatory article about the French economic model (*The Economist*, 2009). If France was indeed a beacon of a new enlightened capitalism, as Sarkozy was suggesting at the height of the crisis, then French solutions should lead the way out of the crisis. But this state of grace did not last long, and as other economies started to bounce back, while the euro crisis deepened and French exports and competitiveness declined, analysts went back to deriding the French model.

The balance sheet of Sarkozy's attempt to manage the global economic order is not overwhelmingly positive. In his speech on the financial crisis pronounced in Toulon in September 2008, he had declared that 'a certain idea of globalization ends with the end of a financial capitalism that had imposed its logic on the whole economy and had contributed to pervert it' (Sarkozy, 2008a). He said that it was time to be 'imaginative and audacious' in coming up with solutions to the crisis and creating a 'new form of capitalism' that puts 'finance at the service of business and citizens'. Under his leadership, France indeed made many ambitious proposals and declarations, such as reform of global economic governance, regulation of hedge funds, a clampdown on financial offshore centres and tax havens, and caps on bonuses for traders and CEOs.

Few of these ambitions, however, had materialized into actual policy reforms by the time Sarkozy left office in 2012. His call for abolishing tax havens was well reported in the French media and was a popular proposal, but so far the G20 has not cracked down on these havens and the proposal announced with great fanfare has not been followed by implementation. One partial exception to the lack of measures actually implemented is the greater international economic governance made possible through the institutionalization of the G20, which has now become the de facto premier international economic forum, though it has not delivered real results so far. But even the quasi-institutionalization of the G20, which now regularly meets annually at the head of state level, is not a clear-cut Sarkozy accomplishment. Though he has claimed its paternity, many actors involved in the troubled days and weeks after the collapse of Lehman Brothers suggest a different story, one in which the US wanted a multilateral response, but to which Sarkozy advocated a more restrictive forum with a dozen members. But all concur that Sarkozy amplified these trends and tried to capitalize on the invention of the new format.

Another announcement that has been followed by partial implementation, if only in France, is the so-called Tobin tax on financial transactions. Initially conceived by the anti-globalization movement at the turn of the millennium and characterized at the time by Sarkozy as 'an absurdity', this tax became a pet cause of the French president who suggested in 2009 that it should be adopted by the G20. He tried to convince France's EU partners to adopt the tax to set an example for the rest of the world, and he finally announced in January 2012 that the 0.1 per cent tax on financial transactions would be implemented in France as of August.

The lack of concrete results of France's attempts to manage the global economic order does not come only from the absence of support for its proposals by other leading economies or by the relentless succession of crises demanding immediate attention. It also came because, in regard to other initiatives, such as the Basel III accords on banking supervision, France was a more reluctant follower than a leader.

The changing nature of globalization

In addition to the apparent failures to manage successfully the global economic order, French assessments of globalization changed during the Sarkozy presidency because of a shift in the actual and perceived nature of the phenomenon. In this section I explore in particular three new, related realizations accelerated by the financial crisis and the euro crisis: that Europe cannot deliver on its promise to manage globalization; that globalization is no longer synonymous with Americanization; and that China is now the dominant face of globalization.

Europe cannot deliver on its promise to manage globalization

For over a decade, French policy-makers had reasoned that globalization could be palatable if it could be managed. The phrase 'managed globalization' originated in France as '*mondialisation maîtrisée*' at the height of the anti-globalization fever of the late 1990s (Abdelal and Meunier, 2010). Politicians promised that globalization would deliver economic opportunities while its negative effects would be kept under control by a series of specific policies. The EU was presented as the instrument of choice for managing globalization.

The divisive debate over the 2005 referendum on the European Constitution was in many ways a debate over whether the EU could enable the French to have their cake and eat it too: that is, to benefit from an open area where people, goods and services could circulate freely while being protected from the economic disruptions and realignments engendered by such freedom. The rejection of the Constitutional Treaty was a warning sign that the French were losing faith in the process of European integration, which they felt had exposed them to globalization instead of protecting them. This trend continued during the Sarkozy presidency. The growing French disillusionment with European efforts to manage globalization was accelerated by two shocks: the American financial crisis and the sovereign debt crisis of the eurozone, neither of which these efforts had been able to prevent or contain.

Surveys confirm both France's growing disillusionment with the EU's potential to manage globalization and its idiosyncrasies when it comes to perceptions of globalization. The Eurobarometer survey asked whether the EU helps to protect from the negative effects of globalization. In 2010, 42 per cent believed this to be the case, while 38 per cent did not. France was the outlier in the survey, with the smallest percentage of responses out of 27 countries believing in the protective role of the EU against globalization (29 per cent) and the second largest number of responses after Greece believing that the EU was not protecting French citizens from the effects of globalization (54 per cent) (European Commission, 2010). The responses are similar to a related question, asking Europeans whether the EU enables citizens to benefit more from the positive effects of globalization: France and Greece are the only two countries where a majority of respondents think that the EU cannot help them to reap the positive effects of globalization.

By the end of Sarkozy's presidency, the French no longer believed that European integration had played the role of a bulwark against globalization. Instead, they perceived that the EU had acted as a Trojan Horse accelerating the process of globalization and amplifying its negative effects into France.

Globalization is no longer synonymous with Americanization

A second French perception of globalization which has evolved during the years of the Sarkozy presidency is the American nature of the phenomenon. Ten years ago, the French equated globalization with Americanization, and the US was perceived to be its main driver and main beneficiary. The American imprint on globalization was seen everywhere. The number of McDonald's, the spread of Starbucks or the ratio of Hollywood versus national blockbusters had become proxies for measuring globalization. The '*altermondialiste*' movement focused on globalization as an instrument of American imperialism and as a cultural steamroller.

The problem for the US was that, while Europeans in general, and the French in particular, were then ambivalent or enthusiastic about the opportunities offered by globalization, many people tended to blame the US for what they did not like about globalization: the increasing gap between the rich and the poor, the increasing pollution of the planet and the impacting negatively on national culture. There was no doubt that the US was the main driver and the main beneficiary of globalization then, and therefore was responsible for the negative side effects of it.

What has changed in the last decade is that the US has moved from a position of culprit to a position of victim when it comes to globalization. Today, few in France believe that the US still holds the keys of globalization. While the US still has, by far, the world's largest economy, only 29 per cent of the French believe this is the case – the fourth lowest score of all countries polled by the 2012 Pew Global Attitudes Project (2012). At least three kinds of changes have contributed to the broad decoupling of globalization and Americanization.

First, the French have increasingly recognized that their own ambivalence about globalization is matched by American ambivalence. Outsourcing, deindustrialization and loss of global competitiveness have stricken American workers as they have the French, and surveys point to a negativity towards globalization almost as great in the US as it is in France nowadays. The financial crisis of 2008 revealed American vulnerabilities and weakened the international prestige and power of the US, precipitating the perceived demise of the country as the holder of the keys of globalization.

Second, as for the fear of cultural homogenization, which used to be the most distinguishing characteristic of the French reticence towards globalization, it has all but disappeared from the national debate. Globalization has not ushered in the feared American-led cultural homogenization. To be sure, the Champs-Elysées glitters with billboards and store signs with American brand names. But many of these signs, from New York to Shanghai, also say 'Louis Vuitton', 'Cartier' and 'L'Occitane'. Moreover, globalization has also meant diversity, with the easier access to wider cultural content and the availability to broadcast to the entire world.

China as the main driver and beneficiary of globalization

A third recent evolution is the perception that, today, China has become the main driver and the main beneficiary of globalization. For the French, it is now clear that China is already the world's largest economic power – even if these perceptions are a far cry from reality. Indeed, in 2012 a sizeable majority (57 per cent) of citizens in France, as elsewhere in Europe, believes that, today, China is already the world's biggest economic power, whereas only 29 per cent think it is still the US (ibid.).

This power shift is worrisome to the French because they share a strong suspicion that their interests are very different from those of the Chinese when it comes to globalization. According to a 2010 Eurobarometer survey, 23 per cent of EU citizens think that China and Europe have the same interests when dealing with globalization, while 52 per cent believe that their interests are different (European Commission, 2010). The French have the lowest percentage in all of Europe in thinking that their interests are different (14 per cent), and one of the highest percentages in thinking that their interests are the same (67 per cent).

The rise of China has brought forward a new set of concerns that have little to do with American competition. When globalization was perceived as American, the main reproaches were that it acted as a cultural steamroller (the 'coca-colonization', 'Disneyification', 'McDoization' of the world) and was heightening the American values of individualism and competition to the detriment of the French values of equality and solidarity (Kuisel, 2012). Today, the concerns about globalization are markedly different. They focus mostly on the lowering of all standards and the ineluctable loss of unemployment to perceived unfair competition.

The tergiversations of France's foreign and economic policy towards China under the Sarkozy presidency reflect the unease towards this power shift. Sarkozy has given both the cold shoulder and a pompous reception to Chinese president Hu Jintao. He played a difficult balancing act of taking a moral stance by meeting with the Dalai Lama, which angered the Chinese government, while simultaneously conducting economic diplomacy to obtain potentially lucrative Chinese contracts for French companies. Chinese foreign direct investment in France is both courted and vilified. Even during the course of the French G20 presidency, policy alternated between alliance with or against China on currency matters. Like they were when globalization presented an American face, the French are now the most worried in Europe of globalization with a Chinese face. But unlike the US, which has long been a security ally and shared common values with France, China, with its exotic culture and fundamentally different political and value system, appears to be a more serious challenge to French identity and its role in the world.

Globalization and 'démondialisation' in the 2012 election

The Sarkozy presidency, which started by focusing on domestic issues and rehabilitating neo-liberalism, came to be defined instead by attempts to manage the global economic order and old-fashioned railing against Anglo-Saxon capitalism. The combination of the financial crisis, the euro crisis and deeper structural power shifts put the topic of globalization back at the centre of political rhetoric during the 2012 presidential campaign: how France had been victimized by globalization; why the EU had been an agent of, instead of a bulwark against, globalization; how to protect the country from its negative effects. In this section I explore how the theme of globalization was used in the 2012 election and beyond.

The French globalization consensus

Globalization made a comeback in French electoral politics, but more as a consensual bogeyman that everyone lashes out against than as a subject of real debate. With their penchant for pessimism, the French focus almost exclusively on the negative consequences of globalization, not the opportunities it has offered or will offer. The consensus in public opinion is striking. The most recent poll on this issue reveals that more than four out of five French people believe that globalization has had overall negative consequences on employment in France (Cochez, 2012). Moreover, polls have shown repeatedly that the French see their country as the least well positioned in the global economy.

Partisan affiliation does not seem to matter, as 71 per cent of PS sympathizers and 75 per cent of Sarkozy's UMP party favour protectionism (Ifop, 2011). The same poll on perceptions of globalization in ten countries reveals that France was judged the least well placed in international economic competition by its own citizens (with 34 per cent of respondents saying 'well placed' and 'very well placed', against 40 per cent in the US, 70 per cent in the Netherlands and 79 per cent in Australia). French respondents were at the extreme of almost all questions asked in the poll, whether on their favourability towards capitalism and the market economy system (15 per cent of favourable responses in France versus 65 per cent in China!), the imminent probability of another economic and financial crisis, and the necessity to block foreign takeovers.

That the health of the French economy is so heavily dependent on globalization does not seem to matter, because these arguments are hardly audible in such a political context. The disconnect between reality and the imaginary in the approach to globalization comes in part from the singular relation that the French entertain with their companies. They hardly see a convergence between the interests of firms and the interests of citizens, between private interest and national interest. The problem is not, as George W. Bush famously said in an involuntary pun, that the French have no word for 'entrepreneur'. The problem is that, in France, '*entreprise*' ('firm') often feels like a dirty word. This can be explained by the very low rate of unionization in France, which has created a culture of individualism and corporatism instead of corporate bargaining, as well as by the absence of basic private sector culture among French politicians, for whom politics has been a lifelong career – starting with Nicolas Sarkozy and Francois Hollande, the two main contenders in the spring 2012 presidential contest.

As a result, the mistrust and fear of globalization is spread out all across the French political spectrum, creating the appearance of a globalization consensus. If the anti-globalization (*alterglobalisation*) movement no longer has the same visibility in France that it did a decade ago, it is not because the French converted to neo-liberalism in the meantime. Rather, it is because its central themes and pet peeves have been co-opted and absorbed into mainstream politics – starting with the Tobin tax on financial transactions, which Sarkozy put on the agenda of the 2011 French presidency of the G20, has tried to sell to Angela Merkel in the European context, and then reaffirmed as a centrepiece of his electoral platform in January 2012.

'Démondialisation' and protection in the 2012 campaign

In reaction to the twin financial and sovereign debt crises, 'deglobalization' and 'protectionism' became some of the keywords of the 2012 presidential campaign – not as real objects of debate, but rather as givens that candidates must deal with. Arnaud Montebourg, an eloquent, ambitious, young Socialist, surprisingly came in third in the party's primary contest in October 2011 after running on a platform of '*démondialisation*' ('deglobalization') (Montebourg and Todd, 2011). That concept spread in the public debate like wildfire. Indeed, *Le Monde* published 73 articles talking about '*démondialisation*' between January 2011 and April 2012, compared to no articles on 'deglobalization' in *The New York Times* during the same period, according to my own count on Lexis/Nexis.

'Protection' was the other keyword of the 2012 campaign. From the far Left to the far Right, with anchors in the PS and the UMP, everyone advocated protection, though this newfangled protectionism was almost systematically qualified with epithets: 'European protectionism' (Jean-Luc Mélenchon, FG); 'new wave protectionism' (Arnaud Montebourg, PS); 'modern protectionism' (Laurent Wauquiez, UMP); 'social and economic protectionism' (Marine Le Pen, FN). Even Sarkozy, who had been misinterpreted initially by American commentators as a neo-liberal reformer, had declared in his first big speech on globalization in 2006 that his first duty would be to protect (Sarkozy, 2006).

As the campaign progressed, attacks on globalization became more virulent, and so did calls for protection from all four major candidates. Le Pen declared that 'globalization goes profoundly against human nature' (Gauvin, 2012). Jean-Luc Mélenchon and the FG, heir apparent to the *altermondialiste* movement and the 'no' vote to the referendum on the European constitution, campaigned on the theme of 'another globalization' and fustigated neo-liberalism and finance. Socialist candidate Francois Hollande also designated global finance as the main enemy in his speech in Le Bourget in January 2012: 'my real adversary has no name, no face, no party; it will never be a candidate and yet it governs. That adversary, it is the world of finance' (Hollande, 2012). Sarkozy also tried to play the protectionist card. In March 2012 he focused his speech in Villepinte on the need to provide protection, including by creating a 'Buy European Act' that would institutionalize a European preference for public procurement (Sarkozy, 2012a). In April, he published his platform in a 'Letter to the French people' in which he mentioned globalization 26 times and insisted on the duty of protection (Sarkozy, 2012b).

This dual theme of globalization/protection featured even more centrally towards the end of the campaign. In his last attempt to convince the electorate in between the two rounds, Sarkozy gave a speech in Toulouse on borders and national identity. Alluding to the scores of 17.9 per cent obtained by Le Pen and 11.1 per cent obtained by Mélenchon in the first round, Sarkozy insisted on the 'crucial importance of borders in globalization' and declared that 'I do not want to let France be diluted in globalization, that is the central message of the first round' (Sarkozy, 2012c).

In the end, since Hollande and Sarkozy shared a general consensus regarding the nature and the drawbacks of globalization, the electoral contest could not play out in the global economic policy sphere. It had to play out elsewhere: in matters of domestic politics, social issues and personality.

Beyond the 2012 campaign

The presidential election that brought Hollande to power in France in May 2012 happened during turbulent times for European economies: there was the fallout from the financial crisis, acute uncertainties about

the future of the eurozone, rampant deindustrialization and a sentiment of Western decline compared to the rising economic powerhouses
of the East. Indeed the second round of the French presidential election
occurred on the same day as a Greek legislative election that sent
shockwaves throughout Europe, and throughout the world, when a
majority of Greek voters expressed their discontent with the pursuit of
austerity measures enacted to deal with the sovereign debt crisis.
Managing France's place in the new global economic order, in part by
managing the European order, will certainly be the defining challenge
of Hollande's presidency.

So far not much has happened on this front, outside of the management of the euro crisis and the governance of the EU of course. The
Hollande administration has sent mixed messages about how it intends
to tackle the challenges posed by globalization. After his election,
Hollande sent a strong signal that he would continue to 'manage' globalization by appointing Arnaud Montebourg to the government as the
minister of the tailor-made, and yet to be defined, 'ministry of productive recovery'. From publicly shaming car-maker Peugeot about its proposed lay-offs to redirecting French automobile production through
targeted subsidies, from provoking a showdown with steel industrialist
Lakshmi Mittal to defending 'made in France' products on magazine
covers, the minister seems to be devising a contemporary industrial
policy to deal with global economic challenges.

But in several instances this ministry has already seemed at odds
with the ministry of finance, headed by Pierre Moscovici, who is operating more in the shadows than the flamboyant Montebourg. This
tension was revealed publicly on several occasions, for instance the creation of the French Public Investment Bank, one of Hollande's keystone initiatives. Supposed to be operational by late 2012 and
bolstered by a capital of €30 billion, this bank is designed to help
small and medium-sized enterprises. In addition to the conditions in
which the bank was created, the two ministries (and ministers) dis-
agreed on the objectives and criteria for financing projects – whether to
encourage innovation and exports or to rescue failing companies and
prevent bankruptcies.

Six months into the Hollande presidency, it is still not clear whether
France will adapt an offensive posture, trying to project itself internationally in order to take advantage of globalization, or a defensive
posture, protecting itself from competition through a variety of measures such as the promised 'Arcelor-Mittal' bill that would force companies intent on closing a factory to find a suitable alternative owner.

Conclusion

All advanced industrialized economies are nowadays confronted with mass and long-term unemployment, deindustrialization and as a result growing resentment vis-à-vis globalization. France is still singular, however, in possessing strong anti-capitalist feelings at the root of its hostility to globalization. Of ten major countries polled in 2011 on perceptions of globalization, France came in first by far in its outright rejection of capitalism and the market economy as the best economic system (33 per cent) and last in expressing clear support (only 15 per cent). Ironically, the most ardent defender of capitalism according to this poll was China (Ifop, 2011).

Yet for all the talk about the loss of any margin of manoeuvre, the necessity of protection and the ineluctability of decline, the French discourse on globalization, left and right, ignores the fact that the deterioration of French competitiveness and trade position happened above all vis-à-vis the country's European partners. While China has displaced a sizable number of jobs to be sure, it is also a scapegoat in explaining why France seems to fare so badly in the globalized world. The competitive position of France has deteriorated in the past decade compared to the rest of Europe, and the record-breaking trade deficit, expected to reach €100 billion in 2012, is mostly incurred in Europe.

The dominant perception in France, on the left as on the right, is that the state's capacity to act and margin of manoeuvre need to be restored in order to protect the French from the unfair competition coming from the rest of the world. France is certainly not unique among its peers in fearing this competition and resorting to protective reflexes against it. But it is singular in the underestimation of its capacity to adapt and in the overestimation of its power to control and direct the global economic environment.

Chapter 16

French Foreign and Security Policy: In Search of Coherence and Impact

JOLYON HOWORTH

On 6 May 2012, President Nicolas Sarkozy was narrowly defeated in his bid for a second term by François Hollande, who thus became the seventh president of the Fifth Republic. During his election campaign, Hollande studiously avoided any major pronouncements in the field of foreign and security policy, conscious that the election would be won or lost in the realm of economics and jobs. Yet Hollande's first month as president was overwhelmed by the foreign and security policy agenda. This has indeed been the case with all his predecessors, who have considered international affairs to be a presidential prerogative (*domaine réservé*; Cohen, 1986). Continuity in these areas has, over the decades, been more prevalent than change. French foreign and security policy under the Fifth Republic has been structured around three broad frames: the transatlantic; the European (see Chapter 14); the Mediterranean/African. Under President Sarkozy (2007–12), all three saw high levels of activity, although there is little evidence that French diplomacy embarked on any radically new departures. Nor is there evidence that Sarkozy's activism succeeded in substantially increasing French influence over regional and global affairs.

France perceives itself as an important player on the international stage. Every president is concerned to preserve what is considered to be France's 'rank' in the international pecking order – usually measured against a Gaullist yardstick (Vaisse, 1998). New presidents do not step into a vacuum. Their policy options are largely dictated by the structure of the international system they inherit and by France's own self-perceptions as a global player. A president's personality can make some measure of difference, but only around the margins. François Hollande, who campaigned on the slogan that he intended to be a 'normal president', is unlikely to do any better, or any worse, than his predecessor, although his style will certainly be different. Sarkozy tended to centralize decision-making at the Elysée Palace, thereby marginalizing both the foreign ministry and, to some extent, even the defence ministry (Meunier, 2012). Hollande made clear his intention of opening up the *domaine réservé* to allow for greater involvement of both government ministries and the National Assembly. Whether he will deliver on this promise remains to be seen.

Transatlantic relations

Arguably *the* key foreign policy challenge for every French president is to establish a good working relationship with the United States (Cogan, 1994). Since the 1980s, the traditional French diplomatic preference has been for what is called 'Gaullo-Mitterrandism', according to which France has a special role to play, *outside* of the Western family of nations, with respect to the Global South and/or the rising powers. By contrast, 'Atlanticism' posits that France's overseas activities should be tightly coordinated with those of her Western allies (Charillon, 2011; Boniface, 2012). This dichotomy hardly corresponds to anything tangible or sustainable. One can find elements of both approaches in the actions of all French presidents of the Fifth Republic, including in those of de Gaulle himself. The eminently 'Gaullo-Mitterrandist' triptych *'ami, allié, non-aligné'* ('friend, ally, non-aligned') coined by Mitterrand's foreign minister Hubert Védrine (2007) has nevertheless become the acid test of France's approach towards the US. The reality is that France, as a medium-sized power, generally embraces a policy of bandwagoning with the US, while at the same time constantly attempting to float autonomous trial balloons. It is questionable whether this translates into either policy coherence or serious international influence (Lagrange, 2012).

On his election in 2007, Sarkozy had long enjoyed a reputation as an Atlanticist – even though the evidence for this lay more at the economic and cultural level than in the strategic and political spheres. His appointment of the socialist Bernard Kouchner as foreign minister was seen as an Atlanticist gesture, Kouchner having been a rare left-wing supporter of US military intervention in Iraq (Gresh, 2008). This interpretation overlooked the fact that Sarkozy's *first* choice for foreign minister had been the anti-Atlanticist Hubert Védrine. Nevertheless, the fact that Sarkozy elected to spend his 2007 summer vacation in New England (a symbolic 'first' for a French president), and the tenor of his speech to the US Congress in November 2007, in which he made an impassioned attempt to turn the page on the transatlantic tensions over Iraq by celebrating more than two centuries of Franco-American friendship and alliance (Sarkozy, 2007d), consolidated the widespread impression that one of the president's top priorities was to re-cement France's ties to its 'oldest ally'. What few noticed in his speech to

Congress was that he used the opportunity of renewing Franco-American friendship to warn the USA that the world would no longer tolerate the frenzied speculation on the global markets that was about to produce a global financial crisis, to suggest that the USA was not being true to its deepest values by ignoring the dangers of climate change, and to argue that the USA had not really understood that Europe needed to emerge as an autonomous military actor in order to be an effective ally. And he ended his speech with this unequivocal reminder of the Gaullo-Mitterrandist triptych: '*je veux être votre ami, votre allié, votre partenaire. Mais je veux être un ami debout, un allié indépendant, un partenaire libre*' ('I want to be your friend, your ally, your partner. But a friend who stands tall, an independent ally and a free partner'). De Gaulle himself could not have put it more succinctly. France under Sarkozy did indeed play a full and active role in the Atlantic Alliance, but it did not hesitate to distance itself from US policy over several key issues (the Middle East; relations with Russia; NATO's core mission; further NATO enlargement; Latin America). In short, 'coherence' involved neither unquestioning alignment with the US, nor blind opposition, but the assertion of the right to be different.

François Hollande came to the presidency with virtually no reputation in the foreign and security field, although the PS saw itself as the champion of Gaullo-Mitterrandism (Védrine, 2008). Hollande's first choice of foreign minister, former Prime Minister Laurent Fabius, is expected to adopt a pragmatic yet creative approach to international affairs. During his first major interview after taking office, when pressed repeatedly to pronounce himself either a 'Gaullo-Mitterrandist' or an 'Atlanticist', he rejected these categories as misleading. The only objective, he insisted, was to ensure that France wielded influence in international affairs, as Fabius (2012) has noted. That is indeed the key challenge for any French president, but Fabius has not elaborated on how it is to be achieved or measured. While Hollande discovered, during his visit to the US in May 2012, that he had much in common, both philosophically and politically, with Barack Obama (Vaisse, 2012), the real test of Franco-American relations will come in the encounter with specific policy challenges in a world in which many believe that the transatlantic relationship is under threat as the US 'pivots' away from Europe towards the Asia–Pacific region (Leonard, 2012).

France's 'return' to NATO

President de Gaulle withdrew France from NATO's integrated command structure in 1966 in order to make three points. First, that French forces, and particularly French nuclear assets, should not be subordinated to a US command chain over which Paris had no political control. Second, to protest about the adoption by NATO of the policy of 'flexible response' which implied a watering down of the allied strategy of nuclear deterrence in favour of conventional war-fighting. Third, to argue that Europe as a whole, by free-riding on US military protection, was abandoning all prospect of becoming autonomous in defence (ICDG, 1992). France nevertheless remained a member of the Atlantic Alliance and made formal arrangements to engage her forces alongside those of NATO if war ever came to Europe. But French officials took no part in the major strategic discussions within NATO's key committees. Since NATO was never activated during the Cold War, this was a policy which offered substantial benefit for Paris. However, from the day the Berlin Wall fell, France faced three huge NATO dilemmas. How to reconcile her semi-detached status within the Alliance (Vaïsse et al., 1997) with her growing participation in the real military missions of the post-Cold War world? How to ensure that her voice carried its full weight in the ongoing debates about where the Alliance was heading? How to square the growing development of an autonomous EU Common Security and Defence Policy (CSDP) with Alliance transformation (Howorth, 2005)?

Sarkozy's decision to return France to NATO's integrated command structures, far from being a symbol of his 'Atlanticism', was in fact the logical continuation of policy orientations initiated by all French presidents since de Gaulle. The much-heralded return was formally announced at the Alliance's sixtieth anniversary summit in Strasbourg-Kehl on 4 April 2009. This seemingly major shift contained elements of both the 'Prodigal Son' and the 'Trojan Horse' (Howorth, 2010). There were two compelling reasons for the decision: one military, the other political.

The military reason had to do with the opportunity costs of staying out. The military lessons drawn from the 1991 Gulf conflict all pointed in the same direction. It was France's *absence* from NATO's integrated structures which presented the greatest obstacle to her performing militarily according to her own perception of 'rank' (Ecole de Guerre, 1991). Once the French armed forces, which had basically sat out the Cold War without adopting NATO procedures, began to find themselves involved in real military operations, it became obvious that their exclusion from the NATO mainstream was a liability. French troops in the 1990s were under fire and increasingly under NATO command. François Mitterrand rejoined NATO's Military Committee in 1993. On 14 June 1995, his newly elected successor, Jacques Chirac, spent more than an hour in *tête-à-tête* with Bill Clinton and persuaded him to use NATO bombers against the Bosnian Serbs (Holbrooke, 1999). Ironically, it was thus France (the 'non-member') which persuaded NATO to engage in military combat for the first time in its history.

Under Jacques Chirac, the country rejoined every NATO committee but two. The real question in 2009, therefore, was not why France was rejoining, but why it had taken so long?

Chirac had indeed tried to return to the fold in 1996/97. His bid for reintegration on two conditions (deep structural reform of the Alliance; and a major European/French command (AFSOUTH) in Naples) was rejected by President Clinton (Brenner and Parmentier, 2002). This had major implications for France during the Kosovo war of 1999. The French ambassador to NATO had to sit out the key strategic meetings of the Defence Planning Committee and then drive over to the US ambassador's residence to learn what had been decided that day in his absence – and France was the second largest force contributor during that war. For the Afghan campaign, in 2002, Chirac deployed a quarter of France's entire navy. The opportunity costs of remaining outside NATO's command structures were very high. At this first, purely military level, Sarkozy simply took the logical and inevitable last step. This was the return of the Prodigal Son. The rewards were appreciable. France received one of NATO's two strategic command posts, Allied Command Transformation, in Norfolk, Virginia, and NATO's Regional Command in Lisbon.

The second reason for reintegration was political. By the mid-2000s, it was clear that the next major challenge for the Alliance was to decide – *politically* – what NATO should become post-Afghanistan. Sarkozy intended to be fully involved in that conversation. During the internal French debates over NATO reintegration in spring 2009, the Socialist opposition charged that Sarkozy's policy amounted to realignment with the US and abandonment of the Gaullo-Mitterrandist triptych. They argued, somewhat disingenuously, that if France had been a full member of NATO in 2003, she would have been obliged to join the Bush war in Iraq and that with reintegration she would in future be under greater obligation to participate in NATO missions (Bozo, 2008). But there was never any reason to assume that NATO reintegration would have a constraining effect on France's diplomatic independence. Germany had long been a core member of the Alliance, but had no compunction, in 2002–03, in utterly rejecting Bush's policy on Iraq. As for France's influence *inside* the Alliance, the picture is unclear. Sarkozy tied up a number of loose *military* ends but took a rather large *political* gamble on the future (Lellouche, 2009). At the political level, reintegration was no Prodigal Son syndrome; it smacked more of the Trojan Horse. The big debate post-Libya is whether NATO will become a true global alliance (as the US and the UK appear to want) or will return unequivocally to the European area and underpin regional stability for the EU (a prospect favoured by France and one or two other EU member states) (Howorth, 2012a). Meanwhile, in July 2012, François Hollande established a commission of enquiry, headed by

Hubert Védrine, to report on the consequences, for France, of the return to NATO. This is almost certainly a cosmetic gesture, designed to reassure the PS's many anti-Atlanticists that the new president is not simply embracing Sarkozyism hook, line and sinker.

Sarkozy proved to be a reliable and enthusiastic ally during military operations in Afghanistan, playing an active and growing role in NATO's International Stabilization and Assistance Force (ISAF) as well as alongside the separate American Operation Enduring Freedom. He progressively increased French troop levels from just over 1,000 in early 2007 to almost 4,000 in 2011. In addition, the country deployed significant naval assets as well as C-135F refuelling planes, Mirage 2000 fighters and Gazelle helicopters. The official objectives of these forces were threefold: to support the gradual empowerment of the Afghan National Army (ANA); to secure the province of Kapisa; and to enable Afghan troops in the district of Surobi to take over all security missions in that area, a task which was accomplished in late 2011.

French troops suffered significant casualties: by summer 2012, there were 86 dead and several hundred wounded (Merchet, 2008). When, in January 2012, four French soldiers were killed by a member of the ANA, the episode became embroiled in electoral politics. Sarkozy hinted that he might withdraw all French forces before the agreed deadline of 2014, and Hollande insisted that he would withdraw all 'combat troops' in 2012. Hollande's stance at the May 2012 NATO summit in Chicago, less than a week after assuming office, was uncompromising. His electoral promise was quietly endorsed by his NATO partners, all of whom were also seeking the exit door. The semantic distinction between 'combat troops' and 'non-combat troops' is a fudge. In 2013, 1,200 French troops remained in Afghanistan to help train the Afghan army. However, if they were required by the US for combat duty, they would be ready and able. Up until the final withdrawal date of December 2014, 400 French troops will remain alongside their allies. As with many other countries that became embroiled in the Afghan War, France was initially motivated by considerations of rank, while becoming increasingly unclear about the precise strategic objective (Notin, 2011). By 2011, over 75 per cent of French people were opposed to the war. NATO was proving to be a mixed blessing.

CSDP: the European alternative to NATO?

One of the main charges brought against Sarkozy by the Socialist opposition was that his reintegration of NATO threatened the infant CSDP. France assumed the six-month presidency of the EU from July to December 2008. One of the top priorities for that presidency was to give a significant boost to the CSDP. The EU should, France suggested, be able to generate the capacity to engage, *simultaneously*, in a broad spectrum of overseas operations: two significant stabilization and reconstruction operations, each involving 10,000 troops over two years; two rapid reaction operations using battle-group formations; one major emergency evacuation operation; one maritime and/or air surveillance and interdiction operation; one civil-military humanitarian mission lasting three months; and about ten civilian nation-building missions of variable duration. The French presidency devoted considerable energy to the delivery, by December 2008, of a package of agreements on new military hardware and to the drafting of a 'Declaration on Strengthening Capacities'. Several new developments were also announced in the defence industrial sector, including support for the European Defence Agency's (EDA) strategy for a 'robust and competitive European defence technological and industrial base'.

It is difficult to evaluate this considerable package of announcements, since very little has yet materialized. But there are two reasons for cautious optimism. The first is that the methodology of European capacity generation is now widely accepted. All member states, including the large ones, accept the inevitability of rationalization, pooling, sharing and specialization (Maulny and Liberti, 2008; Biscop and Coelmont, 2011; EDA, 2012). Secondly, the EU has both a normative responsibility to contribute more to twenty-first century humanitarian crisis management and nation-building, and the empirical ability to assume a growing share of that global burden. The Obama administration has made it clear that what it expects of the EU is the generation of usable capacity (Gates, 2012). That is likely to be the real price of partnership in any revitalized transatlantic relationship.

France's capacity to intervene in the EU's crisis management missions was a key theme of the long-awaited White Paper on defence published in mid-June 2008 (Livre Blanc, 2008). Its principal ambitions were threefold. First, to make French conventional forces more usable within a European and alliance framework. Second, to lay the groundwork for ever-increasing European cooperation on counter-terrorism. Third, to show a lead in fleshing out the contours of a future, genuinely European, grand strategy.

The traditional trumpeting of France's nuclear capacity also underwent important shifts during Sarkozy's presidency. Speaking at the launch of France's fourth strategic nuclear submarine, *Le Terrible*, in March 2008, the president made unprecedented reference to the deterrent value of the NATO Alliance, but also suggested that France's EU partners derived security from the French nuclear deterrent (Sarkozy, 2008b). Under Sarkozy, the US and the EU were equally important strategic partners. In the White Paper, the army turned out to be the sacrificial lamb. Defence spending would be held at around 2 per cent of GDP, but the overall force levels in the army would be cut from 154,000 to 131,000. The air force saw its fighter aircraft fleet reduced from 330 to 300 and transport aircraft cut from 100 to 70. The navy suffered a frigate fleet reduction from 25 to 18, with continuing uncertainty over the hypothetical second aircraft carrier. There were 54,000 jobs cut in support or administrative services and the budget ratio was reversed from 60 per cent personnel/40 per cent equipment to 40/60 per cent. The bottom line was that France could no longer afford the traditional trappings of 'rank'. Under François Hollande, the defence budget will be cut even more drastically.

The signature of the Franco–British Defence and Security Cooperation Treaty in November 2010 was a further step towards recognition, by both countries, that their national ambitions to play a major role on the international stage were being compromised by budgetary realities and that the only way to retain a modicum of international influence was through cooperation (Jones, 2011; Menon, 2011). Several key areas were highlighted: a combined joint expeditionary force; an integrated aircraft carrier strike group; a common support plan for the fleets of transport aircraft; joint development of equipment and technologies for the next generation of nuclear submarines; military satellite communications; unmanned air surveillance; and eventually combat systems. These assets go to the heart of both countries' military ambitions over the coming decades and the Treaty represents further recognition of their shared strategic interests. While both countries insisted that they had 'a shared vision as to the future of the NATO alliance', the UK supports NATO-led international expeditionary operations of the Afghan type, whereas France is much more reticent about NATO becoming a global alliance. The question most analysts asked after the signature of the Treaty was whether it would function as a *complement* to the CSDP or as an *alternative*.

President Hollande, and particularly his defence minister Jean-Yves Le Drian, made it very clear immediately that France intended to prioritize the consolidation of the CSDP. A new White Paper (*Livre Blanc*) was commissioned in June 2012. It was widely predicted to emphasize France's need to integrate its defence thinking ever more closely with that of its European partners. By 2012, the Franco-British defence relationship was in troubled waters. Quite apart from growing doubts about the UK's long-term commitment to the EU itself, several technical decisions were taken in London which, in effect, broke with the November 2010 agreements (the British decision not to fit its aircraft carriers with the catapults which would allow French Rafales to use them). Hollande has insisted that he wants as many EU member states as possible to participate in integrated defence programmes, whereas London wishes the Franco-British cooperation to remain exclusive (Valasek, 2012).

European security and relations with Russia

When the Russo-Georgian War broke out on 7 August 2008, Nicolas Sarkozy, in Beijing for the Olympics, returned immediately to Paris, and, within five days, as the then president of the European Council, was on his way to Tbilisi and Moscow to broker a peace agreement. This was a case of the right man in the right place at the right time. By 12 August, the embattled Georgian President Mikheil Saakashvili was more than ready for an international 'honest broker' to engage in damage limitation by persuading the Russians to accept a peace agreement. By that time, Moscow had begun to realize that it had probably achieved all the gains it could hope for in Georgia and was not unhappy to call it a day. Sarkozy arrived in both Tbilisi and Moscow at the opportune moment. The so-called six-point cease-fire plan which he negotiated with Dmitri Medvedev was in fact a largely cosmetic rearrangement of the new situation on the ground. A second visit to Moscow, on 8 September, succeeded in persuading Russia to withdraw all its troops from Georgian territory and to accept the dispatch of 200 peace monitors from the EU. To claim these achievements as a triumph of Sarkozian diplomacy would be massively to stretch a point. The EU was the only actor capable at that time of brokering a peace deal – and both Russia and Georgia were ready to sign one. Sarkozy, as president of France as well as the EU, enjoyed credibility and legitimacy in both Moscow and Tbilisi. He succeeded, in part through his energy and leadership qualities (and dollops of luck), in maximizing the opportunity handed to him by history. He emerged from the crisis with enhanced stature – both inside and outside France. Thereafter, he significantly deepened relations with Dmitri Medvedev's Russia, which was overtly supportive of French efforts to reform the international financial and institutional system (see Chapter 15). France has been the Western country which has been most open to discussion of Medvedev's plan for a new European security architecture (Traynor, 2008) and has incurred the wrath of many senior US officials by negotiating the sale to Russia of advanced Mistral-class amphibious assault vessels. However, in summer 2012, Russian resistance to French and European efforts to broker a cease-fire in civil-war-torn Syria produced a massive cooling of relations between François Hollande and the newly re-elected Vladimir Putin.

The Mediterranean and the Middle East: activism with little to show

One of the most controversial proposals made by candidate Nicolas Sarkozy in the spring of 2007 was for the creation of a Union for the

Mediterranean (UfM). The original aim was to create, between the countries on the two shores of the Mediterranean, a separate regional regime on the model of the EU (Dotoli and Stétié, 2010). Sarkozy presented this scheme in big-picture terms as the ultimate (French) solution to the clash of civilizations, allowing the world 'to overcome hatred and to make way for the dream of peace and civilisation', including between Israel and Palestine, and as 'the pivot of a grand alliance between Europe and Africa ... the counterweight to Asia and America' (Sarkozy, 2007a, p. 105). From the outset, the UfM ran into serious opposition. German leaders were irritated at the explicit exclusion from the scheme of non-Mediterranean-shore EU members, who were nevertheless invited, as mere 'observers', to assist in its creation. Support for the idea was stronger south of the Mediterranean, where 22 of the 25 states potentially involved appeared to be favourably disposed – particularly Morocco, Tunisia and Israel. Turkey, however, was deeply concerned that the UfM would emerge as an alternative to membership of the EU. Despite the high-profile formal launch of the UfM at a 43-state summit in Paris in July 2008, the project turned out to be a damp squib as the organization demonstrated its total irrelevance during the Arab Spring of 2011 (Iremciuc, 2012). France's influence over events in the Mediterranean appeared to be waning rapidly.

Paris was caught totally off-guard by events in Tunisia (a former colony) and in Egypt. In the former case, the embarrassing December 2010 offer, made by the then French foreign minister Michelle Alliot-Marie to Tunisian President Zine el-Abidine Ben Ali, of French tear gas and riot police to help control the protesters, was only marginally compensated for when Sarkozy refused the Tunisian first family access to French air space during their precipitate flight from Tunis on 15 January 2011. France was hardly more imaginative when, on 25 January, Egypt also erupted and the government found itself, like its counterparts in other Western capitals, faced with deciding how to react to the likely downfall of a long-time ally, President Hosni Mubarak. On 10 February, Sarkozy came out in support of democracy in Egypt and gambled on the eventual fall of Mubarak, but then immediately warned that the West could not afford to connive in the rise to power in Egypt of the Muslim Brotherhood. In short, incoherence and drift marked French policy in the early stages of the Arab Spring.

Sarkozy tried hard to correct for France's inadequate responses in Tunisia and Egypt by his policy towards Libya. In a prime-time television address on 27 February 2011, the president announced his determination to 'accompany, support and assist people who have chosen to be free'. He immediately engaged both London and Washington over possible military action, was the first to call for Gaddafi to step down, the first formally to recognize the Benghazi-based Transitional

National Council (10 March), and energetically co-sponsored the 17 March UN Resolution 1973 on the imposition of a no-fly zone (Howorth, 2012b; Chivvis, 2012). In all of this he was way ahead of his foreign minister, Alain Juppé, who counselled against most of these actions. France was also the first country, on 19 March, to engage Colonel Gaddafi's forces with military action, in an effort to prevent a bloodbath in Benghazi, even before the UN coalition had been formally created. Faced with President Obama's reluctance to lead the anti-Gaddafi coalition, Sarkozy attempted to persuade David Cameron to operationalize the Franco-British Treaty by creating a European command centre; but Cameron insisted on a NATO frame. Sarkozy was nevertheless the driving force behind the interventionists with Cameron tagging along behind (Cameron, 2012). Resigning itself to accepting a NATO framework, France nevertheless became, along with the UK, the lead nation in Operation Unified Protector, flying between 30 and 40 sorties per day throughout the course of the operation, which lasted from late March until October. The air campaign was supported by the deployment of an aircraft carrier group around the *Charles de Gaulle* comprising a refuelling tanker, four frigates, a nuclear attack submarine and a full complement of helicopters. France also played a major role, in contravention of UN resolutions, in supplying weapons and training to the rebels. Sarkozy thus turned the Libyan mission into a major demonstration of France's capacity for power projection in Europe's near-abroad. Sceptics accused him of hoping to capitalize on the Libyan campaign in his 2012 presidential re-election bid (Garton Ash, 2011), but the more likely explanation was his conviction that Libya offered France a perfect opportunity to take a lead in all three major theatres of French foreign and security policy: the transatlantic, the continental European and the Mediterranean/African (Chivvis, 2012).

However, the French reaction to the crisis in Syria in 2011–12, under the leadership of both Sarkozy and Hollande, was marked by extreme caution and a reluctance to go beyond diplomacy and sanctions. In 2009–10, France engaged in regular top level talks with Syria in a fruitless attempt to broker direct negotiations between Damascus and Israel as well as to help engineer an effective government of national unity in Lebanon. France risked the displeasure of the US, which maintained severe reservations about the al-Assad regime. But once the 2012 Syrian crisis became front-page news, it became clear that Paris, in the twenty-first century, in a former French dominion, has virtually no influence whatsoever, either directly with the Bashar al-Assad regime, indirectly through the United Nations, the EU or the Arab League, or even bilaterally, through discussions with Russia, Turkey or Israel. But then Syria confounded the best efforts of all international players, including the US (ICG, 2012).

Israel/Palestine: rhetoric and reality

On the Israel–Palestine conflict, the world waited to see how the new president's reputation as a firm friend of Israel would manifest itself in terms of 'rupture' with the allegedly pro-Arab policy of his predecessor? In the event, no such shift was perceptible. When Israeli foreign minister Shimon Peres visited Paris in March 2008 for a five-day state visit, the media focused on Sarkozy's declaration that the Jewish state must halt its 'colonization' on the West Bank as an indispensable step towards peace. Further settlements, he argued, threatened the creation of a viable Palestinian state. In May 2008, Kouchner made headlines when he announced that France had been engaged in 'contacts' with Hamas. France's pronouncements on Israel/Palestine did not fit the image of a country which had broken with Gaullism in order to embrace Atlanticism. On his first presidential visit to Israel in June 2008, Sarkozy continued to press for resumption of direct peace talks between Israel and the Palestinian Authority, emerging as the sternest critic both of continued settlement expansion and of the Iranian nuclear programme. The French position on a peace settlement was crystal clear: two states, living within the 1967 borders; Jerusalem as the capital of both states; an exchange of territory; and discussions on refugees. Sarkozy became progressively frustrated with Prime Minister Netanyahu's continued expansion of the settlements and was caught, in a sensitive on/off microphone incident, murmuring to Barack Obama that he thought Netanyahu was 'a liar'. In February 2010, Bernard Kouchner went so far as to imply that if, as had been suggested, the Palestinian Prime Minister Salam Fayyad were simply to proclaim the existence of a Palestinian state irrespective of the outcome of negotiations, France would recognize that state. This was then denied by the Elysée. And when, in September 2011, Palestinian leader Mahmoud Abbas attempted to generate United Nations recognition of the Palestinian state, Sarkozy, faced with a US threat to veto the proposal, attempted (unsuccessfully) to dissuade Abbas from submitting the bid to UN Secretary General Ban Ki-moon. Yet when, in October 2011, the Palestinian Authority was formally admitted to UNESCO, France voted in favour while the US voted against. If there was coherence in the French line, it was hard to detect. Ultimately, as in Syria, France proved to be a vociferous, but largely rhetorical, player. Israeli leaders understand the difference between rhetoric and influence and, despite Sarkozy's exceedingly tough line on Iranian nuclear ambitions, Jerusalem remained unimpressed with the ability of French diplomacy to bring about constructive change.

Nevertheless, Sarkozy remained the firm favourite of Israelis for re-election in 2012. Of the 10,000 French citizens living in Israel, 92 per cent voted for Sarkozy. This was largely because Hollande's views on

Israel/Palestine were unknown – and probably unknowable. Hollande had never visited Israel and, during the election campaign, attempted, whenever questioned, to express a strictly neutral position. In February 2012, he despatched Laurent Fabius to the Middle East to reassure both Israeli and Palestinian leaders that nothing would change if he were elected, though the Israeli media were aware that significant sections of the French Left have, in the past, expressed unqualified support for the Palestinians and that one of the candidates for the prime-ministership, Martine Aubry, had a reputation in Israel for being hostile to the Jewish state (Ravid, 2012). After his election, Hollande tried hard to insist that French policy would not change, but Israelis were not reassured when he and Fabius pushed for the reopening of nuclear negotiations with Iran at the same time as they opposed any 'military solution' to the Iranian crisis.

Africa: new direction or more of the same?

Nicolas Sarkozy campaigned for president in 2007 indicating that the phenomenon of 'Francafrique', under which his predecessors, using networks of personal influence and patronage, had essentially run large tracts of Africa from inside the Elysée Palace, was a thing of the past (Verschave, 2003). He got off to a bad start by making a highly insensitive (many said racist) speech at the University of Dakar (Sarkozy, 2007b) which criticized the 'African peasant' for his alleged inability to break with 'a way of life driven by the seasons' and which patronizingly enjoined his astonished hosts 'not to be ashamed of the values of African civilisation' (Denard, 2007). But he subsequently sought to promote a view of Africa which was geared not at perpetuating colonial ties but at underpinning regional stabilization, the development of normal market transactions and the control of immigration flows. In a widely praised visit to South Africa in March 2008, Sarkozy declared that France's long-standing defence agreements with several former colonies would be revised to reflect the genuine needs of Africa as a whole, and that France no longer intended to play a policing role in the continent. He outlined new aid packages amounting to €2.5 billion, purportedly designed to help 2,000 African companies create 300,000 jobs. His major concern remained immigration, given that 65 per cent of the 200,000 annual immigrants into France are African and that 500,000 illegal immigrants enter the EU every year, the majority of them from Africa (Thomas, 2013). Sarkozy's major initiative in this area was the immigration bill which was adopted by the French parliament in October 2007, instituting language exams and DNA testing for prospective immigrants and making family regrouping more difficult.

But in February 2010, switching course, Sarkozy embarked on a new tour of the continent, designed to repair frayed ties with several former allies. In Gabon, despite France's ongoing investigations into the corrupt financial holdings of the Bongo family, he was able to establish a good rapport with Ali Ben Bongo whose controversial 2009 succession to his father Omar had created tensions with Paris. In Rwanda, he succeeded in overcoming 15 years of bad blood between Paris and Kigali (leading to the breaking of diplomatic relations in 2006) by acknowledging that France had made 'grave errors of judgement' in its handling of the 1994 genocide. Despite the early presidential calls for a comprehensive new relationship between France and Africa, transcending 'Francafrique', Sarkozy engaged in more continuity with past practices than innovation (Foutoyet, 2009). In the protracted stand-off in Ivory Coast between the outgoing president Laurent Gbagbo and the universally recognized winner of the November 2010 presidential election, Alasanne Ouattara, France played a decisive military role. As the conflict degenerated into a civil war, French forces were able to create the conditions under which Ouattara's troops could arrest the former president, thus bringing the increasingly deadly conflict to an end. Sarkozy capitalized on this success by attending Ouattara's inauguration ceremony in Abidjan on 21 May 2011, putting an end to over a decade of French decline in this former colony. Sarkozy's personal friendship with Ouattara and his French wife Dominique was a factor in his decision to reverse a plan, outlined in the 2008 Defence White Paper, to abandon the French military presence in Ivory Coast. His Cape Town announcement, in 2008, that France 'will not maintain forces in Africa indefinitely' appeared to have been forgotten. Once again, Sarkozy succeeded in contradicting his own foreign minister Alan Juppé, who had declared, in January 2011, that 'France is no longer in Africa to intervene in the internal affairs of states' (*Le Monde*, 13 January 2011).

President Hollande personally has far fewer links with major African leaders than any of his predecessors, and his latest book devotes only one page to African issues (Hollande, 2012). The president and his foreign minister, like Sarkozy before them, have affirmed their intention of crafting a new relationship with Africa, jettisoning the traditional channels of *Françafrique* and instead working with the African Union and the primary stakeholders to help develop the continent's own immense resources. That, of course, is easier said than done. Hollande's first real test became that of helping to stabilize Northern Mali, which following the fall of Gaddafi had, in 2012, been taken over by Islamic extremists threatening the legitimate government in Bamako. In early 2011, Sarkozy had already launched a 'Sahel Plan' to offer military assistance to the governments of Mauritania, Mali, Algeria and Niger, which at the time were facing increasing incursions from al-Qaeda in the Maghreb, who were also responsible for the kidnapping and murder of several French hostages.

The foreign policy orientations of the Hollande government were made clearer during the annual Conférence des Ambassadeurs in August 2012. The president himself prioritized France's position on Syria, stealing a lead on the international community by announcing that Paris would recognize a 'transitional government' as soon as one was formed, a determination that was widely regarded as premature at best, risky at worst. This determination was also the key point in Laurent Fabius's closing speech to the same conference in which he announced, without specifics, that France would do everything in its power to 'put an end to the domination of the criminal Assad clan'. Another main priority which emerged was a determination to take seriously the threat of an emerging al-Qaeda-dominated void in the Mali–Sahel region. But it was also made clear that France would only act in concert with the EU, the Economic Community of West African States (ECOWAS), the African Union and the UN. Fabius made a point of stressing that Africa, in the long term, was *'un continent d'avenir'*, with which France intended to be a strong partner for mutual benefit.

The third main point emerging from the conference was the absolute priority to be accorded to the EU, not only in solving the crisis of the eurozone, but also in promoting stronger security and defence policies. In all of this, Germany was to be the 'fundamental' partner – while not becoming an 'exclusive' partner. Defence relations with the UK were clearly being re-evaluated in the light of defence cuts on both sides of the Channel. An October 2012 report on Franco-NATO relations by Hubert Védrine ended the internecine battles over Sarkozy's 2009 reintegration by confirming the status quo, while opening up new prospects for NATO–CSDP coordination. There were signs in late 2012 that Germany might finally be moving towards becoming the proactive defence partner that France had always sought and failed to find.

France and the 'emerging powers'

France's role as an international commercial traveller was highlighted in several ways. First, the long-delayed agreement with Russia to supply four Mistral-class amphibious assault ships was signed in January 2011, providing the Saint Nazaire shipyard with 1,200 jobs and the Russian navy with significant assets for its Pacific fleet. Second, a framework agreement between Areva, the French state-controlled nuclear company and India's nuclear Power Corporation, signed in December 2010, to supply two nuclear reactors, highlighted the two countries' shared nuclear interests and secured France the principled support of India for its G-20 agenda. The 2012 sale of Rafale fighter jets to India – the first overseas market (worth an estimated $15 billion) for this hugely expensive and politically controversial aircraft – was an important breakthrough. Third, relations with China were generally positive, major state visits in both directions taking place in 2010. China, like Russia, is outspokenly supportive of France's proactivism in the area of international institutional and financial reform. Hu Jintao endorsed Sarkozy's talk of a new 'multipolar monetary world order'. Sino–French cooperation intensified in the fields of nuclear technology (a joint venture to build two third-generation European pressurized reactors (EPRs) in Taishan), aeronautics (France is helping to build the engine for the first Chinese-constructed large aircraft, the C-919, and has partnered China in constructing the medium utility helicopter, the Z-15), the environment, agriculture and agri-business. Both sides speak of a new departure in Sino–French cooperation. However, the relationship was complicated by Sarkozy's shifting position on human rights (opportunistic rather than principled whenever major business deals were involved) and over his controversial meeting with the Dalai Lama in December 2008, after he had initially caved in to pressure from Beijing not to meet the Tibetan leader earlier that year. China pulled out of the EU–China summit in protest.

Sarkozy also made serious efforts to emerge as a significant partner of Brazil. Through the overseas department of Guiana, which shares 700 kilometres of frontier with Brazil, France is a close neighbour of South America's geopolitical giant. In a January 2010 referendum, 70 per cent of the Guianese electorate voted to reject independence from France. Sarkozy visited Brazil three times in 2009, cheer-leading the familiar discourse about a new institutional and financial world order in which Brazil must play a major role. But above all, the trips were dominated by military transactions. Brazil agreed to purchase from France four Scorpène diesel-electric attack submarines and to retrofit a fifth one with nuclear propulsion. Brasilia agreed to supply Paris with a dozen KC-390 Embraer transport aircraft. Helicopters and sophisticated army equipment were also part of the deal. But the real negotiations revolved around the prospect of Brazil emerging as the first ever client for France's Rafale fighter jet, which has been consistently unsuccessful in the international export market. To increase the attractiveness of the French offer, Sakozy agreed to significant technology transfer arrangements. Moreover, despite his hard-line stance on Iran, he even went so far, in May 2010, as to support the Brazilian–Turkish proposal to recycle Iranian enriched uranium, in effect undermining Western attempts to impose tougher sanctions via the UN Security Council. However, the 2011 election of Dilma Rousseff as President of Brazil called the Rafale contract back into question. Where arms sales are concerned, there are very real limits to France's occupation of the moral high ground. In Sarkozy's policy towards the emerging powers, commercialism and markets rode roughshod over strategic clarity. There is every reason to believe that Hollande will follow directly in his footsteps.

Conclusions

President Sarkozy's record in foreign and security policy was exceedingly patchy. After a number of apparently early successes, his ability to influence world events became bogged down, in part because of his practice of centralizing all decisions in the Elysée and of marginalizing the Quai d'Orsay, and in part because the problems themselves became more and more intractable. His decision to rejoin NATO's integrated command structures was logical and inevitable, but for many French analysts, the future of NATO remains quite opaque (Perruche, 2012). France's relations with the US will continue to respond to both events and personalities in ways which remain unpredictable. Sarkozy's frenetic activism across the Middle East and Africa resulted in few discernible advances – either for those regions or for France itself. French policy was beset with incoherence at best, irrelevance at worst. The Libyan campaign in mid-2011 allowed Sarkozy to claw back some semblance of honour from the wreckage of his Tunisian and Egyptian mistakes, but Libya, as an exercise in international relations, was probably a one-off. France remains a member of the United Nations Security Council P-5, a nuclear power, an important member of the EU and of all other international institutions.

The Organisation Internationale de la Francophonie comprises 56 member states and governments, three associate members, and 19 observers. France retains some ability to project power to distant theatres. But her instincts remain those of a traditional medium-sized nation state and former colonial power – in a world which is increasingly being structured by huge, continental-scale post-colonial units. If President Hollande is to make his mark in foreign and security policy, it can only be through finding a strikingly different, almost certainly European, strategic objective for his country in the twenty-first century.

Guide to Further Reading

Chapter 1

The Sarkozy period has been the object of a number of books and academic articles in English. For the early period of the presidency, the reader is directed to Marlière (2009) and Szarka (2009). A fine synthesis of the paradoxical nature of Sarkozy's presidency is given by Knapp (2013). Cole (2012b) provides an overview of Sarkozy's 'fast presidency'. Raymond (2013) provides the most exhaustive account in English. In French, the key work is that of de Maillard and Surel (2012). Of the various accounts of the 2012 presidential election, the key reference is that of Kuhn and Murray (2013). For the Left, the 2012 elections and the early days of the Hollande presidency, see Clift (2013).

Chapter 2

For an overview of political institutions in France, see Elgie (2003). More specifically, on the operation of the presidency under Sarkozy, François (2009) provides a critical reflection on the early period. Gaffney (2012) offers an original perspective on political leadership in France. Hewlitt's (2011) monograph on Sarkozy is a thorough account. The 2008 constitutional reform is well analysed in Pierre-Caps (2009) and Benetti and Sutter (2009). Foucaud (2010) gives a very valuable overview of the office of the General Secretary of the Elysée, so important under Sarkozy.

Chapter 3

Several classic books have been written on the French Parliament. Williams (1969) is still worth consulting on the early Fifth Republic. The institution has received sparse attention in recent years, but Kerrouche (2006) provides a robust response in defence of the thesis that the French Parliament performs a more active role than it is usually given credit for. Knapp (2005) provides a very useful overview of the Parliament in the broader context of checks on executive power. Dupoirier and Sauger (2010) demonstrate the impact of presidential election outcomes on legislative elections. Smith (2009) has written the major work on the Senate of the Fifth French Republic. Boyer (2007) offers insights into the relationship of the Left and the Senate since 1945. Magnette et al. (2004) provide a good comparative overview of the renewal of legislatures in Europe.

Chapter 4

Stone (2000) most fully develops the concept of judicialization. Lijphart (1999) provides the classic overview of patterns of popular and constitutional democracy. The tense relation between politics and the judges under Sarkozy is covered by Mouhanna (2012). Mény (2008) is good on the legal status of the French president. The Defender of Rights is analysed by Renaudie (2011). Surel (2008) provides an account of EU law and national adaptation in the French case. At a more general level, Cassese (2003) is the key reference on the Europeanization of legal processes, and Falkner and Treib's (2008) study on the worlds of compliance of EU states to EU law is important, if contested.

Chapter 5

Loughlin (2007) provides a thorough account of sub-national government and territorial politics in France. Pasquier (2012) offers an ambitious and comprehensive account of French regions from a comparative European perspective. Pasquier et al. (2007) combine conceptual sophistication with some good empirical accounts of new forms of territorial governance in France. On the turn in decentralization policies, see Le Galès (2008). For developments under Sarkozy, see Cole (2010, 2011, 2012b).

Chapter 6

The main work on the UMP is that of Haegel (2012). A much earlier article in English by the same author (Haegel, 2004) is invaluable as an account of how and why the UMP came to be formed. Knapp (2004) provides an exhaustive overview of the UMP that remains a central reference, though now becoming somewhat dated. Knapp (2013) also offers an interpretation of the Sarkozy presidency in terms of paradoxes that are germane to this chapter. Shields (2007) provides the most sophisticated and complete account of the extreme right in France. Lubbers and Scheepers (2002) present an overview of micro- and macro- perspectives on the FN. Hester (2009) addresses the question of whether the mainstream Right has co-opted the issue of immigration under pressure from the FN.

Chapter 7

The classic book on the PS in English is Clift (2003). Knapp and Sawicki (2008) provide a useful overview of the PS in the context of the broader party system. Cole (2011) addresses the party's radical discursive tradition. Hanley (2008) offers a fairly recent interpretation of the changing PS. Crespy (2008) is good on internal party divisions over Europe. Lefebvre and Sawicki (2006) provide the main account of the Socialists in French and Lefebvre (2011) is very good on the Socialist primaries of 2011. On the Communists, Pudal (2009) provides a historical overview. In English, Bell's (2000) account remains a useful summary of the misfortunes of the Communist party, and Wolfreys (2003) is good on the far Left. Finally, the Greens are discussed by Spoon (2007).

Chapter 8

The main work in English on the politics of the French media is that of Kuhn (2011), a study that examines inter alia ownership, pluralism, policy-making, executive news management and celebrity politics. Kuhn (2013) focuses on campaign coverage of the 2012 presidential campaign by television and the internet from the perspective of both the main candidates' usage of the media (candidate communication) and the media's coverage of the campaign (political reportage and commentary). Hewlett (2011) contains a short section on Sarkozy and the media. Stanyer (2013) is a cross-national comparative study of publicity, privacy and the personal lives of politicians in media saturated democracies, including France. In French Gerstlé (2008) is the standard academic work on political communication, with case studies based on the French experience. Piar (2012) provides a detailed academic work on the influence of television news on French election campaigns and voters.

Chapter 9

Levy (1999, 2006) offers a solid intellectual background for many of the issues raised in this chapter. Rosanvallon (2004, 2008a, 2008b, 2012) is the key French writer for sophisticated discussions about the state and civil society in France. Grossman and Saurugger (2006) offer an interesting account (in French) of interest groups in France. Cole

(2008) discusses the role of interests in French governance. Moravcsik (1998, 2000) addresses the interplay of the state and domestic interests in France's EU policy.

Chapter 10

The special issue of *Parliamentary Affairs* edited by Kuhn and Murray (2013) contains a range of analyses of the 2012 presidential and parliamentary elections. Evans and Ivaldi (2013) have written a monograph on the 2012 electoral series. On the 2007 electoral series and the argument of realignment, see especially Martin (2007a). On French presidential elections in general, from an economic voting perspective, see Lewis-Beck et al. (2012). Bréchon's (2009) book is a standard account of voting patterns in France. Escalona et al. (2013), Fauvelle-Aymar (2011) and Gougou and Labouret (2010) all discuss French regional elections. Gougou (2008) provides an account of the 2008 municipal elections; and Gougou and Labouret (2011a) discuss the 2011 cantonal elections. To understand the articulation between electoral and party systems, see Blais (2010).

Chapter 11

Readers interested by the concept of the mood and its political implications ought to refer to Stimson (1991, 2004) and Soroka and Wlezien (2010). Several sources address the issues relating to the evolution of values in France. Bréchon and Galland (2010) provide a very good synthesis of the issues starting from the 1980s. The annual CNCDH reports, available on the internet, provide a comprehensive account of the evolution of xenophobia in France. On the cultural and social logics of voting, the key references are Grunberg and Schweisguth (1997), Chiche et al. (2000) and Tiberj (2012).

Chapter 12

Algan and Cahuc (2007) are crucial to an understanding of how France's complex, multi-layered social welfare system may have fostered a greater sense of distrust among the citizenry, which might shed light on the public's resistance to reform. Consult Vail (2010) for a study of what *has* changed in France's welfare state in earlier years. Chauvel (2006) examines the social consequences of downward mobility. The arguments developed in this chapter are given a fuller exposition in Smith (2004).

Chapter 13

Readers who would like to deepen their knowledge of citizenship regimes in general and in France especially would benefit from the special issue of the *Journal of Ethnic and Migration Studies* (2010) or the review by Bloemenraad et al. (2008) in the *Annual Review of Sociology*. Weil (2008a) provides a classical comprehensive overview of the history of citizenship in France. The French debate on integration has fostered many publications, in French and in English. Favell (1998) gives an excellent account of the French 'philosophy of integration'. A more recent overview of the literature is provided by Amiraux and Simon (2006).

Chapter 14

In addition to the titles suggested by Kassim (2008), a number of other works are of note. Sutton (2007) provides an impressive account of the 'geopolitical imperative' behind France's role in the EU during 1944–2007, and identifies his work 'as an exercise in contemporary history'. Guyomarch et al. (1998) and Gueldry (2001) are still relevant references, as is Chapter 14 of Knapp and Wright's (2006) book, for its breadth and depth of detail. French scholar Olivier Rozenberg (2012) is valuable for its comprehensive and up-to-date coverage of literature in French and English on the subject of the Europeanization of France. Alistair Cole's chapter on Europeanization in his 2008 volume usefully situates the topic of France–EU relations within the broader literature of government, governing and governance; and Dimitrakopoulos *et al.* (2009) review France and the EU under Sarkozy after the first 18 months of his presidency. Finally, it is instructive to return to Ladrech's pioneering article on 'Europeanization' in the case of France (1994).

Chapter 15

For a historical overview of France's complex embrace and rejection of globalization and Americanization, see the work of American historian Richard Kuisel (1997, 2012). Gordon and Meunier (2001) first highlighted the paradox of France as a bastion of anti-globalization sentiment while also being one of the main actors in it. A similar argument is made by Waters (2012). Ancelovici (2002) has written about the anti-globalization movement in France, as has Fougier (2013). On the link between globalization and Europeanization, consult Schmidt (2007), and Abdelal and Meunier (2010).

Chapter 16

Cogan (1994) provides the classic account of Franco-US relations, a field that Vaisse (2012) revisits after the election of Hollande as president. Howorth (2010) exposes the dilemmas of returning to NATO. Menon (2011) analyses the Franco-British defence treaty. Thomas (2013) provides a rigorous account of relations between France and Africa. In French Meunier (2012) presents an overview of foreign policy during the Sarkozy presidency.

Bibliography

Abdela, R. and Meunier, S. (2010) 'Managed Globalization: Doctrine, Practice and Promise' *Journal of European Public Policy* 17(3): 350–67.

Adorno, T. (1950) *The Authoritarian Personality*, New York: Harper & Row.

Albert, P. (2008) *La presse française,* Paris: La documentation française.

Algan, Y. and Cahuc, P. (2007) *La Société de défiance. Comment le modèle social français s'autodétruit* Paris: Editions rue d'Ulm.

Allport, G. (1954) *The Nature of Prejudice,* Cambridge: Addison-Wesley.

Amiraux, V. and Simon, P. (2006) '"There Are No Minorities Here". Cultures of Scholarship and Public Debates on Immigration and Integration in France', *International Journal of Comparative Sociology* 47(3–4): 191–215.

Ancelovici, M. (2002) 'Organizing against Globalization: The case of ATTAC in France', *Politics and Society* 30(3) 427–63.

Arzheimer, K. (2009) 'Contextual Factors and the Extreme Right Vote in Western Europe, 1980–2002', *American Journal of Political Research* 48: 335–58.

Attali, J. (2008) Quoted in *Problèmes économiques,* 3 September, p. 15.

Auguste, O. (2010) 'Retraites', *Le Figaro* 26 May.

Aust, J. and Crespy, C. (2009) 'Napoléon Renversé? Institutionalisation des PRES et réforme du système académique français', *Revue Française de Science Politique* 59(5): 915–38.

Bachelot, R. (2012) *A feu et à sang,* Paris : Flammarion.

Balme, R. (1999) *Les Politiques de néo-régionalisme,* Paris: Economica.

Bancel, N. (2011) 'La Brèche. Vers une radicalisation des discours publics?', *Mouvements*, special issue: 'La France en situation post-coloniale', pp. 13–28.

Barone, S. (2008) 'Le Train des régions. Régionalisation des transports collectifs et rerompositions de l'action publique', Unpublished PhD dissertation, University of Montpellier 1.

Bartnik, M. (2012) 'En Europe, le salaire minimum pâtit de la crise', www. lefigaro.fr, 24 April.

Baumgartner, F., de Boef, S. and Boydstun, A. (2008) *The Decline of Death Penalty and the Discovery of Innocence,* Cambridge: Cambridge University Press.

Bazin, F. (2009) *Le Sorcier de l'Élysée,* Paris: Plon.

Beauchemin, C., Hamel, C. and Simon, P. (eds) (2010) 'Trajectoires et Origines. Enquête sur la diversité des populations en France. Premiers résultats', Working paper no. 168, Paris: INED.

Bell, D. (2000) *Parties and Democracy in France: Parties under Presidentialism,* Aldershot: Ashgate.

Belot, C. and Bouillaud, C. (2008) (eds) 'Amours et désamours entre Européens: Vers une communauté politique de citoyens?', *Politique européenne*, 26, special issue.

Benetti, J. and Sutter, G. (2009) 'Le parlementarisme après la révision constitution-nelle de 2008: tout changer pour ne rien changer?', *Politeia*, 15: 367–86.

Berthet, T. (2010) 'La Formation professionnelle des régions. Une compétence dis-crète pour une capitale politique accrue', Paper presented at the Nouvelles

Perspectives sur les politiques régionales colloquium, University of Montpellier 1, 29 January.

Bertossi, C. (2009) 'La République modèle et ses discours modélisants: l'intégration performative à la française', *Migrations Société* 122(21): 39–76.

Betbèze, J.-P. (2004) *La peur économique des français,* Paris: Odile Jacob.

Biscop, S. and Coelmont, J. (2011) 'Pooling and Sharing: From Slow March to Quick March?', Brussels, Egmont Institute, Policy Brief No. 23.

Blais, A. (2010) 'The French Electoral and Party System in Comparative Perspective', *French Politics*, 8(1): 79–82.

Blanchard, P., Bancel, N. and Lemaire, S. (eds) (2005) *La fracture coloniale: la société française au prisme de l'héritage colonial,* Paris: La Découverte.

Bloemenraad I., Korteweg, A. and Yurdakul, G. (2008) 'Citizenship and Immigration: Multiculturalism, Assimilation, and Challenges to the Nation-State', *Annual Review of Sociology* 34: 153–79.

Boniface, P. (2012) 'Quelle politique étrangère la gauche et la droite vont-elles choisir?', *Le Monde,* 12 January.

Börzel, T. and Risse, T. (2003) 'Conceptualizing the Domestic Impact of Europe'. In K. Featherstone and C. Radaelli (eds), *The Politics of Europeanization,* Oxford: Oxford University Press, pp. 57–80.

Bouilhaguet, A. (2010) *La carpe et le lapin,* Paris: Éditions du Moment.

Boy, D. and Mayer, N. (1997) 'Que reste-t-il des variables lourdes?'. In D. Boy and N. Mayer (eds) *L'électeur a ses raisons,* Paris: Presses de Sciences Po, pp. 101–38.

Boyer, V. (2007) *La gauche et le seconde chambre de 1945 à nos jours,* Paris: L'Harmattan.

Bozo, F. (2008) *France and NATO under Sarkozy: End of the French Exception?,* Paris: Fondation pour l'Innovation Politique.

Brady, H. (2012) 'Why France is Threatening to Leave Schengen', London: Centre for European Reform, 30 April.

Bréchon, P. (2008) 'Un nouveau centrisme électoral'. In P. Perrineau (ed.), *Le vote de rupture,* Paris: Presses de Sciences Po, pp. 175–95.

Bréchon, P. (2009) *La France aux urnes,* Paris: La Documentation Française.

Bréchon, P. and Galland, O. (2010) *L'individualisation des valeurs*, Paris: Armand Colin.

Brenner, M. and Parmentier, G. (2002) *Reconcilable Differences: US–French Relations in the New Era,* Washington, DC: Brookings Institution.

Brinbaum, Y. (2010) 'Discriminations'. In C. Beauchemin, C. Hamel and P. Simon (eds), *Enquête sur la diversité des populations en France,* Paris: Institut national des études démographiques.

Brouard, S. and Guinaudeau, I. (forthcoming) 'Nuclear Politics in France: High Profile Policy and Low Salient Politics'. In W. Müller and P. Thurner (eds), *Nuclear Policy in Europe*, Oxford: Oxford University Press.

Brouard, S. and Tiberj, V. (2005) *Français comme les autres? Enquête sur les citoyens d'origine maghrébine, africaine et turque,* Paris: Presses de Sciences Po.

Brouard S., Costa O. and König T. (2012) *The Europeanization of Domestic Legislatures: The Empirical Implications of the Delors' Myth in Nine Countries,* New York: Springer.

Burns, J.-M. (1978) *Leadership,* New York: Harper & Row.

Burricand, C., Houdré, C. and Seguin, E. (2012) 'Les niveaux de vie en 2010', *INSEE Première* 1412, September, p. 2.

Cadenel, N. and Ménard, S. (2010) 'Peut-on compter le nombre de personnes qui entrent chaque année en France pour y vivre?', *Regards croisés sur l'économie française* 8: 212–17.

Cahuc, P. and Algan, Y. (2007) *La société de défiance: Comment le modèle social français s'autodétruit*, Paris: Éditions Rue d'Ulm.

Cahuc, P. and Zylberberg, A. (2004) *Le chômage, fatalité ou nécessité?*, Paris: Flammarion.

Cahuc, P. and Zylberberg, A. (2009) *Les réformes ratées du président Sarkozy*, Paris: Flammarion.

Caillé, A. and Vatin, F. (2009) 'Onze modestes propositions pour une réforme démocratique de l'Université française', *Revue du MAUSS permanente*, May 25.

Cameron, A. (2012), 'The Channel Axis: France, the UK and NATO'. In A. Johnson and S. Mueen (eds), *Short War, Long Shadow: The Political and Military Legacies of the 2011 Libya Campaign*, London, Royal United Services Institute.

Campbell, A., Converse P., Miller, W. and Stokes, D. (1960) *The American Voter*, New York: John Wiley.

Capdevielle, J. (1981) *France de gauche, vote à droite*, Paris: Presses de la FNSP.

Caporaso, J., Green Cowles, M. and Risse, T. (2001) (eds) *Transforming Europe*, Ithaca, NY: Cornell University Press.

Carnegy, H. (2012) 'French Government Raises Minimum Wage', *Financial Times*, 26 June.

Cassese, S. (2003) *Lo spazio giuridico globale*, Rome: Laterza.

Cette, G. (2004) 'Productivité et croissance'. In G. Cette and P. Artus (eds), *Productivité et croissance*, Paris: La Documentation française.

CEVIPOF (2012) 'L'Election présidentielle de 2012'. Available at: *http://www. cevipof.com/fr/2012/*; accessed 3 February 2013.

CFDT (2008) 'La réforme des retraites 2008 et les retraités'. Available at: *http:// www.cfdt-retraites.fr/La-reforme-des-retraites-2008–et*; accessed 3 February 2013.

Chandernagor, A. (1967) *Un parlement pourquoi faire?*, Paris: Gallimard.

Charillon, F. (2011) *La Politique Etrangère de la France*, Paris: Documentation française.

Chauvaux, F. and Yvorel, J.-J. (1994) *Histoire de la carte judiciaire*, Paris: Ministère de la Justice.

Chauvel, L. (2006) *Les classes moyennes à la dérive*, Paris: Seuil.

Chevallier, J. (2011) 'Présentation', *Revue française d'administration publique*, 139: 335–7.

Chiche, J., Le Roux, B., Perrineau, P. and Rouanet, H. (2000) 'L'espace politique des électeurs français à la fin des années 1990', *Revue française de science politique* 50(3): 463–87.

Chivvis, C. (2012) *Toppling Qaddafi: Libya and the Future of Liberal Intervention*, Cambridge: Cambridge University Press.

Chojnicki, X. and Ragot, L. (2011) 'L'immigration peut-elle sauver notre système de protection sociale?', *La lettre du CEPII*, 311, June.

Chojnicki, X., Docquier, F., and Ragot, L. (2005) 'L'immigration "choisie" face aux défis économiques du vieillissement démographique', *Revue économique* 56(6): 1359–84.

Chrisafis, A. (2012a) 'Nicolas Sarkozy's Worst Election Fear Realized with Loss of AAA Rating', *The Guardian*, 13 January.

Chrisafis, A. (2012b) 'Nicolas Sarkozy: How a Once Popular President became a Toxic Brand', *The Guardian*, 10 February.

Clerc, D. (2008) *La France des travailleurs pauvres,* Paris: Grasset and Fasquelle.

Clift, B. (2003) *French Socialism in a Global Era: The Political Economy of New Social-Democracy in France,* London: Continuum.

Clift, B. (2013) 'Le Changement? French Socialism, the 2012 Presidential Election and the Politics of Economic Credibility amidst the Eurozone Crisis', *Parliamentary Affairs* 66(1): 106–23.

Cluzel-Métayer, L. (2011) 'Réflexions à propos de la saisine du Défenseur des droits', *Revue française d'administration publique* 139: 447–60.

Cochez, P. (2012) 'Les Français veulent relever les barrières douanières', *La Croix*, 11 April.

Cogan, C. G. (1994) *Oldest Allies, Guarded Friends: The United States and France since 1940*, Westport, CT: Praeger.

Cohen, S. (1986) *La Monarchie Nucléaire: Les Coulisses de la Politique Etrangère sous la Cinquième République,* Paris: Hachette.

Cohen-Seat, N. and Détraigne, Y. (2012) 'La réforme de la carte judiciaire: une occasion manquée'. Rapport d'information de Mme Nicole Borvo Cohen-Seat et M. Yves Détraigne, fait au nom de la commission des lois no. 662 (2011–2012), 11 July 2012, Paris: Sénat.

Cole, A. (1989) 'Factionalism, the French Socialist Party and the Fifth Republic: An Explanation of Intra-party Divisions', *European Journal of Political Research* 17(4): 77–94.

Cole, A. (2006) *Beyond Devolution and Decentralisation: Building Regional Capacity in Wales and Brittany*, Manchester: Manchester University Press.

Cole, A. (2008) *Governing and Governance in France,* Cambridge: Cambridge University Press.

Cole, A. (2010) 'State Reform in France: From Public Service to Public Management?', *Perspectives on European Politics and Society* 11(4): 343–57.

Cole, A. (2011) 'Prefects in Search of a Role in a Europeanised France', *Journal of Public Policy* 31(3): 385–407.

Cole, A. (2012a) 'The French State and Its Territories', *Public Administration* 90(2): 335–50.

Cole, A. (2012b) 'The Fast Presidency? Nicolas Sarkozy and the Political Institutions of the Fifth Republic', *Contemporary French and Francophone Studies* 16(3): 311–21.

Cole, A., Levy, J. and Le Galès, P. (2005) *Developments in French Politics 3,* Basingstoke: Palgrave Macmillan.

Cole, A., Levy, J. and Le Galès, P. (2008) *Developments in French Politics 4,* Basingstoke: Palgrave Macmillan.

Cole, A. and Pasquier, R. (2012) 'The Impact of European Integration on Centre/Periphery Relations: Comparing France and the United Kingdom', *Politique européenne* 36: 160–82.

Comité Interministériel de Contrôle de l'Immigration (2011) *Les orientations de la politique de l'immigration et de l'intégration. Eighth* report to French Parliament, December.

Commaille, J. (1996) *Les enjeux politiques de la territorialisation des fonctions de justice. Contribution à une socio histoire de la carte judiciaire française,* Paris: CEVIPOF.

Commaille, J., Dumoulin L. and Rober, T. C. (2010) (eds) *La juridicisation du politique,* Paris: LGDJ/Lextenso.

Commission Mazeaud (2008) 'Pour une politique des migrations transparente, simple et solidaire. Rapport au ministre de l'intérieur de la commission sur le cadre constitutionnel de la nouvelle politique d'immigration', Paris: Interior Ministry.

Converse, P. (1966) 'The Concept of a Normal Vote'. In A. Campbell, P. Converse, W. Miller and D. Stokes, *Elections and the Political Order,* New York: John Wiley, pp. 9–39.

Costa, O., Roger, A. and Saurugger, S. (2008) (eds) 'Les remises en cause de l'intégration européenne', *Revue internationale de politique comparée,* 15(4).

Cotta, M. (2008) *Cahiers secrets de la Vème République, tome II 1977–1986,* Paris: Fayard.

Couderc, M. (1981) 'La bataille parlementaire contre le temps', *Revue française de science politique* 31(1), February, 85–120.

Courtois, G. (2010) 'Comment effacer 2007 pour l'emporter en 2012', *Le Monde,* 12 October.

Crespy, A. (2008) Dissent over the European Constitutional Treaty within the French Socialist Party', *French Politics* 6(1): 23–44.

Dagnaud, M. (2000) *L'État et les médias,* Paris: Éditions Odile Jacob.

Danet, J. (2008) 'Cinq ans de frénésie pénale'. In L. Mucchielli (ed.), *La frénésie sécuritaire, retour à l'ordre et nouveau contrôle social,* Paris: La Découverte, pp. 19–29.

Darnis, J.-P. (2012) 'François Hollande's Presidency: A New Era in French Foreign Policy?', IAI Working Papers 12/19, Rome: Istituto Affari Internatzionali.

Dehousse, R. and Menon, A. (2009) 'The French Presidency', *Journal of Common Market Studies,* 47, Annual review, pp. 99–111.

Delporte, C. (2007) *La France dans les yeux,* Paris: Flammarion.

Delporte, C. (2012) 'Sarkozy and the Media', *Contemporary French and Francophone Studies* 16(3): 299–310.

Demontés, C. and Leclerc, D. (2010) *Rapport d'Information fait au nom de la mission d'évaluation et de contrôle de la sécurité sociale ... sur le rendez-vous 2010 pour les retraites,* Paris: Senate.

Denard, J. (2007) 'Le Discours de Nicolas Sarkozy à Dakar: rupture conceptuelle ou écran de fumée?' Available at: *http://www.cellulefrancafrique.org/Le-discours-de-Nicolas-Sarkozy-a.html;* accessed 7 August 2012.

Dézé, A.(2012) *Le Front national: à la conquête du pouvoir?,* Paris: Armand Colin.

Dimitrakopoulos, D. G., Menon, A. and Passas, A. G. (2009) 'France and the EU under Sarkozy: Between European Ambitions and National Objectives?', *Modern and Contemporary France* 17(4): 451–65.

Dotoli, G. and Stétié, S. (2010) *L'Union pour la Méditerranée: Origines et perspectives d'un processus,* Paris: Editions du Cygne.

Downs, A. (1957) *An Economic Theory of Democracy,* New York: HarperCollins.

Downs, W. D. (2001) 'Pariahs in Their Midst: Belgian and Norwegian Parties React to Extremist Threats', *West European Politics* 24(3): 23–42.

Drake, H. (2009) 'What Difference Did a (French) Presidency Make? FPEU08 and EU Foreign Policy', *CFSP Forum* 7(1): 1–4.

Drake, H. (2013) 'Everywhere and Nowhere: Europe and the World in the French 2012 Elections', *Parliamentary Affairs* 66(1): 124–41.

Drake, H. and Lequesne, C. (2010) 'France: from Rejection to Return?' In M. Carbone (ed.), *National Politics and European Integration: From the Constitution to the Lisbon Treaty,* Cheltenham: Edward Elgar, pp. 34–50.

Duchesne, S. (2003) 'French Representations of Citizenship and Immigrants: The Political Dimension of the Civic Link', *Immigrants and Minorities* 22(2–3): 262–79.

Duhamel, A. (2009) *La marche consulaire,* Paris: Plon.

Duhamel, O. and Parodi, J.-L. (1982) 'Images du communisme 2: Sur l'effet Kaboul ... et quelques autres', *Pouvoirs* 22: 159–72.

Duhamel, O. and Parodi, J.-L. (1988) (eds) *La Constitution de la Ve République,* Paris: Presses de la FNSP.

Dupoirier, E. and Sauger, N. (2010) 'The Impact of Presidential Election Outcomes on Legislative Elections in France', *French Politics* 8(1): 21–41.

Duprat, Jean-Pierre (1996) 'L'évolution des conditions du travail parlementaire en France: 1945–1995', *Les Petites Affiches* 13, 26 January.

Dupuy, C. (2010) 'Politiques publiques, territoires et inégalités. Les politiques régionales d'éducation en France et en Allemagne (1969–2004)', Unpublished Ph.D. dissertation, Paris: IEP.

Ecole de Guerre (1991) *Quelle Sécurité en Europe à l'Aube du XXIe Siècle?,* Paris: Armée de Terre.

Economist, The (2009) 'Back in the Driving Seat', 14 March.

EDA (European Defence Agency) (2012) 'Taking Pooling and Sharing to the Next Level', *European Defence Matters,* 1.

EIU (Economist Intelligence Unit) (2011) 'Democracy Index 2011: Democracy under Stress'. *Available at: https://www.eiu.com/public/topical_report.aspx?campaignid=DemocracyIndex2011*; accessed 7 July 2012.

Elgie, R. (2003) *Political Institutions in Contemporary France,* Oxford: Oxford University Press.

Elysée (2012) 'Script – Interview du 14 juillet du Président de la République'. *Available at: http://www.elysee.fr/president/les-actualites/conferences-de-presse/2012/script-interview-du-14–juillet-du-president-de.13612.html*; accessed 15 July 2012.

Epstein, R. (2005) 'Gouverner à distance. Quand l'Etat se retire des territoires', *Esprit* 11: 96–111.

Escalona, F., Labouret, S. and Vieira, M. (forthcoming) 'France: Regional Elections as "Third-order" elections?' In R. Dandoy and A. H. Schakel, (eds), *Regional and National Elections in Western Europe: Territoriality of the Vote in Thirteen Countries,* Basingstoke: Palgrave Macmillan.

EurActiv.fr (2012) 'Elections. Sarkozy, l'Européen intéressé'. Available at: *http://www.euractiv.fr/sarkozy-europeen-interesse-dossier*; accessed 20 July 2012.

European Commission (2006) 'Internal Market Scoreboard: Best Result Ever'. Available at: *http://ec.europa.eu/internal_market/score/docs/relateddocs/single_market_governance_report_2006_en.pdf*; accessed 30 October 2012.

European Commission (2010) *Standard Eurobarometer,* 73.

European Commission (2011) 'Making the Single Market: Annual Governance Check-Up 2011'. Available at: *http://ec.europa.eu/internal_market/score/docs/relateddocs/single_market_governance_report_2011_en.pdf*; accessed 30 October 2012.

European Council (2012) 'Conseil européen 9 décembre 2011, Conclusions'. Available at: *http://www.consilium.europa.eu/uedocs/cms_Data/docs/pressdata/fr/ec/126719.pdf*; accessed 17 August 2012.

Evans, J. and Ivaldi, G. (2013) *Alternation, Protest or Conservation? The 2012 Presidential and Legislative Elections in France,* Basingstoke: Palgrave Macmillan.

Fabius, L. (2012) 'Entretien avec Laurent Fabius', *Le Monde,* 30 May.

Falkner, G. and Treib, O. (2008) 'Three Worlds of Compliance or Four? The EU-15 Compared to New Member States', *Journal of Common Market Studies* 46(2): 293–313.

Fassin, D. and Mazzouz, S. (2007) 'Qu'est-ce que devenir Français? La naturalisation comme rite d'institution républicain', *Revue Française de Sociologie,* 48(4) : 723–50.

Fauvelle-Aymar, C. (2011) 'Participation in the 2010 French Regional Elections: The Major Impact of a Change in the Electoral Calendar', *French Politics* 9(1): 1–20.

Favell, A. (1998) *Philosophies of Integration: Immigration and the Idea of Citizenship in France and Britain,* New York: Macmillan.

Featherstone, K. and Radaelli, C. (2003) (eds) *The Politics of Europeanization,* Oxford: Oxford University Press.

Ferrand, O. (2009) *l'Europe contre l'Europe,* Paris: Hachette.

Fiorina, M. (1981) *Retrospective Voting in American National Elections,* New Haven, CT: Yale University Press.

Fortune (2012) *Global Fortune 500 Companies.* Available at: *http://money.cnn.com/magazines/fortune/global500/2011/full_list/index.html.*

Foucaud, F. (2010) 'Le secrétaire général de l'Elysee: éclairage sur la présidentialisation du régime', *Revue française de droit public* 4: 1027–54.

Foucault, M. and Nadeau, R. (2012) 'Forecasting the 2012 French Presidential election', *PS: Political Science & Politics* 45(2): 218–22.

Fougier, E. (2003) *The French Antiglobalization Movement: A New French Exception?,* Paris: IFRI.

Fourquet, J. (2007) 'Le raid réussi de Nicolas Sarkozy sur l'électorat lepéniste', *Revue politique et parlementaire,* 1044: 123–35.

Fourquet, J. (2012) *Le Sens des Carte*s, Paris: Fondation Jean-Jaurès.

Foutoyet, S. (2009) *Nicolas Sarkozy ou la Françafrique décomplexé,* Paris: Tribord.

France Agricole (2012) 'La FNSEA démissionne du Haut-Conseil des biotechnologies'. Available at: *http://www.lafranceagricole.fr/cultures/actu-cultures/biotechnologies-ogm-la-fnsea-demissionne-du-haut-conseil-des-biotechnologies-53261.html*; accessed 3 February 2013.

François, B. (2009) *La Constitution Sarkozy,* Paris: Odile Jacob.

French Senate (2012) 'Rapport d'information fait au nom de la commission des lois constitutionnelles, de législation, du suffrage universel, du Règlement et d'administration générale par le groupe de travail sur la réforme de la carte judiciaire'. *Available at: http://www.senat.fr/rap/r11–662/r11–6621.pdf*; accessed 18 August 2012.

Gaffney, J. (2012) *Political Leadership in France: From Charles de Gaulle to Nicolas Sarkozy,* Basingstoke: Palgrave Macmillan.

Garton Ash, T. (2011) 'France Plays Hawk, Germany Demurs. Libya has Exposed Europe's Fault Lines', *The Guardian,* 24 March.

Gastaut, Y. (2008) 'Le sport comme révélateur des ambiguités du processus d'intégration des populations immigrées', *Sociétés Contemporaines*, 69: 49–71.

Gates, R. (2012) 'The Security and Defense Agenda: The Future of NATO'. Speech by Secretary of Defense, Robert M. Gates, 10 June 2011. *Available at:* http://www.defense.gov/Speeches/Speech.aspx?SpeechID=1581.

Gauvin, F. (2012) 'Marine Le Pen: La mondialisation va profondément à l'encontre de la nature humaine', *Le Point*, 9 March.

Genestar, A. (2008) *Expulsion*, Paris: Bernard Grasset.

Gerstlé, J. (2008) *La communication politique*, Paris: Armand Colin.

Gerstlé, J. and François, A. (2011) 'Médiatisation de l' économie et fabrication de la popularité du président français (2007–2010)', *Revue française de science politique* 61(2): 249–81.

Giesbert, Franz-Olivier M. *Le Président. Scènes de la vie politique 2005–2011*, Paris : Flammarion, 2011.

Giesbert, F.-O. (2012) *Derniers Carnets*, Paris: Flammarion.

Gillespie, R. (2011) 'The Union for the Mediterranean: An Intergovernmentalist Challenge for the European Union?', *Journal of Common Market Studies*, 49(6): 1205–25.

Glad, V. (2010) 'Régimes spéciaux: la réforme des retraites ratée de Sarkozy', www.slate.fr, 17 May.

Goldhammer, Art (2007a): *Available at: http://artgoldhammer.blogspot.com /2007/11/student-movement.html*; accessed 24 November 2012.

Goldhammer, Art (2007b): *Available at: http://artgoldhammer.blogspot.com /2007/06/reforming-university.html*; accessed 24 November 2012.

Goldhammer, Art (2007c) *Available at: http://artgoldhammer.blogspot.com/ 2007/11/worker-speaks.html.*

Goldhammer, Art (2008): *Available at: http://artgoldhammer.blogspot.com/ 2008/01/tampering-with-science.html*; accessed 24 November 2012.

Goldhammer, Art (2009a): *Available at: http://artgoldhammer.blogspot.com/ 2009/03/lamont-on-university-crisis.html; accessed 24 November 2012.*

Goldhammer, Art (2009b): *Available at:* http://artgoldhammer.blogspot.com/ 2009/12/billion-here-billion-there.html; *accessed 24 November 2012.*

Goldhammer, Art (2009c): *Available at: http://artgoldhammer.blogspot.com/ 2009/01/unions.html*; accessed 24 November 2012.

Goldsmith, M. J. and Page, E. (eds) (2010) *Changing Government Relations in Europe: From Localism to Intergovernmentalism*, London: Routledge.

Goodman, S. W. (2010) 'Integration Requirements for Integration's Sake? Identifying, Categorising and Comparing Civic Integration Policies', *Journal of Ethnic and Migration Studies*, 36(5): 753–72.

Gordon, P. and Meunier, S. (2001) *The French Challenge: Adapting to Globalization*, Washington, DC: Brookings Institution.

Gougou, F. (2008) 'The 2008 French Municipal Elections: The Opening and the Sanction', *French Politics* 6(4): 395–406.

Gougou, F. (2012) 'La droitisation du vote des ouvriers en France. Désalignement, réalignement et renouvellement des générations'. In J.-M. de Waele and M. Vieira (eds), *Une droitisation de la classe ouvrière en Europe?*, Paris: Economica, pp. 142–72.

Gougou, F. and Labouret, S. (2010) 'The 2010 French Regional Elections: Transitional Elections in a Realignment Era', *French Politics* 8: 321–41.

Gougou, F. and Labouret, S. (2011a) 'The 2011 French Cantonal Elections: The Last Voter Sanction Before the 2012 Presidential Poll', *French Politics* 9(4): 381–403.

Gougou, F. and Labouret, S. (2011b) 'Participation in the 2010 Regional Elections: The Minor Impact of Change in the Electoral Calendar. A Reply to Fauvelle-Aymar', *French Politics* 9(3): 240–51.

Gougou, F. and Martin, P. (2013) 'L'émergence d'un nouvel ordre électoral? Les élections de 2012 à l'aune de la théorie des réalignements'. In V. Tiberj (ed.), *Des votes et des voix. La France des urnes de Mitterrand à Hollande.*

Gougou, F. and Tiberj, V. (forthcoming 2013) 'Les électeurs du Parti socialiste. Sociologie de l'électorat d'un parti en reconversion (1981–2009)'. In R. Lefebvre and F. Sawicki (eds), *Sociologie des socialistes.*

Grangé, Jean (1990) 'Les déformations de la représentation des collectivités territoriales et de la population au Sénat', *Revue française de science politique* 40(1): 5–45.

Greenpeace (2012) *Available at: http://www.greenpeace.org/france/fr/campagnes/ogm/*; accessed 24 November 2012.

Grémion, P. (1976) *Le pouvoir périphérique*, Paris: Seuil.

Gresh, A. (2008) 'Le Quai d'Orsay, c'est moi', *Le Monde Diplomatique*, July.

Grossman, E. and Saurugger, S. (2006) *Les groupes d'intérêt: Action collective et stratégies de représentation*, Paris: Armand Colin.

Groux, G. (2009) 'Les syndicats contestataires ont-ils le vent en poupe?' *Available at: http://www.telos-eu.com/fr/societe/social-et-societal/les-syndicats-contestataires-ont-ils-le-vent-en-po.html*; accessed 24 November 2012.

Grunberg, G. (2008) 'Vers un espace politique bipartisan?'. In P. Perrineau (ed.), *Le vote de rupture*, Paris: Presses de Sciences Po, pp. 253–70.

Grunberg, G. and Haegel, F. (2007) *La France vers le bipartisme? La présidentialisation du PS et de l'UMP*, Paris: Presses de Sciences Po.

Grunberg, G. and Schweisguth, E. (1990) 'Libéralisme culturel, libéralisme économique'. In CEVIPOF (ed.), *L'électeur français en questions*, Paris: Presses de Sciences Po, pp. 45–70.

Grunberg, G. and Schweisguth, E. (1997a) 'Les recompositions idéologiques'. In D. Boy and N. Mayer (eds) *L'électeur a ses raisons*, Paris: Presses de Sciences Po, pp. 139–78.

Grunberg, G. and Schweisguth, E.(1997b) 'Vers une tripartition de l'espace politique'. In D. Boy and N. Mayer (eds), *L'électeur a ses raisons,* Paris: Presses de Sciences Po, pp. 179–218.

Grunberg, G. and Schweisguth, E. (2003) 'La tripartition de l'espace politique'. In P. Perrineau and C. Ysmal (eds), *Le vote de tous les refus. Les élections présidentielle et législatives de 2002*, Paris: Presses de Sciences Po, pp. 341–62.

Guardian, The (2009) *Available at: http://www.guardian.co.uk/world/2009/apr/01/boss-hostage-france-caterpillar*; accessed 24 November 2012.

Guardian, The (2011a) 'Europeans Are Liberal, Anxious, and Don't Trust Politicians', 25 March.

Guardian, The (2011b) 'Sarkozy and Merkel Promise "EU Government" to Save Euro', 17 August.

Gueldry, M. (2001) *France and European Integration: Towards a Transnational Polity?*, Westport, CT: Praeger.

Guilluy, C. (2010) *Fractures françaises*, Paris: François Bourin.

Guiral, A. (2010) 'C'est indigne d'une démocratie', *Libération,* 17 June.

Guiraudon, V. (2010) 'Les effets de l'européanisation des politiques d'immigration et d'asile', *Politique européenne* 2(31): 7–32.

Giesbert, Franz-Olivier (2011) *M. Le Président. Scènes de la vie politique 2005–2011*, Paris: Flammarion. Guyomarch, A., Machin, H. and Ritchie, E. (1998) *France in the European Union*, Basingstoke: Palgrave Macmillan.

Haegel, F. (2004) 'The Transformation of the French Right: Institutional Imperatives and Organizational Changes', *French Politics*, 2(2): 185–202.

Haegel, F. (2007) 'Le pluralisme à l'UMP'. In F. Haegel (ed.), *Partis et système partisan en France*, Paris: Presses de Sciences Po, pp. 219–54.

Haegel, F. (2011) 'Nicolas Sarkozy a-t-il radicalisé la droite française? Changements idéologiques et étiquetage politique', *French Politics, Culture and Society*, 29(3): 62–77.

Haegel, F. (2012) *Les droites en fusion*, Paris: Presses de Sciences Po.

Hajjat, A. (2012) *Les frontières de l'identité nationale. L'injonction à l'assimilation en France métropolitaine et coloniale*, Paris: La Découverte.

Hall, P. (2006) 'Introduction'. In P. Culpepper, P. Hall and B. Palier (eds), *Changing France: The Politics that Markets Make*, Basingstoke: Palgrave Macmillan.

Hanley, D. (2008) 'Changing the Parti Socialiste: Renewal or Adaptation?', *Journal of Contemporary European Studies* 16(1): 83–97.

Harguindéguy, J.-B. and Cole, A. (2009) 'La politique linguistique de la France à l'épreuve des revendications ethnoterritoriales', *Revue Française de Science Politique* 59(5): 939–67.

Haut Conseil à l'Intégration (HCI) (1993) *L'intégration à la française*, Paris: UGE.

Haut Conseil à l'Intégration (HCI) (2011) *La France sait-elle encore intégrer les immigrés?*, Paris: La Documentation Française.

Hayward, J. (1983) *Governing France*, London: Weidenfeld & Nicolson.

Hebert, D. (2012) 'Le quinquennat de Sarkozy en 5 chiffres', *Le Nouvel Observateur*, 15 February.

Held, D. and McGrew, A. (2002) (eds) *Governing Globalization. Power, Authority and Global Governance*, Cambridge: Polity Press.

Hester, R.-J. (2009) 'Coopting the Immigration Issue within the French Right', *French Politics* 7(1): 19–30.

Hewlett, N. (2011) *The Sarkozy Phenomenon*, Exeter: Imprint Academic.

Hine, D. (1982) 'Factionalism in West European Parties: A Framework of Analysis', *West European Politics*, 5(1): 36–53.

Hirsch, M. (2008) 'Le revenu de solidarité active, plus que jamais'. Available at: www.la vie des idées.fr, 19 June.

Holbrooke, R. (1999) *To End a War*, New York: Modern Library.

Hollande, F. (2012) *Changer de Destin*, Paris: Robert Laffont.

Hollifield, J. (1994) 'Immigration and Republicanism in France: The Hidden Consensus'. In W. Cornelius, P. Martin and J. Hollifield (eds), *Controlling Immigration: A Global Perspective*, Palo Alto, CA: Stanford University Press, pp. 143–75.

Hollinger, P. (2010) 'Pension Tensions', *Financial Times*, 27 May.

Houtman, D., Achterberg, P. and Derks, A. (2008) *Farewell to the Leftist Working Class*, London: Transaction Publishers.

Howorth, J. (2005) 'France and the US: from Desert Storm to Iraq: Influence, Internationalism and Independence'. In G. Jeffrey and P. Dennis (eds),

Entangling Alliances: Coalition Warfare in the 20th Century, Canberra: Australian Army, pp. 222–53.

Howorth, J. (2010) 'What's in It for France? Prodigal Son or Trojan Horse?', *European Security* 19(1): 11–28.

Howorth, J. (2012a) 'CSDP and NATO post-Libya: Towards the Rubicon?', Egmont Institute Security Policy Brief 35, July.

Howorth, J. (2012b) 'La France, la Libye, la PSDC et l'OTAN: Changement de Paradigme sécuritaire?', *Annuaire Français de Relations Internationales,* Paris: La Documentation Française.

Huber, J. D. (1996) 'Restrictive Legislative Procedures in France and the United States', *The American Political Science Review* 86(3): 675–87.

Huret, M. (2010a) 'Retraites: La bataille de l'equité', *L'Express,* 23 June.

Huret, M. (2010b) 'RSA: Débuts précaires', *L'Express,* 2 June.

ICDG (Institut Charles de Gaulle) (ed.) (1992) *De Gaulle en son siècle, Vol. 4, La Sécurité et l'Indépendance de la France,* Paris: Plon.

ICG (International Crisis Group) (2012) 'Syria's Mutating Conflict', *Middle East Report* 128.

Ifop (Department of Opinion and Business Strategies) (2011) 'Regard sur la mondialisation dans 10 pays'. Available at: *http://www.ifop.com/media/poll/1390–1–study_file.pdf.*

Inglehart, R. (1977) *The Silent Revolution: Changing Values and Political Styles among Western Publics,* Princeton, NJ: Princeton University Press.

Iremciuc, A. (2012) *Echec de l'Union pour la Méditerranée: Essai d'explications,* Sarrebruck: Editions Universitaires Européennes.

Jabko, N. (2011) 'International Radicalism, Domestic Conformism: France's Ambiguous Stance on Financial Reforms', Paper delivered to the meeting of the Society for the Advancement of Socio-Economics (SASE), Madrid, 23–25 June.

Jadot, A. (2000) 'Mobilité, rationalité? Une exploration des itinéraires électoraux, 1973–1997'. In P. Bréchon, A. Laurent. and P. Perrineau (eds), *Les cultures politiques des Français,* Paris: Presses de Sciences Po, pp. 377–400.

Jaffré, J. (2012) 'Ce que signifie le vote du 6 mai', *Le Monde,* 5 June.

Jamet, J.-F. (2008) 'L'influence économique de la France dans l'Union européenne', Fondation Robert Schuman, *Questions d'Europe* 101: 2 June.

Jarreau, P. (2012) 'Bayrou: La France est dans un état critique', *Le Monde,* 6 April.

Jérôme, B. and Jérôme-Speziari, V. (2004) 'Forecasting the 2002 Elections: Lessons from a Political Economy Model'. In M. S. Lewis-Beck (ed.), *The French Voter: Before and After the 2002 Elections,* Basingstoke: Palgrave Macmillan.

Jobert, B. (ed.) (1984) *Le tournant néo-libéral en Europe,* Paris: L'Harmattan.

Jobert, B. (ed.) (1994) *Le Tournant neo-libéral en Europe: Idées et recettes dans les pratiques gouvernementales,* Paris: L'Harmattan.

Jobert, B. and Théret, B. (1994) 'France. La consécration républicaine du néolibéralisme'. In Jobert, B. (ed.) *Le tournant néolibéral en Europe. Idées et recettes dans les pratiques gouvernementales,* Paris: L'Harmattan, pp. 21–86.

Joffrin, L. (2008) *Le roi est nu,* Paris: Robert Laffont.

Jones, B. (2011) 'Franco-British Military Cooperation: A New Engine for European Defence?', Paris, EU-ISS Occasional Paper 88.

Joppke, C. (2007) 'Beyond National Models: Civic Integration Policies for Immigrants in Western Europe', *West European Politics* 30(1): 1–22.

Jourdain, L. (2008) 'Peut-on laisser un gouvernement définir l'identité nationale?', *Terra*, Recueil Alexandries, Collections Esquisses, no. 20.

Journal du Dimanche (2012) 'Quand Sarkozy ne veut pas être "le candidat d'une petite élite"'. Available at: http://www.lejdd.fr/Election-presidentielle-2012/Actualite/Sarkozy-le-candidat-contre-les-elites-decryptage-487992; accessed 24 November 2012.

Journal of Ethnic and Migration Studies (2010) Special issue on 'Migration and Citizenship Attribution: Politics and Policies in Western Europe', 36(5).

Juppé, A. and Schweitzer, L. (2008) (eds) *La France et l'Europe dans le monde. Livre blanc sur la politique étrangère et européenne de la France 2008–2010*, Paris: Diplomatie.gouv.fr. Available at: http://www.diplomatie.gouv.fr/fr/IMG/pdf/2LIVREBLANC_DEF.pdf; accessed 20 August 2012.

Kassim, H. (2008) 'France and the European Union under the Chirac Presidency'. In A. Cole, P. Le Galès and J. Levy (eds), *Developments in French Politics 4*, Basingstoke: Palgrave Macmillan, pp. 258–76.

Kellstedt, P. (2003) *The Mass Media and the Dynamics of American Racial Attitudes*, Cambridge: Cambridge University Press.

Kepel, G., Arslan, L. and Zouheir, S. (2011) *Banlieue de la République*, Paris: Institut Montaigne.

Kernell, S. (1986) *Going Public: New Strategies of Presidential Leadership*, Washington, DC: Congressional Quarterly Press.

Kerrouche, E. (2006) 'The French Assemblée Nationale: The Case of a Weak Legislature?', *Journal of Legislative Studies* 12(3–4), December.

Kerrouche, E., Deiss-Helbig, E., Schnaterrer, T. and Brouard, S. (2011) 'Les deux Sénats', *Pôle Sud 35*.

Key, V. O. (1955) 'A Theory of Critical Elections', *Journal of Politics*, 17(2): 3–17.

Kinder, D. R. and Sears, D. O. (1985) 'Public Opinion and Political Action'. In G. Lindzey, G.and E. Aronson (eds), *The Handbook of Social Psychology, Vol. II*, New York: Random House, pp. 659–741.

Klau, T. (2011) 'Merci, mon Général, bonjour Monsieur Monnet', *Financial Times*, 8 October, p. 10.

Knapp, A. F. (2004) *Parties and the Party System in France. A Disconnected Democracy*, Basingstoke: Palgrave Macmillan.

Knapp, A. (2005) 'Prometheus (Re-)Bound? The Fifth Republic and Checks on Executive Power'. In A. Cole, P. Le Galès and J. Levy (eds), *Developments in French Politics 3*, Basingstoke: Palgrave Macmillan, pp. 88–104

Knapp, A. (2013) 'A Paradoxical Presidency: Nicolas Sarkozy, 2007–2012', *Parliamentary Affairs* 66(1): 33–51.

Knapp, A. and Sawicki. F. (2008) 'Political Parties and the Party System'. In A. Cole, P. Le Galès and J. Levy (eds), *Development in French Politics 4*, Basingstoke: Palgrave Macmillan, pp. 42–59.

Knapp, A. and Wright, V. (2006) *The Government and Politics of France*, London: Routledge.

Kramarz, F. and Michaud, M.-L. (2004) 'The Shape of Hiring and Separation Costs', Institute for the Study of Labor, IZA Discussion Paper 1170.

Kuhn, R. (2011) *The Media in Contemporary France*, Maidenhead: Open University Press.

Kuhn, R. (2013) 'The Box Trumps the Net? Mediatising the 2012 Presidential Campaign', *Parliamentary Affairs* 66(1): 142–59.

Kuhn, R. and Murray, R. (eds) (2013) 'Special Issue: French Presidential and Parliamentary Elections 2012', *Parliamentary Affairs* 66(1).

Kuisel, R. (1997) *Seducing the French: The Dilemma of Americanization,* Berkeley, CA: University of California Press.

Kuisel, R. (2012) *The French Way: How France Embraced and Rejected American Values and Power,* Princeton, NJ: Princeton University Press.

Labouret, S. (2012a) 'La défaite annoncée de Nicolas Sarkozy: que reste-t-il de la rupture de 2007?', *Revue politique et parlementaire,* 1063–4.

Labouret, S.(2012b) 'La débâcle de l'UMP et de ses alliés aux législatives: l'amplification du vote sanction', *Revue politique et parlementaire,* 1063–4.

Ladrech, R. (1994) 'Europeanization of the Domestic Politics and Institutions: The Case of France', *Journal of Common Market Studies* 32(1): 69–88.

Lagrange, Delphine (2012) 'La France face aux Etats-Unis pendant la crise irakienne: 'ressources démocratiques" d'une puissance moyenne', PhD thesis, Institut d'Etudes Politiques, Paris.

Lambert, C. (2006) *La société de peur,* Paris: Plon.

Lamont Michèle (2009) 'L'expertise des chercheurs doit être au centre du dispositif d'évaluation'. Available at: *http://www.nonfiction.fr/article-2361–p1–michele_lamont_lexpertise_des_chercheurs_doit_etre_au_centre_du_dispositif_devaluation. htm*; accessed 3 February 2013.

Landré, M. (2010) 'Hausse de 10% des "heures sup" déclarés en un an', *Le Figaro,* 3 July.

Landrin, Sophie (2009) 'Nicolas Sarkozy invoque de Gaulle pour justifier sa pratique du pouvoir', *Le Monde,* 6 February.

Le Boucher, E. (2011) 'Le bilan de Sarkozy est illisible', www.slate.fr, 9 May.

Le Figaro (2008b) 'Divorce: la solution du notaire écartée'. Available at: *http:// www.lefigaro.fr/actualite-france/2008/06/23/01016–20080623ARTFIG00274– divorce-la-solution-du-notaire-ecartee.php*; accessed 3 February 2013.

Le Galès, P. (1995) 'Du gouvernement local à la gouvernance urbaine', *Revue Française de Science Politique* 45(1): 57–95.

Le Galès, P. (1999) 'Le desserrement du verrou de l'Etat', *Revue internationale de politique comparée* 6(3): 627–52.

Le Galès, P. (2006) 'Les deux moteurs de la décentralisation: concurrences politiques et restructuration de l'Etat jacobin'. In D. Culpepper, P. A. Hall and B. Palier (eds), *La France en mutation 1980–2005,* Paris: Presses de Sciences Po, pp. 303–41.

Le Galès, P. (2008) 'Territorial Politics in France: le calme avant la tempête'. In Cole, A., Le Galès, P. and Levy, J. (2008) *Developments in Frensh Politics 4,* Basingstoke: Palgrave Macmillan.

Le Lidec, P. (2007) 'Le jeu du compromis: l'Etat et les collectivités territoriales dans la décentralisation en France', *Revue française d'administration publique* 121–122: 111–30.

Le Monde (2008) 'Une nuit de solidarité avec les sans-abri et les mal-logés en plein cœur de Paris'. Available at: http://abonnes.lemonde.fr/societe/article/2008/02/ 22/une-nuit-de-solidarite-avec-les-sans-abri-et-les-mal-loges-en-plein-c-ur-de-paris_ 1014348_3224.html?xtmc=enfants_de_don_quichotte&xtcr=50; accessed 24 November 2012.

Le Monde (2009a) 'Lettre ouverte au Président de la république'. Available at: http://medias.lemonde.fr/mmpub/edt/doc/20090105/1138173_cpulcsbjfchronique_ d-une_crise_annoncee.pdf; accessed 24 November 2012.

Le Monde (2009b) 'Le RSA n'aura pas un impact significatif sur l'emploi', 15 April.

Le Monde (2009c) 'Nicolas Sarkozy veut "changer l'Europe"', 5 May.

Le Monde (2010) 'Retraites: les régimes spéciaux épargnés par la réforme', 26 May.

Le Monde (2012) 'Entretien avec Christine Taubira', 20 September, p. 12.

Le Nouvel Observateur (2007) 'Rachida Dati en vacances avec les Sarkozy', 7 August.

Le Point (2009) '45 des 83 universités françaises ont été touchées par la contestation'. Available at: http://www.lepoint.fr/actualites-societe/2009–06–04/45–des-83–universites-francaises-ont-ete-touchees-par-la/920/0/349667; accessed 24 November 2012.

Le Point (2010) 'Le mouvement perpétuel selon Sarkozy', 17 June.

Leca, J. (1996) 'La démocratie à l'épreuve du pluralisme', *Revue française de science politique*, 46(2): 225–79.

Lefebvre, R. (2011) *Les primaires socialistes. La fin du parti militant*, Paris: Raisons d'agir.

Lefebvre, R. and Sawicki, F. (2006) *La Société des socialistes. Le PS aujourd'hui*, Bellecombe-en-Bauges: Editions du Croquant.

Lellouche, P. (2009) *L'Allié Indocile: La France et l'OTAN de la guerre froide a l'Afghanistan*, Paris: Editions du Moment.

Leonard, M. (2012) 'The End of the Affair', *Foreign Policy*, 25 July. Available at: http://ecfr.eu/content/entry/commentary_the_end_of_the_affair; accessed 1 August 2012.

Leparmentier, A. (2012) 'Les bons conseils de Schröder à Hollande', *Le Monde*, 1 November.

Levy, J. (1999) *Tocqueville's Revenge: State, Society, and Economy in Contemporary France*, Cambridge, MA: Harvard University Press.

Levy, J. (2006) *The State after Statism: New State Activities in the Age of Liberalization*, Cambridge, MA: Harvard University Press.

Levy, J. D., Cole, A. and Le Galès, P. (2008) 'From Chirac to Sarkozy: A New France?'. In A. Cole, P. Le Galès and J. Levy (eds), *Developments in French Politics 4*, Basingstoke: Palgrave Macmillan, pp. 1–21.

Lewis-Beck, M. (1988) *Economics and Elections: The Major Western Democracies*, Ann Arbor, MI: University of Michigan Press.

Lewis-Beck, M. (2000) 'Economic Voting: An Introduction', *Electoral Studies* 19: 113–21.

Lewis-Beck, M., Bélanger, E., and Fauvelle-Aymar, C. (2008) 'Forecasting the 2007 French Presidential Election: Ségolène Royal and the Iowa Model', *French Politics* 6: 106–15.

Lewis-Beck, M., Nadeau, R. and Bélanger, E. (2012) *French Presidential Elections*, Basingstoke: Palgrave Macmillan.

Lhaïk, C. (2010) 'Retraites: Soupçons sur une réforme,' *Le Figaro*, 6 May.

Libération (2008a) 'Magistrats et avocats unis contre Dati'. Available at: http://www.liberation.fr/societe/0101164364–magistrats-et-avocats-unis-contre-dati; accessed 24 November 2012.

Libération (2008b) 'Dati fragilisée, Sarkozy prend le ministère de la justice'. Available at: http://www.liberation.fr/societe/0101164996–dati-fragilisee-sarkozy-prend-le-ministere-de-la-justice?xtor=RSS-450; accessed 24 November 2012.

Libération (2008c): 'Insatisfaction totale des magistrats après une rencontre avec Rachida Dati'. Available at http://www.liberation.fr/societe/0101164786–insatisfaction-totale-des-magistrats-apres-une-rencontre-avec-rachida-dati; accessed 24 November 2012.

Libération (2010) 'Sarkozy gruge sur le pouvoir d'achat', 8 May.

Lichfield, J. (2010) 'Sarkozy follows Europe in raising retirement age', *The Independent*, 27 May.

Lijphart, A. (1999) *Patterns of Democracy: Government Forms and Performance in Thirty-six Countries*, New Haven, CT: Yale University Press.

Lipset, M. and Rokkan S. (1967) *Party Systems and Voter Alignments*, New York: The Free Press.

Livre Blanc (2008), *Livre Blanc sur la Sécurité et la defense nationale*, Paris: Documentation française.

Lochak, D. (2006) 'L'intégration comme injonction. Enjeux idéologiques et politiques liés à l'immigration', *Cultures and Conflits* 64. *Available at: http://conflits.revues.org/2136*; accessed 15 December 2012.

Lochak, D. (2011) 'Rupture ... ou engrenage?', *Plein Droit* 88: 3–7.

Los Angeles Times (2012) 'Bank of France Urges Tougher Labor Regulations', 10 July.

Loughlin, J. (2007) *Subnational Government: The French Experience*, Basingstoke: Palgrave Macmillan.

Lubbers, M. and Scheepers, P. (2002) 'French Front National Voting: A Micro and Macro Perspective', *Ethnic and Racial Studies* 25(1): 120–49.

Mabileau, A. (1991) *Le système local en France*, Paris: Montchrestien.

Magnette, P, Costa, O. and Kerrouche, E. (2004) *Vers un renouveau du parlementarisme en Europe*, Brussels: Presses de l'Université de Bruxelles.

Maillard, J. de, and Surel, Y. (2012) (eds) *Les politiques publiques sous Sarkozy*, Paris: Presses de Sciences Po.

Maillard, S. (2012) 'Nicolas Sarkozy définit les contours de sa "nouvelle Europe"', *La Croix*, 8 January. Available at: http://www.la-croix.com/Actualite/S-informer/Europe/Nicolas-Sarkozy-definit-les-contours-de-sa-nouvelle-Europe-_NG_-2012–01–08-755275; accessed 20 August 2012.

Marianne (2009) 'Patrick Weil: "Que fait Valérie Pécresse?"'. Available at: http://www.marianne2.fr/Patrick-Weil-Que-fait-Valerie-Pecresse_a85288.html; accessed 24 November 2012.

Marlière, P. (2009) 'Sarkozysm as an Ideological Theme Park. Nicolas Sarkozy and Right-Wing Political Thought', *Modern & Contemporary France* 17(4): 375–90.

Martin, P. (2000) *Comprendre les évolutions électorales. La théorie des réalignements revisitée*, Paris: Presses de Sciences Po.

Martin, P. (2007a) 'Les scrutins de 2007 comme "moment de rupture" dans la vie politique française', *Revue politique et parlementaire* 1044: 167–75.

Martin, P. (2007b) 'L'élection présidentielle des 22 avril et 6 mai 2007', *Commentaire* 118: 397–412.

Martin, P. (2007c) 'Législatives de 2007: Un nouveau "moment de rupture"?', *Commentaire* 119: 731–42.

Martin, P. (2010) 'L'immigration, un piège pour la droite?', *Commentaire* 132: 1027–36.

Martin, P. (2012) 'L'élection présidentielle des 22 avril et 8 mai 2012', *Commentaire*, 138: 415–25.

Martin, P. and Labouret, S. (2009) 'L'état des partis en France', *Commentaire*, 125: 121–31.

Martinez, J. (2011) 'Politiques d'immigration: bilan d'un échec', *Cités*, 46: 33–46.

Matonti, F. (2007) 'La singularité française. La campagne électorale de Ségolène Royal', *French Politics, Culture and Society* 25(3): 86–101.

Maulny, J.-P. and Liberti, F. (2008) *Pooling of Member States Assets in the Implementation of ESDP*, Brussels: European Parliament, March.

Maurin, E. (2009) *La peur du déclassement*, Paris: Seuil.

Mayer, N. (1998) *Ces Français qui votent FN*, Paris: Flammarion.

Mayer, N. (2007) 'Comment Nicolas Sarkozy a rétréci l'électorat Le Pen', *Revue Française de Science Politique* 57(3–4): 429–45.

Mayer, N., Michelat, G. and Tiberj, V. (2012) 'Racisme et xénophobie en hausse: retournement historique ou effet de contexte?', *Commission nationale consultative des droits de l'homme, La lutte contre le racisme et la xénophobie*, Paris: La Documentation Française, pp. 35–49.

Mazeaud, P. (2008) *Pour une politique des migrations transparente, simple et solidaire*, Paris : Documentation française.

Mediapart.fr (2011) 'Comment Nicolas Sarkozy a perdu pied on Europe', 27 October.

Meguid, B. (2008) *Party Competition between Unequals: Strategies and Electoral Fortunes in Western Europe*, Cambridge: Cambridge University Press.

Menon, A. (2011) 'Double Act: Anglo-French Defence Cooperation Pact', *Jane's Intelligence Review*, February.

Mény, Y. (2008) *Le système politique français*, 6th edn, Paris: Montchrestien.

Merchet, J.-M. (2008) *Mourir pour l'Afghanistan*, Paris: Jacob-Duvernet.

Meunier, S. (2003) 'France's Double-Talk on Globalization', *French Politics, Culture and Society* 21(1): 20–34.

Meunier, S. (2010) 'Globalization, Americanization, and Sarkozy's France', *European Political Science* 9(2): 213–22.

Meunier, S. (2012) 'La Politique Etrangère de Nicolas Sarkozy: rupture de fond ou de style?'. In J. de Maillard and Y. Surel (eds), *Politiques Publiques sous Sarkozy*, Paris: Presses de Sciences Po.

Michelat, G. and Tiberj, V. (2007) 'Gauche, centre, droite et vote', *Revue française de science politique* 57(3): 371–92.

Ministère de l'intérieur (2011) *Les collectivités territoriales en chiffres*, Paris: Interior Ministry.

Monde solidaire (2012) 'Faucheurs d'OGM'. Available at: http://www.monde-solidaire.org/spip/spip.php?rubrique131; accessed 24 November 2012.

Monroe, K. (1984) *Presidential Popularity and the Economy*, New York: Praeger.

Monso, O. (2008) 'L'immigration a-t-elle un effet sur les finances publiques?', *Revue Française d'Économie* 23(2): 3–56.

Montebourg, A. and Todd, E. (2011) *Votez pour la démondialisation!*, Paris: Flammarion.

Moravcsik, A. (1998) *The Choice for Europe: Social Purpose and State Power from Messina to Maastricht*, London: Routledge.

Moravcsik, A. (2000) 'De Gaulle Between Grain and Grandeur: The Political Economy of French EC Policy, 1958–1970', *Journal of Cold War Studies*, part 1, 2(2): 3–43; part 2, 2(3): 4–68.

Mouhanna, C. (2012) 'Nicolas Sarkozy et la justice pénale: les artifices d'une politique volontariste'. In J. de Maillard and Y. Surel (eds), *Les politiques publiques sous Sarkozy*, Paris: Presses de Sciences Po, pp. 259–78.

Mueller, J. (1973) *War, Presidents and Public Opinion*, New York: John Wiley.

Murard, N. (2011) 'Organisation et fonctionnement du protection sociale'. In *L'Etat de la France, 2011–2012*, Paris: La Découverte.

Musso, P. (2009) *Télé-politique: Le sarkoberlusconisme à l'écran*, Paris: Éditions de l'aube.

Nay, Catherine (2012) *L'Impétueux. Tourments, tourmentes, crises et tempêtes*, Paris: Grasset & Fasquelle.

Noiriel, G. (2007) *A quoi sert l'identité nationale?*, Marseille: Agone.

Notin, J.-C. (2011) *La Guerre de l'Ombre des Français en Afghanistan 1979–2011*, Paris: Fayard.

Nouvel Observateur (2007) 'Dray et Hollande pour des "garanties financières"'. Available at: http://tempsreel.nouvelobs.com/speciales/social/le_mouvement_etudiant/20071119.OBS5568/dray_et_hollande_pour_des_garanties_financieres.html; accessed 24 November 2012.

OECD (2008) *Created Unequal?*, Paris: OECD.

OECD (2009) *Economic Survey of France*, Paris: OECD.

OECD (2011) *Employment Outlook 2011: How Does France Compare?*, Paris: OECD.

OECD (2012) *Incidence of Full-time, Part-time Employment – Common Definition*. Available at: http://stats.oecd.org/Index.aspx?DatasetCode=FTPTC_I; accessed 5 February 2013.

Official Journal of the European Union (2007), C306, Vol. 50, 17 December. Available at: *http://eur-lex.europa.eu/LexUriServ/LexUriServ.do?uri=OJ:C:2007: 306:0158:0159:EN:PDF*; accessed 21 July 2012.

Padis, M.-O. (2007) 'Manipulation ou saturation médiatique', *Esprit* 339: 43–51.

Palier, B. (2000) 'Does Europe Matter? Européanisation des politiques sociales des pays de l'Union européenne', *Politique européenne* 2: 7–28.

Palier, B. and Surel, Y. (2007) (eds) *L'Europe en action*, Paris: L'Harmattan.

Panebianco, A. (1988) *Political Parties: Organization and Power*, Cambridge: Cambridge University Press.

Parodi, J.-L. (1983) 'Dans la logique des élections intermédiaires', *Revue Politique et Parlementaire* 903: 43–70.

Pasquier, R. (2004) *La capacité politique des régions. Une comparaison France/ Espagne*, Rennes: Presses universitaires de Rennes.

Pasquier, R. (2012) *Le Pouvoir régional*, Paris: Presses de Sciences Po.

Pasquier, R., Simoulin, V. and Weisbein, J. (2007) (eds) *La gouvernance territoriale*, Paris: LGDJ.

Peillon, L. (2010a) 'Retraité, le fisc aussi est ton ami', *Libération*, 15 June.

Peillon, L. (2010b) 'Retraite: Les français contre les pistes du gouvernement', *Libération*, 11 May.

Perruche, J.-P. (2012) *L'Europe de la Défense post-Lisbonne: illusion ou défi?*, *Etudes del'Irsem No. 11*, Paris: IRSEM.

Petitfils, A-S. (2007) 'L'institution partisane à l'épreuve du management. Rhétorique et pratiques managériales dans le recrutement des "nouveaux adhérents" au sein de l'Union pour un Mouvement Populaire (UMP)', *Politix* 79(3): 53–76.

Pew Global Attitudes Project (2012) 'Global Opinion of Obama Slips, International Policies Faulted'. Available at: *http://www.pewglobal.org/2012/ 06/13/global-opinion-of-obama-slips-international-policies-faulted/*.

Peyrelevade, J. (2008) *Sarkozy: l'erreur historique,* Paris: Plon.

Phelps, E. (2012) 'Germany Is Right to Ask for Austerity', *Financial Times,* 19 July.

Piar, C. (2012) *Comment se jouent les élections,* Paris: INA.

Pierre-Caps, S. (2009) 'Une révision constitutionnelle en trompe-l'oeil ou la constitutionnalisation du présidentialisme majoritaire?', *Politeia,* 15: 305–20.

Pontusson, J. (2006) *Inequality and Prosperity: Social Europe versus Liberal America,* Ithaca, NY: Cornell University Press.

Pouvoirs (2011) 'Question prioritaire de constitutionnalité', 137 (special issue).

Présidence de la République (2011) '4 ans d'action, Mai 2007–May 2011'. Available at: http://www.elysee.fr/president/les-dossiers/4-ans-d-action/4-ans-d-action.11149.html; accessed 26 June 2011.

Public Sénat (2012) 'Sarkozy contre les "corps intermédiaires": "soit il n'y croit pas, soit il fait du populisme"'. Available at http://www.publicsenat.fr/lcp/politique/sarkozy-contre-corps-interm-diaires-soit-il-n-y-croit-pas-soit-il-fait-populisme-21059; accessed 24 November 2012.

Pudal, B. (2009) *Un monde défait. Les communistes français de 1956 à nos jours,* Bellecombe-en-Bauges: Éditions du Croquant.

Putnam, R. (1988) 'Diplomacy and Domestic Politics: The Logic of Two-Level Games', *International Organization* 42(3): 427–60.

Radaelli, C. (2001) 'Europeanization of Public Policy'. In K. Featherstone and C. Radaelli (eds), *The Politics of Europeanization,* Oxford: Oxford University Press, pp. 27–56.

Ravid, B. (2012) 'Will France's New President François Hollande Be Good for Israel?', *Hareetz,* 7 May.

Ravinet, P. (2011) 'La coordination européenne "à la bolognaise": réflexions sur l'instrumentation de l'Espace européen d'enseignement supérieur', *Revue française de science politique* 61(1): 23–49.

Raymond, G. (ed.) (2013) *The Sarkozy Presidency: Breaking the Mould,* Basingstoke: Palgrave Macmillan.

Renaudie, O. (2011) 'La genèse complexe du Défenseur des droits', *Revue française d'administration publique* 139: 397–408.

Rondin, J. (1985) *Le sacre des notables,* Paris: Fayard.

Rosanvallon, P. (2004) *Le modèle politique français,* Paris: Seuil.

Rosanvallon, P. (2008) *La contre-démocratie,* Paris: Seuil.

Rosanvallon, P. (2010) *La légitimité démocratique,* Paris: Seuil.

Rosanvallon, P. (2012) *La société des égaux,* Paris: Seuil.

Rozenberg, O. (2011) 'Monnet for Nothing? France's Mixed Europeanisation', *Les Cahiers européens de Sciences Po,* 4, December.

Rozenberg, O. (2012) 'Genuine Europeanization or Monnet for Nothing?'. In S. Bulmer and C. Lequesne (eds), *The Member States of the European Union,* Oxford: Oxford University Press.

Salmon, C. (2007) *Storytelling,* Paris: La Découverte.

Sarkozy, N. (2006) 'Address to the "Friends of Europe" Association'. Available at: http://www.europesworld.org/NewEnglish/Home_old/Article/tabid/191/ArticleType/articleview/ArticleID/20662/language/en-US/Default.aspx; accessed 20 August 2012.

Sarkozy, Nicolas (2007a) *Ensemble,* Paris: XO Editions.

Sarkozy, Nicolas (2007b) 'Discours de M. Le Président de la République à l'Université de Dakar', 26 July. *Available at: http://www.archives.elysee.fr/*

president/les-actualites/discours/2007/discours-a-l-universite-de-dakar.8264.html; accessed 1 August 2012.

Sarkozy, N. (2007c) *Testimony*, New York: Harper Perennial.

Sarkozy, N. (2007d) 'Discours de M. Le Président de la République Devant le Congrès des Etats Unis', Speech by the President to the US Congress, 7 November.

Sarkozy, N. (2007e) 'L'Europe sera un grand idéal ou ne sera plus', Speech to the European Parliament, 13 November.

Sarkozy, N. (2008a) 'Le discours de Nicolas Sarkozy à Toulon', *Le Monde*, 25 September.

Sarkozy, N. (2008b) 'Discours de M. Le Président de la République. Présentation su sous-marin nucléaire lanceur d'engins Le Terrible', 21 March. *Available at: http://www.archives.elysee.fr/president/les-actualites/discours/2008/presentation-du-sous-marin-nucleaire-lanceur.1944.html*; accessed 1 August 2012.

Sarkozy, N. (2012a) 'Discours de Nicolas Sarkozy'. Réunion publique nationale, Villepinte (Seine-Saint-Denis), 11 March. Available at: http://www.u-m-p.org/sites/default/files/fichiers_joints/articles/11_03_discours_villepinte.pdf; accessed 17 August 2012.

Sarkozy, N. (2012b) 'Lettre de Nicolas Sarkozy au peuple français', April. Available at: http://ump-6eme-circonscription.hautetfort.com/media/01/02/1108009623.pdf; accessed 23 July 2012.

Sarkozy, N. (2012c) 'Nicolas Sarkozy en meeting et en multiplex depuis Toulouse'. Available at: *http://www.lcp.fr/videos/reportages/135825–nicolas-sarkozy-en-meeting-et-en-multiplex-depuis-toulouse.*

Sauger, N. (2007) 'Le vote Bayrou', *Revue française de science politique* 57(3–4): 447–58.

Sayad, A. (1993) 'Naturels et naturalisés', *Actes de la Recherche en Sciences Sociales*, 99: 26–35.

Schain, M. (2006) 'The Extreme-Right and Immigration Policy-making: Measuring Direct and Indirect Effects', *West European Politics* 29(2): 270–89.

Schmidt, V. (2007) 'Trapped by Their Ideas: French Elites' Discourses of European Integration and Globalization', *Journal of European Public Policy* 14(4): 992–1009.

Schonfeld, W. (1980a) 'La stabilité des dirigeants des partis politiques. Le personnel des directions nationales du Parti socialiste et du mouvement gaulliste', *Revue française de science politique* 30(3): 477–505.

Schonfeld, W. (1980b) 'La stabilité des dirigeants des partis politiques: la théorie de l'oligarchie de Robert Michels', *Revue française de science politique* 30(4): 846–66.

Schweisguth, E. (2007) 'Le trompe-l'œil de la droitisation', *Revue française de science politique* 57(3): 393–410.

Sénat (2010) 'Rapport d'Information fait au nom de la mission d'évaluation et de contrôle de la sécurité sociale … sur le rendez-vous 2010 pour les retraites', Christiane Demontés and Dominique Leclerc, Sénateurs, 18 May, Paris: Senate of France.

Sheriff, M. (1996) *Common Predicament: Social Psychology of Intergroup Conflict and Cooperation*, New York: Houghton Mifflin.

Shields, J. (2007) *The Extreme Right in France*, London: Routledge.

Shields, J. (2012) 'Marine LE Pen and the "New" FN: A Change of Style or Substance?', *Parliamentary Affairs* 66(1): 179–96.

Simon, P. (2006) 'La crise du modèle d'intégration', *Cahiers Français*, 330: 62–7.

Simon, P. (2009) 'Les discriminations et l'émergence des minorités ethniques en France', *Cahiers Français*, 352: 83–7.

Simon, P. (2010) '"Race", ethnicisation et discriminations: une répétition de l'histoire ou une singularité post-coloniale?'. In N. Bancel *et al.* (eds), *Ruptures post-coloniales. Les nouveaux visages de la société française*, Paris: La Découverte, pp. 357–68.

Simon, P. and Sala-Pala, V. (2009) 'We're Not All Multiculturalist Yet: France Swings between Hard Integration and Soft Anti-discrimination'. In S. Vertovec and S. Wessendorf (eds), *The Multiculturalism Backlash: European Discourses, Policies and Practices*, London: Routledge.

Simon, P. and Tiberj, V. (2012) 'Les registres de l'identité: les immigrés et leurs descendants face à l'identité nationale', Working paper 176, Paris: INED.

Slama, S. (2006) 'Les politiques d'immigration en France depuis 1974', *Regards sur l'actualité* 326: 5–25.

Smith, E. (1989) *The Unchanging American Voter*, Berkeley, CA: University of California Press.

Smith, P. (2009) *The Senate of the Fifth French Republic*, Basingstoke: Palgrave Macmillan.

Smith, T. (2004) *France in Crisis*, Cambridge: Cambridge University Press.

Soroka, S. C. and Wlezien C. (2010) *Degrees of Democracy: Politics, Public Opinion, and Policy*, Cambridge: Cambridge University Press.

Spanje, J. van and Brug, W. van der (2007) 'The Party as Pariah: The Exclusion of Anti-Immigration Parties and Its Effect on Their Ideological Positions', *West European Politics* 30(5): 1022–40.

Spoon, Jae-Jae (2007) 'Evolution of New Parties: Evidence from the French Greens', *French Politics* 5(2): 121–43.

Stanyer, J. (2013) *Intimate Politics*, Cambridge: Polity Press.

Stimson, J. (1976) 'Public Support for American Presidents: A Cyclical Model', *Public Opinion Quarterly* 40(1): 1–21.

Stimson, J. (1991) *Public Opinion in America: Moods, Cycles, and Swings*, Boulder, CO: Westview Press.

Stimson, J. (2004) *Tides of Consent: How Public Opinion Shapes American Politics*, New York: Cambridge University Press.

Stimson, J., Tiberj, V. and Thiébaut, C. (2011) 'Le mood, un nouvel instrument au service de l'analyse dynamique des opinions: application aux évolutions de la xénophobie en France (1999–2009)', *Revue française de science politique* 60(5): 901–26.

Stone, A. (2000) *Governing with Judges: Constitutional Politics in Europe*, Oxford: Oxford University Press.

Stone, A., Sandholz, W. and Fligstein, N. (eds) (2001) *The Institutionalization of Europe*, Oxford: Oxford University Press.

Sundquist, L. (1973) *Dynamics of the Party System: Alignment and Realignment of Political Parties in the United States*, Washington, DC: Brookings Institution.

Surel, Y. (2008) 'Checks, Balances and the New Rules of the Political Game'. In A. Cole, P. Le Galès and J. Levy (eds), *Developments in French Politics 4*, Basingstoke: Palgrave, pp. 141–55.

Sutton, M. (2007) *France and the Construction of Europe, 1944–2007*, Oxford: Berghahn Books.

Szarka, J. (2009) 'Nicolas Sarkozy as Political Strategist: *Rupture Tranquille* or Policy Continuity?', *Modern and Contemporary France* 17(4): 407–22.

Taguieff, P.-A. (1995) 'L'identité nationale: un débat français', *Regards sur l'actualité* 209–210: 13–28.

Tajfel, H. (1978) *Differentiation between Social Groups: Studies in the Social Psychology of Intergroup Relations,* London: Academic Press.

Tapinos, G. (1975) *L'Immigration étrangère en France,* Paris: Presses Universitaires de France.

Terra nova (2012) 'Nicolas Sarkozy 2007–2012: le dépôt de bilan. Partie V International et Europe: Une France moins influente'. Available at: http://www.tnova.fr/essai/nicolas-sarkozy-2007–2012–le-d-p-t-de-bilan; accessed 21 July 2012.

Thierry, X. (2008) 'Les migrations internationales en Europe: vers l'harmonisation des statistiques', *Population & Sociétés* 442(2).

Thomas, D. (2013) *Africa and France: Postcolonial Cultures, Migration, and Racism,* Bloomington, IN: University of Indiana Press.

Thomson, R. (2009) 'Same Effects in Different Worlds: The Transposition of EU Directives', *Journal of European Public Policy* 16(1): 1–18.

Tiberj, V. (2008) *La crispation hexagonale, France fermée contre France plurielle, 2001–2007,* Paris: Plon.

Tiberj, V. (2012) 'La politique des deux axes: variables sociologiques, valeurs et votes en France (1988–2007)', *Revue française de science politique* 62(1): 71–108.

TNS-SOFRES (2012) 'Barometre de confiance dans les media 2012', 6–9 January 2012. Paris. Available at http://www.tns-sofres.com January (last accessed 13 February 2013).

Transatlantic Council on Migration (2012) *Rethinking National Identity in the Age of Migration,* Washington, DC: Bertleman Stiftung and Migration Policy Institute.

Traynor, I. (2008) 'Sarkozy Backs Russian Plans for Pan-European Security Pact', *The Guardian,* 15 November.

UE2008.fr (2008) 'Présidence française du Conseil de l'Union européenne. Programme de Travail, 1 juillet–31 décembre 2008. Une Europe qui agit pour répondre aux défis d'aujourd'hui'. Available at: http://www.eu2008.fr/webdav/site/PFUE/shared/ProgrammePFUE/Programme_FR.pdf; accessed 20 August 2012.

US Department of Defense (2012) 'Sustaining US Global Leadership: Priorities for 21st Century Defense'. *Available at: http://www.defense.gov/news/Defense_Strategic_Guidance.pdf;* accessed 1 August 2012.

Vail, M. (2010) *Recasting Welfare Capitalism: Economic Adjustment in Contemporary France and Germany,* Philadelphia, PA: Temple University Press.

Vaisse, M. (1998) *La Grandeur: politique étrangère du Général de Gaulle,* Paris: Fayard.

Vaisse, J. (2012) 'Franco-American Relations after the Election of François Hollande', Washington, DC: Brookings Institution, 22 May. *Available at: http://www.brookings.edu/research/papers/2012/05/22–us-france-vaisse;* accessed 1 August 2012.

Vaïsse, M., Mélandri, P. and Bozo, F. (1997) *La France et l'OTAN 1949–1996,* Brussels: Editions Complèxes.

Valasek, T. (2012) 'Is the Franco-British Defence Treaty in Trouble?', *Centre for European Reform* 85(8–9): 6.

Védrine, H. (2007) *Rapport pour le Président de la République sur la France et la Mondialisation*, Paris: Fayard.

Védrine, H. (2008) *Continuer l'Histoire*, Paris: Flammarion.

Verschave, F.-X. (2003) *Françafrique: le plus long scandale de la République*, Paris: Stock.

Waters, S. (2012) *Between Republic and Market: Globalization and Identity in Contemporary France*, London: Continuum.

Weaver, K. (1986) 'The Politics of Blame Avoidance', *Journal of Public Policy* 6(4): 371–98.

Weil, P. (2005) *Qu'est-ce qu'un Français? Histoire de la nationalité française depuis la Révolution,* Paris: Gallimard.

Weil, P. (2008a) *How to Be French: Nationality in the Making,* Durham, NC: Duke University Press.

Weil, P. (2008b) *Liberté, égalité, discriminations. L''identité nationale' au regard de l'histoire*, Paris: Grasset.

Williams, P. (1969) *The French Parliament, 1958–1967,* London: George Allen & Unwin.

Wlezien, C. (1995) 'The Public as Thermostat: Dynamics of Preferences for Spending', *American Journal of Political Science* 39: 981–1000.

Wolfreys, J. (2003) 'Beyond the Mainstream: *la gauche de la gauche'*. In J. Evans (ed.), *The French Party System*, Manchester: Manchester University Press, pp. 91–106.

Index

Printed and bound in Great Britain by
CPI Antony Rowe, Chippenham and Eastbourne